PHILOSOPHICAL IDEALISM

AND CHRISTIAN BELIEF

PHILOSOPHICAL IDEALISM
AND CHRISTIAN BELIEF

Alan P. F. Sell

St. Martin's Press
New York

PHILOSOPHICAL IDEALISM AND CHRISTIAN BELIEF
Copyright © 1995 by Alan P. F. Sell

For information, address:

St. Martin's Press, Scholarly and Reference Division, 175 Fifth Avenue, New York, N.Y. 10010

Printed in Wales, UK, by Dinefwr Press, Llandybïe

ISBN 0-312-12746-4

Library of Congress Cataloging-in-Publication Data

Sell, Alan P. F.
     Philosophical idealism and Christian belief / by Alan Sell.
          p.   cm.
     Includes bibliographical references and index.
     ISBN 0-312-12746-4 (cloth)
     1. Idealism, English.   2. Philosophy and religion.
     3. Philosophical theology--History of doctrines--19th century
     4. Philosophical theology--History of doctrines--20th century
     I. Title
     B1616.I5S45   1995
     141--dc20   95-17944
                                                                       CIP

First Edition 1995

To Roger and Christina
in their anniversary year

Contents

There is nothing heroic about 'keeping the mind open' on all questions, simply because we are too indolent to give ourselves the trouble of shutting a door. Nor is it well to leave all doors indiscriminately open, for, though the open door often provides an avenue for the entrance of much that is welcome, it also, as we too often forget, affords an exit through which what we can least afford to lose may disappear. The important thing is to judge rightly which doors should be left open and which should be shut.

(A. E. Taylor, *The Faith of a Moralist,* II, 108)

Preface

The relations between philosophy and theology never cease to intrigue me. In this book I seek to show what happens when Christian beliefs encounter, or are articulated in terms of, post-Hegelian idealism in its friendliest guise. Though a sufficiently large task entailing a good deal of textual analysis, this is a clearly delimited project. I do not here set out to provide a defence of what I take to be the broadly classical Christian position in the light of which I view the idealists. This is by no means to deny that there is a work of exposition and defence to be undertaken – indeed, I regret that for a variety of reasons apologetics is currently somewhat in the doldrums. But that task must wait; for the present book, though it may stand as a study in its own right, represents but one of two soundings in Enlightenment and post-Enlightenment thought which I have it in mind to take. The second, on the influence of Locke on the eighteenth-century divines will, I trust, follow shortly. If it should transpire that the rationalism of the eighteenth century, no less than the post-Hegelian idealism of the period 1870–1950, provides a less than adequate vehicle for the articulation of what is taken to be Christian truth, the questions of the nature of that truth and of its viable statement and defence will clamantly be raised. I hope to turn to these questions before the dawn of the third Christian millennium.

The project of which this work is a part has been taking shape over a number of years. It seemed to me that a considerable amount of groundwork in philosophy, theology and intellectual history was required before I could proceed with any hope of success. I have built upon foundations laid under the tutelage of Dorothy Emmet, Eric Gilman, Jonathan Harrison, D. P. Henry, Ronald Hepburn, George Phillips, Ronald Preston, James Richmond and John Heywood Thomas. To all of these I am indebted in a variety of ways. With regard to the present book I am most grateful to my friend D. O. Thomas for bringing his considerable erudition and well-honed editorial skills to bear upon my draft. I have found our discussions as instructive as they were enjoyable.

Thanks are due to Ned Thomas, Director of the University of Wales Press, for his willingness to undertake this project, and to Ceinwen Jones for her prompt and exemplary editorial work.

I cannot find words adequate to express my gratitude to Karen, my wife, whose support never wanes and whose tolerance is limitless.

Alan P. F. Sell
Aberystwyth

1

The Provenance of British Idealism

To set out in the grand manner, let us take a 'text' from that most homiletic of philosophers, Henry Jones. Writing in 1910, he declares,

> To become the teacher of his times [the philosopher] must learn from his times, and be their foremost pupil. He will be the more effective critic and reformer, the more ardent his discipleship. I should be inclined to estimate the value of a philosophic theory by its affinity to [*sic*] the general thought of its time . . . It is a strong presupposition [?presumption] in favour of a philosophic theory that it is in essential accord with the spirit of the period in which it flourishes.[1]

Every sentence here calls for comment. In the first, Jones correctly perceives that if philosophers wish to communicate with their generation, and still more if they wish to 'teach' it something, they must pay heed to their socio-intellectual environment: this on analogy with the old agricultural principle that for the best results one must know the soil into which the seed is to be sown. Moreover, Jones was not unjustified in thinking that philosophical idealism (especially when construed in evolutionary terms) was in accord with a major intellectual trend of his day – a trend in which many poets, religious teachers and social reformers were alike caught up. But what if philosophers do not wish to teach their age or, to come to the second sentence, to criticize and reform it? Jones assumes without argument that these are the obligations of the philosopher, and they were certainly among the duties which he himself sought to fulfil. Many philosophers, however, would feel distinctly uneasy if they were required to assume a mantle so similar, if not at times identical, to that of the prophet. For them philosophy is a matter of the analysis of concepts, the elucidation of arguments – their own and those of others. However it may be in other aspects of their lives, they may well, *qua* philosophers, manifest little historical sense or social concern.

In Jones's next sentence, the proposal that we should estimate the value of a philosophical theory according to the degree of its affinity with the 'general thought of its time' would, if literally construed, rule out the prophetic philosophical critic from the start. Jones would here seem to overlook both the fickleness of public opinion (and his own Edwardian optimism), and the fact that some of the most instructive philosophers – Kierkegaard comes to mind – have, in their own time, been thoroughly out of accord with the prevailing intellectual mood. *A fortiori*, to say that the truth of a philosophical theory turns upon its 'essential accord' with that mood is to appeal to a most unphilosophical criterion of truth. We are inclined to ask, 'Was the version of absolute idealism which Jones espoused theoretically disproved by the advent of the First World War?' The war certainly prompted the erstwhile idealist J. B. Baillie's desertion of idealism in favour of a philosophy based upon 'critical common sense', which emphasized the concrete individuality of human beings.[2] But was this a good philosophical ground for a change of view? If so, why did not Jones, consistently with his stated criterion, abandon idealism also? He did not; and to the end he proclaimed his doctrines fervently – not least in his Gifford Lectures, *A Faith that Enquires* (1922). The possible inferences to be drawn are either that philosophers have difficulty in assessing 'the spirit of the period', or that in practice they do not always heed their assessments; or (which seems most likely) that the truth of a philosophical position is not so bound to the prevailing climate of opinion as Jones declared it to be. In fact Jones remained faithful to absolute idealism because it seemed to him to be preferable to any other *philosophical position*.

As already noted, idealism was to Jones the philosophy most in accord with the spirit of the age. He deemed it a presumption of its value that musicians and poets had welcomed its emphases, and observed: 'The theory of Hegel differs from that of Locke and Hume not more than the poetry of Goethe or Wordsworth from that of Pope and Swift . . .'[3] But idealism was, of course, a multifaceted phenomenon. One year later than the publication of

Jones's words, J. R. Illingworth observed, cautiously yet justly, that

> a really complete survey of contemporary opinion would disclose in it variety rather than unity – a multitude of incoherent and often incompatible points of view, all of which may in a sense be called modern, though many have ancient analogues; but none of which can claim to be typically representative of the age.[4]

Materialism, agnosticism, the new realism and rising pragmatism – all of these, in addition to idealism, claimed supporters at the time of Illingworth's writing. Furthermore, where idealism is concerned we may say that, as with peaks in a mountain range, the greater the distance between the viewer and the objects the more symmetry there appears to be. To pile metaphor upon analogy, we may say that idealism has numerous peaks – and not a few troughs.

Thus, to illustrate in a deliberately bald way, whereas Berkeley proposed what is sometimes known as psychological idealism, in which all existents have their being in being perceived by a mind – either ours or God's, Kant reinstated an objective order of phenomena, but left a realm of strictly unknowable noumena. Hegel, so many absolute idealists thought, had healed that breach though, according to those who became known as personal idealists, he had lost individual distinctiveness in the process. As if this were not enough, John Cook Wilson, who deserted the epistemological idealism of his teachers for a version of realism, nevertheless continued to maintain the reality of both spirit and matter, so that his pupil, C. C. J. Webb, placed him in the line of *Platonic* idealism.[5] These cryptic utterances must suffice for the present. An important part of my purpose is to elucidate those varieties of idealism which bear upon theological questions as I proceed. The desire to avoid the appearance of pedantry alone restrains me from enclosing the terms 'idealism' and 'idealist' within inverted commas every time I use them. These commas are, however, to be understood.

Is there any good reason for entering upon such an arduous labour? Was not the death-knell of idealism sounded long ago? As early as 1914 Bertrand Russell, himself a convert from idealism, proclaimed to his readers that that philosophy was an amalgam of 'stupid and trivial confusions'.[6] In 1934 Rudolf Metz wrote of the British idealist movement that it had 'about entirely receded into history'.[7] Undeniably, British idealism did not have force of numbers on its side after 1920, but however much its form may have varied, it has never entirely died out – as the work of such philosophers as T. M. Knox, H. J. Paton, A. C. Ewing and C. A. Campbell amply testifies.[8] That the last-named published his Gifford Lectures, *On Selfhood and Godhead* (1957), more than twenty years after Metz's verdict is instructive. Not indeed that Campbell was an 'old-fashioned' absolutist; rather, it was his emphasis upon the role of judgement in the acquisition of knowledge that kept him within what might be called 'Broad Church' idealism.

However, the mere survival of strands of thought, though a fact to be noted against any who may feel that philosophical theories are ever absolutely disproved and finally shelved, and against philosophers who may too eagerly compose epitaphs for movements of thought to which they are hostile, would not by itself suffice to motivate the writing of this book. What does move me is the fact that many British idealists of the period 1870–1950 sought to present their religious convictions through the medium of, or in some kind of relationship to, their favoured philosophical 'ism'. Were they thus led into methodological quagmires? Did they, perhaps, attenuate the Christian Gospel? In a word, our concern is with these philosophers *qua* proponents of a world view deemed to be in general harmony with Christianity, even if not identical at all points with Christian doctrine. Nor is our interest antiquarian only. Even if many philosophers have departed from, or have never embraced, any form of idealism, idealistic thought forms pervade the thought of Paul Tillich, for example, and are to this day drawn upon by process theologians, by such European theologians as Moltmann and Pannenberg, and by some who are in quest of a tolerable theology of religions. It is not therefore altogether 'irrelevant' to return as dispassionately as possible to a significant group of philosophers whose approach was from the standpoint of idealism. From one point of view our study might be regarded as a meditation upon two verdicts upon Hegelianism which are, perhaps, capable of extension to other varieties of idealism. In the mid-nineteenth century, before the heyday of British post-Hegelian idealism, J. D. Morell declared that 'Religion, if not destroyed by the Hegelian philosophy, is absorbed in it, and, *as religion,* for ever disappears.'[9] As if to echo this, McTaggart, nearly sixty years on, warned that Hegelianism was for theologians 'an enemy in disguise – the least evident but the most dangerous'.[10]

My principal concern, together with the mention of McTaggart's name, prompts some remarks upon the method to be followed here. Of McTaggart, A. E. Taylor wrote that in his book, *Some Dogmas of Religion* (1906), he 'offers a rare example of the combination of a fervent belief in the fundamental righteousness of the universe and in human immortality with an equally fervent denial of the existence of God'.[11] On the other hand, of F. H. Bradley and Bernard Bosanquet, Clement Webb wrote that 'To neither does the evidence of a future life seem strong, still less convincing.'[12] Without in any way denying the philosophical importance of McTaggart, Bradley and Bosanquet, I must point out that by my criterion of selection they will be accorded a peripheral place in this book. If, as I believe, the attempt to express Christian thought through the medium of idealism fails at certain crucial points, it is important that the idealists chosen for study should represent those who made the most persuasive attempts to succeed in this matter, and were most closely aligned to the main lines of Christian orthodoxy. T. H. Green, who mused upon the attractions of the unitarian position, might be thought by some to be thereby disqualified; but he is the fountain-head of so much that followed, and for that reason as well as for his own sake he cannot justifiably be omitted. Of all those to be discussed here in some detail : Green, Edward Caird, Henry Jones, A. S. Pringle-Pattison, J. R. Illingworth, Clement Webb and A. E. Taylor, it may with justice be claimed that they stood closer to what passed for Christian orthodoxy in their day than did McTaggart, Bradley and Bosanquet. Certainly the judgement of J. H. Muirhead (himself a pupil of Edward Caird) that 'British Idealism from the first has been in essence a philosophy of religion'[13] conveys an inaccurate sense of the motivation, and too narrow an impression of the breadth of concern of many idealist philosophers. Nevertheless, if the idealistic philosophical-theological marriage fails when my selection of idealists presides over it, it is not likely to work anywhere else. Given the general sympathy of the seven selected idealists with Christianity, the differences between them will be the more interesting, and their pupils' parting of the ways – with the philosophers Watson, MacKenzie and Muirhead remaining faithful to idealism, and the theologians Orr, Denney, Forrest,

Robert Mackintosh and Garvie deserting it – the more telling.

Three further methodological points must be made. First, I regard it as of great importance that, as far as possible, the idealists shall speak for themselves. I wish readers not merely to grasp their main ideas, but to hear their very different tones of voice. This will assist the assessment of the validity of any judgements which may be forthcoming. Secondly, I am thoroughly committed to the view that simply to treat of the 'great names' in any period can have a distorting effect. Hinterland thinkers are of great importance – not least those who set their faces against prevailing or significant intellectual tendencies. For this reason I have gone to some trouble to unearth lesser-known books, articles and reviews which will reveal the reception accorded to the main subjects of this study by their contemporaries. Thirdly, it is not to my present purpose to provide an account of idealism's retreat before realism, positivism and allegedly anti-metaphysical linguistic analysis.[14] My concern, to repeat, is with the bearing of post-Hegelian philosophical idealism upon Christian belief.

It goes without saying that others, among them Hastings Rashdall and James Ward, might have been selected for detailed examination. The seven under review do, however, raise the points crucial to Christian doctrine, and, from the activities of Green and Caird in the 1870s to the death of Webb in 1954, they encompass the period of British post-Hegelian idealism's peak, decline and (almost entire) fall.[15]

In the next chapter I shall introduce my seven selected idealists, providing for each a brief biographical sketch, and paying particular attention to the main lines of their thought, and to the verdicts passed upon them by their contemporaries and successors. A chapter on God, the absolute and the idealists will follow, and then I shall focus upon the ethical (and, to a lesser extent, the social) motif which informs so much of theistic idealism. We shall then be in a position to examine the views of our authors on specific Christian doctrines, and to assess the viability of the attempt to express Christian thought in terms of philosophical idealism. I shall conclude by drawing the several strands of the discussion together in a chapter on the legacy of idealism *vis-à-vis* Christian thought. Not indeed that I think we have heard the last of idealism (and hence the term 'legacy' is perhaps not the most suitable); but an attempt to take stock of the situation to date will be appropriate and necessary.

For the sake of clarity I must emphasize that my way of conducting this enquiry should not to be taken as implying that I think that there is a box labelled 'Christianity' and another labelled 'idealism', and that the philosophers under review sought to mix the contents of the one with those of the other. The situation was – to use a word beloved by some of them – more organic than that. They grew up breathing intellectual air impregnated by romanticism, evolutionary thought, and increasing interest in those of other faiths, and neither the Christianity they received nor the philosophy they imbibed can be divorced entirely from one another. By the same token, while I shall find it necessary to query some of their arguments on philosophical grounds, when indicating pitfalls in their writings from the point of view of the Christian faith, I by no means imply that I alone have grasped the Gospel perfectly, or that my understanding of the Christian faith has not been influenced by my context, which is in many ways different from theirs. In a word, my attitude is not at all sectarian, and I regard this project as an attempt to scrutinize 'intellectual portraits' in a family album, and not at all as a heresy-hunting expedition. I need hardly explain that it is not for jingoistic reasons that I confine myself to British thinkers. It is simply that some of our thinkers were pupils of others, some were in correspondence with others, they reviewed one another's books and, even where personal acquaintance was slight or non-existent, the younger ones were well versed in the thought of all. Lacking the structure of a school, and too geographically spread in most cases to become close personal friends, they, for all their differences of opinion, jointly represent a relatively coherent philosophical approach which was of considerable significance in their time, and which is not without its echoes to this day.

Since philosophical idealism did not have its origin *ex nihilo* in T. H. Green, we shall do well first to enquire how the philosophical idealism of our chosen period found its way to Britain; why it found such fertile soil; and what were the philosophical loose ends which its exponents thought they were able to tie by utilizing it. These matters will occupy us for the remainder of this chapter. As we proceed it will be helpful, even before introducing our principal subjects and their constructive work, to view the philosophical heritage as far as possible through their eyes.

I

The great advances in the understanding of the cosmos, associated with the names of Copernicus, Kepler, Galileo and Newton, could only result in intellectual friction so long as they were accompanied by pre-critical views of the Bible. Hence what Clement Webb, with reference to the dualistic solution favoured by many Christian thinkers, described as the 'double-mindedness' of the seventeenth and eighteenth centuries.[16] The material phenomena were to be investigated by scientific processes and evaluated by criteria appropriate to empirical studies; religion was deemed to be concerned with the transcendent order, with the several varieties of deism as the terminus; and it was only a matter of time before the observable results of the sciences prompted some to question the continuing relevance of the supernatural. Thus to materialism, naturalism and, later, agnosticism.

Romanticism's objective was that of healing the dualism bequeathed by the Renaissance. Its therapy entailed the advocacy of an immanent God, absolute, rational principle, world soul – the nouns varied according to the predilections of the several writers. Spinoza (1632–77), though by no means to be labelled a Romantic, provided impetus in this direction. His immanent absolute – *Quicquid est, in Deo est*[17] – which imparted a pantheistic hue to his theory, led to the charge that he had obliterated all important distinctions, not least that between good and evil. On 12 October 1665, Henry Oldenberg wrote to Spinoza to ask 'how each part of Nature accords with the whole of it, and in what way it is connected with all the other parts'. In his reply of 20 November, Spinoza explained that there are, by God's design and not by our judgements, degrees of perfections, and that he does not 'attribute to Nature beauty or ugliness, order or confusion. For things cannot, except with respect to our imagination, be called beautiful, or ugly, ordered or confused.' Rather, he means that the several parts of Nature mutually adapt themselves to one another in such a way as to minimize opposition.[18] To some the concession regarding degrees of perfection was the Achilles' heel of his system. Even so, the notion of the organic unity of all things exercised a powerful sway in Europe, where it found impressive literary expression, supremely in the writings of Goethe.

In addition to the ontological dualism with which we have so far been concerned, there is also in idealism's hinterland an epistemological dualism whose fountain-head is Descartes (1596–1650). As is well known, Descartes, having in his quest of certainty resolved to doubt all received opinion, discovered that he could not doubt that there existed a doubting thinker. He therefore adopted as his secure philosophical base the proposition *cogito ergo sum.* To Descartes the ego was an impersonal substance, for ever distinguished from the material world. When Descartes took the further step of supposing that if he ceased to think he would cease to exist, he made that fatal leap from epistemology to ontology which has plagued so much of subsequent philosophy.[19] If we state Pringle-Pattison's criticism of Descartes at this point we shall supply our first piece of evidence for the fact that one may be an idealist in ontology and a realist in epistemology: 'As thinking . . . in whatever form we take it, implies the relation of the thinker to an objective world, it must be fallacious to start as if one side of the antithesis could enjoy an independent existence.'[20] In this remark we see also the influence of that post-Kantian hindsight which enabled Webb to say that 'it was Descartes that with his *Cogito ergo sum* originated the subjectivist trend which has marked so much of modern thought and which culminates in the Kantian criticism.'[21] (By contrast, and as a harbinger of discussions to come, we may note Henry Jones's view that

> the most significant of all the discoveries of modern Epistemology [is] that an idea is an idea, and a judgment is true or false, in virtue of their relation to a *system* of ideas or judgments; that their certainty rests not in themselves, but in the system of knowledge of which they are a part; and that their certainty grows as the system of knowledge expands.[22]

Here is affirmed the coherence theory of truth, the epistemological staple diet of consistent absolute idealists, but viewed askance by personal idealists in general, and by personal idealists with a dash of Scottish common-sense realism in particular).

To resume: by his 'Copernican revolution' in philosophy to the effect that 'objects must conform to our cognition'[23] – that is to say, that the mind actively participates in the creation of knowledge out of what is empirically presented to it – Kant (1724–1804) set about removing one kind of epistemological dualism. While agreeing with Hume that what is given in knowledge is sensation, and that sensation cannot yield necessity, Kant invoked the mind in such a way as to bring ideas and objects into vital relation with each other. This move, declared Henry Jones, 'constitutes the transition from Naturalism (or Materialism) to Idealism'.[24] On the other hand, by virtue of his distinction between phenomena, which are knowable by the human mind, and noumena, or things-in-themselves, which are not, he bequeathed his own brand of epistemological dualism to his successors. As Jones forthrightly put it,

> the subjective origin of Kant's speculative effort rendered it a vain and impossible endeavour to reach things as they are, or things in themselves, which, so far from 'conforming to our cognition', remained absolutely beyond its reach as unknowable and empty entities. What Kant succeeded in demonstrating was that 'our cognition does not conform to objects' *if objects are to be regarded as they were conceived by Hume and the Associationists,* that is to say, if they are conceived as independent facts and events really disconnected, though outwardly and contingently combined in our knowledge by means of purely mental relations. He showed, as against his predecessors, that the only Nature which could be knowable by us is a Nature which is systematic, and which owes its systematic character to a principle that is analogous to the supreme unity of self-consciousness.[25]

We have here an echo of T. H. Green's earlier lament to the effect that Kant's alleged phenomena–noumena dualism, whose sway over British minds Green attributed to William Hamilton's baneful interpretation of Kant, had come to overshadow

> The really prolific element in his system, the view of the 'noumenon', which he calls the ego, as the source of the categories, and thus at once of the order of phenomena and our knowledge of it, and again as itself constituting an intelligible world of ends freely pursued . . .[26]

Green commends Caird for showing that, having broken with Wolff's mistaken identification of self-consistency with truth, Kant, in his treatise of 1766, did hold that 'experience of an actual, but intrinsically unintelligible, sequence of phenomena teaches us all that we know, and that the office of metaphysics is only to warn us against the pretence of knowledge otherwise founded.' This, Green declares, is 'the position which most of [Kant's] English assailants have never left'.[27] But both Green and Caird, like the latter's pupil Jones, found the clue to the resolution of the difficulty in Kant himself (albeit a Kant construed in Caird's and Jones's case through Hegelian eyes).[28] Caird contends that while Kant did maintain a 'sharp antithesis between the phenomenal and the real or intelligible worlds', he

> was also the first to supply the conclusive means of refuting it. For, while he treated the world of experience as a system of objects – which are external to each other in space, and pass through successive phases in time, according to necessary laws of coexistence and succession – he showed also that this world of necessity stands in essential relation to the unity of the self that knows it. Hence, any explanation of the world, or of any object in it, which does not take account of this relation, must be regarded as abstract and imperfect.[29]

So too in the realm of morals: Caird was utterly convinced that the opposition between theoretical and practical reason, as posited by Kant, vitiated morality, for it rendered the realization of the good for ever unattainable in the phenomenal world.[30] His sepulchral verdict was that as between the two spheres of reason there was 'a "great gulf fixed" . . . and moral freedom moves safely in a vacant "kingdom of ends", where it never comes in contact with any necessity of nature.'[31]

The truth would seem to be that as with Augustine, so with Kant: by selective reading opposed parties could claim his endorsement of their own views. Thus both nineteenth-century agnostics who recalled the dualism between the knowable and the unknowable, and the same century's transcendental idealists who invoked Kant's categories of reason, could claim him as their own. But not even the latter position satisfied all anti-agnostics. With some justification, Robert Mackintosh, like Jones a pupil of Caird, concluded that 'The great critic of [Humean] scepticism has diverged from idealism towards idealism again, or has given his idealism a sceptical colour, mitigated – but only mitigated – by faith in the moral consciousness.'[32]

Let us dwell for a little longer upon Kant's ambiguous legacy to religious thought. Kant's searching criticism of the traditional ontological, cosmological and teleological arguments for the existence of God, coupled with his apparent scepticism concerning our ability to know the abstract thing-in-itself which exists beyond the phenomenal realm, had a direct impact upon received understandings of the certitude of God's existence and the reality of a future life. Adjustments had to be made, and some concluded that Kant had legitimated agnosticism concerning God and immortality, and naturalism and materialism concerning our understanding of the cosmos. In 1890 Pringle-Pattison went so far as to say that 'The so-called Kantian revival, of which so much has been heard of late, . . . has been for the most part a popularising of Kant's Agnostic results.'[33]

On the other hand, and in amplification elsewhere of his remark quoted above, Green wrote in exposition of Kant,

> It has become a commonplace among us that all which we know consists of phenomena and their relations, but the true import of this doctrine is seldom realised. In its common application, it tends rather to hinder us from recognising the function of thought in the constitution of the known world, than to deliver us from the oppression by the outsideness and beyondness under which we have learnt to figure the relation of that world to ourselves. Yet if it means anything, it means that the world, which alone we know or can know, consists in relations to consciousness and in relations of those relations. Space, time, matter, motion, force, are not indeed modes of consciousness, but apart from consciousness they would not be.[34]

While some – Pringle-Pattison among them – would not have agreed with the last sentence here, he did value Kant's contribution (not agnostically construed) for two things in particular. First, Kant had asserted 'the necessity of a permanent subject of knowledge . . . Connection or relatedness of any sort – even Hume's association – is possible only through the presence of such a [subject–object] unity to each term of the relation.'[35] Secondly, Kant had upheld and bequeathed to all subsequent idealist philosophy the 'conception of intrinsic value as the clue to the ultimate nature of reality'.[36] Most British idealists would, however, have endorsed Muirhead's summary of Caird's view that Kant 'had broken the spell that sets subject and object in irreconcilable opposition to each other. On the other hand he is himself still under the spell of the opposition of knowing and being.'[37] Or, as Henry Jones lyrically expressed it,

Sense and spirit, the material world and the mind of man, natural necessity and moral freedom, the blank despair of Materialism and the empty void of scepticism on the one hand, and, on the other, the reasoned hope of a destiny to whose spiritual splendour there are no bounds, remained for Kant opposed to one another till the evening twilight wrapped his great mind in its folds.[38]

Less poetically, Webb drew out the religious implications of Kant's method in some detail. The combination of Kant's suspicion of Schwärmerei, 'enthusiasm', and his quest of a religion within the bounds of reason with his epistemological principles, according to which God can be an object of faith only, led him to reject the concept of the supernatural, and with it the idea of *revealed* religion. When to this is added what Webb calls his 'markedly *unhistorical* temper of mind', we have the seeds of a recurring suspicion that, where our seven idealists are concerned, much that is of importance for their religion cannot easily be accommodated within their philosophy.[39]

It would be premature at this juncture to write, 'Enter Hegel', for that philosopher's contribution will not adequately be understood unless we see how he adjusted himself to the responses of his contemporaries – Schleiermacher (1768–1834), Fichte (1762–1814) and Schelling (1775–1854) – to the legacy of Kant.

Schleiermacher's response was that of throwing down the gauntlet before the cultured despisers of religion of his day. Whereas they were persuaded that the traditional arguments for God's existence had successfully been demolished, and therefore that the grounds of religious belief had been removed, he rebuked them for supposing that a religion thus grounded was truly religion at all: 'If you have only given attention to these dogmas and opinions . . . you do not yet know religion itself, and what you despise is not it.'[40] Indeed, he continues, 'if you regard the systems in all schools, how often are they mere habitations and nurseries of the dead letter.'[41] Schleiermacher's advice to the cultured despisers was to 'turn from everything usually reckoned religion, and fix your regard on the inward emotions and dispositions, as all utterances and acts of inspired men direct'.[42] 'Belief,' he affirms, 'must be something different from a mixture of opinions about God and the world . . . Piety cannot be an instinct craving for a mess of metaphysical and ethical crumbs.'[43] It is not that Schleiermacher wishes to separate knowledge and piety, or piety and action; rather, he maintains their distinctness but also their inseparability. But this unity is grounded in the pious feeling, and this feeling, the very root of real religion, is a feeling of absolute dependence.

In the course of his exposition Schleiermacher invites the despisers to

> Offer with me reverently a tribute to the manes of the holy, rejected Spinoza. The high World-Spirit pervaded him; the Infinite was his beginning and his end; the Universe was his only and his everlasting love.[44]

No doubt, as W. B. Selbie wrote, 'the Spinoza Schleiermacher knew and reverenced was in some respects a creation of his own',[45] not least because of Schleiermacher's insistence, against Spinoza, that there could be reciprocal relations between the believer and God. The fact remains, however, that from Spinoza Schleiermacher drew the clue to the unity of reason, emotion and piety, the source of which was the immanence of the God who works in all things. Thus,

> The usual conception of God as one single being outside of the world and behind the world [that is, the deistic view] is not the beginning and the end of religion . . . [T]he true nature of religion is . . . immediate consciousness of the Deity as He is found in ourselves and in the world . . . In the midst of finitude to be at one with the Infinite and in every moment to be eternal is the immortality of religion.[46]

Like Schleiermacher, Fichte spurned Kant's unknowable Absolute, but unlike that of 'the father of modern theology' his thought was of an intellectualist rather than an affective type. While agreeing with Kant that the noumenal transcends the phenomenal, he resolved the dualism of the two realms by making the free rational ego the sole source of deductions regarding space, time and the categories of quality, quantity, relation and modality, which Kant had deemed to be inexplicable characteristics of phenomena as distinct from things-in-themselves. His results, which he designated idealism or criticism, Fichte distinguished from what he called dogmatism, namely, the doctrine that we must set out from the investigation of phenomena. In his view the logical consequence of dogmatism – even in its more spiritual Spinozistic form – was materialism. As Pringle-Pattison reminds us, 'Fichte described his own system as an inverted Spinozism, in which the Absolute Ego stands in place of Substance, thus conserving the rights of the self-conscious life, and justifying the name Idealism.'[47] He further explains that whereas 'Kant was under no temptation to separate the transcendental and the empirical self, because the former was for him simply the logical unity of thought in general', Fichte identified the transcendental self with what was variously named as 'the divine or creative Self', or 'the Absolute Ego, or the universal consiousness'. Herein lies the distinctive feature of neo-Kantianism, which recurs in the writings of T. H. Green.[48]

As Fichte's thought developed, he for a time left phenomena even further behind, so to speak, and arrived at the absolute *qua* ground of being about which nothing could be known or said. Hence Hegel's jibe concerning the night in which all cows are black. Later still Fichte posited an ideal knowledge, the object of which (since there can be no knowledge which is not knowledge of something or someone) is God. But knowledge and God are not identified. On the contrary God, being absolute and self-subsistent, does not enter into process, or come to be. All that can be said is that the absolute is. Despite this, and in accordance with the teleological thrust in his exposition, our life must consist in striving to become the image of God. What is more, the ideal knowledge does not require a subject. Hence Pringle-Pattison's dry remark,

> The final disappearance of the empty Ego is hardly a cause for wonder or regret . . . [Nevertheless] Thought *exists* only as the thought of a thinker; it must be centred somewhere. To thought *per se* we can attribute neither existence nor causal activity; and this being so, it can have no place in metaphysics as a theory of Being.[49]

Edward Caird's verdict upon Fichte was equally blunt:

> The error that clings to Fichte's speculations is . . . that he treats consciousness merely as a necessary illusion which exists simply with a view to self-consciousness, and hence is led to regard self-consciousness itself – because it is essentially related to this necessary illusion – as a schema or image of an unknowable absolute. In fact, in the end Fichte falls back upon the abstract identity in which Kant had found his noumenon, and his philosophy seems to lose itself in mysticism.[50]

Originally sympathetic towards Fichte's subjective monism, Schelling, whose aesthetic sensitivities were acute, eventually left the path of stern intellectualism, and sought to restore the relations between natural phenomena and an ideal spirit which manifested itself within them. To Schelling, nature was an organism which achieves consciousness in the thinking self. As Caird put it,

> Unfortunately, in correcting Fichte's over-statement of one of the two sides of the Kantian philosophy, Schelling fell into an equal over-statement on the other side . . . [T]o say that the absolute equally manifests itself in nature and spirit, is almost equivalent to saying that it does not manifest itself at all; for if the distinguishing characters of mind and matter are treated as unimportant, and their identity alone is insisted on, what distinctions *can* be of importance? The absolute unity becomes necessarily a pure 'indifference', as Schelling calls it, an absolute which rests in itself and withdraws itself from all contact with the intelligence . . .[51]

We are now in a position to review the adjustments to the foregoing positions which were supplied by Hegel (1770–1831). While he assented to Spinoza's doctrine of immanent causality, Hegel's absolute is subject, not substance.[52] Over against Kant's subjective treatment of the categories, Hegel insisted that 'Thoughts do not stand between us and things, shutting us off from the things; they rather shut us together with them.'[53] As Henry Jones neatly expressed it, since Kant set out from the subject–object distinction (although the ever-more-shadowy things-in-themselves did not entirely disappear), his 'task to the end was that of reconciling differences, that of Hegel was to differentiate a unity'.[54] In this way, according to Caird, Hegel overcame the dualism between the pure intelligence and its object, the intelligible world, which had been bequeathed to thought by Aristotle.[55] Caird was the first to admit that 'The thought that there is a unity which lies beneath all opposition, and that, therefore, all opposition is capable of reconciliation, is unfamiliar to our ordinary consciousness.' The reason for this is that 'That unity is not usually an object of consciousness, just because it is the presupposition of all consciousness.'[56] Hegel does not intend to obliterate the distinction between being and non-being, however; rather, his point is that if this distinction is made absolute, it vanishes.[57] Thus, for example, substantiality and relativity are one in the sense that neither can be comprehended without the other. If an entity exists, it does so in relation to other entities, and its relativity is an essential feature of its own being.[58] And both the subject–object distinction and the unifying self-consciousness are mutually essential the one to the other.[59]

Consistently with this, Hegel sought 'to connect the ethical as well as the intellectual experience of man directly with the divine life, and by so doing to root Kant's abstract individual in the historic life of humanity'.[60] As free, the human being is self-determined in both knowledge and action: 'he must find *himself* in the object he knows, and realise *himself* in the end to which he devotes himself.'[61] It is not without significance that this intellectual and ethical restoration of the individual coincided with the revolutionary cries of 'Liberty, fraternity, equality' which were echoing around Europe from their revolutionary locus in France, or that Hegel, with hindsight, was to eulogize the Revolution, grounded as it was in the conviction of the reconciliation of the secular with the divine, and to deem Napoleon a 'world-soul'.[62] As J. E. Toews points out,

> The general ideal of Hellenic 'wholeness' was an inheritance from the neoclassicism of the eighteenth century, but the members of Hegel's generation reinterpreted this ideal in terms of their own particular historical experiences and tasks, focusing on the sociohistorical matrix of the self-sufficient wholeness of the Greek personality and the beauty of Greek art.[63]

In Hegel's writings, accordingly, Kant's abstract distinction between God and human beings is dispensed with.[64] Both Hegel and Schleiermacher sought to surmount the God–humanity dualism, but whereas Schleiermacher spoke, against the philosophers, of 'This miserable love of system', which excludes the perceptions of those 'Seers of the Infinite'[65] who understand that the seat of religion is in the feeling of absolute dependence, Hegel insisted that the sought-after unity could be achieved only by means of rational speculation. As contrasted with Fichte, who landed in an abstract identity of subject and object, and Schelling, the pantheizing tendency of whose thought put the subject–object distinction at risk, Caird remarks that Hegel regarded

> the external world, not as Fichte regarded it, as merely the opposite of spirit, nor as Schelling regarded it, as merely the repetition and

co-equal of spirit, but rather as its necessary manifestation, or as that in and through which alone it can realise itself.[66]

But this emphasis upon realization, becoming, underscores the teleological thrust of Hegel's thought, and, to Pringle-Pattison, 'it may cordially be allowed that [in this respect] Hegel represents what is profoundest and best in modern philosophy.'[67]

Not indeed that Hegel's dialectical method in which art, religion and philosophy are regarded as forming an ascending scale of thesis, antithesis and synthesis in absolute spirit was universally adopted – least of all in Britain. On the contrary, Pringle-Pattison rightly judged that

> The Method, so far as that means an invariable self-repeating formula, has been quietly shelved of late, even by those whose thoughts have been most plainly moulded by Hegel . . . [I]t was only, I think, with the rank and file of the Hegelian army that the dialectic method actually became a fetish.[68]

I have confined my account of Hegel's philosophical legacy to that legacy as perceived by the idealists in whom I am primarily interested. To them, in a word, Hegel resolved the epistemological and ontological dichotomies bequeathed by Kant. As we shall see, some of them thought that Hegel's remedy had few, others that it had more, deleterious side-effects. But Hegel at least came to their assistance. He did so, however, in the wake of a philosophical tradition which was fertilized by Lockean epistemology, Berkeleian psychological idealism, Humean scepticism and Scottish common sense. These factors, whether positively or negatively, influenced British idealists, notably Green, in a neo-Kantian direction, and helped to restrain the absolute triumph of Hegel. Indeed, Pfleiderer welcomed the fact that Kant's influence upon post-Hegelian idealists was more clearly seen in the writings of Caird, Stirling and Green than in those of most German idealists:

> It is really a remarkable phenomenon in national psychology, that in the same years in which in Germany the younger generation discovers the progress of philosophy in a backward movement from Hegel to Kant, and from Kant to Hume and Locke, the younger generation in Great Britain has gone in exactly the opposite direction.[69]

We must therefore turn more directly to the British soil in which

Hegelianism took root if we would understand the varying degrees of enthusiasm with which Hegel was received by our seven idealists.

II

In the seventeenth century the British intellectual climate was significantly influenced by the idealism of the Cambridge Platonists. In the first half of the eighteenth century Berkeley advanced his psychological idealism. The connections between these versions of idealism and between both of them and post-Hegelian idealism are so loose, and the intervening intellectual shifts (supremely that inspired by Kant) are so significant, that it would be improper to speak in terms of any major indebtedness of the British post-Hegelian idealists to these idealistic forebears. Nevertheless a number of the later British idealists took the trouble to adjust their own positions to that of Berkeley,[70] and some of them made reference to the Cambridge Platonists. We shall therefore do well to take up our story, chronologically, with the latter, and then, in order to place Berkeley in sequence, to permit the intervention of Locke.

As with the post-Hegelian idealists, so with their Cambridge predecessors: their thought was by no means homogeneous. While none of the latter would have disagreed with Whichcote that 'The *Spirit of a Man is the Candle of the Lord,* Lighted by God, and Lighting us to God',[71] Henry More (1614–87), for example, emphasized more than others the way in which God's lamp is nourished by external phenomena. Thus, against advocates of the inner light he maintained that

> *This Conscience within them* is not a thing so absolutely within them, that it can take no information from that which is *without.* For it is manifest that this *Lamp of God* that burneth in us, is fed and nourished from external Objects.[72]

Not always careful to distinguish Plotinus from Plato, and drawn to Origen and the Alexandrian theologians, the Platonists opposed the materialism of Hobbes and what they deemed to be the materialistic atheism of Spinoza. As to Cartesian dualism, it was not until his *Divine Dialogues* and *Enchiridion Ethicum* (1667) that

More, who had done much to introduce the writings of Descartes to Cambridge, argued that this dualism was fatal to Platonism and, hence, to Christianity.[73] More especially invoked the concept of 'plastic nature' – that vital force inherent in nature as a whole and in all its parts – to heal the dualism (the fact that Plotinus had borrowed the concepts of *dunamis* and *energeia* from *Aristotle* notwithstanding);[74] while Ralph Cudworth (1617–88), as if in unwitting contradiction of nineteenth-century evolutionists, declared that

> in the universe things did not thus ascend and mount, or climb up from lower perfection to higher; but, on the contrary, descend and slide down from higher to lower: so that the first original of all things was not the most imperfect, but the most perfect being.[75]

At the same time we find clear indebtedness to Descartes in Cudworth's distinction between sense and thought, and in his understanding of the mind–body relation and of sensation.[76]

Despite his attack upon innate ideas, Locke (1632–1704), no less than the Cambridge Platonists, was a debtor to Descartes. As Pringle-Pattison reminds us,[77] Locke concurred with Descartes in limiting knowledge to the realm of necessary truth, and he presupposed that mind and matter are two distinct substances. Hence, and given their sharp distinction between the knowable and the unknowable, the supreme task of philosophy for Descartes and Locke was to determine the limits of human reason, and to close the subject–object gap. With a view to the latter they both had recourse to the theory of representative perception. In Locke's words,

> Since the things the mind contemplates are none of them, besides itself, present to the understanding, it is necessary that something else, as a sign or representation of the thing it considers, should be present to it: and these are ideas.[78]

It is not that, for Locke, the mind knows only its own states; rather, 'Ideas seem to possess for him a quasi-substantive existence between the knower and the real things,'[79] these last remaining for ever unknowable. Thus Locke, no less than Kant, has his unknowable, and if this aspect of the latter's thought was hailed by nineteenth-century agnostics, Locke handed Hume his sceptical weapon – but only after Berkeley's attempted improvement of the epistemological condition.

Where Locke understood secondary qualities to be a series of effects produced upon the mind by the independent world of material and unknowable substances, Berkeley (1685–1753) contended that the whole of our sense experience – appearance and essence – is communicated to us by the divine will. Knowledge is thus an entirely 'internal' matter, and accordingly there is no need to concern ourselves with the passage from 'internal' to 'external'.[80] As he forthrightly put it, the claim that 'unthinking things have a subsistence of their own distinct from being perceived by spirits' is 'a most groundless and absurd notion', and 'the very root of scepticism'.[81] In the opinion of Caird's pupil, J. S. Mackenzie, his teacher did well to resist all such subjectivism, for

> It is that false idealism, more than anything else, that blocks the way to the true. For it is easy to see that the false type of idealism leads by inevitable steps to the devouring gulf of solipsism, from which the mind at once recoils. If once we allow that the existence of things consists only in their being known, it is soon seen to be impossible to exempt spiritual substance or any other kind of reality from this fatal doom.[82]

This, of course, is exactly what Hume (1711–76) demonstrated. Locke, he argued, had no right to conclude from ideas in the mind to transcendent real objects, for

> to form the idea of an object, and to form an idea simply, is the same thing; the reference of the idea to the object being an extraneous denomination, of which in itself it bears no mark or character.[83]

Following A. Campbell Fraser, Pringle-Pattison avers that while it is true that Locke ignored the distinction which Hume here denies, he is unjustly handled by Green, who

> seeks to pin Locke down to his sensationalist formulae, interpreted with the utmost rigour of the law, in the light of Hume's deductions, whereas it is apparent on every page of the Essay that Locke never dreamt of their bearing such a meaning.[84]

On the other hand, Berkeley's

> Idealism or Spiritualism which does not guarantee the rights of the object is a lop-sided theory which has no defence against the further inroads of its own logic. Put forward as a short and easy method with

the sceptics, Berkeleianism only preluded to the sceptical nihilism of Hume.[85]

Positively, Hume contended that all knowledge is derived from sensation, and that our sense impressions yield ideas which, for reasons which Hume does not supply, happen to form associations. Our understanding of cause and effect is thus, for example, to be construed in terms of the regularity with which sensation B follows sensation A. On all of which Percival Chubb remarked,

> This doctrine of the association of ideas is a wonderful solvent; it not only dissolves cause and effect, but it dissolves the idea of a mind, an Ego, an external world. If ideas make their associations on their own responsibility, there is obviously no need of a master of ceremonies, a director, or a referee.

The doctrine, he continues, was revived more elaborately and with reference now to states of consciousness by Herbert Spencer (1820–1903), but 'the flux of the mind's thoughts and sensations . . . is still a straggling, disorderly procession with no spectator to view it, or know it as a procession.'[86]

As he reviewed the earlier phases of the debate just described, Pringle-Pattison summed matters up thus:

> [I]dealism, materialism, and Humism have meaning only with reference to the assumption of a duality of self-existing substances to which experience is referred as to its causes. These theories exist as the denial of one of the factors, or as the assertion of the impossibility of proving either, but they do not attack the abstraction on which this hypothesis of dual existence was originally founded. Hume is a sceptic because he cannot prove either mind or matter to be real in the sense in which Cartesian and Lockian metaphysics understood reality. But if such realities are no more than fictions of abstract thought, then a sceptical disproof of our knowledge of them is so far from being a final disproof of the possibility of any real knowledge, that it is rather to be taken as indispensably preliminary to the attainment of a true notion of what reality is.[87]

At this point the contribution of Thomas Reid (1710–96) must briefly be noted, for Pringle-Pattison in particular and, at a later stage in his career, A. E. Taylor were indebted to Scottish common-sense philosophy, notwithstanding the fact that they would have agreed with Mackenzie that

The objection to such a realism as that of Reid is not that [against Hume] it recognises that we are in contact with an objective order; but that it is too naïve in its interpretation of that order.[88]

On the other hand, while commendably anticipating Kant's view of the logical place of judgement in apprehension,[89] 'it went beyond Kant in refusing to be deluded of its significance by interpreting the "judgment" as referring after all to mere appearance.'[90] Reid thus crusaded against Berkeley's view that the objects of our knowledge are ideas in our own minds,[91] and contended that the theories of Descartes, Malebranche, Locke, Berkeley and Hume alike land us in scepticism because they rest upon the theory of ideas, which is but an unproved hypothesis. Against them all he argued that perception and relationless sensations may not be identified if our perceptions are to have objective reference. 'I am ready to admit', declared Pringle-Pattison,

> that, in their zeal against subjective idealism, [Reid and his followers] often over-stated their case, and maintained the independence of the world in terms which imply the old two-substance doctrine. But the Natural Dualism of the school, as it is sometimes called, does not in itself involve this doctrine. On the contrary, it might be argued that, by maintaining a theory of Immediate Perception, Scottish philosophy destroys the foreignness of matter to mind, and thus implicitly removes the only foundation of a real dualism.[92]

He further emphasizes the fact that the common-sense philosophers did not set out to be ontologists: they were epistemologists opposing what they took to be a sceptical virus in the form of representative perception.[93] No doubt their dogmatically asserted theory of immediate perception is inadequate, but to the extent to which Reid saw that it is only because of their borrowing from realism that the idealistic substitutes for a trans-subjective real world can be stated and discussed he bequeathed a philosophical legacy of real importance.[94]

It cannot be denied that in Britain the way was paved for the reception of German philosophy more by men of letters than by professional philosophers. Prominent among the former was Coleridge (1772–1834), who had spent fourteen months in Germany, and had imbibed something of the Romantic spirit from lectures he heard there. For this he was vastly teased by his literary contemporaries. In delightful prose Hazlitt explains how, having been 'engaged with Hartley's tribes of mind', having flirted with Priestley's materialism, 'where he felt himself imprisoned by the logician's spell, like Ariel in the cloven pine-tree, [Coleridge] suddenly became enamoured of Bishop Berkeley's fairy-tale world . . .', thence *inter alia* through 'Cudworth's Intellectual System (a huge pile of learning, unwieldy, enormous)' to unitarianism. Thereafter 'Spinoza became his God, and he took up the vast chain of being in his hand', until 'poetry redeemed him from this spectral philosophy.' The pilgrimage continued, and at one point Coleridge 'wandered into Germany and lost himself in the labyrinths of the Hartz Forest and of the Kantean philosophy, and amongst the cabalistic names of Fichte and Schelling and Lessing, and God knows who . . .' With delicate irony Hazlitt confides, 'It was not to be supposed that Mr Coleridge could keep on at the rate he set off . . .'[95]

A few years later Coleridge, now under the *alias* Mr Flosky is found, together with other thinly disguised literary figures, in Thomas Love Peacock's *Nightmare Abbey* (1818). Peacock explains the derivation of his name in a footnote: 'A *corruption* of Filosky, quasi *philoskios,* a lover, or spectator, of shadows'.[96] At first an enthusiastic supporter of the French Revolution, Flosky, dismayed by the failure of that movement to fulfil its promise, concluded that

> the overthrow of the feudal fortresses of tyranny and superstition was the greatest calamity that had ever befallen mankind; and that their only hope now was to rake the rubbish together, and rebuild it without any of those loopholes by which the light had originally crept in. To qualify himself for a coadjutor in this laudable task, he plunged into the central opacity of Kantian metaphysics, and lay *perdu* several years in transcendental darkness, till the common daylight of commonsense became intolerable to his eyes.[97]

He embarked upon synthetic philosophy, which has for its goal 'some unattainable abstraction', and which proceeds by deducing a third assumption from the union of two unprovable assumptions: 'The beauty of this process is', he declares,

> that at every step it strikes out into two branches, in a compound ratio of ramification; so that you are perfectly sure of losing your way, and

keeping your mind in perfect health, by the perpetual exercise of an interminable quest; and for these reasons I have christened my eldest son Emanuel Kant Flosky.[98]

I introduce these literary references not by way of light relief, nor out of self-indulgence, but in order to show (a) that Coleridge's mental lineage was, according to one's degree of sympathy with him, manifold or muddled; (b) that he unquestionably introduced German ideas into Britain; (c) that writers who draw too straight a line of indebtedness between Coleridge and the post-Hegelian idealists overlook both his post-Revolution temperamental conservatism and his lack of reference (except in marginalia and notebooks)[99] to Hegel; (d) that there was in Britain a general cultural as well as a more specifically philosophical barrier to German thought; and (e) that the maintenance of this barrier could, and in the case of the literary men we have just encountered did, lead to some serious misrepresentations of Coleridge. Thus, for example, he cannot simply be construed as a Kantian, for unlike Kant, to whom God, freedom and immortality were postulates, conditions of thought, but not objects of knowledge, to Coleridge they could be apprehended by reason. Nor was he a rationalist pure and simple. On the contrary, he elevated the moral and spiritual, and not simply the intellectual, aspects of the God–humanity relation. In this way he goes beyond both Kant and the Cambridge Platonists John Smith and Henry More, to whom he declared himself indebted.[100]

Turning now to the philosophical barrier against German thought, I find that there is some justification for Pringle-Pattison's remark that 'the enlightenment of one century lives on, as dogma and prejudice, to impede the higher thought of the next.'[101] Thus, although John Stuart Mill could say of Coleridge that his was a 'seminal mind',[102] the philosophical advantage was, at least until the 1860s, with the empiricism of Bentham and the utilitarianism of James Mill and his son in England, and with the heirs of common sense in Scotland.

Hence where Britain was concerned, Kant, whose works gradually became known from about 1790 onwards, had to make his way in the face of some misunderstanding of his position. We have already noted two literary caricatures, but now our concern is with philosophers. As F. D. Maurice noted, Kant's philosophy had been received in Britain more as 'transcendental' than as 'critical'. In consequence of this,

> The notion that Kant was, in some sense, reversing the decrees of Locke, by bringing in *a priori* truths has blinded us to the fact that the German had an even greater horror than the Englishman of that 'ocean' which he forbade us to approach.[103]

But if Kant was not adequately understood by some of his successors, it is equally certain that he would have found it hard to understand some of them. Indeed, he would strongly have repudiated the neo-Kantian identification of the transcendental ego with the divine self-consciousness. To Kant the latter is 'a non-discursive understanding, the very possibility of which we are unable to comprehend'.[104] He regretted the way in which 'The logical exposition of thought in general is mistaken for a metaphysical determination of the object.' On which Pringle-Pattison remarks, 'The words are spoken of the metaphysical psychologists, but it would be impossible to characterise more aptly the fallacy which underlies the Neo-Kantian deification of the abstract unity of thought.'[105]

Among philosophers who may be said imperfectly to have received Kant was Thomas Brown (1778–1820). He discussed Kant in *The Edinburgh Review* of 1803, but it was a Kant seen through the eyes of the French philosopher, Villers,[106] Brown himself having no German. Brown's predecessor in the Chair of Moral Philosophy at Edinburgh, Dugald Stewart (1753–1828) was self-confessedly innocent of German, and he likewise drew on French sources for assistance in writing a less than fully comprehending chapter on 'Kant and the Other Metaphysicians of the New German School'.[107] Stewart declares that his lack of German

> would have prevented me from saying anything of the philosophy of Kant if the extraordinary pretensions with which it was first brought forward in this island, contrasted with the total oblivion into which it soon after very suddenly fell, had not seemed to demand some attention to so wonderful a phenomenon in the literary history of the eighteenth century.[108]

Stewart's particular debt was to Madame de Staël's *De l'Allemagne* (1810), a work which portrayed the German philosophers as

Romantic sentimentalists – a more than sufficient reason in Stewart's eyes for deeming them beyond the pale from the point of view of Scottish common-sense philosophy.

But a new lease of life in Britain was at hand for Kant – or, at least, for what Pringle-Pattison called a 'lop-sided' version of Kant. This was the contribution of William Hamilton (1788–1856). He welcomed Kant's demolition of the older rationalistic metaphysics, believing, however, that human reason's incompetence depended,

> not, as with Kant, on what might be a peculiarity of *human* reason – its limitation by the forms of space and time – but on the impossibility of knowledge, which is essentially a relation, having for its object that which, as 'absolute' is essentially *out of* relation – a disability which, it would appear, must attach to *any* knowledge whatsoever.[109]

Thus, thought Hamilton, the way was left open for a transcendental object of faith, the Unconditioned. But this entailed his departure from Reid's natural realism, and landed him in scepticism and subjectivism.[110] Of Hamilton, Masson drily remarked that 'he did more than any other man to reinstate the worship of Difficulty in the higher mind of Great Britain.'[111]

Dean Mansel (1820–71), in his Bampton Lectures, *The Limits of Religious Thought* (1858), sought to make Christian apologetic capital out of the Hamiltonian reading of Kant. For contending that the failure of old-style metaphysics and the incompetence of human reason paved the way for faith in God and required submission to scriptural revelation, he was adversely criticized by F. D. Maurice among others.[112] The nub of the criticism was that along the proposed line of argument there was no ground for preferring the supernaturalism of Mansel to the agnosticism of Herbert Spencer or T. H. Huxley. As Clement Webb remarks:

> even those who, in their indifference to the philosophical bearings of doctrines which they themselves accepted merely on authority, and shrank from venturing to bring into close relation with any free speculation, might not have been indisposed to welcome an argument which seemed to place the traditional dogmas once for all out of reach of philosophical criticism, were soon startled to find the philosophical tenets of the Bampton Lectures openly adopted by Herbert Spencer in 1862 among the 'First Principles' of his system . . . It is by a singular irony of fate that the ingenious champion of the ancient creeds who

would fain have put the aspiring human reason helpless under the feet of a wholly transcendent revelation has his niche in the history of philosophy as the immediate forerunner of Herbert Spencer, the most ambitious projector of a system of pure naturalism that the nineteenth century knew.[113]

As Pringle-Pattison suggests, the following words of Reid 'might almost have been written in view of the subsequent development':

Some good men have been led to depreciate the human understanding, and to put out the light of nature and reason, in order to exalt that of revelation. These weapons which were taken up in support of religion, are now employed to overturn it . . . Atheists . . . join hands with theologians in depreciating the human understanding, that they may lead us into absolute scepticism.[114]

For an idealist's view of the route thus far travelled we may turn to Percival Chubb. In 1888 he writes of the course of British philosophy with the confidence of one who has seen the light (and read the Old Testament genealogies):

If we call over the roll of philosophers we shall see that for the most part they have been the descendants of Hume – all with a marked family likeness. Scotland has produced a few recalcitrants – Reid, Stewart, Hamilton; but they were not big enough to turn the current, and indeed had not 'the root of the matter in them', to use a favourite expression of Green's. Tracing the main line of descent in England, we find that Hume begat Hartley, Hartley begat James Mill and Bentham, who begat John Stuart Mill; but here the type undergoes a little modification through alliance with another family – the physical scientists. Darwin and the Evolutionists appear and prove immensely attractive to the philosophers. The union produces the full-fledged scientific, materialistic philosophy of Lewes and Spencer and their adjutants . . . [T]he philosophy of evolution . . . has carried all before it, and Herbert Spencer is now the ruling light in the philosophic firmament. But already his beams have begun to pale by the rising of a new and larger light.[115]

With this we come to Hegel. It has been fashionable among historians of British philosophy to express surprise at Hegel's belated arrival in England. Indeed, Muirhead, himself an idealist, seems positively wounded by it: 'Whence this belated arrival in England of the greatest thinker of his time?'[116] He attributes the calamity to British insularity, antipathy to all things German, Humean philosophy, and the 'curse' of the 'theological bias' as found in Maurice.[117] A. M. Quinton largely follows this interpretation, though he is uncharacteristically confused on the matter. Thus, he writes, 'Poor communications with the philosophy of the outside world were the result of the parochialism, inertia, and markedly practical bias of the British philosophy of the age.' But he at once contrasts Hegel's reception with Kant's earlier and swifter welcome (when communications were no better); and he refers to the first British mention of Hegel's name by Hamilton in 'The philosophy of the Unconditioned' (1829), to the 1832 translation and abridgement of Tennemann's history of philosophy, and to J. D. Morell's account (deficient in neglecting the *Phenomenology*) of Hegel in his *An Historical and Critical View of the Speculative Philosophy of Europe in the Nineteenth Century* (2 vols., 1846). Granting that this last is the most substantial of early native comments upon Hegel, a time-lag of fifteen years since Hegel's death is not unduly great. Remarking upon the fact that 'Hegel's importance was not acknowledged in Britain until well into the 1840s', Bradley pertinently comments, 'But even nowadays this would not be too unusual a time-scale for the recognition of foreign work.'[118] Finally, Quinton does not note that earlier British philosophers such as Brown and Stewart were not parochial *vis-à-vis* France.

As with Kant, so with Hegel: literary figures were the harbingers of his thought in Britain. If Coleridge did much to introduce Kant, Carlyle's opposition to British 'mud philosophy' paved the way for Hegel. 'Carlyle spoke', said Mackenzie, 'not only for himself, but with all the added weight of thinkers whose names were hardly known in England – Goethe and Fichte, Schiller and Richter and Novalis.' Not, indeed, that Carlyle had a metaphysic to propound – on the contrary, he was highly suspicious of metaphysical pretensions; but 'In his *Sartor Resartus* Carlyle tells us that the world is no dead machine, but palpitates with the life of a single principle.'[119] When the British idealists – most notably Henry Jones – sprinkle their writings with quotations from Wordsworth and Browning, they are doing more than display their literary taste; they are testifying to the close ties between a prominent aspect of the literary mood of the day and the philosophical position they embraced.[120] Again, by publishing her

translation of D. F. Strauss's *The Life of Jesus* in 1846, Marian
Evans (George Eliot) propagated left-wing Hegelianism among
British intellectuals; when the popular version of her translation
appeared in 1864 alarm bells were set off in many conservative
Christian minds.

J. F. Ferrier (1808–64) may stand as a philosopher whose ideas
to a certain extent paved the way for Hegel in Britain. This
emerges in his *The Institutes of Metaphysic* (1854). He is by no
means a methodological Hegelian, and the fact that Stirling found
him in desperation perusing Hegel upside down because he had
failed to understand him the right way up should caution us
against regarding him as an authority on Hegel.[121] But his
starting-point is the conviction that any intelligence must have
some knowledge of itself, and he does, as H. D. Lewis has
reminded us, conclude that 'there must be "a supreme and infinite
and everlasting mind in synthesis with all things." This is very
close to what the major idealists were to hold later in the
century.'[122]

John Grote (1813–66) of Cambridge must be numbered among
those who prepared the soil for Hegel's reception in Britain. Against
phenomenalism and positivism he maintained that we can know the
truly real, the thing-in-itself, because it partakes of the same nature
as our minds. However, the bulk of Grote's work was published
posthumously – part II of his *Exploratio Philosophica* not until 1900,
by which time his pioneering work had been superseded.

It was left to James Hutchinson Stirling (1820–1909) to produce
the first major work on Hegel in Britain (though T. C. Sandars's
account of Hegel's *Philosophy of Right* in *Oxford Essays* (1855)
should not be overlooked). Of Stirling's *The Secret of Hegel* (1857)
Caird said, 'To English readers Hegel was first introduced in the
powerful statement of his principles by Dr Hutchinson Stirling.'[123]
On the other hand (as it is *de rigueur* for writers on this subject to
point out), it was at the time remarked that 'if Mr Hutchinson
Stirling knew the secret of Hegel he had managed to keep it to
himself.'[124] Well-nigh pulverized by the 'Swabian lout', Stirling's
prodigious labours were sustained by his optimistic view that

> Kant and Hegel – all but wholly directly both, and one of them quite
> wholly directly – have no object but to restore Faith – Faith in God –
> Faith in the immortality of the Soul and the Freedom of the Will – nay,

Faith in Christianity as the Revealed Religion – and that, too, in perfect harmony with the Right of Private Judgment, and the Rights, or Lights, or Mights of Intelligence in general.[125]

Caird also paid tribute to the pioneering work of William Wallace of Oxford, who published his translation of Hegel's 'lesser Logic', *The Logic of Hegel* in 1874,[126] and William T. Harris of St Louis, editor of *The Journal of Speculative Philosophy*. Elsewhere, Caird remembered the important role played by Benjamin Jowett, Wallace's and Green's teacher, who became Master of Balliol. As early as 1844 Jowett was in Germany with A. P. Stanley, imbibing the current philosophy and seeking the advice of Erdmann as to the best way of tackling Hegel.[127] As Quinton has it, although through teaching and conversation Jowett did much to introduce Hegel to England, his

attitude to Hegel itself underwent a dialectical change. By the 1870s, suspicious of the effect of Green's earnest obscurities on the undergraduates of Balliol, he was complaining that 'metaphysics exercises a fatal influence over the mind.' But by 1884, accepting the gift of a bust of Hegel for the Balliol library from Lord Arthur Russell, he adopted a more favourable posture. 'Though not a Hegelian', he wrote, 'I think I have gained more from Hegel than from any other philosopher.' Of the bust itself he added, 'Hegel looks quite a gentleman.' We may perhaps see this as a symbol of the satisfactory absorption of Hegelianism into British intellectual life.[128]

III

We now stand at the threshold of the period occupied by our seven selected idealists. Before introducing them, however, it is appropriate briefly to take stock of the situation. This I shall do, first, by summarizing what were thought to be the positive and negative advantages of idealism by those who embraced it; and secondly, by recounting three testimonies which will indicate contrasting attitudes towards idealism, with special reference to its bearing upon Christian belief.

I have sought to delineate the route by which post-Hegelian idealism reached Britain, and to sketch the British philosophical background which ensured that any reception of Hegelianism would entail its modification – not least by neo-Kantianism (as in Green) and Scottish common-sense philosophy (as in Pringle-Pattison). Not for nothing did F. H. Bradley write, 'As for "the Hegelian School" which exists in our reviews, I know no one who has met with it anywhere else.'[129] Nevertheless, if not a school, there was a decided post-Hegelian tendency in many British writers from the 1870s onwards. What, in summary form, did they deem the benefits of idealism to be?

In the first place, they welcomed idealism's therapy. Here, they thought, was the medicine which would heal the ontological and epistemological dualisms which had pervaded British philosophy from the moment the writings of Descartes had become known. Blending (or, as some would have said, confusing) ontology and epistemology, Green concludes that

> the real world is essentially a spiritual world, which forms one inter-related whole because related throughout to a single subject . . . [Even so], a knowledge of [the world] in its spiritual reality – such a knowledge of it as would be a knowledge of God – is impossible to us. To know God we must be God . . . That there is one spiritual self-conscious being, of which all that is real is the activity or expression . . . [and] that this participation is the source of morality and religion; this we take to be the vital truth which Hegel had to teach.[130]

On the ontological point, and against a caricature of Hegel, Jones insists that

> To regard Hegel as dealing with thought-determinations, as generating abstract conceptions out of one another, as needing in the end to leap out of the sphere of mere thoughts into a sphere of reality, is to attribute to him that dualism by repudiating which *alone* he was able to gain his starting-point. Go where Hegel will, he cannot escape from the Reality. He finds it active in all thinking, in all being. No *idea* of the reality interposes between him and it.[131]

This is not to say that the British idealists followed Hegel in supposing it to be possible to map out a complete systematic description of reality as a whole: they were more modest than that. Nevertheless the immanent spiritual principle which they found at the heart of all encouraged their breadth of thought. They were genuinely concerned, albeit to varying degrees as between one writer and another, with the ethical, socio-political and religious realms. As Green said, it was the 'professed object' of Hegel's philosophy 'to find formulae adequate to the action of reason as exhibited in nature and human society, in art and religion'.[132]

Implicit in the foregoing, and in harmony with the inward thrust of romanticism, is the further benefit that in idealistic immanentism was found the answer to eighteenth-century deistic transcendence. 'The Deism', writes Jones,

> which witnessed to a God benevolent but remote, has no defence whatsoever against the Agnosticism which dares not affirm and the Scepticism which must deny. Belief in such a God has perished of inanition, which is the most complete of all refutations. But what other God is possible? . . . [T]he alternatives are those of complete negation or a new interpretation.[133]

Such an interpretation has been offered by Hegel.

Again, idealism was deemed to provide weapons against unacceptable theories. Robert Mackintosh appraised aspects of the nineteenth-century intellectual environment thus:

> Herbert Spencer . . . though scantily enough imbued with the better elements of Kant's teaching, stands in direct filiation to Kant, and has borrowed from him the assertion that the Absolute is unknowable. Even Positivism itself, the most pretentious and the most Philistine of all competitors in the forum of thought, echoes the parrot-cry, 'we can know only phenomena', as if any intelligence confined to phenomena could be an intelligence at all, or if it were could possibly know that it was *confined* to phenomena. It is due to Kant that we have to face neither deism nor dogmatic materialism, but agnosticism; and the prevalence of agnosticism warns us that the old Natural Theology is dead.[134]

It was the spiritual principle, as enunciated by Green and his successors, which, according to his pupil Henry Scott Holland, so gripped readers of the *Prolegomena to Ethics* that 'Materialism appeared to have been absolutely displaced out of the field.'[135] Others, among them Pringle-Pattison, pointed to the contradictions within Spencer's agnosticism itself: 'To describe as unknowable "the Power *manifested* to us through all existence" is a plain *contradictio in adjecto,* and yet that is his constant usage.'[136] Relating Spencer's agnosticism and Huxley's materialism, Caird declared that these writers have adopted the odd, and we might even say irrational, expedient of telling us that we may regard the world *either* as a collection of the phenomena of mind, *or* as a collection of the phenomena of matter, but that we can never bring these two ways of looking at things together – a view which supposes man to be afflicted with a kind of intellectual *strabismus,* so that he can never see with one of his mental eyes without shutting the other.[137]

From this optical deficiency idealism is, once more, the deliverer. As for Comte's half-positivism ('half' because, while denying a transcendent object to religion, it allowed room for the religion of humanity), the nub of Caird's case against Comte is that 'there can be no religion of Humanity, which is not also a religion of God.'[138] Concerning the positivist's desire to opt for system in human affairs and to deny it everywhere else, this attempted compromise, Caird elsewhere avers,

> unites the difficulties of both of the extremes it would avoid: the difficulties of an absolute philosophy, which seems to go beyond the limits of human knowledge, and the difficulties of a scepticism which leaves the moral and intellectual life of man without a principle of unity.[139]

In opposition to rationalism, idealism was held to advocate a fuller treatment of human experience. In the words of Webb, 'Rationalism is not really so much an excess of confidence in reason as a want of confidence in it; since it does not attempt to understand a great part of human experience.'[140] Over against the empiricism of Mill, Bain and Spencer, which was predominant in the Oxford University curriculum, and was said by H. P. Liddon to have 'fatally undermined' serious theology there,[141] idealism placed its conviction that reality is one and spiritual, and that the immanent principle, operative in all phenomena, holds them in a union which empiricism, confined as it is to sensationalism and atomism, logically cannot conceive. While welcoming the working of the immanent principle in pragmatism, the idealists denied its subjectivism in favour of objective reality.[142]

In relation to materialism and naturalism, idealism was preferred because of its elevation of the spiritual as supreme. Thus in his Bampton Lectures for 1894, Illingworth chided the materialist:

He first isolates by abstraction certain elements of his total experience, and calls them 'force' or 'matter'; he then substantiates or solidifies these 'abstract ideas' through his imagination, till they look as if they existed by themselves, and so is able to picture them as creating the mind by which, in fact, they have been created.[143]

Similarly, those who espouse naturalism omit an important aspect of reality: the mind. 'Merely "natural" objects', declared Jones, idealism

> finds unknowable or mere-things-in-themselves. What ordinary and naturalistic thought deemed to be independent of experience, it showed to be objects *of* experience, and *already* in relation to sense and thought.[144]

As if to beat the materialists and naturalists at their own game, the idealists embraced the theory of evolution, widespread discussion of which was prompted by the publication of Darwin's *The Origin of Species* in 1859. This theory might have seemed the final witness to the truth of materialism and naturalism, but the idealists read it as witnessing to the activity of the immanent spirit, and as underwriting their developmental and teleological interests which had been stimulated in some cases by Herder, Schelling and Goethe. The point was not lost upon Henry Calderwood who, writing as a Scottish common-sense philosopher with a debt to Kantian transcendentalism, declared that in connection with the idealists' understanding of progress from nothing, through matter and spirit to the absolute, 'it would seem as if science had been unwittingly preparing an auxiliary demonstration ready to the hand of the Hegelian.'[145] Pringle-Pattison further explains:

> the doctrine of evolution seemed at first . . . to thrust man ruthlessly back into the lower circles of nature and to make for an all-engulfing materialism. But, in another perspective, the process of evolution as a whole, with man as its crowning product, may be held to reintroduce into nature, on a grander scale and in a more tangible form, the idea of end or aim which the theory of natural selection had done its best to banish from the details of her procedure . . . Man appears, according to the doctrine of evolution, so interpreted, as the goal and crown of nature's long upward effort.[146]

Along this latter line of interpretation evolutionary considerations were pressed into apologetic service by many theologians and preachers,[147] not least by those High Church members of the Church of England who contributed to *Lux Mundi* (1889).[148] In that work Illingworth, writing on 'The Incarnation and development', extolled the new thought thus:

> Evolution is in the air. It is the category of the age . . . And our religious opinions, like all things else, that have come down on the current of development, must justify their existence by an appeal to the past. [This appeal to tradition is not nearly as strong in Pringle-Pattison as in the ecclesiastic Illingworth, behind whose thought, no doubt, there lies J. H. Newman's doctrine of development]. It is the object of the following pages to consider what popular misconceptions of the central doctrine of our religion, the Incarnation [here is an example of the Anglican recovery of Alexandrian Logos theology], have been remedied; what more or less forgotten aspects of it have been restored to their due place; what new lights have been thrown upon the fulness of its meaning, in the course of our discussion of the various views of evolution.[149]

If idealism assisted those who embraced it to turn the edge of materialism and naturalism, it also fostered the study of history and offered an escape-hatch from the more awkward particularities of biblical history. Under Hegelian inspiration, the biblical criticism of Baur and the Tübingen school prompted a diversity of responses, some of which were hostile – not least those emanating from conservative Christians who were out to 'guard the ark'. If the geologists had called the creation narratives of Genesis into question, the biblical-historical critics, of whom in Britain the authors (among them Jowett) of *Essays and Reviews* (1860) were the heralds, were now, it seemed, cutting the Bible into fragments, and casting doubt upon the historicity of large tracts of it. Hence the insistence of the idealists that, by transposing biblical history into matter illustrative of ideas of permanent worth, they were protecting the faith from the ravages of the new criticism. Hence the equally strong insistence of their opponents that they had idealized Christ off the stage of human history.[150] Of the most extreme culprit in this regard, D. F. Strauss, Sanday remarked that

> It was on the strength of his Hegelian Christology that he felt himself emancipated from any servile dependence upon the Gospels. So long

as he remained true to the idea of the union of Godhead and Manhood, the historical facts in which that idea was supposed to be expressed were indifferent to him, and he exercised freely the most trenchant criticism upon them.[151]

To the idealists with whom we are principally concerned, an important blessing of idealism was its openness to the aesthetic, the ethical and the religious. About the last two of these we shall have much more to say, but meanwhile we may record a comment from Pringle-Pattison upon idealism's ethical thrust, and one from Webb concerning religion. The former writes, 'Idealism takes its stand on the essential truth of our judgements of value, and the impossibility of explaining the higher from the lower.'[152] And Webb points out that

> The tendency of the British Idealists . . . was to insist upon the claim of Religion not either to be left on one side or explained away as illusion or misunderstanding, but rather to be interpreted as a form of human experience at least as significant as the moral, the aesthetic, or the scientific. At the same time this very insistence of theirs upon the significance of Religion implied a claim on the part of Philosophy to deal no less freely with the religious than with any other form of experience, and to deny the right of any authority, whether ecclesiastical or biblical . . . to interfere with and restrain a liberty which must be regarded as inseparable from the very nature of Philosophy.[153]

The advocacy of the human–divine unity, the healing of older dualisms, the slaying of religiously hostile philosophical bogeymen – small wonder that idealism's advent was greeted with enthusiasm by some. By some, but not by all, and not by all Christian thinkers. I conclude this chapter, in which I have sought to view the coming of post-Hegelian idealism to Britain through the eyes of those who were positively influenced by it, by setting down three testimonies which are diverse to the point of being discordant.

In a most revealing autobiographical article Andrew Martin Fairbairn (1838–1912), who went on to become the first Principal of Mansfield College, Oxford,[154] recounts his pilgrimage from despair over the Westminster Standards, through a period as 'an unchurched wanderer, conscious mainly of one thing, that I had been called of God to preach another gospel than I had been trained in',[155] to liberation under the influence of German thought. From Edinburgh he went to study in Germany, and there, amidst the controversies over the philosophy of history, Christology and biblical criticism, he became impressed by the Hegelian notion that Christianity was a system of ideas with the Christ of history as its supreme symbol. As to the results of his German experience:

> (i) The doubts which had been hidden like secret sins lost their power to harm, and ceased to cause shame . . . (ii) . . . [T]heology changed from a system doubted to a system believed . . . (iii) . . . [T]heology was reborn and with it a new and higher faith . . . (iv) Nor could the old narrow notion which made salvation rather an affair of a future state than of this life survive in the face of those larger ideas . . . I believed then what I still believe, that the Christ I had learned to know represents the largest and most gracious truth God had ever communicated to man.[156]

Fairbairn's younger Scottish contemporary, the theologian James Denney (1856–1917)[157] was at the opposite pole – and this despite the fact the he had not only been a pupil of Caird, and a friend of his fellow-student Henry Jones, but had won the Gold Medal in Caird's class. To his friend J. P. Struthers Denney wrote,

> The last unprofitable labour I have done was to read Edward Caird's Gifford Lectures. That put me in mind of a remark by a wiser man than Law: 'After that in the wisdom of God the world by its own wisdom knew not God, it pleased God to dispense with philosophers, etc. etc., and to save the world in an absurd way.' The philosophers, however, are irreconcilable still, and think themselves in a position to patronise Heaven. It is pitiful.[158]

For more public consumption Denney identified what was for him the most serious defect of post-Hegelian idealism:

> it assumes certain relations between the human and the divine, relations which foreclose the very questions which the Atonement compels us to raise. To be brief, it teaches the essential unity of God and man . . . On such a system there is no room for atonement in the sense of the mediation of God's forgiveness in Jesus Christ.[159]

In face of idealistic pantheizing tendencies which seemed to obliterate moral distinctions Denney thundered, 'Christ *died* for the difference between right and wrong.'[160]

Our third testimony comes from Fairbairn's and Pringle-

Pattison's teacher, A. Campbell Fraser (1819–1914), whose intermediate position is prompted by the dual conviction that the Enlightenment is not to be thrown overboard in its entirety, and that the (in his day) ascending idealism was something less than a philosophical cure-all:

> On the one hand there was scientific Naturalism, with its dogmatic assumption of progressive and regressive evolution as final synthesis, – all beyond this, the darkness of the Unknowable. On the other side was the new gnostic Idealism, bound by its profession to eliminate all mysteries, and at last to reach infinite science of Reality . . . I found myself on a *Via Media*, repelled alike from an agnostic science wholly ignorant of God, and from a gnostic science which implied Omniscience.[161]

The testimonies of Fairbairn, Denney and Campbell Fraser set the parameters within which much of our subsequent discussion will move. But first we must become more closely acquainted with our seven idealists.

2

Seven British Idealists

Not least because of their philosophical and, especially in the case of Green, Caird and Jones, their practical concern for the whole of human experience, we shall do well to introduce the lives as well as the thought of our seven idealists. With the exception of Green, whom I place first because of his role as intellectual catalyst, I shall present the philosophers in chronological order. This will enable us to monitor developments within idealism as such, and within the thought of each author. We shall find that whereas the majority of them remained true to philosophical stances adopted early in their careers, Taylor increasingly found that idealism required to be tempered by insights drawn from Thomism and Scottish realism. I shall note the seven idealists' main philosophical contributions insofar as these relate to their understanding of the Christian faith. I shall not, for example, dwell upon Green's political theory, or upon the contributions of Webb and Taylor to medieval and classical studies respectively. Finally, I shall in each case review verdicts pronounced upon the seven idealists by their contemporaries and others. My objectives are to lay the foundation for the thematic chapters to come, and to provide evidence of the variety of thought within this group.[1]

I

In a lay sermon on 'The witness of God' (I Corinthians 5: 7–8), delivered in Balliol College chapel, T. H. Green makes this self-revealing observation:

In this place how much cleverness, and more conceit of cleverness, goes to how little true spiritual achievement . . . How much of our real interest is going to the quest after truth and God, how much to the attainment of skill in writing clever articles and saying 'good things' . . . ?
. . . [I]f in reading and thinking we look merely for a testimony to our own cleverness, we shall find probably what we seek, but no higher witness.[2]

These words indicate the motivating force of Green's life, and bring us face to face with his integrity, his hatred of sham, and his disdain for cant. For all that some have caricatured idealistic philosophy as being ethereal and out of touch with life, Green was intensely down-to-earth. Of him William Sanday declared that 'He was a unique compound of Hegelianism in philosophy, Liberalism in politics, and Puritanism in religion.'[3] I have already indicated, and closer inspection will confirm, that Green's was a tempered Hegelianism; and as for Puritanism, I have good reason to think that many divines of that type would have weighed Green doctrinally and found him wanting. But insofar as Sanday presumably refers to the principled sobriety which 'Puritanism' had come to denote, his comment is apt. Of Green's black or dark grey attire a colleague said that this placed him 'with plain people of the working or middle class rather than the upper, the puritans of the past and the non-conformists of the present, Germans and all that is sober-suited and steady going'.[4]

Thomas Hill Green, born on 7 April 1836, was the youngest of four children of Valentine Green, the evangelical rector of Birkin, a village which has one of the most notable Norman churches in Yorkshire. Green's mother, the eldest daughter of Edward Thomas Vaughan, vicar of St Martin and All Saints, Leicester, died when Green was one year old. After a somewhat isolated childhood, Green was sent at the age of fourteen to Rugby School, then under the headmastership of Dr E. M. Goulburn. He was not a brilliant scholar, only a dutiful athlete, and was temperamentally a loner. His one real school friend died of insanity. He knew Henry Sidgwick, who later pitted his utilitarianism against Green's ethics, but was not close to him. Green's intellectual potential was recognized (in 1855, to Sidgwick's surprise, he gained the prize for Latin prose composition), as was his indolence. He was respected for his uncharacteristic abstinence from alcohol, and likened to his hero Cromwell. Not at ease in 'society', he valued his contacts with country folk and tradespeople. He had a sense of humour, but his directness could also, unintentionally, hurt. Green was his own man, and made his own judgements. As early as 1854 he read F. D. Maurice's *Theological Essays,* concluding that 'its merits, as is usually the case, seem to be in exact counter-proportion to the abuse which has been heaped upon it.'[5] (Maurice, it will be recalled, was deposed from his Chair at King's College, London, in 1854 for denying the eternity of punishment.) The writings of Carlyle also exercised a formative influence upon him, and he was later to commend Wordsworth for having 'delivered literature from bondage to the philosophy that had naturalised man'.[6]

Green entered Balliol College, Oxford, in October 1855, worked less than zealously and was placed in the second class in Classical Moderations in 1857. Urged on by his tutor, Benjamin Jowett, he gained a first in 'Greats' (Literae Humaniores) and then, after six months of cramming, a third in Law and Modern History. He became an original and an active member of the Old Mortality Club, founded by John Nichol in 1857, whose members were graduates who were, or had recently been, in a 'weak or precarious' condition of bodily health.[7] The Club heard and discussed papers on a wide range of literary and philosophical subjects.

In 1860 Green taught Ancient and Modern History at Balliol in the absence of W. L. Newman, and was elected to a Fellowship there. A visit to Germany in the following year inspired Green to immerse himself in German philosophers from Kant to Hegel, and also introduced him to the work of F. C. Baur (part of whose *Geschichte der christlichen Kirche* Green translated) and the Tübingen school of biblical critics. The Hegelianism of these last, he felt, enabled them rationally to establish what was of permanent value in Christianity, while at the same time it played down the miraculous elements in the Bible and skirted the objections to the scriptural text which were being advanced by the newer historians. Melvin Richter adduces evidence from Mrs Humphrey Ward, who cast Green as Mr Grey in her *Robert Elsmere* (1888), and Henry Nettleship to support the view that Green surrendered the mythological aspects of Christianity only with the very greatest difficulty, and that his piety remained of the Protestant and Evangelical type to the end.[8] Nevertheless, although his family and Jowett had marked him as a candidate for ordination, Green informed his father in January 1861 that 'I don't think I am ever likely to take orders.'[9] In the same year he opined that 'a modified unitarianism suits me very well.'[10] Unenamoured of the law, Green, though devoted to speculative thought, had no strong passion for teaching: indeed, he found Oxford undergraduates an obnoxious breed. He toyed with the idea of applying for a position at Owens College, Manchester, where the type, if not the presumed ability of the students attracted him, but Jowett advised against the move;[11] in 1863 he was offered the editorship of the fledgeling *Times of India,* but was dissuaded from accepting by Jowett, and by fears for his health if he went to Bombay; and he mused upon the possibility of writing a heterodox book and becoming a Dissenting minister. Meanwhile his teaching at Balliol was meeting with increasing success, and he felt more contented there. He pioneered the understanding of philosophy as a professional discipline in its own right – which is to say, that he loosened the grip of classical scholarship upon the subject, and this despite Jowett's distress at the baneful influence of metaphysics as destroyer of 'the power of observation and of acquiring knowledge'.[12] In addition he frequently gave lectures on the Pauline and Johannine writings.

In 1864 Green applied for the Chair of Moral Philosophy at St Andrews, made vacant by the death of J. F. Ferrier. On this occasion Jowett supported him, and both he and the candidate were very disappointed when Green did not succeed. Green attributed his failure to the fact that 'in order to give oneself a fair chance, all sorts of private agencies have to be set to work', and to the fact that he had been presented in Scotland as a devoteee of Comtism and materialism.[13] In Jowett's opinion Green's jargon-laden article on Aristotle, the only published item from a planned but aborted edition of Aristotle, had proved incomprehensible to the Scots in whose *North British Review* it was published. Principal John Tulloch of St Andrews clearly favoured Stephen Baynes. In a letter to R. H. Story he wrote: 'Notwithstanding Mr Green, a famous Balliol man, of course, about whom Dean Stanley writes to me, Baynes is, of all men I know, the man competent for the chair . . . ' To Dr Mitchell he wrote: 'I have received strong testimonies in Mr Green's favour from Dean Stanley and others, but we may have enough of even such good things as "Balliol men".'[14] In the event, on John Veitch's translation to Glasgow,

Baynes succeeded to the Chair of Logic, Robert Flint to that of Moral Philosophy.

During the last nine months of 1865 and in the spring of 1866, Green had a taste of life outside Oxford. He was appointed to serve the Royal Commission of inquiry into 'the schools attended by the children of such of the gentry, clergy, professional and commercial men as are of limited means, and of farmers and tradesmen'.[15] Green was assigned to Warwickshire and Staffordshire, and was subsequently required to visit the endowed grammar schools in Buckinghamshire, Leicestershire and Northamptonshire. Nettleship comments,

> It must strike anyone who reads his lectures on education and his report, that while as a matter of fact his teaching power was almost entirely spent in a university, his strongest sympathies were with the education of the middle classes, whom the universities were only just beginning to touch.[16]

Prominent among the middle classes were the Nonconformists and, not surprisingly in view of Green's own tincture of Dissent, he encouraged the establishment of a Nonconformist college in Oxford, writing to R. W. Dale of Birmingham, one of the promoters of the cause, in these terms:

> The opening of the national universities to Nonconformists has been, in my judgment, an injury rather than a help to Nonconformity. You are sending up here, year after year, the sons of some of your best and wealthiest families: they are often altogether uninfluenced by the services of the Church which they find here, and they not only drift away from Nonconformity – they drift away and lose all faith; and you are bound, as soon as you have secured the opening of the universities for your sons, to follow them when you send them here, in order to defend and maintain their religious life and faith.[17]

The education commission served, Green returned to his teaching. In 1866 he was appointed tutor at Balliol, and was probably the first layman to hold this office. In the following year he unsuccessfully applied for Oxford's Waynflete Chair of Moral and Metaphysical Philosophy, which went to Henry Chandler; and he decided not to pursue a vacancy at Edinburgh. He did, however, in 1867 deliver four lectures on 'The English Revolution' to the Edinburgh Philosophical Institution. When Jowett was appointed Master of Balliol in 1870, Green assumed 'practically the whole subordinate management of the college'.[18] In 1871 he married Charlotte Symonds, whose father's settlement of ten thousand pounds upon the couple ensured their financial security.

That Green was no armchair Liberal is clear from his activities as an Oxford town councillor (elected 1876), as a supporter and benefactor of Oxford High School, and as a temperance campaigner. He joined the United Kingdom Alliance in 1872, subsequently becoming a vice-president; he established a coffee tavern in St Clement's in 1875; he was active in the Church of England Temperance Society, and President of the Oxford Band of Hope Temperance Union. Though not at first an abstainer, he became one, influenced both by sorrow over his drunkard brother, and by the damage done to working folk by the 'demon drink'. In an address to the Liberals of Leicester he appealed to the citizens of England

> by law to put a restraint on themselves in the matter of strong drink. We ask them further to limit – or even altogether to give up – the not very precious liberty of buying and selling alcohol, in order that they may become more free to exercise the faculties and improve the talents which God has given them.[19]

With the objectivity of one who was neither an Oxford man nor a disciple of Green, Robert Mackintosh wrote,

> If Hegel was a greater philosopher, Green was greater as a man. He served the Idea not merely in scholarly abstraction, but in the routine of the Oxford City Council and in the despised paths of temperance reform.[20]

Collingwood's verdict is also of interest:

> The school of Green sent out into public life a stream of ex-pupils who carried with them the conviction that philosophy, and in particular the philosophy they had learnt at Oxford, was an important thing, and that their vocation was to put it into practice. This conviction was common to politicians so diverse in their creeds as Asquith and Milner, churchmen like Gore and Scott Holland, social reformers like Arnold Toynbee . . . Through this effect on the minds of its pupils, the philosophy of Green's school might be found, from about 1880 to about 1910, penetrating and fertilizing every part of the national life.[21]

In this connection we may note that Green encouraged Bernard Bosanquet to leave Oxford for social work in London, and that his influence was felt in such diverse circles as the *Lux Mundi* theologians, Toynbee Hall and Oxford House, London, the Christian Social Union and the London Ethical Society.[22]

In 1878 Green became Whyte's Professor of Moral Philosophy. He had already published some articles in *The Contemporary Review*, and a substantial Introduction to an edition of Hume's *Works* (1874–5). He now began to devote himself to the adumbration of an ethical system. However, from 1879 onwards his health began to decline, and in August of that year he wrote in a letter that 'I must make a push now, or I shall leave the world with nothing done.'[23] He hoped to complete his *Prolegomena to Ethics,* but by his death on 26 March 1882 from ulcerated tonsils and pyemia,[24] his hope was denied. 'We shall never know a nobler man', wrote a friend on hearing of his death.[25] The Greens had no children.

Was Green a Hegelian? Was he a Christian? These questions have drawn affirmative, negative and carefully qualified anwers down the years. In sketching the main lines of his thought as they bear upon religious questions I shall set out from the former question and conclude with the latter.

Geoffrey Thomas has noted that W. H. Walsh designates Green and others as British Hegelians, and that Green's Oxford contemporaries, the philosopher Thomas Case, and the economist F. Y. Edgeworth, in his *New and Old Methods in Ethics* (1877), likewise describes him.[26] To these we may add Henry Calderwood;[27] A. M. Quinton, who argues that British idealism 'owed more to Hegel than to anyone else';[28] and the somewhat more ambivalent Robert Mackintosh. The latter, writing of the British neo-Kantians, says that they, 'with the very doubtful exception of T. H. Green – agree with Hegel much more than they do with Kant'. He later declares, 'The gist of the British Hegelian position is best seen in T. H. Green.'[29] Thomas finds, on the other hand, that to James Ward the influence of Hegel upon Green was 'slight or non-existent', that Sidgwick deemed him a Kantian, and that others labelled him 'neo-Kantian'.[30] Referring to Green and others, Collingwood was quite definite:

The philosophical tendencies common to this school were described by its contemporary opponents as Hegelianism. This title was repudiated by the school itself, and rightly. Their philosophy, so far as they had one single philosophy, was a continuation and criticism of the indigenous English and Scottish philosophies of the middle nineteenth century.[31]

Collingwood's last sentence here, however, while it rightly indicates Green's starting-point, plays down the German contribution to his criticism. Pringle-Pattison's judgement is more apt:

> It is a serious mistake to suppose that, in Green, for example, we have simply a revival of Kant, or a revival of Hegel, or a combination of the two. Materials certainly have been drawn from both these thinkers; but the result is a type of thought which has never existed before, and of which it is absurd, therefore, to speak as an importation from Germany.[32]

Green and others, as we saw in the first chapter, were concerned to answer Locke, Hume and their successors, and to surmount the epistemological dualism bequeathed by Kant. This objective served as their Ockham's razor, and governed what they took from Hegel and what (notably the method of thesis, antithesis and synthesis) they left behind.[33] No doubt some, supremely the Cairds and Henry Jones, took more than others from Hegel and, indeed, it is in his review of John Caird's *An Introduction to the Philosophy of Religion* (1880) that Green, confirmed by his reading of Lotze in the view that reality is essentially relational, shows himself quite other than a clone of Hegel. The following quotation will both distance him from Hegel and Caird, and introduce the position from which he encountered empiricists, materialists and naturalists alike:

> Hegel's doctrine has been before the world now for half a century, and though it has affected the current science and philosophy to a degree which those who depreciate it seem curiously to ignore, yet as a doctrine it has not made way . . . When we think out the problem left by previous inquirers, we find ourselves led to it by an intellectual necessity; but on reflection we become aware that we are Hegelian, so to speak, with only a fraction of our thoughts – on the Sundays of 'speculation', not on the weekdays of 'ordinary thought' . . . As a follower of Hegel [John Caird] must and does hold that the objective world, in its actual totality, is thought, and that the processes of our intelligence are but reflections of that real thought under the conditions of a limited human nature. But he does not sustain himself at this point

of view. It may be that no one can; but till it is done our idealism, though we may wish it to be 'absolute', remains only 'subjective' . . . . [It must be] made more clear that the nature of that thought, which Hegel declares to be the reality of things, is to be ascertained, if at all, from analysis of the objective world, not from reflection on those processes of our intelligence which really presuppose that world . . . It comes to this, that in his method, though not in his conclusion, we think [John Caird] has been too much overpowered by Hegel . . . [H]e . . . seemed to arrive at his conclusion as to the spirituality of the world, not by interrogating the world, but by interrogating his own thoughts . . . That there is one spiritual self-conscious being, of which all that is real is the activity or expression; that we are related to this spiritual being, not merely as parts of the world which is its expression, but as partakers in some inchoate measure of the self-consciousness through which it at once constitutes and distinguishes itself from the world; that this participation is the source of morality and religion; this we take to be the vital truth which Hegel had to teach.[34]

As Edward Caird was later to remark, Green 'regarded the actual Hegelian system with a certain suspicion as something too ambitious, or, at least, premature. "It must all be done over again", he once said.'[35]

It was, nevertheless, idealism which provided the vantage point from which Green criticized his philosophical predecessors. In his view idealism supplied the corrective to, and rose from the ashes of, the train of philosophy set in motion by Locke and Hume:

> The genius of Locke and Hume was their readiness to follow the lead of Ideas: their spirit was the spirit of Rationalism – the spirit which, however baffled and forced into inconsistent admissions, is still governed by the faith that all things may ultimately be understood. We best do reverence to their genius, we most truly appropriate their spirit, in so exploring the difficulties to which their enquiry led, as to find in them the suggestion of a theory which may help us to walk firmly where they stumbled and fell.[36]

Setting on one side my conviction that Green is not altogether fair in the criticism of his predecessors,[37] I take the nub of his case to be that Locke stumbled and fell over the question of consciousness. Locke held that ideas, by nature distinct from the mind, were presented to the mind which receives impressions of them. This seemed to make the self a complex of sensations held together by association, rather than a vital, originating actor; for sequences of sensations could not be known as sequences. Green argued that Humean scepticism was the only possible outcome of this epistemological false start. Again, on a mechanistic view of the mind such as Hume's, there could be no ethical freedom or responsibility:

> it is obvious that to a being who is simply a result of natural forces an injunction to conform to their laws is unmeaning. It implies that there is something in him independent of those forces . . .[38]

Here is the kernel of Green's response to Hume's notion that reason is the slave of the passions. On the contrary, says Green, reason and the passions are not external to one another; rather reason is the prior condition of experiencing the passions, which it can order and tame. Human beings are not simply acted upon as from without by pleasures, pains, circumstances in general; they are self-conscious moral beings possessed of moral freedom, capable of rising to ever new heights through the vanquishing of adversities and the pursuit of the good.

Against empiricism Green contends for self-consciousness, the prior condition of sensations, as the ultimate reality; and for a universe the several parts of which are inherently relational in character, these relations being the product of mind. As he says, 'Events, unrelated, could not be a succession.'[39] It is the work of mind to combine sensations into experience of the real world (the strong echoes of Kant are heard at this point). 'A sensation', he declares, 'can only form an object of experience in being determined by an intelligent subject which distinguishes it from itself and contemplates it in relation to other sensations . . .'[40] The universe as a whole is a system in which all the elements mutually presuppose one another, and reality as such has as its correlative 'an eternal thinking subject . . . without which nature could not be'.[41] In these words we have Green's greatest debt to Hegel. Reality is not an objective world of entities standing apart from thought – an 'outer' as opposed to the mind's 'inner'. Rather, the real is the rational. In elucidating this point Percival Chubb wrote, 'That which requires thought for its comprehension implies thought in the constitution of it'[42] – at which point Ingram Bywater's loathing of 'men who say "imply"' comes to mind.[43]

Just as the human consciousness unifies the diversity by which it is confronted, so the eternal subject unifies all particulars, while not being identified with any. The eternal subject, which may be called God, reproduces itself in human beings in a manner consistent with their nature, motivates their actions and gives them a sense of purpose. This, said H. H. Price, yields an 'excessively immanent God',[44] and of this we shall hear much more in the sequel. For the moment we should note that Green's intensely practical religion, the social results of which we have already noted, was derived directly from his sense of the immanence of the eternal spirit as making for a universal wholeness of relations which challenged teleologically orientated human moral effort as its counterpart and expression. This explains his somewhat acerbic remarks on learning that his former pupil, Gerard Manley Hopkins, had become a Jesuit:

> I imagine him – perhaps uncharitably – to be one of those, like his ideal J. H. Newman, who instead of simply opening themselves to the revelation of God in the reasonable world, are fain to put themselves into an attitude – saintly, it is true, but still an attitude. True citizenship 'as unto the Lord' (which includes all morality) I reckon higher than 'saintliness' in the technical sense . . . It vexes me to the heart to think of a fine nature being victimised by a system which in my 'historic conscience' I hold to be subversive of the Family and the State, and which puts the service of an exceptional institution, or the saving of the individual soul, in opposition to loyal service to society.[45]

Just or not to the Jesuits, these words are more than a little revelatory of Green's understanding of religion – with which I return to the question posed earlier: Was Green a Christian?

Here, as Nettleship observed,

> the answer must depend on what 'to be a christian' means. If it means to believe that every man has God in him, that religion is the continual death of a lower and coming to life of a higher self, and that these truths were more vividly realised in thought and life by Jesus of Nazareth and some of his followers than by any other known men, then without doubt he was a christian. If it means to believe that the above truths depend upon the fact that Jesus was born and died under conditions impossible to other human beings, then equally without doubt he was not a christian.[46]

We may observe in passing that these are not the only alternative definitions of 'Christian', and we may suspect that if the former is a characteristically exemplarist-rationalistic attenuation of the Gospel, the latter is an equally characteristic biblicist-legalistic attenuation. To both we may retort, for example, 'What if Christians are those who, by grace, have been enabled to respond to a redemptive act?' H. D. Lewis significantly (even ominously) remarked, 'it is very uncertain whether the Synoptic Gospels mattered at all' to Green.[47]

Green was convinced that

> There is . . . an inner contradiction in that conception of faith which makes it a state of mind involving peace with God and love towards all men, and at the same time makes its object that historical work of Christ, of which our knowledge depends on evidence of uncertain origin and value.[48]

This claim will be subjected to close scrutiny in due course, but for the present we simply record Green's response to his perceived contradiction. He plays down the historical and declares that 'the primary christian idea is that of a moral death into life, as wrought for us and in us by God . . .'[49] Of this dying and rising, Christ's death and resurrection are symbolic. This is in accordance with his conviction (which begs a question of central importance in this book) that 'Christian dogma . . . must be retained in its completeness, but it must be transformed into a philosophy.'[50] Only so can the miraculous and supernatural encumbrances of belief, and the untoward restrictions of dogma be sidestepped. He testifies:

> I have definitely rejected dogmatic theology for a certain sort of philosophy. This does not to my own consciousness essentially separate me from orthodox Xtians, but I fear it must (if known) do so to theirs. The position of dogmatic theology is that true ideas about God and things spiritual are derived from miraculous events. Now on the matter of the truth of the ideas I don't essentially differ from it, except that the way in which it derives them limits the scope of the ideas. It is the derivation from miraculous events that I reject, holding that the belief in the events was derived from the ideas (of which philosophy is the true intellectual expression), not the ideas from the real happening of the events. The result is that from orthodox Christianity, as expressed in prayer, and in the ordinances of Protestant worship, I find no alienation, while I could not subscribe to one of the creeds.[51]

As he elsewhere said, 'Inability to adopt the creeds of christendom in their natural sense . . . need not disqualify us from using its prayers.'[52] There is an unresolved puzzle here. It might appear that the act of formal subscription was the primary obstacle for Green; for the use of the Book of Common Prayer's collect for Trinity Sunday, for example, would commit the sincere worshipper to Trinitarian doctrine. Yet we know that he was at home with Unitarian doctrine. Two incidents concerning his pupil, the Congregationalist R. F. Horton, are instructive at this point. Of Green Horton wrote,

> Never can I forget his expression when one day he found that I had a real and vivid faith in Christ. His own faith was philosophical and ethical; but Christ, as a Person, had been dissolved by criticism. 'You are very fortunate', was his brief, intense comment.

Again, when in 1881 Horton was wondering whether to leave Oxford for the pastorate at Hampstead, Green said, 'You are likely to do much good here, because you do believe, more than most of us, in the old doctrines.'[53] Is it fanciful to detect a note of wistfulness here?

Be that as it may, many modernists welcomed Green's idealizing policy, while from their very different vantage point some Anglo-Catholics were able to invoke his support for an immanent God, whom they proceeded to rebaptize in the Alexandrian incarnational theology. But the same policy also prompted the charge of pantheism against Green, and from the following quotation we can see how this could happen:

> There must be eternally such a subject which is all that the self-conscious subject, as developed in time, has the possibility of becoming . . . [God] is not merely a Being who has made us, in the sense that we exist as an object of the divine consciousness in the same way in which we must suppose the system of nature so to exist, but that He is a Being in whom we exist; with whom we are in principle one; with whom the human spirit is identical, in the sense that He *is* all which the human spirit is capable of becoming.[54]

Must there? As Robert Mackintosh declared, 'Green scarcely took sufficient pains to justify his supreme interest in righteousness and in its divine source.'[55] Furthermore, in the words just quoted, Green, the opponent of Kant's phenomena–noumena dualism, articulates a dualism of eternal thought and nature which, while no doubt required by his critique of naturalism, appears to undermine his foundational conviction concerning those internal relations whereby all things comprise a logical order whose origin is rational/spiritual.

Again, Green steadfastly maintains that

> God is not wisely trusted when declared unintelligible . . . God is for ever reason; and his communication, his revelation, is reason; not, however, abstract reason, but reason as taking a body from, and giving life to, the whole system of experience which makes the history of man.[56]

That system is intrinsically moral, and of the challenges posed to those who are in the process of fashioning their history Green said,

> Faith in God and duty will survive much doubt and difficulty and distress . . . But if once we have come to acquiesce in such a standard of living as must make us wish God and duty to be illusions, it must surely die.[57]

Here is the dualism between the perfect and the imperfect which Green, 'a living man among living men',[58] with his concern for human personality and his recognition of the problem of evil, could not deny. It may be questioned, however, whether his philosophical standpoint adequately allows for this deliverance of his humanity. Henry Jones, expecting the answer, 'Of course not!' asked, '[C]an anyone discover cold Intellectualism in Burke, or Bentham, or Carlyle, or Mill, or Green, the latest of the great exponents of the nature of human society?'[59] Leaving the other thinkers on one side, I suggest that if Green's intellectualism was not 'cold', it was because it was inconsistently saved by his practical human experience. Thus the man who could declare that 'God is not something outside and beyond the consciousness of him',[60] could also write:

> Who is there that has not known a simple, self-denying christian, and known that if he would, he might become like him? Perhaps, wrapped closely in the fleece of conceit, we think lightly of such a one. He is not clever, or he has awkward manners, or a mean appearance. His bodily presence is weak and his speech contemptible. Yet . . . he is exhibiting that power of the resurrection which still sends healing to the broken-

hearted, deliverance to the captives and recovery of sight to the blind
. . . because it is the spring of that charity which seeketh not her own
and rejoiceth in the truth.[61]

However it may have been practically, theoretically Green leaves
us with an idealized Christ: 'To the modern philosopher the idea
itself is the reality. To him Christ is the necessary determination of
the eternal subject, the objectification by this subject of himself in
the world of nature and humanity.'[62] This was more than the
Scottish divine, James Iverach, could take: '[I]f philosophy can exist
only by attenuating [Christ] to an idea, then so much the worse for
philosophy.'[63] Even the Unitarian Martineau referred to Green's
position as a 'curious type of vague or semi-theism', and said that

> It reveals a state of mind which I suspect to be very prevalent, but
> which can never set into any form of permanent influence. It is either
> the last faint streak of a dissolving nebula, or the first visible undulation
> of an ethereal medium that must condense into a central sun.[64]

In less poetic terms than Martineau's, my questions are: Can
Green's idealistic immanentism allow for the genuinely personal?
Can it surmount the problem of evil? Can it make room for a real
incarnation? In subsequent chapters I shall return to these
questions. For the present I conclude my remarks upon Green by
referring to some of the judgements passed upon his philosophical
work.

It is more than usually the case that from the verdicts recorded
upon Green's work we may learn a good deal about the judges.
The verdicts are mutually contradictory. If, to J. H. Randall,
Green was 'the keenest critical mind to appear in Britain since
Hume',[65] to C. D. Broad he was 'a thoroughly second-rate
thinker', who diffused 'a grateful and comforting aroma of ethical
"uplift"'.[66] Whereas Randall found Green strong on criticism and
weak on construction,[67] in R. B. C. Johnson's opinion Green's
constructive exposition of the significance of reality was 'one of
the most valuable contributions to the metaphysical thinking of
Britain during the last twenty-five years'.[68] A. C. Bradley said that
he owed his soul to Green, and, deep doctrinal differences
notwithstanding, Scott Holland testified to Green's 'profound
Evangelical heart which made all that he taught us intellectually
become spiritual and religious in its effect'.[69] To Hugh Price
Hughes, remembered as much for his social conscience as for his

Methodism, Green was 'the most splendid Christian that I ever knew',[70] and to the Evangelical Anglican F. J. Chavasse, more impressed when a student at Oxford by Green than by anyone else, he 'seemed to have more of the prophet about him than any man I have had the honour of meeting'.[71]

One final verdict of a more technical nature will lead us forward. If I suggested that Green's practical concerns and his humanity saved him from the more devastating consequences of ultra-intellectualism, Henry Jones regretted that Green had not been more consistently monistic:

> The dualism of Kant . . . is only moderated by T. H. Green. It is true that Green finds the spiritual and natural to be related positively, but he has left such a priority to the former as to make it possible to understand him to establish, not a single system revealing in every part and operation the presence and activity of the principle, but the natural *plus* the spiritual, *plus* a relation between them. The externality and contingency of the relation are not overcome. They may, or may not, be brought together. They are not seen by him to be *aspects*, or *elements* of a single real.[72]

But Jones, we recall, was a pupil and disciple of Caird, and to the latter I now turn.

II

Edward Caird was born on 23 March 1835, the fifth of seven sons of John Caird, a partner in an engineering firm in Greenock, and his wife Janet, daughter of Roderick Young of Paisley. The oldest son, John, to whom Edward owed a great deal, became Principal of the University of Glasgow.[73] When his father died in September 1838 Caird went to live with his aunt, Jane Caird, a devout if somewhat narrow member of the Free Kirk. He attended Greenock Academy, and was relieved when the fearsome Dr Brown was succeeded as rector by a university contemporary of his brother John, David Duff, who in 1876 became Professor of Church History at the Theological Hall in Edinburgh of the United Presbyterian Church.[74] On leaving the Academy, Caird entered Glasgow University, where he read arts and divinity. In poor health, he removed to St Andrews University for the session

1856–7, and whilst there he lived with his Aunt Jane. Thence to the manse at Errol, Perthshire, where John was now minister. He returned to Glasgow in 1857 to complete his attendance at the divinity classes. At university Caird excelled in classics, but 'there is no record of any special achievement in the classes of Logic or Moral Philosophy.'[75] He was not naturally given to autobiography, and little is recorded of Caird's opinion of his teachers. It is, however, difficult not to detect a certain affection in his recollection of George Buist. Buist had been Professor of Ecclesiastical History at Glasgow since 1823 and his lectures, which set out from creation, never passed Og, King of Bashan. Of the latter the Bible records that his height was 'like the height of the cedars'. To Buist, however, Og's 'stature was so large that while his feet were in the torrid zone and his body in the temperate, eternal snows rested on his head'.[76]

As with Green and many others, so with Caird: a formative influence on his developing intellect was Carlyle who, according to Henry Jones, 'pointed, as through the bars of a prison-house, the way out of the narrow and cramping orthodoxies into the broad, generous, natural-supernatural world outside'.[77] In Caird's words Carlyle, 'the greatest literary influence of my own student days',

> was the first in this country who discovered the full significance of the great revival of German literature, and the enormous reinforcement which its poetic and philosophical idealism had brought to the failing faith of man . . . He spoke, therefore, from what was recognisably a higher point of view that that of the ordinary sects and parties which divided opinion in this country . . . [H]e was inspired with a passion for social reform, which, at least in this country, was then felt by few.[78]

This 'higher point of view' appealed greatly to Caird, who was temperamentally unsuited to controversy, and who ever looked for the unity which he was convinced lay behind and beyond differences of all kinds.

His speculative interests and his dislike of Scotland's ecclesiastical rough-and-tumble, appear to have been among the factors which turned Caird's mind away from ordination to Oxford and an academic vocation. In 1860 he went to Balliol College as Snell Exhibitioner, and in the following year he won the Pusey and Ellerton Hebrew Scholarship. Older than other undergraduates, and already a graduate of Glasgow, Caird was elected a member of the Old Mortality Club, where his friendship and intellectual sympathy with Green blossomed. On his subsequent appointment to the Mastership of Balliol, Caird said that the College had given him 'the best of my friends; for in Green I found one whose brotherly sympathy and inspiring example has stimulated me, more than any other single influence, in the prosecution of my philosophical work.'[79] In 1862 he was placed in the first class in Classical Moderations; in 1863 he achieved the same result in Literae Humaniores, and secured the degree of BA. For a while he taught philosophy privately, until on 18 May 1864 he was elected a Fellow of Merton. In 1865 his first article, 'Plato and the other Companions of Socrates', was published in the *North British Review*. This was

> ostensibly a review of Grote's work under that title, but really an independent treatise, displaying perfect familiarity and mastery of the whole philosophy of Plato in its inner development, and indicating an equal acquaintance, to those who could read between the lines, with the doctrines of Kant and Hegel.[80]

On 28 May 1866, the year in which Green secured his Tutorship, Caird was unanimously elected Professor of Moral Philosophy at Glasgow University. The other candidates for the post were Henry Calderwood, John Cunningham, Robert Flint, Simon S. Laurie, John Campbell Shairp and James Hutchinson Stirling. Caird told R. M. Wenley that 'he had done nothing', which enigmatic phrase Wenley took to mean that amidst the Scottish ecclesiastical and philosophical parties Caird had 'not committed himself to his harm'.[81] His dislike of controversy was constant. He once gently rebuked the more pugilistic Henry Jones: 'Can't you philosophise without "fechtin"?'[82] And some years later, for example, in a reference to his sermon on Job, he said that his objective had been to 'try to put things in a way that would avoid either orthodoxy or heresy and found it easier than I had expected'.[83]

Caird's strength, like that of Green, was not in philosophical synthesis, but in criticism. '[I]t was rather characteristic of his method of exposition', wrote J. S. Mackenzie,

> that he seldom paused to sum up its final outcome. He had a strong conviction that the results of philosophy, apart from the process by

which they are reached, are almost worse than useless; and, though I think he would have agreed that a process without any definite outcome, a mere dialectical exercise, is equally worthless, yet he probably considered on the whole that the danger on that side is not as great.[84]

Even if he stopped short of final synthesis, however, Caird's critical method was nevertheless of the constructive kind, Green's of the adversarial and destructive. Whereas Green, sometimes one-sidedly, saw the need to trounce empiricist philosophers with whom he disagreed, Caird, bringing his favoured posture of 'Kant-corrected-by-Hegel' to bear upon his predecessors, positively extracted from them what would support his synoptic vision, whilst passing by contrary positions. Thus, as Jones said,

> Session after session passed and no allusion, near or remote, was made to the 'Scottish School' of Common Sense, whose psychological doctrines were confused with Metaphysics, and in the agnosticism of which there was supposed to be support for religious faith. No Scottish name later than that of David Hume passed his lips.[85]

The result was that Caird delivered his conclusions (albeit not in a pontificating manner) without feeling obliged to compare and contrast them with the views of such continuing Scottish Hamiltonians as Fraser, Calderwood and Veitch.[86] If Green went back into the past with a view to demolition, and thence to reconstruction out of the rubble of past philosophy, Caird declared that

> in the first instance at least, we must read development *backward* and not *forward*, we must find the key to the meaning of the first stage in the last; though it is quite true that, afterwards, we are enabled to throw new light upon the nature of the last . . . by carrying it back to the first.[87]

This principle, enunciated here with reference to religion, likewise informed Caird's philosophical criticism, and characterized his attitude to life as a whole: 'If he could not find the germ of good in things evil, he not only turned away from them, but seemed to delete them.'[88] The comments of two of Caird's pupil-disciples will confirm the likeness and the contrast between Caird and Green. Muirhead who, having sat under Caird at Glasgow proceeded to Oxford, reflected thus: Caird seemed to be one always walking on the mountain tops. When one came across others, like Green and Nettleship, one was in a different atmosphere. They were as men in the valley, their eyes no doubt on the mountain tops, but engaged rather in taking bearings and planning routes than in leading the way.[89]

Or, in the words of Henry Jones, [Caird] 'was not more earnest than Green in maintaining that "The real is the rational" and that the rational is the spiritual; but one thinks of him as more "rapt" by the vision.'[90]

Since reference has already been made to some of Caird's professionally academic pupils – Jones, Watson, Mackenzie and Muirhead – who continued in his line; and to others – Denney and Robert Mackintosh – who did not, it may be instructive to note the comments of Charles Silvester Horne, whose talents lay in other directions, and who became well known as the Congregational minister of Whitefield's Tabernacle and MP for Ipswich. Horne writes to his mother:

> I see now that Father was right when he said I had not a philosophical mind. As I write an essay, I consider how it would sound to an audience, the result being an essay in a popular rather than philosophical spirit. I fear I have not, and shall not acquire that great spiritual gift of dryness which is essential to the successful philosopher. Caird says my essay was well written, many expressions being very happy, but it lacked 'firmness of thought', which I presume is, being interpreted, long philosophical technicalities arranged in rigid logical sequence.[91]

Two months later Horne writes, 'Caird's final exam. was on Saturday – a very stiff paper – almost, if not quite, unfair.'[92]

In 1867 Caird married Caroline Frances, the eldest daughter of the minister of Carluke, Lanarkshire, John Wylie. Like the Greens, the Cairds had no children. Also like Green, Caird gave himself to community activities of various kinds. In Glasgow, together with Mrs Caird, he staunchly supported moves to facilitate the higher education of women and to extend the franchise. With others he established the University Settlement Association along the lines of Toynbee Hall in London, as a centre from which students could undertake social work; and he was prominent in the Women's Protective and Provident League, the objective of which was to secure improved conditions for working women and children.

George Adam Smith, Principal of Glasgow University, did not exaggerate when, following Caird's death, he described him as 'one of the greatest citizens Glasgow ever had'.[93]

In 1891–2 Caird visited St Andrews to deliver his first series of Gifford Lectures, *The Evolution of Religion* (1893). Of these he wrote, 'I confess to having more of a personal interest in them than other things I have written, as I have put more of my own experience into them.'[94] He delivered a second series of Gifford Lectures at Glasgow in 1900: *The Evolution of Theology in the Greek Philosophy* (1904).

Meanwhile on Jowett's death in 1893, Caird was elected Master of Balliol. Although 'it was one of the hardest things in going to Oxford to want the almost daily talk over things with my brother', and despite the fact that 'My own incapacity for affairs and for society is a greater hindrance than I had expected', he felt that in Oxford, 'I should have my hand on the heart of England.'[95] Devastated by the early death of Green, Caird became an active governor of Oxford High School, which Green had done so much to found. He continued in Oxford his advocacy of education for women, admitted women to his lectures, and read their essays.

On the death of William Wallace in 1897 Caird, like Wallace a President of London's Ethical Society, failed to secure the Whyte Professorship of Moral Philosophy. His distinction was, however, recognized in other ways: honorary doctorates were bestowed upon him by the universities of St Andrews, Glasgow, Oxford, Cambridge and Wales, and in 1902 he was elected a Fellow of the British Academy. Caird continued to teach and write, but in 1905 he suffered a paralytic stroke, and resigned the Mastership in 1907. He died on 1 November 1908, and was buried in St Sepulchre's cemetery beside Jowett, Henry Smith (a Balliol scientist and mathematician) and Green.

Something of Caird's philosophical approach – notably his principle of reading development backwards – has already become clear. What did he see as he reviewed the course of philosophy? His pupil Muirhead concisely supplies the answer:

> Caird's philosophy was an attempt to do justice to different elements in human experience which certain tendencies in the thought of his time had severed and treated in abstraction from one another. On the one hand was the Idealism commonly called Subjective, which, with its

sceptical corollaries, had infected English philosophy from the time of Berkeley. On the other hand, there was the Realism or Naturalism which sought to eliminate the element contributed by the subject and to explain everything in terms of nature conceived of as a mechanical system and held to be not only the one thing that could be known, but the ultimate reality of things. Against the first Caird maintained the doctrine of the essential intelligibility or rationality of a universe in the fullest sense objective. Against the second he asserted the necessity of interpreting the Whole, within which Nature and Mind appeared as related elements, by the light of and therefore as kindred to our own highest or self conscious experience.[96]

More particularly, and in the wake of such organic views as those of the German Romantics, Coleridge and F. D. Maurice, Caird believed that under the presently prevailing intellectual conditions a return to monism – supremely represented by the greatest of the Greek philosophers – was required in order to prevent the further erosion of thought at the hands of dualists whether Cartesian or Kantian. (Of Kant, Caird said that 'He started from both ends of the road at once, but he never met himself.')[97] With reference to Goethe's idea of a self-revealing unity, Caird declared that 'The great question of philosophy is whether such a unity in totality, such a self-determined principle of infinite change, can in any sense be verified, or made an object of knowledge.'[98] To this question Caird returned an affirmative answer, and he overcame the agnosticism which on this point remained with Green who, in his review of John Caird's *An Introduction to the Philosophy of Religion*, cautioned that

> when we have satisfied ourselves that the world in its truth or full reality is spiritual . . . we may still have to confess that a knowledge of it in its spiritual reality – such a knowledge of it as would be a knowledge of God – is impossible to us. To know God we must be God.[99]

Caird insisted, however, that

> If philosophy is incapable of a universal synthesis, it cannot make any synthesis at all. If it admit any absolute division, whether between the ego and the non-ego, or between man and nature, or even between the finite and infinite, it is driven of necessity into scepticism. Unless it reconciles us with the universe, it cannot even reconcile us with ourselves.[100]

Caird's goal is not, of course, a unity in which all distinctions are obliterated. He construes Plato with approval thus: 'objects can be recognised as real, only if, and so far as, they have that unity in difference, that permanence in change, that intelligible individuality, which are the essential characteristics of mind.'[101] He admits that 'The greatest task of philosophy . . . is just to consider how the constant presence of this unity modifies the contents both of the subjective and of the objective consciousness.'[102] But there can be no absolute distinction as between subject and object, and no ultimate epistemological dualism as between phenomena and noumena, for reality is one spiritual, knowable whole. In this way Caird 'corrected' Kant, who had mistakenly sought an undifferentiated unity beyond the knowable, by recourse to Hegel – albeit to a carefully selected Hegel; for Caird never expounded Hegel's system as a whole. Like other British 'Hegelians' he left the 'method' on one side, and he had reservations concerning some of Hegel's criticisms of Kant and regarding Hegel's categorial schema.[103] Not surprisingly, Caird commended Carlyle for his

> attempt to show, not that spirit interferes with matter, or miraculously works upon it from without, but that the material or sensible world is itself, in its deepest essence, rational, spiritual.[104]

Scientific developments – especially those of the past hundred years – had, he thought, converted the long-standing 'belief that in some sense the world is a rational or intelligible system' into 'a palpable assurance'.[105]

It follows that to Caird the supreme importance of religion was its ever-developing ability to assist humanity in the comprehension of the spiritual reality at the heart of all. The developmental motif is here crucial. In fact

> the great reconciling principle of Development . . . has made it possible for us to understand the errors of men in the past as partial and germinating truths . . . The idea of development . . . enables us to maintain a critical spirit without agnosticism, and a reasonable faith without dogmatism; for it teaches us to distinguish the one spiritual principle which is continuously working in man's life from the changing forms through which it passes in the course of its history.[106]

Thus, where religion is concerned, later expressions fulfil and correct what has gone before. Caird denies that Jesus intended to emphasize his originality, and lays considerable weight on the latter's declaration that he came not to destroy, but to fulfil the law and the prophets.[107] Accordingly, we must not 'seek for something which is *common* to all religions, but rather for that which *underlies* them all as their principle'.[108] In practical terms, religion

> delivers [man] from himself and the difficulties of his immediate life by reverence for that which is above him; and . . . it teaches him to regard that power which he thus reverences as manifested both in nature and in the society to which he as an individual belongs.[109]

In Jesus' confidence that all evils will be remedied, and in his confidence of union with God, we have the bases of 'a faith beyond which religion cannot go, except in two ways, namely, in the way of understanding them more adequately, and of realising them more fully'.[110]

Of Caird's method with respect to the truths enunciated by other philosophers, it was said that 'He constrained the truths to expose their one-sidedness and abstractness, and to exhibit their need of their opposites.'[111] In the result, and because of his personal humility and humanity, he inspired many. William Temple described himself as 'a loyal pupil of Edward Caird';[112] Henry Jones declared that as far as Caird's students were concerned, 'There was nothing to rival the sway of their reverence for his strong, calm, thought-laden personality except their affection.'[113] 'As he was speaking', recalled Mackenzie,

> the fire burned; and some were apt to think him overconfident, almost too much of a prophet in the promulgation of his creed. Others complained of a certain hesitancy on ultimate issues, lack of detailed applications and positive results . . . [In fact Caird] was silent where he did not know. He gave the reins to his thought, but not to his fancy.[114]

This more balanced judgement of the generally sympathetic Mackenzie leads us on one side to examples of pupils who escaped the master's intellectual net.[115] Given that Caird's Glasgow class comprised up to 250 hearers, it is not surprising that some who, like Silvester Horne, were not primarily philosophers, and others who were more than competent in the field should have had their misgivings. Of these last I summon two.

Alfred Ernest Garvie, theologian, ecumenist, and Principal of New College, London, found Caird to be

> one of the most attractive teachers and most influential personalities I have ever met. In no class was there as close attention or as warm appreciation as in his. He shaped the minds of his students to the likeness of his own; by the spell he cast over them he captured them for his Neo-Hegelian philosophy. Only after they had passed from his classroom did some of his students 'hae their doots'.

Garvie's doubts were such that his subsequent 'abandonment of Neo-Hegelianism disappointed' Caird.[116] In a more technical context Robert Mackintosh had earlier revealed the nature of Caird's 'spell'. Speaking of the way in which Caird transformed 'Hegel's coldly hostile examination of Kant into a sympathetic eliciting of the hints of constructive idealism from behind the prejudices or hostile principles with which Kant was hampered', he remarked, 'While we read, we are "under the spell of the magician". Difficulties vanish, and the demonstration seems complete. It is only when we close the book that difficulties begin to return.'[117] More particularly,

> as we proceed under Dr Caird's guidance from Kant's starting-point to Hegel's goal, we lose touch with the familiar world. Kant, Dr Caird explains, shows that our thought constitutes reality; there is no reason for saying with Kant, *phenomenal* reality; but an *individual* thought could not constitute objective reality; therefore we must take Kant to mean that *thought as such* constitutes *absolute* reality. The starting-point is therefore transformed or is knocked to pieces in the course of our further movements. That is quite in order, upon the principles of Hegelianism. But the appeal to Kant for a new way into Hegel was designed to help British minds too deeply immersed in common sense to be capable of receiving Hegel's Hegelianism. It is to be feared that the difficulties of the new road are almost as great as those of the old.[118]

Mackintosh's prescription is that

> If we are to criticise such arguments . . . with success, we must criticise, not what is argued for, but rather what is taken for granted. Is a formula drawn from logic or metaphysics adequate to determine the contents of morality and religion?[119]

This question will haunt us throughout the remainder of this book.

Following Caird's death Clement Webb wrote,

> even those of us who stood at some distance were sensible that in the
> late Master of Balliol we had among us one whose thought about
> Religion, while it deserved, if ever thought did, the honourable name of
> 'free thought', was always the thought of one who knew in his own soul
> as present life and power the thing which was its object.[120]

If idealism facilitated Caird's free thought, how did it serve one
whose sense of vocation placed him within holy orders? Enter
Illingworth.

III

> There is much need . . . now as ever, for work in the field of theology.
> But 'pectus facit theologum' – the heart makes the theologian – the
> heart that has been given to God. Intellect combined with mental
> tendency is not enough. The Christian student's is not a life of literary
> ease, directed to theological subjects . . . The life of the theologian is
> before all things a life of prayer . . . The crown of the Christian intellect
> has been called a crown of thorns. Theology is a matter of vocation.[121]

With these solemn words John Richardson Illingworth characterized the high calling which he himself strove to fulfil. At once we
suspect that, however much Green and Caird lived their religion –
and they did – in Illingworth's works the religious spirit is much
closer to the surface, though far from superficial.

Illingworth was born in London on 26 June 1848. His father,
the Reverend E. A. Illingworth, was chaplain to Coldbath Fields
Prison; his mother, Mary Taylor, was possessed of considerable
intellectual gifts. A shy boy who nevertheless made firm friends, he
was educated at St Paul's School, London, under Dr Kynaston,
for whom he had great respect and affection. He won an
exhibition to Oxford University and a scholarship at Corpus
Christi College, distinguishing himself with first class honours in
Classical Moderations and Literae Humaniores. He proceeded in
1872 to a Fellowship at Jesus College, and in the same year
became a tutor at Keble College. He was ordained deacon in 1875
and priest in 1876. He did not take ordination lightly, deciding as
early as 1871 that although it was his wish to take orders, 'I feel

that I must have two or three years of reflection before I can hope
to be ordained; if indeed I can ever be ordained at all . . .'[122]

Henry Scott Holland has provided an illuminating account of
Illingworth's impact upon his students:

> As a young tutor at Keble . . . he swept the hearts and imaginations of
> the young fellows who came to his lectures on philosophy. They were
> agog with the intellectual turmoil of those days when the power of
> T. H. Green was put out to shatter the idols of Empiricism. The
> currents of the new thought were running strongly, and the ancient
> strongholds were breaking, and the formulas of J. S. Mill were going
> under. But Green was cruelly inarticulate: and his message was tough
> and tangled: and the Hegelian jargon was teeth-breaking, and head-
> splitting: and the way of speculation was hard and grim to tread. And
> lo! here was a man who was at home in that strange world, it would
> seem, and yet whose speech was clear and quick as the song of a bird.
> As his limpid sentences dropped from his lips in their certainty of
> rhythm and sequence, everything became intelligible . . . This man
> could say at once what he had to say: and yet it was not easy or cheap.
> It did not keep on the surface. It went down deep . . . All this had its
> perils. The men who followed along his illuminating speech with such
> delight thought that they understood more than they really had
> mastered. But this only increased their enthusiastic devotion to the
> man who could do such great things with them and for them.[123]

In his student days Illingworth had been a member of what was
humorously known as the Association of Bigoted Catholics; he
had fasted and worn a hair shirt. In later life he denied himself the
theatre, music and an annual visit to London 'because he found
them too exciting to allow him to settle down again readily to that
pursuit of the presentment of truth to which he had set
himself'.[124] At the same time, his awareness of the pitfalls of the
ascetic path is clear from a letter to 'M.C.L.' of May 1903 on the
subject of Lent:

> Surely all asceticism belongs to the negative side of religion (touch not,
> taste not), and must therefore assume less and less importance in
> proportion as the positive side (to know the love which passeth
> knowledge) develops – and all this was meant to be. To attempt,
> therefore, to invent fresh negatives when the old ones have ceased to be
> felt, just because they have passed into one's life and done their work, is
> to go backwards. More positives are what we want. I know you agree
> with all this, but can't get rid of a certain sensual craving to hurt

yourself a little more, just for the niceness of it. But I should struggle against that.[125]

To complete the portrait of Illingworth, it should be noted that although he could appear aloof, was by nature reserved and often in indifferent health, he played fives and enjoyed climbing, had a sense of humour and, according to a former student of his, J. C. M. Brown,

> there was a strong feeling in college that Mr. I. was himself a bit of a rebel, and that infractions of rules and regulations were regarded by him with a somewhat lenient eye.[126]

In 1875 the first of a series of meetings of what Scott Holland called 'the holy party' was held. This group was to some extent continuous with the later *Lux Mundi* party, whose leader was E. S. Talbot, then Warden of Keble and later Bishop of Winchester. In 1883, his health causing concern, Illingworth accepted the living of Longworth, Oxfordshire, and there he remained, declining offered positions on four occasions, for the rest of his life. In the following year he married Agnes Louisa Gutteres, a nurse, who survived him, and published a biography of her late husband. Like the Greens and the Cairds – and also the Webbs – the Illingworths had no children. *Lux Mundi* appeared in 1889, and the group continued to meet at Longworth until 1914.

On arriving in Longworth, Illingworth repaced the quarterly communion service with a weekly one; he instituted daily worship, and communion monthly on a weekday at noon. He would not have a surpliced choir, and he would not have the singers in the chancel: 'He maintained that the singing in a parish church should be congregational, and that the best chance of making it so was to have the choir at the back.'[127] At first he was quite out of touch with the way of life of many of his flock. He did not know that a sum of money less than half-a-crown could be of use to anyone. He did not undertake routine pastoral visitation, but he conscientiously and effectively called upon the sick and the distressed. He was no committee man, and saw little of the neighbouring clergy. On the contrary,

> Guided by the bold and shrewd insight of his wife, he shut himself up inside his hidden parish. He refused to be persuaded to go beyond it.

He made it his sole pulpit: and it proved amply sufficient. He reached far, far more people than we can do by racing up and down the earth and occupying every pulpit open to us.[128]

This is borne out by the fact that Illingworth's writings appeared in Japanese and Chinese, and that the Bishop of Tinnevelly – a stranger to Illingworth – wrote from South India to say how much he had enjoyed reading *Divine Immanence* whilst travelling by bullock-cart over the sandy wastes.[129] It is noteworthy that Illingworth's limpid prose, which flows so easily, was achieved only with much effort: his wife recalls his making about thirty attempts at one sentence.[130]

Though living a retired yet not reclusive life (he preferred to work in the room where his wife was, rather than in his study), Illingworth as far as possible kept himself *au fait* with theological developments, though he did lament his inability to afford all the books he would have liked to purchase. On at least two occasions he fired off elegant, albeit oblique, salvos against what he regarded as damaging views. First, in 1911 J. M. Thompson of Magdalen College, Oxford, a disciple of the Catholic Modernist Loisy, published his *Miracles in the New Testament*. He argued that the miracles were but the psychologized accounts of non-miraculous events. For this he was censured by E. S. Talbot, and against this position Illingworth took up his pen, arguing in *The Gospel Miracles* (1915) that the miracles are 'intrinsically congruous with the Incarnation, considered as the great enfranchisement of human life by its deliverance from the slavery to sin',[131] and concluding that

> the attempt to eliminate these miracles, in the supposed interest of a more rational Christianity, apart from its other difficulties, involves a serious misconception of what the Christian Faith has historically been. It would substitute an ideal for an eventful religion, a theory of the wise and prudent for the revelation to babes.[132]

Secondly, Illingworth by implication rebutted R. J. Campbell's *The New Theology* (1907). This book was a nine-day wonder written by the then minister of London's City Temple, who subsequently recanted and returned to the Church of England.[133] Campbell advocated an immanentist understanding of a God who made his appeal to human feeling, and the experience of whose nearness was the only ground of religion. To Illingworth this entailed a capitulation to 'the psychological bias', and a repudiation of the authority of the Christian tradition – 'The element of authority in religion must always be strong.' Moreover, it was not balanced by the fact of transcendence – an idea which 'We do not postulate . . . because our feelings need it'.[134]

In 1900 Illingworth was invited to give the Gifford Lectures in 1902. He did not think that the two years allowed for preparation would enable him to do his best, and he did not wish to do less than his best. Accordingly, in 'one of the great renunciations of his life', he declined. He did, however, accept the honorary degree of Doctor of Divinity of the University of Edinburgh, which was offered in the same year.[135]

As he lay dying, this most unworldly man 'would beg us with tears in his eyes to pray that he who had preached to others might not himself be a castaway'.[136] The end came on 21 August 1915.

Illingworth's wife testified that 'no ill-natured word was ever present in John Illingworth's heart or on his lips.' As Charles Gore said,

> He retired to his quiet parish, and there, loved and honoured, he occupied himself in undistracted meditation on God and the world and mankind in the light of the light of the Incarnation.[137]

Integral to his understanding of the Incarnation was his appreciation of beauty wherever he found it. In others he saw the beauty of holiness, among them 'some who little thought that by their simple following they were helping him to write his books'.[138] He was much moved by the death of Ruskin, and in January 1900 wrote to 'M.C.L.':

> I always feel that whereas many people appreciate beauty as being a kind of expression or manifestation of goodness, I have always felt that goodness was only a kind of manifestation of beauty – a fascinating but far more dangerous creed.[139]

His emphasis upon the eye as well as the ear is not unrelated to his strong sacramentalism. However, any dangers inherent in his aesthetically weighted creed were held in check by his strong intellectualist strain. In a letter to Wilfrid Richmond he welcomed Pringle-Pattison's *Hegelianism and Personality* for its 'strong defence of personality', and continued,

Someone is wanted on our side to keep up the touch of abstract thinking – as circumstances seem driving most of us to one form or another of 'applied' thought, and the only people who are doing the other seem to be the Greenites of the Left (Bosanquet, Bradley?). And yet we know the Greenites of the Right are the only true interpreters.[140]

None could deny that, with a remarkable consistency throughout his career, Illingworth devoted strenuous thought to fundamental philosophico-theological issues. He was convinced that 'we are living in one of those epochs when a resetting of the Truth, a restatement of it in more adequate language, has become imperatively necessary.'[141] Eleven years later, in his preface to *Lux Mundi* Gore explained that the contributors were anxious 'to attempt to put the Catholic faith into its right relation to modern intellectual and moral problems'.[142] The emphasis upon the resetting and restatement of the catholic faith of the ages under-lines the *conserve*-ative motive: the objective was by no means that of concocting a new faith; the inescapability of modern critical methods, of scientific advance, of increasing recognition of world faiths other than the Christian – these were among the stimuli to relevance. When reading Illingworth and his colleagues we are much more aware of the impact of the mid-nineteenth-century revival of Classics at Oxford, with its repercussions in Patristics, than when reading Green or Caird – for all the 'Johannine' emphases of these last. The Alexandrian logos theology is overtly at work in the Incarnationalism of the *Lux Mundi* men, and is deemed by them both to harmonize with the evolutionary-immanentist thought of their time, and to demand a counterbalancing emphasis upon the divine transcendence. None was more definite on these points than Illingworth himself.

Thus he called upon the Church to welcome scientific discoveries and to clear the air on evolution, 'in the direction of showing that it is the name of a process or method, and can never account for any "origins"'.[143] He was convinced that, properly understood, theology and science were complementary and could not contradict one another:

Science may resolve the complicated life of the material universe into a few elementary forces . . . but of the origin of energy . . . it knows no more than did the Greeks of old. Theology asserts that in the beginning was the Word, and in him was life . . . He is the source of all that energy . . .[144]

In a sermon on 'Eternity' he pointed out that

> intellectual satisfaction is not to be found in science . . . Why was it all
> thus? Why did universal history take this course and not another? Show
> me not only that it was so, but that it could not have been otherwise.
> And science cannot answer you. Its results are empirical, contingent,
> probable. It cannot satisfy the postulates of reason. It is at best a grand
> *perhaps*.[145]

All of which throws into relief the importance of the
philosopher-theologian's task. Both the 'philosophical outworks'
and the 'theological centre' clamoured for attention.[146] As to the
former,

> the aim of philosophy is concrete knowledge of the world as a whole. It
> surveys all the different parts of experience . . . with a view to
> ascertaining their mutual relations and total significance; what is the
> nature of their connexion; what is their meaning as a whole.[147]

From the theological side comes the co-ordinating, personal
spiritual principle – God, transcendent and immanent. Just as we
know the distinctions between body and soul, and spirit and
matter only in combination, so we can conceive of the eternal
transcendent spirit as immanent within the created order.[148] Both
deism and pantheism are excluded by the fact that 'Spirit which is
merely immanent in matter, without transcending it, cannot be
spirit at all.'[149] But this is no impersonal spirit (we recall
Illingworth's welcome of Pringle-Pattison's emphasis upon
personality). It is the divine spirit made known to us in the
Incarnation of Christ. Because of this revelation the Christian
philosopher, unlike his secular counterpart, 'must view the
universe in that new light which the Incarnation had cast upon its
meaning'.[150] This, at any rate, is what Illingworth says the pioneer
philosophers of the early Christian centuries had to do; but his
words aptly summarize his own view of the matter.

The fact of the eternal immanent spirit, together with the
concept of development, allows us – even requires us – to adopt a
positive stance *vis-à-vis* world religions other than the Christian.
Indeed,

> there can be no greater mistake – from an apologetic point of view –
> than to depreciate the ethnic religions in the supposed interests of an

exclusive revelation. For if it were granted that the majority of the religions in the world had existed unsustained by any kind of inspiration, this would constitute a strong presumption that the remainder were in similar case. The world's religion is too much of a piece to be torn asunder in this way. There is too obvious a solidarity about it. Its higher stages are inseparably joined with the lower steps that have led up to them . . . [151]

Elsewhere he writes,

the spiritual experience of mankind, with all the thoughts that it suggests, is after all the most important element in our total body of experience, of which scientific knowledge is only a part; while it is upon this total body of experience, and not on any isolated part of it, that our general view of the world, our ultimate philosophy is founded. And it is this ultimate philosophy that is our final court of appeal in the discussion of religious questions . . . [152]

Not indeed that any system of philosophy 'can ever become adequate or final';[153] but continual effort must be made to reach an ever less unsatisfactory view of the world.

For Illingworth the Trinity is the archetype of the always incomplete human personality (itself an ultimate fact, and not simply a succession of states of consciousness), which comprises reason, will and love. Hence to ethics. Christianity provides an absolute ethical end: 'Be ye perfect, even as your Father'; it supplies a standard in Christ the Son; it imposes a sanction: 'That ye may be the children of your Father'; and in the Holy Spirit it provides a resource.[154] It is particularly interesting to observe that whereas, when commenting on Christian thought since the Reformation, Illingworth regretted that 'the religion of the Incarnation was narrowed into the religion of the Atonement',[155] when ethics were under consideration he could write, 'The conquest of sin, then, being the first requisite of Christian life, the Atonement necessarily, as the pledge of that conquest, stands in the forefront of Christian ethics.'[156] Here is the note of redemption, subdued by that of illumination in Green, which, together with his devotion to the sacraments, his commitment to the tradition and authority of the Church, and his counter-balancing of immanence with transcendence, distinguishes Illingworth's content from that of his illustrious predecessor. In method also Illingworth differed from both Green and Caird. If

Green proceeded on the basis of the destructive criticism of his philosophical foes, and Caird by distilling the helpful from, and bypassing what he deemed misguided in, the work of his predecessors, Illingworth positively expounded a theologized – at times a devotionalized – idealism which drew overtly on Christian tradition, but did not involve detailed historical analysis or philosophical criticism of his intellectual forebears.

Illingworth's books were widely and courteously reviewed. His wife perceptively remarked that he 'set himself all along, as it were, more to the study of the forest, than of the trees which grow therein'.[157] That at least one of his reviewers wished for more argumentative trees is clear from his remark on *Personality Human and Divine*, that 'The book is of value for its indications of ethical and spiritual insight rather than for the cogency of its formal argument.'[158] His friend Scott Holland candidly observed that 'The intellectual appeal to reason was always there . . . but it was touched with an artistic imagination that perhaps disguised the necessity for intellectual wrestling.' The same writer also admitted that there was 'a certain sameness' in what Illingworth had to say. This, he felt, 'was the inevitable price that he paid for the security and peace of the unchanging background which alone enabled him to do his work'.[159] On the other hand, of *Reason and Revelation*, which Illingworth himself felt to be his best work,[160] that doughty demolisher of weak arguments, James Iverach of the United Free Church of Scotland, declared that the book was 'one of the ablest treatises on apologetics which we have had the good fortune to read'.[161] What cannot be denied is that many would have endorsed the following words of the Revd H. Stewart:

> The name of John Illingworth stands, and will stand very high in the rôle of those who in our time have interpreted the ways of God to man; and for his help and guidance we should this day bless God, and by our effort to express his teaching in our lives declare that he who lived so little to himself still lives in those who were privileged to know him in the flesh and to hear his voice.[162]

IV

Between the temperaments and careers of Illingworth and Henry Jones – full of Celtic fervour, man of affairs and eager controversialist – there could scarcely be a greater contrast. Neither were their upbringings at all similar. Jones's folk, with a weekly income of a little over one pound, would certainly have known the value of a sum of money less than half-a-crown. And Illingworth could not have valued education more than Jones, neither did he have to work so hard to obtain it.

Henry Jones,[163] born at Llangernyw, Denbighshire, on 30 November 1852, was the eldest son of Elias Jones, the village shoemaker, and his wife Elizabeth (née Williams). It was a devout, Presbyterian (Calvinistic Methodist) home, and in his Sunday school Jones learned much from Robert Hughes, a neighbouring farmer, whom he recalled in *Old Memories* as 'one of the best teachers I ever had'. He attended the village school for about eight years, until he was apprenticed to his father at the age of twelve and a half. At this time he had two ambitions: 'One was to become a first-rate shoemaker, and the other was to be made an elder in the little Calvinistic Methodist chapel, when I was a man.'[164] He worked a twelve-hour day, studied into the night, found time to participate in local eisteddfodau, and secured admission to Bangor Normal College. In 1873 he became schoolmaster at the Amman Ironworks School, Brynamman, south Wales, and whilst there he was enrolled as a Presbyterian lay preacher.

In 1875 a punishing five months of study was rewarded with a Dr Williams Scholarship to the University of Glasgow, where he found Veitch's Hamiltonianism 'rich in bones and poor in meat', but was enthused by Nichol on English literature and, above all, by Edward Caird, to whom he was profoundly indebted for his own philosophical position. From Caird he derived a world-and-life view which enabled him to cleave to the kernel of the Christian faith, whilst sitting loose to the more doctrinaire deliverances of confessionalism. As he said, 'I was born in Llangernyw in 1852, and born again in 1876 in Edward Caird's class-room.'[165] Though never an exact scholar, Jones nevertheless achieved first class honours, and was awarded the University's George A. Clark Fellowship, which kept him for the next four years, during which time he studied (including an unsatisfying term as a non-collegiate student in Oxford) and assisted Caird as a private tutor. In 1882 he married Annie Walker of Kilbirnie, Ayrshire, by whom he had six children, two of whom died young, and one of whom was killed during the First World War.

In 1882 Jones accepted a call to a prominent Calvinistic
Methodist church in Liverpool, but Caird persuaded him to
withdraw. Accordingly, in the same year he took up a lectureship
in philosophy at the college in Aberystwyth. His relations with the
Principal, the Revd Thomas Charles Edwards, staunchly orthodox
and possibly less than adept in human relations, were not easy,
and when it was decided that his lectureship should become a
professorship Jones failed to apply for the post. Unknown to him,
an advertisment was published, and the position went to one who
had formally applied for it. This left Jones without regular work for
fifteen months from Easter 1883. He acted as an external
examiner for Glasgow University, and was engaged by William
Rathbone MP to draft the constitution for the proposed North
Wales College, Bangor. In 1884 he applied for the Principalship of
this institution, but was awarded the Professorship of Philosophy
there. Notwithstanding his conviction that 'They also serve who
only stand and think',[166] Jones preached regularly in the chapels
around Bangor, staunchly supported the Liberal Party, and
actively advocated the establishment of Welsh intermediate
schools. Here too he wrote his first book, *Browning as a
Philosophical and Religious Teacher*, which was published in 1891. In
the same year he applied for the Chair of Logic and Metaphysics
at Edinburgh University, but was defeated by Pringle-Pattison.
The latter's translation left open the Chair of Logic at St Andrews,
and to that position Jones was appointed. At that time the College
in Dundee was a constituent of St Andrews University, and it
transpired that Jones was largely supported by Dundee
representatives; but the friction thus caused was soon overcome.
At St Andrews Jones was required to teach English literature as
well as philosophy – no hardship this to him, for he strongly
believed that true philosopher and true poet alike see things
whole, and that the world shows itself to be rational and poetic
'under the same conditions, namely, when it is viewed *sub specie
aeternitatis*'. He could without difficulty declare Hegel, Goethe,
Carlyle and Wordsworth 'unique amongst their peers' for 'they
teach the world as it never was taught before, in any age, how
sacred it all is and how interfused with the light divine';[167] and
although he feared that at times Browning sailed too close to
pantheism, he nevertheless welcomed his emphasis upon the
divine immanence which pervaded humanity and nature alike.

Before leaving St Andrews, Jones wrote the first and only volume of his projected two-volume critical analysis of the philosophy of Lotze. While appreciating Lotze's insistence on the importance of personality, Jones held that Lotze's dualism of subject and object was deficient, and that insofar as he achieved consistency, it was only by smuggling more of the intellect into reality than his presuppositions, when strictly adhered to, sanctioned.

As we have seen, Caird was appointed to the Mastership of Balliol in 1893, and Jones succeeded him at Glasgow in 1894. There can be no doubt that the master was well satisfied to be followed by this pupil. In 1891 he had written, 'Jones is one of the best men we have had here in my time, with a remarkable combination of Celtic fervour and lecturing power with capacity for philosophy.' A few years later, with reference to Jones and the Professor of Logic, Robert Adamson, he could say,

> I think that they will work well together, especially as they supplement each other, Adamson being a man of great learning and a strongly analytical and critical spirit, while Jones is – as you know – a fervid Celtic idealist.[168]

Jones's comment on succeeding Caird was, 'I will not be disappointed if I fail to fill Mr Caird's place, because I do not expect to do so.'[169]

As in Bangor, so in Glasgow: Jones threw himself into his teaching, and into numerous other good works besides. Social work in the slums of Glasgow, the Glasgow Civic Society, the Western Infirmary, Scottish education reform – all of these fell within his purview. Indeed, in 1899 Caird reported,

> I have been scolding [Jones] much for taking up too many things beyond his Chair . . . [his] influence is growing in Glasgow, but he must resist the pressure it brings on him to be useful in all directions.[170]

In 1901 Jones declined the invitation to succeed Viriamu Jones as Principal of University College, Cardiff; in 1907 he was interested in, but failed to secure, the Principalship at Glasgow, which was made vacant by the death of Robert Herbert Story, who had succeeded John Caird in the post. Jones's university contemporary, James Denney, thought that while 'the betting is in favour of Jones', and that George Adam Smith came next, 'Smith would be a far better man of business than Jones. He is besides a far more thoroughly educated man, except in philosophy. Both would be immensely popular with the students . . .' Ten days later he wrote, 'The Government, and at least Lloyd George, want Jones in Wales, and that is in Smith's favour.'[171] In the event Donald Macalister was appointed.

Jones was elected a Fellow of the British Academy in 1904; he was knighted in 1912; he received honorary doctorates from St Andrews and Wales; in 1916 he served on the Royal Commission on Education in Wales; and in January 1922, just before he died, he was made a Companion of Honour, and received the medal of the Honourable Society of Cymmrodorion. His last major philosophical task was the preparation of his Gifford Lectures, *A Faith that Enquires* (1922). These were completed with great determination and amidst considerable physical pain. As Jones said,

> The devil has been so busy with me for many a year, and such a bad friend to me, that I must have one good return slap at his affairs before I go to sleep.[172]

Neither his physical state, nor the horrific war through which he had lived, dampened his optimism: 'The universe is so *crammed* with the benevolent will of our Father.'[173] He died on 3 February 1922, and was buried at Kilbride.

Once we know that Jones was a faithful disciple of Caird, it is not difficult to predict what the main lines of his thought will be. But just as he had a Welsh accent and not a Scottish, so his inspiration and point of reference were more moral and practical than epistemological. In his own words:

> The primary function of philosophy is to be a witness to the unity of the world and the wholeness of life. But the task it first performs in exercising its function is that of criticism. It exposes the inadequacy of the principles which the working world has adopted, it knows not whence, nor why. It traces back its unrest, its doubts and its bewilderment to these ideal causes; for in the world of human action there are no causes *except* ideals. It shows, in the last resort, that human ills, social and individual, come from man's ignorance of himself.[174]

In an address delivered at St Andrews in 1891 he lamented that 'All attempts at representing the unity of things have failed', and this he attributed to the fact that 'Philosophy has fallen upon evil

days, if not amongst evil men.'[175] It was not that Jones imagined
that the construction of a final system of philosophy was possible;
he did not favour 'the high *priori* road';[176] but he did regard the
philosopher as under obligation to reflect rationally upon
experience with a view to seeing what could be made of it.

All thought requires premises, and 'Philosophy . . . as reflexion
upon experience, is thought engaged upon thought.'[177] As he
graphically expressed it, 'If you can avoid calling the simile crude,
I should say that nature grows ideas just as she grows apples.'[178]
Experience is organic, and we must approach it with a working
hypothesis in mind. For Jones that hypothesis is that in self-
consciousness we have to hand 'a category which is at once the
intensest unity and the source of the deepest differences',[179] and
neither the one nor the many must be sacrificed. Since the self is
spiritual what it knows must likewise be spiritual. No subject–
object dualism is legitimate, for these terms are correlative. But
precisely because experience is in process, 'a fixed system is not to
be sought . . . a completed doctrine of an evolving process, a static
theory of a dynamic reality, must prove false.'[180] The significance
of his term 'working hypothesis' is precisely that there can be no
final proof of the validity of a philosophical system; there can only
be the satisfaction that this hypothesis rather than those leads us
to the most satisfactory account of the range of human experience
currently attainable. As the concluding chapter of his volume on
Lotze makes plain, Jones's monism was one in which reality
determines thought. This, declared Pringle-Pattison, 'gives
Professor Jones's presentation of Absolute Idealism a degree of
originality which differentiates it from the ordinary versions of
English Hegelianism that descend from Green'.[181] To Robert
Mackintosh, however, Jones's conclusion involves 'a deliberate
repudiation of Idealism', which, whether in its Hegelian dialectical
form, or read with Kantian eyes as by Green, has ever 'staked
everything upon the principle that . . . *thought creates reality*'.[182]

Mackintosh is certainly justified, but Jones's lapse was
momentary only. This emerges, for example, in his denial that
there is a distinct science named epistemology. Early in his career
he took exception to Pringle-Pattison's claim that

> Epistemologically there is a union of subject and object: the knower
> and what he knows are in a sense, as Aristotle says, one. But

ontologically, or as a matter of existence, they remain distinct – the one here and the other there – and nothing avails to bridge this chasm.[183]

Jones objected to the chasm as entailing the view that while there is a relation between knowledge and reality, knowledge is entirely, and reality is not at all, within the subjective consciousness.[184] To him this was a knowledge-denying dualism. Pringle-Pattison returned to the fray, noting that 'Professor Jones has a bitter quarrel with the critics of Hegelianism, and those whom it pleases him to call Epistemologists',[185] and reminding Jones that he had argued that 'Knowledge is an activity, an activo-passive experience of the subject.' He further ruefully observes that

> There is a certain satisfaction in seeing one's own views expressed almost in one's own language, but there is also a feeling of topsy-turvydom in seeing them elaborately proved as a refutation of one's own contentions.[186]

We need not further disturb the cold ashes of this dispute, except to notice that in his book on Lotze,[187] and consistently to the Gifford Lectures at the end of his career, Jones maintained his view:

> There never was and never will be a 'world of ideas' in the sense of a system of mental entities, other than, though somehow true of, the world of facts and events, and, as Lotze thought, needlessly duplicating it. I doubt if there ever was a more persistent or widespread error, which gives philosophers more trouble, than this reification of ideas. Ideas are not like, nor are they symbolic of, nor do they correspond or in any way point to objects. They don't exist. There are minds which in relation to objects carry on a process called knowing, and there are objects which guide and control and inspire their operations. But there is no third world of entities, as men who speak of the world of ideas seem to think.[188]

With none of this would Pringle-Pattison have disagreed. But his warning stands:

> Many thinkers . . . for want of distinguishing clearly between the necessary self-transcendence in knowledge and the impossible self-transcendence in existence, have denied to the individual a knowledge of anything more than his own states.[189]

That way lies scepticism. On the other hand if, beginning as we must with the epistemological question of the relation of the individual knower to the world of reality, we reach positive results, we can then proceed to metaphysical construction: 'If epistemology is not to be confounded with psychology . . . neither is it to be identified with metaphysics.'[190]

It must not be thought that Jones's characteristic optimism blinded him to certain problems attaching to the monistic solution. Supreme among these was the problem of suffering; but even here his optimism surfaced. In acknowledging a letter from Macneile Dixon which was appreciative of *Idealism as a Practical Creed*, Jones declared,

> I am stirred just now with some odd results which have come from looking as closely as I can at that frightful obstacle to all Idealism, viz., animal pain.[191] My optimism has got an impulse from it that is like feeling one's wings in the upper air for the first time.

He went on to suppose that pain may be a 'subjective report of the value of external happenings to the self', and that since pain, though widely distributed, is incommunicable from one individual to another, 'the actual greatest pain in the world is not greater than that which is suffered by him who has it . . .' Furthermore, pain is

> the waving of the red flag . . . pain is a utility . . . and if we take a wider outlook it may be all right. Is all this nonsense, and am I losing my head? or am I discovering something worth saying?'[192]

These are the words of one whose thought was ever on the way. But, as we have seen, this by no means entails that he did not have a definite vantage point from which to view the problems of philosophy and life. And none was more acutely aware than he that his outlook was by no means shared by all. As he remarked in his Inaugural Lecture at Glasgow:

> The spectator of all time and existence, now that time and existence have come to comprehend so much, presents a rather pathetic figure amongst his busy fellows. He is . . . bidden to content himself with a smaller handful than 'the solution of the universe'.

The present-day philosopher

> insists . . . that he is not a 'system-monger', that the last of these was

Hegel, and that he has already been given over to the mob. He does not write a Metaphysic, nor pass judgment on the nature of things; he writes a Science instead – a Science of Psychology, a Science of Knowledge, and a Science of Morals. But the need of a working theory of life . . . is permanent, and all men must think their thoughts into some kind of a whole.[193]

What sustained Jones in philosophy as in life was his commitment to the religious hypothesis. The word is still 'hypothesis', but the religious believer is in no different case than the scientist: both need hypotheses. Nowhere other than in faith

is it more evident that there are some principles so vital to experience and therefore so secured by experience (*which is just the thing that reasons*) that to deny them is to reduce the world into chaos. Doubt of them is impossible: it turns into absurdity and madness.[194]

But this is the doubt which is a logical impossibility. Of doubt as a practical reality Jones was also aware, for in the year of publication of the words just quoted he said in his Martineau centenary lecture,

Burdened with our doubts, baffled by our own reasonings, stumbling all too frequently over our own simplest thoughts, climbing the Hill Difficulty, creeping from fact to fact, as on our hands and knees, those of us who have embraced divine philosophy will prize most highly of all those moments when Religion takes us by the hand and plants us in a purer air where we can see, though from afar, the Golden Gates of the City of God.[195]

At such moments we realize that '*Religion* does not invent its God, it finds Him: and, at its best, it finds Him everywhere. The structure of things is spiritual.'[196] Not indeed that this is the false assurance of feeling or dogma:

I am persuaded that you yield the opponents of religion far too much, perhaps even the central fortress, if you allow to them, and deny yourselves, the help of the formidable forces of reason . . . I believe with all my heart that religion, yea, the Christian religion in its essence, is rational through and through; and I want the Church to take a stronger stand.[197]

Jones returned regularly to this last point:

> I do not deny . . . that the Christian religion furnishes truths which are authoritative . . . But they are authoritative only because they are believed to be true. Hence they cannot suffer from examination . . .[198]

For Christianity to remove its doctrines from the scrutiny of science and philosophy 'is not to establish their authority but to render them suspect, and at the same time it throws the door open for any false prophet to prophesy in its name'.[199] To Jones,

> philosophy . . . when most true and positive, is the process by which reason substantiates the main hypothesis [that word again] of religion and furnishes a rational basis for man's infinite claims, making him no doubt a pilgrim on a road that leads to a very far city. But the way is, at every step, a way of life.[200]

Neither such words as these, nor Jones's manifest religious devotion, sufficed to calm the fears of some more conservative, more exclusive, Christians. Thus James Denney felt that 'a good many who ought to be our students are diverted from the Church – and as I am convinced from the Gospel – by his influence.'[201] This charge was stoutly repudiated by Jones's biographer:

> [I]t is true that he made it difficult for many . . . to accept some doctrines which Denney believed to be fundamental in the Christian faith. But it cannot be maintained that he turned the interest of any of his students away from religion, or gave them anything but a profoundly reverent interpretation of Christianity.[202]

For his part Jones recalled that 'Denney, the best scholar of that year, seemed to belong to another sphere than the merely terrestrial one on which we dwelt.'[203] It must be admitted, however, that Jones could supply tinder for conservative fires – as when he owned to being a Celt, and defined such a one as 'an incorrigible Romanticist. His very reason is fancy-fed . . . he is a dissenter from every creed.'[204]

After his death, verdicts were pronounced upon Jones from many quarters. As a man of affairs 'He was, in his generation, one of the most potent influences in the moulding of public opinion.'[205] He was a greatly loved teacher. Hugh A. Rayburn, then of the University of Cape Town, dedicated his book, *The Ethical Theory of Hegel* (1921), to Jones, 'The greatest teacher whom I have known'. Many felt that he was preaching them a gospel rather than teaching them in a formal university way.[206] But this could be counter-productive. As one student recalled,

> the very forcefulness of his utterance was apt to provoke in the dour temper of the Lowland Scot, a certain suspicion, and even antagonism. The abler students, at any rate, refused to be either daunted or spellbound. They were goaded into thinking, but into a critical thinking which by no means spared the dicta of their professor. And this was as it should be, whether Jones altogether liked it or not.[207]

Jones had but a modest opinion of his own powers as a thinker, and sometimes his adversarial stance and his fluent tongue got the better of him. Hastings Rashdall spoke for others when, in reviewing *Idealism as a Practical Creed*, he wrote, 'I am compelled to say that I have occasionally wished that I could discover in it a little less heat, and a little more light.'[208]

As Henry Jones lay dying he said,

> The ultimate meaning of Reality is Love. If that is true, there must be a soul, a personal God, to do the loving. The task of philosophy is to justify that view.[209]

V

To a greater degree than Jones, and in a less partisan spirit than (in their different ways) Green and Caird, Pringle-Pattison patiently adjusted himself to his philosophical inheritance, as we saw in the first chapter. In this he was like his teacher, Campbell Fraser, but whereas Fraser's positive position was reached after long investigation towards the end of his career,[210] Pringle-Pattison's constant idealism, nourished like that of others by Carlyle and the Romantic poets – especially Wordsworth – was significantly modified in the direction of personal idealism under the influence of the home-grown Scottish common-sense philosophy, and of such exotic influences as that of Lotze. His *contretemps* with Henry Jones over the relation of epistemology to ontology signals his concern that the individual be not submerged under monism.

Andrew Seth was the second of seven children of Smith Kinmont Seth, a clerk with the Commercial Bank of Scotland,

and his wife Margaret (née Little).[211] He was born in Edinburgh on 20 December 1856. In 1898 he inherited The Haining, the 7,000-acre estate of his friend Mrs Pringle-Pattison, a distant relative of the Seths. Under the terms of the will he was required to add her name to his; this he did, and Pringle-Pattison I shall continue to name him in this text.

Pringle-Pattison was educated at the Royal High School, Edinburgh, and at the University of Edinburgh, to which he proceeded in 1873, and where his contemporaries included R. B. Haldane and W. R. Sorley. In 1878 he achieved first class honours in classics and philosophy, owing much of his love of language to the Professor of Humanity, William Young Sellar. For English literature he was in the capable hands of David Masson, and himself wrote verse and loved the theatre and music (especially opera). But none impressed him more than Campbell Fraser, Professor of Logic and Metaphysics who, as Pringle-Pattison was later to remark in his Inaugural Lecture at Edinburgh, opened a new world to him.[212] In his memoir of his brother James, who studied under Fraser from 1876 and who joined his brother on assuming the Chair of Moral Philosophy at Edinburgh in 1898, Pringle-Pattison both encapsulates Fraser's position and suggests the grounds of his own tempering of absolutism:

> [Fraser] had by that time [1876] worked his way to his own characteristic statement of Spiritual Idealism as a philosophy of the universe, involving at its root an element of Faith – a *via media*, therefore, between the Agnosticism then current in scientific circles and the Gnosticism (as he was fond of calling it by way of contrast) represented by Hegelianism, with its apparent claim, as he deemed, to omniscience.[213]

His nomination by J. B. Capper, and the support of James Martineau, secured Pringle-Pattison a Hibbert Travelling Scholarship. This enabled him to travel and study on the Continent for a period of two years, Berlin, Jena and Leipzig being his main centres of interest. In Göttingen he met another Hibbert Scholar, J. G. Schurman. To their disappointment, Lotze was teaching only a junior course at the time, and after a few lectures they left to contentrate on their Hibbert theses.[214] Pringle-Pattison's thesis was subsequently revised and published under the title *The Development from Kant to Hegel, with Chapters on the*

Philosophy of Religion (1881).[215] The most positive aspect of his German adventure was his meeting with Eva, daughter of Albrecht Stropp, whom he married in 1884. They had five children, of whom one died in infancy and another on active service during the First World War. Eva, who had been educated by the Moravians, was keenly interested in German, French and English literature.

Back in Edinburgh, Pringle-Pattison succeeded Sorley as assistant to Campbell Fraser, supplementing his income by writing leading articles for *The Scotsman* on subjects ranging from foreign policy and Bismarck to sabbatarianism and a comparison of the ultramontanism of 'Cardinals Begg and Manning' – a particularly teasing title, since James Begg was a stalwart Calvinist of the Free Church of Scotland.[216] Of more significance for Pringle-Pattison's future career was his developing friendship with A. J. Balfour, who established a lectureship in his own name specifically so that his friend could devote himself to writing with a view to lecturing and publishing. The lectures were delivered in 1885, 1887 and 1891, and issued in *Scottish Philosophy* (1885), *Hegelianism and Personality* (1887), and *Realism*. The third series appeared in *The Philosophical Review*, and was republished posthumously as a book in 1933.

Meanwhile in 1883, at the age of twenty-six, Pringle-Pattison applied for the Principalship of the new University College of South Wales and Monmouthshire. Just as Henry Jones had been denied the Principalship at Bangor, but secured the Chair of Philosophy, so Viriamu Jones became Principal at Cardiff and Pringle-Pattison took the Chair of Philosophy.[217] In the same year *Essays in Philosophical Criticism* was published under the editorship of R. B. Haldane and Seth (as he then was). The book was dedicated to Green, who had died in the previous year, and Caird contributed a preface.

On the death of Stephen Baynes in 1887, the Chair of Logic, Rhetoric and Metaphysics became vacant at St Andrews University.[218] Pringle-Pattison succeeded, and soon proved his worth within the university at large. The new professor's 'sober demeanour' so impressed his students that 'they behaved less like St Andrews students of those days than people waiting for a service in church'. Even so, 'He made Metaphysics not merely interesting but exciting.'[219] On the other hand, to John Laird he was 'a shy man, unready of speech, he hugged the shelter of his manuscript, reading it beautifully to large classes which sometimes were almost openly restive.' To his senior classes he read still more polished lectures, and was no debater. His kindness to his students was, however, 'very notable'.[220] One former student who became a professional philosopher wrote that Pringle-Pattison

> was a great teacher of philosophers: there must be half-a-dozen professors of philosophy at present in the universities of Great Britain alone who owe their first initiation as philosophers to Pringle-Pattison; but I should say that no two of them belong to the same school of thought. They were not so taught.[221]

On the retirement of Campbell Fraser in 1891, Pringle-Pattison became Professor of Logic and Metaphysics at the University of Edinburgh. Robert Adamson, unsuccessful on this occasion, went to Glasgow where, as we saw, he became Henry Jones's colleague; R. M. Wenley was also unsuccessful. With the appointment of Pringle-Pattison, Fraser's hope was, as he wrote, 'happily realized in the appointment of my distinguished successor, who fitly represents philosophy in the city of David Hume, Adam Smith and Dugald Stewart, Sir William Hamilton and James Frederick Ferrier'.[222] Pringle-Pattison became an active member of the Synthetic Society, founded in 1896 to provide a forum for the discussion of scientific and religious questions. In his characteristically patient way he spent the next years publishing articles and smaller works which allowed him to adjust himself to the thought of a variety of thinkers including Kant, Hegel, Lotze, Nietzsche, Bradley, Fraser, Martineau, Kidd and McTaggart. Two collections of papers appeared: *Man's Place in the Cosmos and Other Essays* (1897) and *The Philosophical Radicals and Other Essays* (1907). In addition there appeared *Two Lectures on Theism* (1897), which had been delivered on the occasion of the sesquicentennial celebrations of Princeton University. Pringle-Pattison delivered the Gifford Lectures at Aberdeen in 1912 and 1913, and these were subsequently published as *The Idea of God in the Light of Recent Philosophy* (1917), his most substantial constructive work. In 1922 he delivered a further series of Gifford Lectures, this time at Edinburgh. These, an expansion of his Hibbert Lectures of 1921, were published under the title *The Idea of Immortality* (1922). His *Studies in the Philosophy of Religion* (1930) were partly based upon his Gifford Lectures for 1923.

Meanwhile Pringle-Pattison had retired in 1919, to be succeeded by Norman Kemp Smith, one of his students at St Andrews. The University of Edinburgh conferred an honorary doctorate upon him (as the universities of St Andrews and Durham had already done), and named him Professor Emeritus. He had been elected a Fellow of the British Academy in 1904.

In retirement, and in addition to the preparation of his Edinburgh Giffords, he undertook an abridgement of Locke's *Essay Concerning Human Understanding*, furnishing his volume with a substantial introduction. This appeared in 1924 and was reprinted ten years later. Also in 1924, and just a few weeks after resigning his Chair, James Seth suddenly died. He had never married, and had been very close to Andrew, living with their mother until her death. Andrew's edition of his brother's book, *Essays in Ethics and Religion*, to which the editor prefixed a memoir, appeared in 1926. Two years later Pringle-Pattison's wife died, as did his great friend R. B. Haldane. Lord Balfour followed in 1930, and Pringle-Pattison himself in 1931.

'To be delivered from bad metaphysics is the first step and the most important one towards the true conception of the science.'[223] So wrote Pringle-Pattison in his important early essay, 'Philosophy as criticism of categories'. This was his contribution to *Essays in Philosophical Criticism* (1883), and it was reprinted twenty-four years later in *The Philosophical Radicals*. It may be said to represent the author's philosophical *credo*, and he remained content with its main line of argument.[224] 'What, then, is desirable metaphysics?' He answers in the next sentence: 'True metaphysics lies . . . in that criticism of experience which aims at developing out of the material of science and of life the completed notion of experience itself.'[225] This is one of the more down-to-earth definitions of metaphysics which might be proposed, and Pringle-Pattison contrasted it with the approach of those who go forth 'in quest of some transcendent reason why the nature of things is as it is'; those who, as Lotze put it, attempt to tell us 'how being is made'; and those who seek to explain the whole 'by a principle which is adequate merely to one of its parts or stages'.[226] Again,

All idealism teaches the correlativity of subject and object; they develop *pari passu*, keeping step together, inasmuch as the objective world seems to grow in richness as we develop faculties to apprehend it. But all sane idealism teaches that, in such advance, the subject is not creating new worlds of knowledge and appreciation for himself, but learning to see more of the one world.[227]

Furthermore, a sane idealism will realize that 'The ultimate unity of things is what we stretch forward to, what we divine, but what we never fully attain.'[228]

Here we see the nature of Pringle-Pattison's modest variety of idealism – ever in touch with the real world; we note also his employment of the concept of development so fashionable in his day. His underscoring of the former point and his caution concerning the latter clearly emerge in this passage from his Edinburgh Inaugural Address. Whilst welcoming the 'sonorous utterance' which Hegel gave to the view that all things are relative to man as rational, he qualified his endorsement thus:

> The achievements of the world-spirit do not move me to unqualified admiration, and I cannot accept the abstraction of the race in place of the living children of men. Even if the enormous spiral of human history is destined to wind itself at last to a point which may be called achievement, what, I ask, of the multitudes that perished by the way? 'These all died, not having received the promises.' What if there *are* no promises *to them*? To me the old idea of the world as the training-ground of individual character seems to offer a much more human, and, I will add, a much more divine, solution than this pitiless procession of the car of progress. Happily, however, the one view does not necessarily exclude the other: we may rejoice in the progress of the race, and also believe in the future of the individual.[229]

Properly regarded, the theory of evolution is 'our most essential help' in the interpretation of experience, 'for the divine must be held to be most fully and adequately revealed in the highest aspects of our experience'.[230] It is our experiences of rationality, of moral freedom and of unconditional obligation which supply 'our only indefeasible standard of value, and our clearest light to the nature of the divine'.[231] It is not difficult to detect the influence of Fichte and Lotze at this point.

By what method did he work towards his metaphysic? Once again he is as clear as he is modest: of his first series of Gifford Lectures he wrote,

> although it consists largely of criticism, the interest of the book is

neither critical nor historical, but constructive throughout. The method of construction through criticism is one which I have instinctively followed in everything I have written. I do not claim that it is the best method; I simply desire that its nature be recognised.[232]

Although Pringle-Pattison entered the philosophical arena at a time when terms had to be made with Kant, Hegel, agnosticism and materialism, we should not suppose that his range of interest was narrowly circumscribed. As his book *The Idea of Immortality* shows, he had great sympathy with Plato's ethical motivation; and he owed his grasp of the principle of development at least as much to Aristotle as to Darwin. The classical strand of his philosophical inheritance is clearly seen in a Graduation Address he delivered in 1895: 'That truth, you may be sure, is no truth, which has not room within its confines for the Beautiful and the Good, and all that these imply.'[233] He later confirms this by saying that 'The truth of the poetic imagination is perhaps the profoundest doctrine of a true philosophy.'[234] Again, 'Beauty and goodness are not born of the clash of atoms: they are effluences of something more perfect and more divine.'[235] This, we may observe in passing, was too much for J. B. Baillie – himself by now, significantly, a convert from idealism. In his carping and not entirely accurate assessment of Pringle-Pattison's philosophical work, he made clear his opposition to the mixing of poetry with philosophy, and to the elevation of the former above the latter, whilst grudgingly granting his deceased colleague's 'high-souled devotion to the best that can be found in the pursuit of Truth, Beauty, and Goodness – that trinity of values to which his life was dedicated'.[236]

Turning to his modern philosophical predecessors, and by way of brief supplement to the account given in my first chapter, we see that Pringle-Pattison's method enabled him to utilize resources which he deemd to be of benefit (as did Caird), and to counter arguments and doctrines which he thought were fallacious and ill-advised (as Caird did not). In this respect he closely resembled his teacher, Campbell Fraser. He valued Reid's claim against Hume that at the heart of knowledge is an act of judgement, and his repudiation of epistemological relativity, whilst observing the failure of both Reid and Kant adequately to relate all principles of explanation to the nature of the explaining self.[237] Where epistemological relativity was concerned he felt that Reid had provided the clue to the answer to Kant's phenomenalism. Hegel's importance was that he 'alone of all metaphysicians lifts us completely clear of Relativism'.[238] However, Pringle-Pattison became dissatisfied with neat Hegelianism, and in *Hegelianism and Personality* he revealed himself as a critic from *within* the idealistic camp, and as a pioneer of personal idealism. His common-sense inheritance would not permit his acquiescence in the Hegelian deduction of reality from thought with its attendant undervaluing of struggling, moral individuals, and its relegation of the divine reality to the consciousness of the worshipping community:

> The radical error both of Hegelianism and of the allied English doctrine I take to be the identification of the human and the divine self-consciousness, or, to put it more broadly, the unification of consciousness in a single Self.[239]

Not the least of the unfortunate results of this unification is the undermining of true religion, which requires a willed self-surrender.[240] On the other hand, Pringle-Pattison was alive to the perils of dualism. This emerges not only in his advocacy of suitably tempered idealism –

> The knower is in the world which he comes to know, and the forms of his thought, so far from being an alien growth or an imported product, are themselves a function of the whole[241]

– but also in his opposition to the way in which Albrecht Ritschl and his followers distinguished between judgements of fact and judgements of value:

> Unless the objects of religious faith are real, theology is entirely in the air; and if they are real it is impossible to treat the world of religious belief and the world of fact, as science and philosohpy handle it, as if they were two non-communicating spheres . . . Such a dualism is essentially a surrender to scepticism, and is therefore a seed of weakness in the Ritschlian theology.[242]

As H. F. Hallett correctly saw, Pringle-Pattison, his feet ever firmly on the ground *vis-à-vis* both thoroughgoing monism and subjective idealism, was one for whom

> Idealism is . . . the end of the argument and not the beginning, and

because it is so it is able to include the truth of realism as a subordinate moment in a more complete and profound philosophy.[243]

In Pringle-Pattison's own words:

> I think the Realists are right as against 'the Berkeleian fallacy', or what they call 'the ego-centric predicament'. And their argument applies to Green no less than to Berkeley. In both cases I think we only arrive at a formal Ego, and really nothing is gained by such a point of subjectivity. But however much of a Realist one may be epistemologically, when it is a question of the individual knower, I still hold, ultimately or metaphysically, to what you call 'the over-reaching subject–object relationship'. It is, as you say, simply impossible to take the relation of compresence in time and space as final.[244]

In a word, Pringle-Pattison did what he thought the Scottish common-sense philosophers would have done: he reversed the deductive method of Fichte and Hegel.[245] Others, J. B. Baillie among them, levelled the charge of instability and inconsistency against Pringle-Pattison's position. As Baillie snootily declared before proceeding to 'praise with faint damns', 'There are some things doubtless more important than the achievement of a logically symmetrical system of thought . . .'[246] All who occupy mediating positions run the risk of receiving such treatment; but if mediators often leave theories insufficiently stark to be labelled by their names, they do challenge us to balanced critical thought. We may hope that there will ever be some who prefer this to being deluged by 'truth'.

Having referred to the reactions of some philosophers to Pringle-Pattison's work, I should like to conclude this section by quoting three theologians. The first, one of his pupils, Hugh Ross Mackintosh, wrote of his teacher that

> His mind was preponderantly of a religious cast, though without the least prejudice on the side of orthodoxy, and in the last generation no distinguished philosophical thinker has given to the idea of God a more profound or liberalizing interpretation . . . Not only did he fan intelligence, he made goodness lovable. In manner he was extremely kindly, and even gentle; but behind this gentleness lay all the force of tenacious conviction.[247]

The other two theologians will sharply remind us of the main theme of this book. To Dean Inge, Pringle-Pattison 'was never quite a theist in the Christian sense', and he 'never really got beyond pantheism'.[248] Denis M. Gallagher went still further: Pringle-Pattison's theories, carried to their logical conclusions, 'must inevitably lead to the destruction of true Christianity' – indeed of all religion; for the God who is a focal unity only is not the God of Christian faith.[249] But before testing out such claims I must introduce my two remaining idealists.

VI

Not a man of affairs after the fashion of Green, temperamentally the reverse of the crusading Jones, more outgoing than Illingworth and Pringle-Pattison, and more traditionally Christian than either Green, Caird, Jones or Pringle-Pattison, Webb enjoyed the longest life and the most stationary career of our seven idealists. When he arrived in Oxford as a student in 1886, the influence of Green, who had died four years earlier, was at its height; when he died in 1954 philosophical idealism had been for many years out of fashion in his University.[250]

Clement Charles Julian Webb was born in London on 25 June 1865.[251] His father was the Revd Benjamin Webb, vicar of St Andrew's, Wells Street, and Prebendary of St Paul's Cathedral. His mother, Maria Elphinstone, was the daughter of W. H. Mill, Canon of Ely and Regius Professor of Hebrew at Cambridge. In a brief autobiography Webb informs us that his father was a friend of the hymn-writer John Mason Neale and a Tractarian:

> The religion of my parents combined with a somewhat rigid ecclesiastical theory and with the high standard of morality and duty characteristic of English clerical households a love of beauty and culture which was quite remote alike from Puritan suspicion and from utilitarian contempt of these aspects of life. The requirement or even the approval of such an experience as is called 'conversion' in young people who were already Christian and had not wandered altogether away from the ways of right living had no place in their scheme of piety.[252]

He elsewhere records his surprise when, as a student, he encountered Gore, then Principal of Pusey House, and found in him, though a High Churchman, 'none of that instinctive distrust of Evangelical language about individual conversion'.[253] In yet another place he relates that his father, whilst an undergraduate, was secretary of the Cambridge Camden Society – a body devoted to the practical realization of Tractarian ideals concerning the form and setting of the liturgy.[254] In all of this Pugin and Ruskin were among Benjamin Webb's guides.

Webb was educated at Westminster School ('there was nothing in the "Broad Church" atmosphere of Dean Stanley's Westminster to suggest the thought of . . . a spiritual crisis'),[255] where he met his long-standing friend C. J. Shebbeare, who accompanied him to Christ Church, Oxford, where, during his first year, Webb underwent an experience which was 'a turning-point in my spiritual history'.[256] He had been at once sceptical in a youthful way and contemptuous of the equally boyish pose of the heterodoxy of some of his contemporaries. This

> left me with a profound conviction of the reality of God and of the duty of open-mindedness and intellectual honesty; a belief that it was the first of religious duties to keep one's ears open to any voice, from whatever quarter, which might convey a message from God . . .[257]

This open-minded receptiveness to ideas never left him; none of our selected idealists was more sympathetic towards views other than his own; and this sympathy, coupled with Webb's scholarly care and manifest sincerity, smoothes the reader's passage through his often inordinately long sentences of latinate prose replete with finely balanced subsidiary clauses.

Even as a child Webb had wondered 'What do I mean by *I*?' Like others, he was influenced by the writings of Carlyle, and his strong sense of the continuity of history (stronger than that of any other of our seven idealists), so characteristic of a High Churchman, was fertilized by his youthful reading of Edward Augustus Freeman's *Sketch of European History* and by A. P. Stanley's *Westminster Abbey*. Now, as a student, he devoted himself to the study of philosophy. While Green's recently published *Prolegomena to Ethics* impressed him, it was a translation of *Kant's Principles of the Metaphysic of Ethics*, with its strong presentation of the categorical imperative, which deeply moved him and 'left ineffaceable traces on all my subsequent thought'.[258] Webb's tutor was J. A. Stewart, who taught his students 'to think for themselves, not to repeat the thoughts of their tutor; which, indeed, he was in no particular hurry to impart to them'.[259] During Stewart's absence in America, Cook Wilson deputized. Webb greatly appreciated his patient probing of the philosophical problems implied by human experience, and was receptive to Wilson's brand of realism

> for which spirit is no less real than matter, and the spiritual values of truth, goodness and beauty no mere creations of finite minds, but abiding characteristics of that reality in the apprehension of which all minds capable of apprehending it find their satisfaction.

Such teaching, thought Webb, was much closer to Platonic idealism than 'any form of *epistemological* Idealism'. Wilson, he wrote, was 'a man to whom I owe more than to any other of my philosophical instructors'.[260]

Webb achieved a first class degree in the School of Literae Humaniores in 1888. From 1889 to 1922 he was Fellow and Tutor of Magdalen College, and from 1920 to 1930 he was the first holder of the Oriel (later Nolloth) Chair of the Philosophy of the Christian Religion at Oriel College, of which he became an honorary Fellow. Magdalen similarly honoured him in 1938. His Inaugural Lecture was published under the title, *Philosophy and the Christian Religion* (1920). Among his colleagues Webb felt himself especially indebted to J. A. Smith, H. W. B. Joseph and H. A. Prichard. He also testified to the privilege of having known Friedrich von Hügel, whom he first met on 5 June 1896 at a meeting of the Synthetic Society, of which he and the Baron were devoted members until the society ceased in 1903.[261] He was a keen participant in the meetings of the Aristotelian Society.

Webb's first publication was a review of *Lux Mundi*,[262] and this was followed by a number of studies in medieval thought, among them works on John Scotus Eriugena, John of Salisbury and Anselm. From about 1900 his attention increasingly turned to questions concerning religious experience, and to interaction with his idealist contemporaries and others. A stream of articles, reviews and books followed; and the reception given by his friends on the occasion of his eightieth birthday, and the associated volume containing Grensted's reflections on Webb's career, Webb's lecture on 'Religious Experience', and a twenty-one page bibliography of his works, evidence the esteem in which he was held.

In 1905 Webb married Eleanor Theodora, whose father, Alexander Joseph, was an Honorary Canon of Rochester; she predeceased him in 1942. Also in 1905 Webb became a governor of his old school, and to this he added a similar responsibility at Aylesbury Grammar School in 1938. From 1911 to 1914 he was the first Wilde Lecturer on Natural and Comparative Religion – 'an unsatisfactory lectureship upon a very obscure and unsatisfactory subject', as Grensted later described it.[263] However that may be, Webb's tenure resulted in the highly useful reclamation on behalf of English readers of major facets of the theistic heritage, for the substance of his Wilde Lectures was published as *Studies in the History of Natural Theology* (1913). The two books, *God and Personality* (1918) and *Divine Personality and Human Life* (1920) were the product of his Gifford Lectures delivered in Aberdeen in 1918 and 1919. Webb was the Riddell lecturer (1929), the Hertz lecturer (1930), the Stephanos Nirmalendu Ghosh lecturer in Calcutta (1930–1), the Olaus Petri lecturer at Uppsala (1932), the Forwood lecturer at Liverpool (1933), and the Lewis Fry lecturer at Bristol (1934). From the Riddell, Ghosh, Petri, Forwood and Fry appointments there emerged, respectively, *Religion and the Thought of To-day* (1929), *The Contribution of Christianity to Ethics* (1932), *A Study of Religious Thought in England from 1850* (1933), *Religion and Theism* (1934), and his last book, *The Historical Element in Religion* (1935). Webb was awarded honorary doctorates by the universities of St Andrews, Uppsala and Glasgow, and was elected a Fellow of the British Academy in 1927. In 1924 and again in 1938 Webb was a member of the Archbishop's Commission on Doctrine in the Church of England; and he was a member of the Old Marston Parish Council. He died on 5 October 1954, highly respected for his scholarship, his intellectual wrestling, his friendliness, his loyalty, his modesty and his courtesy.

Throughout his life Webb remained true to the inspiration of his 'conversion' experience: he was 'open to any voice, from whatever quarter, which might convey a message from God'. But his mind, though hospitable, was diverted from certain philosophical fields which his temperament, and his years of teaching and discussion 'have taught me that I do not readily understand or greatly care about; for example, those concerned with logical method and those relating to the nature of perception'.[264] He was undeniably moved, however, to relate Christianity to current thought. Hence his series of inquiries into personality and religious experience (whilst acknowledging his 'reprehensible neglect of [psychological] studies relevant to my own, though not, I will admit, specially attractive to myself').[265] Hence also his dealings with the Modern Churchman's Union, whose determination to pursue rigorous historical criticism he welcomed; whose sometimes positivistic conclusions, which did not shake his relative orthodoxy, he sometimes deplored; and whose grasp of the fact that no statement may be deemed infallible because it appears in Scripture, creeds or as an *ex cathedra* pronouncement of a Roman pontiff he thoroughly applauded.[266] Hence, yet again, the welcome he gave to improved relations between Christians of the several denominations. Webb had lived to see the stimulus provided in Oxford by the Congregational Mansfield College and the Unitarian Manchester College;[267] he rejoiced in the increasing candour and charity which now characterized Christian relations, and he looked for the time when Christianity would be presented by a united Church 'and not by a host of discordant bodies mutually antagonistic and denying each other the right to speak in the name of Christ'.[268]

If Green's idealism was strongly nourished by Kant; if that of Caird and Jones was more avowedly Hegelian, while Pringle-Pattison's was tempered by the Scottish philosophy and Lotze, Webb, to a greater degree even than Illingworth, had Plato looking over his shoulder, as it were. Indeed, he felt that one of the reasons for the isolation of Anglicanism over against the Lutheran and Reformed churches with their (alleged) tendency to drive a wedge between reason and revelation on the one hand, and Rome with its canonical Aristotelianism on the other, was its deep indebtedness to Platonism.[269] Certainly Platonism was in his blood. Thus, for example, in discussing personality he can say, 'we rightly begin with thinking out the ideal and then considering the experienced facts in the light of it.'[270] This is the polar opposite method to that of Pringle-Pattison, yet both of them wished to maintain the place of the individual (though Webb abhorred individualism – especially in religion);[271] and Webb, to a greater degree than his Scottish contemporary, had a great feeling for the historical rootedness of the Christian faith. Thus, for example, he contends that 'the success of Christianity in maintaining a doctrine of

Divine Personality is due to its peculiar doctrine of Divine Incarnation.'[272]

Like all the others we have considered, Webb did not expect the final philosophical system to be produced; rather he gave himself to the patient exploration of philosophical problems suggested particularly by religious faith: 'it is certainly religion that has supplied me with my primary motive in philosophizing', he declared. But he immediately went on to make plain his recognition of the danger of becoming an 'apologist'. Against this he had always sought to guard himself, for 'nothing is to me more unlovely, when detected, than apologetic masquerading as philosophy.'[273]

The words just quoted are from Webb's 'Outline of a philosophy of religion' which is, in brief, his philosophical *credo*. A summary of the first part of this statement affords the most convenient way of encapsulating his understanding of his task. He places himself in the line of Kant insofar as he cannot agree that the world of our experience is completely given through sensation, or that the methods used by natural science in the investigation of objects are adequate to the investigation of the whole of human experience. Unlike Pringle-Pattison, however, he does not think that we can,

> without self-contradiction, attempt to postpone knowledge to an inquiry into the nature of knowledge . . . That an *absolute* standard, not external but immanent, is implied in the very notion of truth, and in the fact that we can detect and correct error, appears to me to be beyond all question; and, on this account, I cannot but reject altogether any doctrine of the relativity of knowledge which ignores this, and any system which, like Pragmatism, demands an external criterion of truth.[274]

The implication of his view, shared by the majority of philosophers from Plato and Aristotle onwards, is that the world we know is rational, and if we accept, as we ought, our aesthetic, moral and religious experience as genuine experience, we seem committed to the view that Beauty, Goodness and Divinity are realities. There can, however, be no final proof that this is so, or that in such experiences we are not deluded by subjective illusion. But he certainly dissented from Kant's view that the relations between religion and morality are symbolic only.[275]

'Philosophy', Webb continues,

cannot, without committing suicide, abandon the quest of an ultimate reality within which may be embraced all the regions of Reality that are revealed to us in the several forms of experience already mentioned.[276]

Naturalism can only explain away morality and beauty; scientific laws cannot be deduced from ethical or aesthetic principles. Webb acknowledges that in his general stance he is in the line of Plato, but he also fully recognizes the sea-change which has swept over philosophy since the classical period. Whereas for the most part the ancient philosophers believed that the object known exists independently of the knowing subject, with Descartes we have the interjection of the principle that the foundation of knowledge is one's knowledge of oneself. Then the problem arises: How can we know what is not ourselves? Descartes's *cogito* 'does not really guarantee the existence of anything in the self other than just this present act of thinking'.[277] Both ancient realism and Cartesian idealism which, against Descartes's own belief, led to the ident-ification of the divine with the human mind (as by Croce – *Deus in nobis et nos*), are, however, found wanting by religious experience, in which the individual is transcended by the divine in such a way that the only appropriate attitude is that of religious worship. Webb is convinced that a God who is less than absolute would be an inadequate object of worship, but

> Around the problem involved in the questions: Is God the Absolute? Is the Absolute God? my thoughts continually revolve, but I could not honestly say that I am satisfied with any suggestions that I can offer towards its solution.[278]

At this point in his statement Webb moves into a discussion of the absolute, and I shall return to this in the next chapter. For the present I wish to complete this indication of his overall stance by making three points.

First, Webb devotes at least as much attention to natural theology and to the discussion of the relations of reason and revelation as any among the other six idealists with whom we are concerned. In one of his more succinct sentences Webb boldly affirmed that 'as all religious truth is revealed, so is all revelation addressed to the reason.'[279] Religious believers have not sold out to irrationality, neither are they shut up in their feelings. Moreover – and here Webb's idealistic anti-dualism is clearly presupposed –

there is no clear distinction between religious knowledge which is supernaturally revealed and that which is revealed in the natural:

> any knowledge of God which may be obtained from the world of nature as distinct from that of spirit is not to be regarded as unrevealed, although we may call the sphere of the spirit, in which he is more clearly revealed, the sphere of Revealed Religion, in contrast to one which, whatever manifestation there is, is in comparison obscure and doubtful.[280]

Finally, we cannot sift our religious knowledge in such a way as to mark off some aspects of it which are infallible and some which are not; for in the case of none of it may we claim infallibility.[281] Consistently with the foregoing, Webb defines natural theology as

> the sphere of general reflection upon the objects of religious experience, so far as this experience is open to all men and not peculiar to a particular race, community, or individual.[282]

Secondly, there is a significant lacuna in Webb's work. On more than one occasion he expressed the opinion that much more work was required on the question of the relation of time and evolution to the eternity and perfection of God.[283] But, unlike the less overtly Christian Pringle-Pattison, he did little to help us here: 'Few philosophers of his eminence have had so little to contribute, positive or negative, to the discussion of the problem of immortality.'[284]

Thirdly, Webb, more autobiographical in his works than any of the idealists here under review, pays attention to a wider variety of theological and ecclesiastical themes than Green, Caird, Jones or Pringle-Pattison, and his conclusions are more orthodox than theirs. Since evidence of the truth of this assertion will emerge as we proceed I shall not delay over the matter here, but shall rather proceed to introduce the last of my seven selected idealists.

VII

Where Jones was raised within the circles of Welsh Calvinistic Methodism, Taylor was brought up in the Arminian atmosphere of a Wesleyan manse. His father, the Revd Alfred Taylor, had been a missionary on the Gold Coast, but was minister at Oundle when

Alfred Ernest was born on 22 December 1869; his mother was Caroline Esther Fax.[285] Taylor's was the life of a scholar: if anything it was less eventful even than that of Webb. Of all of our idealists, he was the most technically erudite, as his classical work (with which I am not primarily concerned) attests; indeed, some felt that his learning obtruded to such an extent as to reduce his purely philosophical powers – a view with which it is difficult at times not to feel a certain sympathy. Of decided opinions upon all manner of subjects, he was reticent about himself. His biographical sketch in *Contemporary British Philosophy* (1924) characteristically opens with a quotation in Italian from Dante's *Purgatorio*, the point of which is that 'It is a rule of good breeding . . . not to speak of oneself without necessity.' Taylor adheres so strictly to this rule as to tell us virtually nothing about his life except insofar as those whom he met at various geographical locations influenced his intellectual development. W. D. Ross managed to glean the information that even as a child Taylor was a voracious reader, who would hide under the table with a book in order to avoid being sent out to play; and that he would amuse his brother and sister by telling them long and complicated stories of his own invention.[286]

Taylor went to the Methodist school, Kingswood, Bath, and thence as a Scholar to New College, Oxford, where he was placed in the first class in both parts of the School of Literae Humaniores. As an undergraduate Taylor would preach in Methodist chapels in the Oxford area, but this activity ceased after graduation, and he subsequently became a member of the Scottish Episcopal Church.[287] He was elected a Fellow of Merton in 1891, and re-elected in 1901. During this period he was much under the influence of Bradley's idealism and, whereas Collingwood recorded that 'although I lived within a few hundred yards of [Bradley] for sixteen years, I never to my knowledge set eyes on him',[288] and Webb recalled that he had never spoken to him,[289] Taylor 'was one of the very few people who could induce Bradley to talk about philosophy'.[290] From Taylor himself we learn that whilst at Merton he had 'the advantage of daily intercourse with Bradley'.[291]

In 1896 Samuel Alexander appointed Taylor to teach classics and philosophy at the University of Manchester; in 1899 Taylor won the Green Moral Philosophy Prize, his first book *The Problem of Conduct* (1901) being largely a reproduction of this essay; in

1900 he married Lydia Jutsum Passmore, an authoress, by whom he had one son; in 1903 he became Professor of Philosophy at McGill University, Montreal, and in 1908 he succeeded Bernard Bosanquet in the Chair of Moral Philosophy at St Andrews University. From 1924 until his retirement in 1941 he held the Chair of Moral Philosophy at the University of Edinburgh. Taylor's Gifford Lectures, delivered at the University of St Andrews, 1926–8, were published in two volumes under the title, *The Faith of a Moralist* (1930, 1931). He died, full of honours – Fellow of the British Academy (1911), Foreign Member of the Accademia dei Lincei, Corresponding Member of the Prussian Academy of Sciences, and honorary Doctor of St Andrews, Manchester, Aberdeen and (again) St Andrews – on 31 October 1945.

A little flesh is put on these bare bones by the reminiscences of John Laird, Taylor's assistant at St Andrews:

> *More suo*, he imposed a certain strain upon his interlocutors, who were expected to make intelligent remarks about Greek dowries, or any other sweeping from the Platonic epistles. But even if one couldn't help, one could admire and be excited. I had never met, or at any rate had never known, a philosopher to whom the Greek or any other past philosophy had been the burning heart of present existence, fresher than the morning's news . . . [H]e seemed to assume, quite undaunted, that we were respectable medievalists as well as passable Grecians. He always spoke as if his own enthusiasms extended over all the literate earth . . . [292]

A junior colleague of a later date recalls the occasion on which the tassel on Taylor's mortar-board caught fire from his pipe, a fact of which the professor was oblivious; he informs us that Taylor was proud of his prose style, that he was 'full of wisdom and humanity, yet oddly cross-tempered', and that he could be pungent in colloquial language, as when he remarked of a philosopher just appointed at Edinburgh, 'another damned plumber'. The same writer recalls that Taylor's impatience in church was rewarded with a rebuke from the pulpit: 'Will Professor Taylor please stop rustling his raincoat?'[293]

It is as true of Taylor as of any of our idealists that most of the excitement in his life occurred inside his head. Indeed as regards his philosophical pilgrimage, which was continuous, and the

religious and intellectual aspects of which were inseparable, he is
the most interesting of the philosophers under review. It is not that
he was of fluctuating opinions – he was no trimmer who varied
with the wind. He was always definite in his views; but he was
definite in different ways at different stages in his life. In this
connection his biographical note of 1924 is most informative, and
I shall be guided by it as I attempt to chart his course.

Taylor tells us that he arrived in Oxford in quest of a defence of
the convictions he felt essential for the conduct of life, 'against
what seemed to be the disintegrating influences of scholarship and
biological science'.[294] He was advised to read the works of Green
and Bradley, and studied Kant through the eyes of Green and
Caird. He also delved into Plato and Aristotle, Kant and Hegel.
Bradley's *Ethical Studies* especially impressed him. In the idealism
of Green and Bradley he found the means he sought of defeating
anti-religious naturalistic theories,

> though I found an insoluble puzzle from the first in what seemed to be
> T. H. Green's conception of a world composed of relations between
> terms of which we could say nothing, except that they were the terms
> of the relation.

Moreover,

> I was not then alive to what I now think the great danger of the whole
> Hegelian way of regarding things, that it dissevers the 'eternal verities'
> from all contact with 'historical' actuality.

(This will be a theme of crucial importance in our sequel.)
Bradley advised him to read Herbart 'as a wholesome corrective of
undue absorption in Hegelian ways of thinking', and to attend to
the findings of empirical psychology. All of which, together with
increasing attention to the principles of science, the reading of
Mach and others, and regular contact with the ever-inquiring and
stimulating Samuel Alexander at Manchester, encouraged him in
the direction of empiricism. Galileo, Descartes and Leibniz – and
notably the 'pan-mathematism' of Leibniz and Plato – fascinated
him and the attraction survived the subsequent historicist turn
which his thought took. At that early period 'I suppose that . . . I
was not far from developing into a kind of "Positivist" . . .' But
from this fate he was rescued when he came under the influence of
G. F. Stout at St Andrews, from whom he learned the importance

of the meaning of history, and the ineradicability of contingency in nature. His thought on these matters began to mature, and by the time he returned from Montreal in 1908 he had come to realize that

> the business of metaphysical philosophy is, in a way, a modest one. It has to be content to recognise that in the sciences, in history, in morality and religion it is dealing with a reality which is in the end simply 'given' and not to be explained away. Its concern is with the various intellectual interpretations of the 'given', and its supreme task is not, as I once used to suppose, the 'unification of the sciences', but the necessarily imperfect and tentative reconciliation of the exigencies of scientific thinking with the imperative moral and religious demands of life. It has not to invent an improved substitute for historically real religion and morality, but to fathom as much as it can of their significance.

None of this can it do infallibly; there can be no final metaphysics. In fact,

> it becomes a question whether, after all, the main service of metaphysical study to the mind is not to 'liberate it from prejudices' and thus prepare it to receive illumination from sources outside metaphysics.

His all too belated study of the neo-Platonists and major medieval philosophers, and the writings of von Hügel, had led him to this view. Taylor also acknowledged a debt to Varisco, and declared,

> I should be ungrateful to the memory of a profound thinker if I did not add that the influence of Reid's writings has come late into my life, but is not the less felt for that.

Let us take some soundings in Taylor's literary *corpus* with a view not to engaging him in discussion at this point, but to illustrating his own account of his philosophical journey. At the turn of the nineteenth century we find him in recoil from Hegel, yet still within the bounds of idealism. He objects to Hegel's

> claim to . . . prescribe to experience a series of successive forms into which it *must* fall, no matter what its contents. It should scarcely be necessary at the present time to repudiate for philosophy any such pretensions to the possession of knowledge acquired by some directer

and diviner way than that of painstaking analysis of the concrete contents of our experience.[295]

Two years later Taylor was arguing that facts are real insofar as they are inseparable aspects of a sentient experience.[296] This prompted G. E. Moore's rejoinder:

> My paper will at least refute Mr Tayor's Idealism, if it refutes anything at all: for I *shall* undertake to show that what makes a thing real cannot possibly be its presence as an inseparable aspect of a sentient experience.[297]

It was this aspect of his thought which was so profoundly modified by Taylor's later discovery of the medieval philosophers, and by his still later discovery of Reid.

That Taylor published *The Problem of Conduct* (1901) when under the influence of empiricism is clear from his assertions that 'It is for empirical psychology to say what qualities are and what are not of "absolute" worth for human beings.'[298] But on the question: What is to be done? such an axiology is silent. Taylor accordingly had recourse to Bradley's recapitulation of the theme of 'my station and its duties'[299] which, though problematic and far from intellectually satisfying, had to be lived with in the absence of any more adequate guidance. Nearly thirty years later, as if in direct repudiation of his earlier view, Taylor declares,

> the every-day moral life of simple discharge of recognised duty transcends the artificial limits we set to it, for our intellectual convenience, when we discriminate between morality and religion. Such a life is, after all, from first to last, a life inspired by 'faith'. The notion that whereas religion makes the demand for faith in the beyond and dimly descried, morality does not, but is a matter of walking in the full daylight, can only arise when we mistakenly think of moral virtue as being nothing more than the routine practice of a set of duties which are perfectly familiar to us all, from our inheritance of social rules and traditions. The life of genuine morality is always something indefinitely more than this . . . Morality itself, when taken in earnest, thus leads direct to the same problems about 'grace' and 'nature', 'faith' and 'works', with which we are familiar in the history of Christianity, the religion which stands supreme above all others in its 'inwardness' and takes the thought of regeneration of the self from its centre with unqualified seriousness.[300]

Gone is the norm of 'my station and its duties'; gone is the appeal to empirical psychology. On the contrary, 'the *raison d'être* of any fact must be a "value".'[301]

In *The Elements of Metaphysics* (1903) we find Taylor still in the intellectual environment of his first book. Not surprisingly, therefore, he was open to J. E. Creighton's charge that

> it appears to me not only contrary to fact, but contradictory of the very notion of experience to regard it as . . . composed of 'psychical matters of fact' which are destitute of all ideal significance. Surely we must say that 'to be experienced' does not mean merely to be felt, or to further or hinder some unconscious psychophysical tendency, but that it also involves being judged, or interpreted, to some extent, in terms of ideas.

The reviewer observes places where Taylor seems to recognize this in principle, but his understanding of experience forbids the development of these hints. What is required is an appreciation of the category of self-consciousness and an application of it to the nature and relations of the absolute and the finite individual. Here, thinks Creighton, Taylor might well learn from Kant and Hegel.[302] At this stage, thought Robert Mackintosh, Taylor 'gives us a fighting chance of immortality, and an Absolute that cannot be called personal or a self'.[303] As we know, Taylor did learn – and not from Kant and Hegel only, but from Plato, the medievals, von Hügel and others, so that in 1926 he could write in a very different accent,

> the specific experience of contact with the divine not only needs interpretation, like all other direct experience, but that, though it is the directest way of access to the 'wholly other', it is not the only way. If we are to reach God in this life, so far as it is permitted, we need to integrate the 'religious experience' with the suggestions conveyed to us by the knowledge of Nature and of our own being.[304]

The explanation of Taylor's philosophical pilgrimage is to be found largely in his religious pilgrimage. These, as I said, were inextricably interwoven, and I am conscious that in starkly isolating some of his earlier and later philosophical verdicts, I have to some extent falsified matters. But at least the philosophical distance over which he travelled has become clear. Now as to his religious experience. In the opinion of the Methodist scholar W. F. Lofthouse, Taylor's fine article of 1921 on 'Theism' for the

Encyclopaedia of Religion and Ethics marked his transition from
theist to Christian.[305] This transition was made notably under the
influence of Aquinas and Kant. From the former he derived the
clue which enabled him to move away from idealistic
immanentism to a restatement of the cosmological argument for
the existence of God and a fresh interpretation of the relation of
reason and faith; to the latter he owed his strong sense of the
categorical imperative on the basis of which he developed the
ethical theism in which he finally came to rest, and which he
construed in distinctly Christian terms:

> To believe in God means to believe that there is a universal world-order
> which is intelligible and justifiable at the bar of our deepest moral
> convictions. To believe in Christianity means further to believe that the
> fullest clue we have to the nature of God, the source of the intelligible
> and moral order pervading the universe, is given us in the person and
> life of Jesus Christ.[306]

If his Gifford Lectures represent the high point of his ethical
theism, his 1924 lecture, *Saint Thomas Aquinas as a Philosopher*,
developed hints present in his article on Theism, and paved the
way for *Does God Exist?* (1945). In the last-named work Taylor, far
from supposing that a complete, logically coercive demonstration
of God's existence was to be had, set out to show that unbelief
rather than belief was the unreasonable attitude. Crucial to his
case is his conviction that

> 'exact science' and knowledge are not coextensive, that 'science' in the
> current sense in which it means knowledge of numerical or quantitative
> formulae verified by precise observation and experiment, is a highly
> specialized and rather narrowly delimited department of knowledge,
> and can itself only exist in virtue of its connection with knowledge
> which is extra-scientific or pre-scientific . . . If we did not come to
> science with the conviction that knowledge is not merely an internally
> coherent way of thinking, but an apprehension of real objects other
> than the thoughts which apprehend them, science could never give us
> the conviction.[307]

In the book just referred to, his last, Taylor incorporates his ethical
theism in the form of a moral argument for God's existence, and
his conviction that believer and unbeliever alike have no option
but to exercise faith.[308] This is consistent with his view of the

unending task to divine the supreme pattern of the real, and so to rationalize it, to the best of our power, knowing well that the element of the disconcerting and perplexing will never be eliminated.[309]

Although Taylor was not a social reformer after the manner of Green or Jones, his interest in philosophy and religion was of a very practical kind, and he felt that society needed, and lacked, the influence of genuine religion. To the individual, religion gave power for the ethical quest, and joy. As for society, 'In our own day the only effect of persuading men that the Most High is a dream appears to be that they transfer their worship to the demonstrably not most high.'[310] However, if the Christian belief in Christ's final victory through suffering is true – with all that that means for morality –

> then we have such a certainty as the world cannot otherwise afford that love and duty are indeed sacred . . . We know, then, that, however appearances may be against them, these values can 'never fail'; they are the foundation-stones on which the frame of things is built.[311]

VIII

I have now done my best to delineate the intellectual environment in which British post-Hegelian idealism took its rise, and to introduce the seven idealists with whom I am principally concerned. I believe that the material as presented both indicates the variety of human temperaments to which this style of philosophizing appealed, and justifies the view I expressed at the outset concerning the variety of thought to be found among idealists. At several points in the present chapter the implications of the philosophical positions taken by the seven idealists for Christian belief have been indicated. But now the time has come to turn to a detailed thematic treatment of matters crucial to Christian belief which are raised by these seven thinkers, whose attitudes were positive and whose personal beliefs, if not always traditionally orthodox, were far from being intentionally hostile to the Christian faith.

God, the Absolute and the Idealists

In his generally rapturous review of the two volumes of *Essays on Literature and Philosophy,* E. H. Blakeney declared of the author that 'Of the few earnest Hegelians which England can boast of to-day, Professor Caird is the recognized champion and leader.' With a confidence which, from my perspective as one who in the declining years of the twentieth century recalls the anti-metaphysical onslaught of the middle decades of the century, savours of the irresponsible, he proceeded to define philosophy as 'simply the struggle to put thought into things'.[1] By no means all, even in his own period, were as bold. Ten years later we find Robert Mackintosh writing of the 'misty ambiguities' of Hegel's thought, and crisply specifying two prominent and widely differing options to which these may lead:

> If, holding a Theistic creed, we take a Theistic view of Idealism, then Hegel teaches us to regard God as the Great Supreme mind. If we are Pantheists, or if we interpret idealism pantheistically, then Hegel must be held to trace the evolution of the average normal (human) mind, though perhaps one so ideally normal as never to have existed.[2]

These divergent attitudes serve to remind us that philosophical idealism is a variegated phenomenon, and we have now to investigate some of the ways in which this variety bears upon the question of God. I shall first focus upon the view of God and the absolute which emerges from the writings of Green, Caird and Jones, noting some contemporary criticisms in passing, and this will raise the issue of the analysis of 'absolute' *vis-à-vis* 'God'. We shall then be prepared for an examination of three consequences of absolutism for Christian belief which are, bluntly expressed, that immanence swamps transcendence; that the Creator–creature distinction is blurred if not denied; and that the individual is put at risk by the absolute process. In connection with this last point I shall reintroduce the protest of the personal idealists, whose views are not free of ambiguity, and who cannot finally be said completely to save the day for the Christian understanding of God.[3] I reserve the most serious charge, that philosophical idealism cannot deal adequately with the problem of evil, until the next chapter.

I

At the heart of Green's thought there lies the conviction that self-consciousness, which entails self and not-self, is the eternal and evolving reality which lies at the heart of all things. 'Nature, or the world of becoming', he declares, 'is not possible except for, or in relation to, a thinking subject.'[4] Indeed, 'all reality lies in relations', though 'It is not that first there are relations and then they are conceived. Every relation is constituted by an act of conception.'[5] Otherwise we should have to suppose either that the world we know begins with our birth and ends with our death, or that there is a world of 'things in themselves' to which our categories have no application. As it is, ' "the real" is an intellectual order, or mind, in which every element, being correlative to every other, at once presupposes and is presupposed by every other.'[6]

Thus far it might be supposed that we have in Green a strong intellectualism which pays less than adequate heed to the objective world around us. But it is by no means his intention to neglect the phenomenal realm. The natural order, for example, comprises a systematic network of relations which presuppose, and reflect, the eternal order. This latter order is objectively real, but not in the sense that it is apart from all or any thinking subjects. On the contrary, they have their being by virtue of its existence. Green, as we saw, criticized John Caird for having allowed himself to become so overpowered by Hegel that he minimized the activity of thought in the objective world and gave undue place to the introspective quest of the capabilities of conception. This, Green argued, would yield only a subjective and not an absolute idealism. The remedy lies in the analysis of the objective world, not in reflecting 'on those processes of our intelligence which really presuppose that world'.[7] After all, 'what other medium do we know of but a thinking consciousness in and through which the separate can be united in that way which constitutes relation?'[8] In Green's opinion such an inquiry would lead to the view that

> the real world is essentially a spiritual world, which forms one inter-related whole because related throughout to a single subject . . . [But] we may still have to confess that a knowledge of it in its spiritual reality – such a knowledge of it as would be a knowledge of God – is impossible to us.[9]

This, which sounds, and is, modest, is also an echo of a Kantian agnosticism which threatens to reduce Green's fundamental declarations to mere rhetoric. For the theory of internal relations would seem to require that a subject, the reality of which comprises all of its relationships, can be known only if all of its relations are known. As it is,

> We must hold . . . that there is a consciousness for which relations of fact, that form the object of our gradually attained knowledge, already and eternally exist; and that the growing knowledge of the individual is a progress towards this consciousness.[10]

But this is a big 'must', and the introduction of the idea of progress as a counterpart to agnosticism, and (apparently in repudiation of his doctrine of relations) of a consciousness which now seems to be independent of the world, received little justification or harmonization from Green. Sidgwick was among those who were disturbed by the latter ambivalence, for he felt that as between Green's earlier view of nature as a system of thought-relations and his later view that this very system 'implies something other than itself, as a condition of its being what it is'[11] there was tension which Green had quite failed to resolve.

These considerations notwithstanding, Green proceeds to identify the eternal self-consciousness with God:

> There must be eternally such a subject which is all that the self-conscious subject, as developed in time, has the possibility of becoming; in which the idea of the human spirit, or all that it has in itself to become, is completely realised. This consideration may suggest

the true notion of the spiritual relation in which we stand to God; that He is not merely a Being who has made us, in the sense that we exist as an object of the divine consciousness in the same way in which we must suppose the system of nature so to exist, but that He is a Being in whom we exist; with whom we are in principle one; with whom the human spirit is identical, in the sense that He *is* all which the human spirit is capable of becoming.[12]

Two important questions are raised by these words. First, does Green consider that the eternal self-consciousness/God has a personal existence? It would seem that the question did not concern him unduly and, with some justification, Richter has maintained that Green returns an equivocal answer:

> If we mean anything else by it [personality] than the quality in a subject of being consciously an object to itself, we are not justified in saying that it necessarily belongs to God and to any being in whom God in any measure reproduces or realises himself.[13]

On this Richter remarks,

> In this, perhaps his most explicit statement, Green failed to specify whether he thought the eternal consciousness to have an individual personality apart from the humans in which it realises itself. No doubt, he would have insisted that the distinction was not meaningful in his terms. Yet the question remains whether he was not being disingenuous in suggesting that Idealist concepts had enabled him to retain everything valued by ordinary Christians.[14]

The theologian James Orr had earlier wondered what, precisely, Green's eternal self-consciousness was; and he concluded that, strictly, it was but the 'ideal unity of the system of thought-relations we call the universe . . . It is Kant's "Synthetic Unity of Apperception" deified.'[15] But, as a student of Balliol remarked, this means that whether in science or religion God may be regarded as '*une quantité négligeable*'. The opinion of C. B. Upton that in Oxford vital interest in theology was as effectively quenched by Green and the neo-Hegelians as by 'the coarser extinguisher which Mr Spencer's agnosticism supplies' is understandable.[16] A. E. Taylor's expostulation is not surprising either:

If all you know of God is that He is an 'eternal self-distinguishing being who, so far from being nature, is the conditon which makes it possible that there should be a nature for us to know', and who somehow 'reproduces himself' in our mental and moral life, you may, no doubt, feel reverence for such a principle, but never the *amor* which is for Christianity the 'great commandment'. When all is said, the deity of Green, against his own will, remains, if we are to be quite candid, an only half-baptized Aristotelian God; Green has not taken the conception of God which the Christian Church brought with it from the study of the Bible to its subsequent study of the Greek philosophers with sufficient *metaphysical* seriousness.[17]

The second question arising from Green's remarks as quoted above concerns the implication that not only are human beings both in relation and *in via,* but so is the absolute, or God:

God is for ever reason; and his communication, his revelation, is reason; not, however, abstract reason, but reason as taking a body from, and giving life to, the whole system of experience which makes the history of man. The revelation, therefore, is not made in a day, or a generation, or a century. The divine mind touches, modifies, becomes the mind of man, through a process of which mere intellectual conception is only the beginning, but of which the gradual complement is an unexhausted series of spiritual discipline through all the agencies of social life.[18]

At first sight it may seem plausible to say that all Green is here contending for is the progressiveness of a revelation gradually communicated to us; he is not explicitly referring to a developing eternal consciousness, absolute, or God. But this would be to overlook his doctrine of relations and his emphasis upon the objectivity of the phenomenal world, in and through which the eternal consciousness gradually comes to self-realization. If, however, we do not overlook these matters we stumble upon two recurring problems in Green's thought: how, given his understanding of the interrelatedness of the eternal self-consciousness with all phenomena, are we really to sustain the particularity of phenomena and of persons which he also wishes to honour (a question raised by Webb among others)?[19] And how, if reality really is 'one all-inclusive system of *unalterable* relations' are we to admit progress and development (on which his *Ethics* turns) at all?

More than a generation on, and in harmony with Green on this point, Jones announced in his Gifford Lectures, 'The Absolute is not static, and the Universe is not dead.'[20] Later in the series of lectures, and now more cautiously, he said,

> I admit that the conception of a moving perfection, or of God as a being who ever expresses himself in new perfections, has its difficulties; but, unlike those of the conception of a static Deity, they are not insurmountable.[21]

How, then, may they be surmounted? Jones does not immediately reply, but contents himself with urging the principle of love against the static position. He here follows a clue left by his teacher Edward Caird, who had written to Mary Sarah Talbot:

> The greatest of all difficulties in the whole theory [articulated in *The Evolution of Religion*] . . . is . . . the union of the conception of God as a self-determining principle manifested in a *development* which includes nature and man, with the conception of Him, as in a sense eternally complete in Himself . . . A clearer conception of the idea that 'God is love' going beyond Himself to be Himself, would probably contain the solution of such difficulties, if one could get it realised and stated.[22]

Later still Jones returns to the charge that 'an Absolute which is subject to temporal conditions, or which changes, is . . . a confused and self-contradictory conception.' He answers that 'This difficulty . . . springs from taking a half truth as the whole truth. For that which changes also persists. Succession implies permanence, and it can take place only in that which has duration.'[23] But this *quasi*-credal response fails to address the nub of the difficulty which is moral: can the absolute improve, become more perfect, aspire to greater depths of love . . . ? Pringle-Pattison considered that from the point of view of the religious consciousness the idea of progress 'is unintelligible as applied to the whole'.[24] It must be said that neither Green nor Jones offers an effective counter-*argument* to this claim.

Before saying anything further about Jones, it will be well to return to his teacher. The running themes in Caird's writings are that the intelligible world is the real world, and that it is intelligible because of its nature as spiritual. The universe is a developing, organic system which is the expression of the eternal self-consciousness. The latter is integral to the former, and Caird resolutely sets his face against that side of Green's teaching which proposed the eternal self-consciousness as prior to, or independent of, the world process.[25] To him

> Reality lies, – not, as common-sense supposes, in the mere individual taken by itself – nor, as science seems to teach, in the mere particular which is related to other particulars; it lies in the relation, or principle of relation, itself, – in the universal which differentiates or particularises itelf and yet is one with itself in its particularity. Or, to express all in a word, 'the real is the rational or intelligible.'[26]

Caird names the principle of unity which holds together subject and object 'God'. He writes:

> The idea of God . . . meaning by that, in the first instance, only the idea of an absolute principle of unity which binds in one 'all thinking things, all objects of all thought', which is at once the source of being to all things that are, and of knowing to all beings that know – is an essential principle, or rather the ultimate essential principle of our intelligence, a principle which must manifest itself in the life of every rational creature.[27]

Again, God is 'the principle of unity in all consciousness',[28] and

> The intelligence is able to understand the world, or, in other words, to break down the barrier between itself and things, and find itself in them, just because its own existence is implicitly the solution of all the division and conflict of things.[29]

But things are not intelligent selves, and hence Caird resorts to the ideas of degrees of reality and evolutionary process – to the disquiet of some of his critics.[30] Again, Caird's identification of the objective reason with the subjective made it appear that God himself was evolving as human beings progressed. Since idea and spirit are equated, the conclusion said Pfleiderer, followed by Caird's pupil Garvie, is panlogism.[31]

If Caird has rightly defined God, what are we to understand by belief in God? His answer is swift if (not least because of the little word 'akin') not altogether clear:

> to believe in God is, in the last resort, simply to realise that there is a principle of unity in the whole, akin to that which gives unity to our own existence as self-conscious beings.[32]

This would seem to make religious faith into a matter of

intellectual assent and, without at all wishing to deny that 'belief in' is inextricably interwoven with 'belief that', there is more to faith than intellectual assent. More serious still is Caird's tendency to leave out of his primary definitions of God everything that makes God lovable, adorable, worthy of being worshipped. Even at the philosophical level the phrase 'principle of unity' is, as Pringle-Pattison declared, 'as bald and abstract a description of God or the Absolute as the much-derided "Being" or "Substance" of earlier philosophies'.[33] Religiously, it is even less adequate. It is 'too exclusively a logical idea, or the standpoint is too narrowly intellectualist', wrote Garvie, 'so that due weight is not given to the witness of the practical and spiritual as of the theoretical reason.'[34] Caird, however, persisted in his convictions on the matter. He thought that the complaint of abstraction was met if it were realized that the infinite is not an abstraction, but a self-determining, evolving principle of unity.[35] This is a mere repetition of his view, not a rebuttal of his objectors. Elsewhere he seems to imply a certain dissatisfaction with his abstract definition of 'God'. He admits that the idea of the principle of unity in all our consciousness is abstract, and promises that he will subsequently treat other conceptions of the divine as they appear in special religions.[36] But this is to raise more than a methodological question: it is a question of logic. Can understandings of the deity in the world's religions be satisfactorily accommodated if the starting-point is an abstract monism? To be more specific, is the God of Christianity to be reached by that route? Can the attributes of God be assimilated to the abstract eternal self-consciousness otherwise than by a Cairdian *fiat*? The question will press as we turn to Henry Jones.

As we have seen, Jones perpetuated Caird's general approach, albeit with more passion and in jauntier style. It is his conviction that only the irrational is unintelligible, and he doubts 'if anything real is irrational except as misunderstood'.[37] Proof requires 'systematic coherence and existential interdependence',[38] and idealism affords these. For whereas naturalism abstracts, dividing object from object, '*Spirit comprises* [the differences within the natural world] *without annulling them:* it possesses them and yet distinguishes itself from them.'[39] Philosophical idealism is thus 'a recoil from the endless negation of the finite'; both it and religion are 'in different ways, the awakened soul's last resort'.[40] Human beings, having a sensuous-rational nature, seek first finite desires. Sooner or later, however, the individual

> is in a far country, and has joined himself to the citizens thereof, and he would fain satisfy himself with husks; till, at last, the hunger of his soul awakens, and he remembers his Father's house, where 'even the hired servants have bread enough and to spare.'[41]

Spirit, according to Jones, has superior rights to the material and the natural: indeed, 'the natural world is itself the symbol or phenomenal manifestation of Spirit.'[42] Human beings derive their existence from the indwelling spirit, and realize themselves as they obey God's will. At the same time, 'The Absolute realizes itself in finite centres; and more fully in that finite centres are spiritual.'[43] This process of self-realization on the part of the absolute may, agreed Jones, appear odd, for 'It looks obvious that what is perfect cannot change except for the worse.' Nevertheless against static notions of the deity he held to

> the idea of God as *the perfect in process,* as a movement from splendour to splendour in the spiritual world, as an eternal achievement and never-resting realization of the ideals of goodness in history.[44]

As he wrote to A. C. Bradley,

> Is it nonsense to think of the most perfect as that which is a self-enriching love, a love growing by its own activity? . . . I don't *like* [an Absolute] who is aye at his *limits.*[45]

For his part, however, J. A. Smith ruefully remarked, 'The sliding basis of "a moving Absolute" is one on which it is difficult to keep one's feet.'[46]

Jones has no compunction about naming the absolute 'God', about insisting that its character is personal, or about declaring that philosophy is incomplete until it concludes that God is love, and that for this datum it must have recourse to religion. 'The God of religion is the same as the absolute of philosophy; and for both alike the universe in the last resort is the scene of a self-manifesting perfection.'[47] At the same time, however, 'God . . . is greater than and transcends the Universe.'[48] Jones refrains from advising us how these two assertions cohere; or, at least, the weight of his argument is in favour of immanence at the expense of transcendence. The further jump to God/the absolute as love seems to be simply a direct import from Christianity at the same time as the term's Christian connotation is left behind, or at least unmentioned in context. With Jones's insistence that 'the demand of philosophy, placed at its highest, is . . . met by a religion whose God is a God of Love',[49] I feel the same unease as with Caird: how viable is the procedure of working up to the Christian God from the starting-point of idealism? Have we done justice to the divine revelation claimed by Christianity if we think of Christianity as the coping-stone of philosophies which start elsewhere? 'If I wanted to get to Tipperary', said the mythical Irishman to the lost traveller, 'I wouldn't be starting from here.'

Jones sets out to be a realist-absolutist, neither giving the natural world less than its due nor landing in philosophical abstractions. The contrast between the sacred and the secular is, for example, false. Both natural science and the philosophy of religon 'have to deal with principles that are at once ultimate and . . . timeless, and which also embody and actualize themselves in temporal events'.[50] Consistently with this, 'Universal and particular exist only as elements in a system, and disappear when separated.'[51] Again, 'Religion could not survive a fundamental discrepancy between the Good and the Real or True.'[52] At the same time the natural world must be given its due. He thinks that while idealists have demonstrated the unity of nature and spirit they have not paid sufficient attention to their difference, and have thus tended towards either abstract monism or unintelligible and chaotic pluralism. 'Having proved that the real world is ideal, [idealism] must prove that the ideal world is real' – that is, that space, time and matter are real.[53] Subjective idealists, materialists and pantheists all overlook the important point that to distinguish between the self and the world is not to separate them.[54] His case against Lotze is that while thought and things are not identical, they are in an unbreakable relation, which Lotze will not allow.[55]

But if Jones did not opt for abstract intellectualism, he certainly did not wish to minimize the importance of intellectual considerations. Thus while agreeing with Tennyson and Browning that 'the universe is spirit-woven' and that God is immanent in it, he raises the 'stern question' of the ground for this conviction. The poets, he charges, wrongly divorce faith from reason, and

Those who rest on *such* a faith, or have recourse to 'intuition' which is only tradition and habit in disguise, or to 'feeling' which in fact can give neither truth nor error, are distinguished from the Agnostic in no wise except that he is better aware of his ignorance and more frank in the confession of it.[56]

On the basis of this brief résumé of the positions of Green, Caird and Jones I shall attempt to address the vexed queston of the relations of the concepts 'absolute/eternal self-consciousness/ spirit' and 'God', using 'absolute' to stand for its alternatives as well, except when quoting from others.

II

Writing of idealist transcendentalism, and at a time when Jones and others were still active, Donald Mackenzie averred,

> Its manner is apt to strike the observer as being haughty and supercilious, and its language would lead one to think that a claim to something like omniscience is arrogated – a claim so contrary to our broken experience as human beings, and so opposed to that humility which serious thinkers have always regarded as the fitting attitude for all searchers after truth.[57]

Undeniably there are passages – even entire works – which justify this lament. But the best of the idealists knew better. Thus, for example, Caird:

> It is involved in the very idea of a developing consciousness such as ours, that while, as an intelligence, it presupposes the idea of the whole, and, both in thought and action, must continually strive to realize that idea, yet what it deals with is necessarily a partial and limited experience, and its actual attainments can never, either in theory or practice, be more than provisional . . .[58]

That this humility did not prevent some fairly large claims concerning our ability to define the absolute has already been made clear.

Since my concern is with Christian belief, let it be said at once that in some sense the idea of the absolute is psychologically and ontologically necessary to Christian faith. This comes out most clearly in connection with the religious attitudes of reverence and awe: 'No conception of God which takes him for less than the ultimate Reality', wrote Webb, 'will satisfy the demands of the religious consciousness'; indeed, he thought that the doctrine that God is not the absolute, as propounded by F. H. Bradley, 'must, . . . if seriously taken, make nonsense of Religion'.[59] What was even more troublesome to personalists such as Webb was Bradley's denial that the absolute was personal, moral, beautiful or true.[60] Bosanquet was later to write to Webb with reference to Bradley and himself, 'we do not think it possible to worship the Absolute. What is worshipped, at once must become less than the whole.'[61] Webb remained unconvinced, and so too did Jones. The latter declared of Bosanquet's conclusion that 'the God of religion . . . is an appearance of reality, as distinct from being the whole and ultimate reality', that 'If I thought that these consequences were involved in the principles of Idealism I should "cultivate my garden".'[62] Pringle-Pattison likewise found Bosanquet's position defective. His particular complaint was that 'In his theory there is no real self at all, either of God or man, but only a logical transparency called the Absolute.'[63] Bosanquet thus substitutes 'the logical analysis of knowledge . . . for an account of living experience', and this yields only Kant's unity of apperception, which 'is no real self (whether human or divine) but simply the ideal unity of systematised knowledge'.[64] For his part Webb, while granting that the divine personality must be free of the limitations which attach to human personality, nevertheless argued against Bosanquet that the human capacity for personal relations with the supreme reality on the part of finite individuals requires 'the presence in the Supreme Reality of whatever is necessary for the existence of such a relation thereto'.[65]

Bradley was similarly taken to task. He had contended in *Appearance and Reality* that while appearances exist, they are not themselves real, but are embraced by the one reality, the absolute, in an all-inclusive harmony.[66] Against this Pringle-Pattison urged that there were in Bradley's position two lines of approach, the one Spinozistic and Schellingian, the other Hegelian. The terminus of the former route was the undifferentiated unity of Spinoza's substance or Schelling's neutrum. By contrast, the Hegelian line prompted Bradley to pay due heed to difference and permanent distinctions – even within the absolute; but this line was finally neutralized by the weight of Spinozistic influence. We are thus left with empty transcendence or shallow pantheism, and these are 'two sides of the same mistake'.[67] Bradley's insistence that all necessary distinctions are retained and preserved is 'nothing more than a *saying*'.[68]

Like Bosanquet, Bradley denied that the absolute was God:

> The Absolute for me cannot be God, because in the end the Absolute is related to nothing [so much for Green's omni-relational eternal self-consciousness], and there cannot be a practical relation between it and the finite will.[69]

Indeed, 'The highest Reality . . . must be super-personal.'[70] Commenting on these passages Henry Jones declared, 'It is on this matter of the significance of personality that I differ most deeply from Mr Bradley – if I understand him correctly.'[71] As he elsewhere remarked, Bradley's 'premises are such that differences must not merely be reconciled or harmonised, and relations not merely be surmounted, but *eliminated*.'[72]

These reactions to Bradley and Bosanquet raise two questions which we must keep in mind as we proceed. First, if, as Pringle-Pattison alleged, Bradley was merely *saying* that in his theory distinctions are preserved, was Jones, on his absolutist principles merely *saying* that God is personal? In other words, how legitimate – even logically possible – is it to import into the absolute such concepts as personality and love (which Jones also attributes to the absolute)? This is the question to which I alluded earlier in connection with Caird and Jones. Is it legitimate to deem the terms 'God' and 'Absolute' synonymous? Secondly, is the personal idealism of Pringle-Pattison in the last resort a stable position? I shall reserve the latter question for a later section of this chapter, and proceed now to address the former.

His criticisms of Bradley and Bosanquest notwithstanding, it must be said that Webb wavers with regard to God and the absolute. He rightly urges the necessity of distinguishing between 'absolute' as meaning 'out of relation', and 'perfect' or 'complete'.[73] In the former sense the absolute is an abstract concept which 'implies that nothing is left out; but it does not say what is there.'[74] It was this consideration which had prompted Taylor earlier to say that there might well be a metaphysically satisfying conception of the absolute *qua* world system which might be 'entirely inadequate as a description of the God or

Absolute of the religious experience'. It might, while satisfying the requirements of logical coherence, leave our ethical demand for 'a really existing object adequately realising our ideals of practical and emotional perfection' quite unmet.[75] Clearly the latter understanding is more congenial to a religious philosopher – especially to a personal idealist such as Webb. Yet there is in places an ambivalence in Webb's position which suggests the dangers which linger when the metaphysical absolute invades the territory of the religious. (I do not mean that we are here dealing with two absolutes, but Webb does think that the term may be used in both a metaphysical and a religious sense). Thus, for example, when he speaks of 'the Spirit which expresses itself in the worshipper's personal love and devotion to God as to a Father' as being 'nothing less than an integral factor in the very life of God himself',[76] we cannot but wonder whether the worship thus offered is really that of a free person. Is Webb on the way to blurring the Creator–creature distinction after the manner of immanentist-absolutists? To say that God enables our worship by his Spirit is one thing; to imply that the worship itself is God's is to suggest a self-worshipping deity and to rule out genuine human worship altogether. We earlier noted Webb's remark to the effect that the question whether or not God was the absolute was one which continually revolved in his mind, and which he had never answered to his entire satisfaction.

Pringle-Pattison traced ambivalence concerning the absolute back to Hegel himself. He finds two lines of thought in Hegel:

> The one starts from the idea of God, which is Neo-Platonically construed as Trinity in unity, but which is simply the idea of knowledge as such, treated as a real being. There is no passage from this hypostasised conception to the facts of the finite world. The second line of thought starts with these facts, and treats the historical development of humanity as the process in which the Absolute comes to itself.[77]

We have found traces of both lines in our idealists – especially, of course, in Green, Caird and Jones. Pringle-Pattison finds that in Hegel's writings the two lines are interwoven, with the result that comprehension of his meaning is rendered difficult. He is clear, however, that 'The Absolute Idea is no more than an ideal drawn by Hegel from his sole datum, the human self-consciousness, and does not of itself lift us beyond our starting-point.'[78] Here is a further allusion to the difficulty we have noted concerning the attempts of Christian idealists to import into their concept of the absolute notions drawn from their religious faith. Despite his appreciation of the problem, however, Pringle-Pattison's own position is not without its ambiguities. He has no qualms about using the terms 'Absolute' and 'God' interchangeably,[79] and when answering those who criticized him for this usage he denied that he intended the terms as 'precise equivalents in the sense that one may be substituted for the other in any context'.[80] Positively, he wishes

> to keep in view at once the transcendent being of God for Himself, which we inadequately figure to ourselves as a self-consciousness or personality on the model of our own, and the creative and illuminative activity of the same Spirit in the beings which live, and are sustained in life, only through its self-communicating presence.[81]

But here, no less than the absolutists, Pringle-Pattison appears to proceed by assertion, and has the same difficulty as they in justifying the content he puts into 'God/Absolute'.

From the evidence adduced it cannot be denied that 'absolute' is employed ambiguously in idealist circles, and this both by absolute and personal idealists. I have agreed with those who argue that the understanding of God as the absolute in the sense of the greatest and worthiest is the inspiration of Christian worship and living, but I seriously doubt whether the idealist metaphysical starting-point yields the Christian God. It seems that those who identify the two terms, and who import Christian meaning into the concept at a later stage, are probably committing a category mistake,[82] and are certainly being selective in the (pleasant as opposed to nasty) attributes they ascribe to God/the absolute. They seem seldom to face up to, or even to notice, this selectivity when discussing the absolute; but at a *later* stage an appeal to revelation is sometimes made. But is it, from the point of view of metaphysical consistency, too late by then? Can the philosophical absolute bear the religious weight which is imposed upon it? At crucial points the idealists seem to proceed by assertion – 'philosophy needs to culminate in love' (Jones), for example – rather than by argument, and to smuggle Christian conceptions into the absolute with little warrant.

With none of this had the theologian A. B. Bruce any patience at all, and after all the subtleties through which we have had to pick our way, it is refreshing to hear the outburst of someone who begins elsewhere:

> I do not wish, if I can help it, to worship an unknown or unknowable God called the Absolute, concerning whom or which all Bible representations are mere make-believe, mere anthropomorphism; statements expressive not of absolute truth, but simply of what it is well that we should think and feel concerning God. I am not disposed to subject my idea of God to the category of the Absolute, which, like Pharaoh's lean kine, devours all other attributes, even for the sake of the most tempting apologetic advantages which that category may seem to offer. A poor refuge truly from unbelief is the category of the Absolute![83]

H. R. Mackintosh, theologian and pupil of Pringle-Pattison, was more temperate but no less critical of absolutism. 'It is true', he wrote,

> Absolutist criticism has done extremely effective work in protesting against a Deistic view of God. Also there is a priceless truth of which Pantheism is a grave but not wholly inexplicable distortion. None the less, to believe in God is a good deal more than to realise the existence of a principle of unity in all things.[84]

That we cannot simply indulge in the substitution of terms was clear to A. E. Taylor:

> [T]he transference of knowledge or thought from one society to another is no mere affair of adaptation to a new vocabulary; it is a matter of adaptation to a different set of habits of mind.[85]

It may also be, I suggest, a matter of attending to a different set of facts on which 'habits of mind' or, more grandly, 'world views' may turn. If Christians wish to think that their God is absolute in some legitimate sense (though most of them would hardly use the term) they are not saying that he is identical with the metaphysical absolute of Green, Caird or Jones, or with the personalized absolute of Pringle-Pattison and (on occasion) Webb. To suppose otherwise is to commit a logical howler. It is to overlook the fact that, when it comes to the expression of Christian thought through the medium of terms whose natural home is elsewhere, the Christian's role must be not that of poacher, but of anabaptist. This

process of anabaptism is an analogical task in which, following
J. M. Keynes,[86] we have to show not only how our terms are like
those of others, but also how and where they differ.[87] An
illustration may make the point clear. In *Lux Mundi* Aubrey Moore
argued that if we surrender the assumption of moral relationship
between God and humanity we shall find ourselves falling back
upon such philosophical terms, supposedly equivalent, as the
Infinite, the absolute, and others. 'But', he continues, 'these terms,
which metaphysicians rightly claim, have no meaning for the
religious consciousness.'[88] The 'no' here is too strong: there may be
Christians who *by analogy* from Christian understandings of God
find some of these terms helpful, though such qualifying phrases as
'absolute in this sense but not in that' would need to be used, or
understood, by the user. Moore correctly continues:

> in metaphysics proper 'God' is as much a borrowed term as 'sin' is in
> non-religious ethics. Moral evil is 'sin' only to those who believe in
> God; and the infinite is only 'God' to those in whom it suggests a
> superhuman personality with whom they are in conscious relation.[89]

Accordingly, to regard 'sin' and 'moral evil' or 'God' and 'infinite'
as synonymous terms is to commit a logical mistake and to leave
out of account some of the most important things which most
Christians wish to say. As James Iverach bluntly declared, 'To
speak of the absolute and unconditioned as synonymous with
God, is simply to alter the conception of God.'[90]

With this cautionary word ringing in our ears we may now leave
terminological questions and proceed to examine the charges that
philosophical idealism puts the Christian Gospel at risk by
swamping transcendence with immanence, by blurring if not
denying the Creator–creature distinction, and by losing the
individual in the absolute process. Clearly, these are variations
upon one theme, but it will be well for us to treat them in turn. I
reserve the most serious charge, that philosophical idealism cannot
adequately deal with the problem of evil, until the next chapter.

III

The determination on the part of philosophers and theologians
alike to bid farewell to deism, the 'inward' thrust of romanticism,

and the impetus of evolutionary thought – these were among the factors which prepared the soil in which immanentism could take root.[91] A further consideration, prominent not least in the thought of Edward Caird, was the desire to avoid the pitfall inherent in mysticism:

> the great error of mysticism was just this, that it thought to reach the deepest reality, the absolute truth of things, by the *via negativa*, the way of abstraction and negation; in other words, that it tried to approach the infinite by turning its back upon the finite, and not by seeking more thoroughly to understand the finite.[92]

Again, Pringle-Pattison welcomes the emphasis upon immanence as a bulwark against Kantian agnosticism:

> The strength of Hegel's system lies . . . in his insistence on the doctrine of immanence . . . The polemical emphasis of the system is directed against the agnostic relativism of the Kantian Critique with its doctrine of the thing-in-itself, and against the easy mysticism of Schelling's Philosophy of Identity.[93]

That not all were sanguine where immanentism was concerned is clear from the way in which A. C. McGiffert speaks of the doctrine of immanence as a refuge for theologians against science which had in the past wrought havoc upon the then current theism; as being seldom treated to close examination by its proponents; and as

> hardly more than an instinctive protest against traditional mechanical and external notions of the relation of nature and the supernatural, or against the deistic banishment of God from the world and from human life . . .[94]

For his part Webb noted that immanentism had modified the understanding of religion, so that instead of its objective being the quest of happiness in a world governed by a supreme being, it became a matter of the satisfaction of an inborn need of evolving humanity, and this without reference to a transcendent reality;[95] while Taylor, in his important article on theism which marked a turning-point in his philosophical pilgrimage, observed that Hegel's appeal to 'professedly Christian theologians' had 'usually led to an extreme "immanence" doctrine of God which at least compromised the theistic position'.[96] The point was not lost upon the theologian

P. T. Forsyth who had earlier welcomed the emphasis upon the
intimacy of God with his world to which immanentism testified,
whilst cautioning against losing God in 'a Monism which is rather
the absolutising of the immanent than the incarnation of the
transcendent'.[97] Earlier still Illingworth, who gave 'immanence
respectability as a theological category',[98] declared that

> we need not fear to transgress the limits of the Christian tradition in
> saying that the physical immanence of God the Word in His Creation
> can hardly be overstated, as long as His moral transcendence of it is
> also kept in view.[99]

Nevertheless there was in many minds more than a suspicion
that the idealist emphasis upon immanence was putting
transcendence and the supernatural at risk.[100] Of Hegel it has
been said that 'His philosophy is indeed theistic; but its views of
man, history and God make it finally a pantheism.'[101] It is difficult
to deny that from Hegel there descend what at the very least are
pantheizing tendencies in philosophy and theology alike, and this
in the service of continuity which took theological form in the
writings of John Caird, for example,[102] and which prompted the
philosopher R. L. Nettleship to go so far as to say,

> I think I shall end my days as something like a Spinozist. At least I get
> more and more to feel that there is absolutely no difference in principle
> between what is called physical and what is called spiritual, and that if
> one can understand a triangle one can understand oneself.[103]

Green set out to reassure his readers that since an assertion of
identity implies difference or change 'We need not be frightened
. . . from the doctrine that man is identical with God on the ground
that it makes God "no more than" man.'[104] In one place Richter
asserts that Green 'abandoned' the doctrine of God's transcendence
for that of his immanence.[105] Later, however, he quotes W. D.
Lamont with approval as saying that Green's religious inheritance
disposed him to think in terms of a transcendent creative mind and
that 'The "theistic" and the "pantheistic" ideas which struggled in
his mind never quite fought the battle out to a finish.'[106] This is the
more accurate judgement, and it is consistent with our earlier
discovery of Green's predisposition to think in terms of an
independent *fons et origo* despite the generally immanentist view of
the eternal self-consciousness which he adopts.

Although Caird was fully alive to the perils of Spinozistic (as of mystical) pantheism,[107] his own strong emphasis upon immanence was found disturbing by some. Thus he denies that the absolute unity is static, existing independently of process, and affirms that it is dynamic, and that it is realized in the process of the Christian life, whereby 'humanity becomes – what it potentially is – the highest organ of the divine self-manifestation.'[108] Leaving on one side the legitimacy or otherwise of the assimilation of Christian ideas to the absolute, the pantheistic tendency is here plainly revealed, for it would seem that individuals are simply phases of the absolute which, for convenience, is frequently called God.

The general result of an overemphasis upon immanence is that the balancing concept of the transcendent receives less than its due. But there are also particular consequences which are, from the point of view of Christian belief, unfortunate, and I must note some of these.

First there is the tendency towards what is tantamount to materialism. This emerges in S. S. Laurie's puzzlement at Green's absolute:

> What an inadequate Absolute – a whirl and whorl of relations giving birth to infinite other relations! Were I to accept this, should I necessarily also accept a self-distinguishing Subject as base, centre, source, and sustainer? I think not. The system of relations includes God Himself; and things are just so. And we have a monistic Pantheism, which anyone may call Materialism, if he chooses.[109]

'What', asked Pringle-Pattison,

> is the difference between Idealism and Materialism, if in the one case human existence is the outcome of an unconscious system of logical conceptions, and in the other the outcome of unconscious matter?[110]

Illingworth agreed:

> Spirit which is merely immanent in matter, without also transcending it, cannot be spirit at all; it is only another aspect of matter, having neither self-identity nor freedom. Pantheism is thus really indistinguishable from materialism; it is merely materialism grown sentimental, but no more tenable for its change of name.[111]

His remedy was to claim a place for both reason and matter in a theology of the Word.[112]

Secondly, a thoroughgoing immanentism cannot leave room for genuine personal relations, and so undermines both ethics and worship. As might be expected, the personal idealists had a good deal to say on this matter. Moral relations were of particular concern to them. Thus Pringle-Pattison argued that 'in our wills we feel a principle of self-hood which separates us even from the Being who is the ground of our existence.' (In fact, that would seem to be impossible, and accordingly I should prefer the word 'distinguishes' to 'separates'). He continues,

> 'Our wills are ours to make them Thine', as the poet finely puts it. But they must be really ours, if there is to be any ethical value in the surrender . . . If there are not two wills involved, then no relation between them is possible . . .[113]

Webb was in general agreement and, as to worship, he noted that while Aristotle's extreme doctrine of transcendence was at the opposite pole to Spinoza's equally extreme doctrine of immanence, neither of them left room for personal communion between God and his worshippers; hence the modifications of Aristotle introduced by Thomas Aquinas.[114]

Thirdly, an overemphasis upon immanence tends to the distortion of a number of Christian doctrines. I shall have more to say on this in the penultimate chapter, but some of the issues may be indicated by reference to two contemporary quotations. Von Hügel wrote that 'every pantheism persistently denies, that the inner life of God is something far fuller and richer than is the whole of His creative and providential activity.'[115] And while agreeing with the immanentists that in God we live and move and have our being, Garvie affirmed that we are dependent upon God and not ourselves God. Hence,

> Any attempt at doctrinal restatement with exclusive emphasis on divine immanence, the identity of God and man, must sacrifice essential features of the Christian faith. If God and man are one, and man cannot sin against God, then forgiveness and atonement become meaningless terms. Philosophy has no warrant to claim this surrender from Christian faith, for its pantheism ignores data that any adequate interpretation of the universe must take into account, man's religious consciousness of distinction from, and dependence on, God, and man's moral consciousness of liberty and abuse of that liberty in sin.[116]

The upshot is that transcendence and immanence must be held together and, moreover, that this view was endorsed even by those idealists whose absolutism made it theoretically least appropriate for them to do so. Those most guilty of seeming to have their cake and eat it were, I think, helped by the ambiguity of both 'transcendence' and 'immanence' – ambiguities over which few dwelt for long. McGiffert did allude to the 'crass and bald' assertion that by transcendence is meant simply that God is larger than the universe; and to the view that the term means that while God is 'eternal' all else is 'temporal'.[117] Interestingly, he did not allude to the view that 'transcendence' may in Christian discourse be said to find its supreme place in reference to the holiness of God *vis-à-vis* the sin and alienation of humanity. Pringle-Pattison comes closer to this when he construes transcendence as indicating the distinction between the perfect and the imperfect, but this does not yet carry the religious significance of the holy and the sinful.[118] He did, however, realize the importance of the distinction between transcendence conceived as a distinction of value or of quality, as over against transcendence understood as 'the ontological separateness of one being from another'.[119] However, for his denial of God's independence of, or priority to, creation, Pringle-Pattison was adversely criticized by Charles Gore.[120]

'Immanence' too is ambiguous. It is one thing to think of God as omnipresent, another to be in a relationship with him established by grace through faith: 'There is . . . a real operational distinction between God's immanence as essence and as presence.'[121] To express the matter otherwise, when immanence as identity of logical relations or of substance is deemed to be synonymous with morally grounded interpersonal relations, and even more when the latter are unceremoniously and illegitimately grafted on to the former, we are on the way to a finally unstable philosophical position.

To repeat, there is general agreement among our seven idealists that transcendence and immanence belong together. In Illingworth's words,

> the divine immanence in man, as conceived by Christians, depends, for
> its very character and value, upon the divine transcendence; upon the
> thought that the same God who 'hath respect unto the lowly', is still

'the High and Holy One that inhabiteth eternity; whose name is Holy'.[122]

Here, once again, is the idea of the holy, conspicuous by its absence from so much of the idealism of the period with which we are concerned. Yet it can hardly be denied that for a religious understanding of transcendence in relation to immanence the experience of Isaiah of Jerusalem affords a paradigm case. He was confronted by the transcendent God, 'high and lifted up', who was immanent to the point of grave moral discomfort: 'Woe is me! I am lost, for I am a man of unclean lips . . .'[123]

It is impossible not to detect a change of tone between Illingworth as just quoted and Caird:

> God is a word that has no significance, unless by it we mean to express the idea of a Being who is the principle of unity presupposed in all the differences of things, and in all our divided consciousness of them. In this sense, then, we must think of God as essentially immanent in the world and accessible to our minds. But from another point of view, the principle of unity in the world must necessarily transcend the whole of which it is the principle . . .[124]

The same idea is developed in closer relation to Christianity elsewhere, but the justification for assimilating Christian concepts to those of philosophical idealism is not clear, and the note of the holy transcendent is not adequately sounded.[125]

Transcendence, wrote Illingworth, saves us from a pantheism which would confuse God with the world; immanence precludes the neo-Platonist separation of God and the world.[126] The divine presence both transcends and sustains and indwells the material order.[127] Webb repeatedly insists that transcendence and immanence must be held together if we are to be true to our religious experience, the outstanding notes of which are ultimacy and intimacy.[128] Jones concurs: the religious consciousness, he avers, 'can yield up neither of the two conceptions, except with its own life'.[129] Finally, a number of writers have urged that Christian doctrine has the resources which will hold the two inseparable concepts in balance. Illingworth believed that the doctrines of the Trinity and the Incarnation well fulfilled this function.[130] But at this point I begin to encroach upon the province of my penultimate chapter. I shall accordingly for the moment conclude with a quotation from David Jenkins, and then proceed to the allegation that immanentism calls into question the Creator–creature distinction. Jenkins writes, 'Transcendence without immanence makes nonsense of God, immanence without transcendence makes nonsense of man. Both are quite untrue to the givenness of Jesus Christ.'[131] These are not the cadences of an Illingworth, but in conviction the earlier and the later Anglican are at one.

V

'A true theism', wrote Clement Webb, 'is never "anthropomorphic" in the sense of drawing no essential distinction between man and God, of merely making God in the image of man.'[132] Nearer to our own time this claim was endorsed in yet grander terms by Nels Ferré: 'There is . . . an unbridgeable, qualitative distinction, eternally real, between God and man and between *God* as immanent and the nature and history in which He is immanent.'[133] The Creator–creature distinction has, however, been under threat from a variety of directions during the course of Christian history. Illingworth, for example, noted the danger that mysticism may seek union with God by obliterating human limitations and underestimating human guilt;[134] and many came to feel that the philosophical idealism of the period with which we are concerned led to the same consequences by traversing the path of immanence. 'Idealism', lamented A. D. Lindsay, 'has seemed to be so occupied in transcending conflicts that it has obliterated all differences and made the world a foggy place where everything looks the same as everything else.'[135]

It must in justice be pointed out that the major idealists were well aware of the need to preserve the Creator–creature distinction. Thus Green, for example, writes,

> Our formula . . . is that God is identical with the self of every man in the sense of being the realisation of its determinate possibilities, the completion of that which, as merely in it, is incomplete and therefore unreal . . . :[136]

But this is Green in the context of ethics, not metaphysics; and even here the questions may be raised: What is the relation between the eternal self-consciousness and the human? – a question to which Green returns no clear answer; and: Does God have an existence independently of humanity in and for himself? – a matter on which, as we saw earlier, Green is ambivalent.[137] Green the metaphysician cannot, it would seem, so easily accommodate the Creator–creature distinction. His doctrine that the eternal self-consciousness reproduces itself in finite beings prompted Robert Mackintosh's verdict that only by 'a masterful exercise of force' could Green introduce

> a God, and men, and a relation between them; but properly philosophy, as he works it out, is merely the abstract image of consciousness or self-consciousness, with scanty ontological implications. Even if we speak of the *creative* power of thought, the analogy between God's creating and man's knowing is too faint to form the backbone of a philosophy, – and what justification has Green for the contrast between God and man? And yet such a contrast is necessary, and Green draws it.[138]

Caird likewise was apprised of the necessity of drawing the Creator–creature distinction, but once again the question is whether his metaphysical doctrine really permits this in any adequate way. Certainly he wished to avoid the perils of pantheism on the one hand and deism on the other,[139] and his positive point was concisely expressed thus:

> We are conscious of ourselves in relation to, and distinction from a world, and therefore, implicitly, of a unity which is beyond this distinction, *i.e.* of God. This is the circle out of which we never get, and within which all knowledge and all our scepticism is necessarily included. Any attempt to establish a dualism which is not merely the relative difference of the elements in this unity seems to be to refute itself . . .[140]

Here once again is the identification of the ultimate unity with (presumably the Christian) God; but the question how far the elements in question – not excluding the evil aspects of the human ones – can be brought to unity if God is as Caird wishes him to be, remains a mystery to which we shall return in the next chapter. In Lindsay's accurate opinion both Caird and Jones habitually

> dealt more gently with an extreme monist than with an unrepentant dualist . . . Balliol men who were reading philosophy with Caird would

in imitation . . . consign a philosopher to outer darkness with the fatal words, 'He's a Dualist.'[141]

At the same time it must be admitted that Caird's remark, 'An absolute difference would be no difference at all; for it would annihilate all relation between the things distinguished, and, in doing so, it would annihilate itself',[142] is very much to the point. What is required, then, is a careful analysis of the nature of the distinction. As between Creator and creature there cannot be an absolute ontological distinction if the life of the latter is derived from the former. Christianity does concur with the unnamed writer who averred, 'In him we live and move and have our being.'[143] Nor, if creation is good, can the distinction turn upon that between matter and spirit. But that our mortal being is not as God's eternal being; that there is an epistemological distinction (we 'know in part', God is omniscient); and that there is, above all, a moral gulf between sinful humanity and holy God – these distinctions are exceedingly difficult to sustain (though not to assert) on the basis of so heavily immanentist a philosophy as Caird's.

Granting that we are not proposing an absolute divorce between God and creatures, it would seem that unless the Creator–creature distinction is sturdily upheld many aspects of Christian belief are placed at risk. How can there be genuine interpersonal relations (whether between human beings or between them and God) within an absolute unity? How, within such a unity, could there be revelation at all? For, as Forsyth pointed out, 'a God conceived as above all things monistic and immanent to the world cannot reveal Himself, because He has no recipient Other.'[144] Yet personal relations, the hearing of the Word and the bestowal and reception of grace are integral to the Gospel. Indeed, the Gospel is fundamentally about the restoration of broken relations. Illingworth made the point clearly, though with an overemphasis which must be queried:

If there is no determinate outline between the creature and the Creator; if our being is *metaphysically involved in that of God, or His in ours,* we lose, together with our personal distinction, our capacity for spiritual communion. Thus however much stress we lay upon God's immanence, or intimate presence in the world, and inspiring guidance of the minds of men; this immanence gains its whole significance and character from the fact that it is the immanence of the Transcendent One, the Eternal, the All-Holy, the Almighty.[145]

The overemphasis lies in the italicized words. First, I have just suggested that if God is the source and giver of life, there cannot but be a metaphysical/ontological relation between human beings and himself. But this relation is not one of absolute identity – otherwise it would be meaningless to speak of relations. Jones earnestly advocated the point:

> complete fidelity to a theory which springs from the conception of man and God as mutually exclusive would condemn it to be either dumb or to assist itself into articulate speech by means of a dogmatic dualism.[143]

Illingworth himself elsewhere acknowledges this when he writes that when Christians think of

> God's indwelling presence or immanence within us, and of Christ being formed within us, and of our bodies becoming temples of the Holy Ghost, the whole significance of this depends upon the fact that God is our eternal Other, and not ourself.[147]

Pringle-Pattison concurs: hence his rebuke of Jones for translating 'ontological relations' into 'ultimate identity'.[148] Jones, like Green before him, conceded the point where ethics were concerned: 'Affirm nothing but the unity of the divine and human will, or, on the other hand, affirm nothing but their independence of each other, and religion becomes impossible.'[149] But, as with Green and Caird, it remains doubtful how far he is justified in this concession by his metaphysics.

In the quotation from Illingworth on p. 133 the last four italicized words introduce our next consideration. For it would seem crucial to Christian doctrine that God does not depend on us for his being as we do upon him; and here Illingworth may be understood as suggesting the contrary. That this was far from his intention is clear from his words earlier in the same chapter:

> All Theists regard God as absolute in the sense of being self-contained and independent of all necessary relation to finite persons or things, meaning by this that finite persons and things are in no way essential to His being what He is, in no way contributory to, or constitutive of His Godhead.[150]

Were it otherwise, and if God had no option but to have dealings with us, grace would be less gracious than the Christian Gospel would have us believe. It may well be a requirement of God's character as love to condescend to sinful humanity, but this is far from saying that were there no human beings – not to mention no sinners – God could not be.[151] To deny this would be to fasten upon that strand in Hegelian thought which issues in materialism, for 'the appearance of man becomes identical with the creation of God; man creates himself, and at the same time brings God to the birth.'[152] We should no longer have a doctrine of the creation of all things by God.

In connection with many other doctrines the maintenance of the Creator–creature distinction is vital, as the following summary points will indicate. It is vital for our understanding of God's holiness and love. His holiness is *the* quality which for ever distinguishes him from us. His love is such that he will let others be in their relative independence, despite their abuse of his gift of freedom.[153] Moreover, we should never know of this love apart from God's gracious revelation – but here again identity of being would vitiate the notion of the revelation of one party to another (something for which Green's philosophy, for example, scarcely allows), just as it would nullify the idea of the believers' genuine reception of God's free gift of salvation. And what, finally, of religious aspiration and worship? Both of these turn upon the conviction that God is other than ourselves. He is, said Illingworth, 'the Object of all our hope and desire'.[154] As to worship, Pringle-Pattison aptly wrote,

> It takes two not only to make a bargain; it takes two to love and be loved, two to worship and be worshipped . . . [T]he most perfect *alter ego* must remain an *alter* if the experience is to exist, if the joy of an intensified life is to be tasted at all.[155]

VI

The third form taken by the protest against immanentism is that it swallows up or envelops individuals and deprives them of genuinely distinct existence. The challenge presented to those most inclined towards absolutism was how to maintain real differences whilst at the same time positing genuine union or continuity within the spatio-temporal order and between it and the realm of spirit. The problem became acute when they extrapolated from the logical axiom of internal relations to ontological and epistemological relations. John Oman bluntly threw down the gauntlet before Hegelianism thus: 'Hegelianism . . . is the profoundest attempt to account for [the individual] on a scheme which, nevertheless, derives all rationality from absorbing him into the process of the Cosmic Reason.'[156]

We have seen that the Hegelian emphases within Green's writings were introduced in the first place as part of his response to the then dominant empiricism extending from Locke to Mill, and it may well be that in his anxiety to avoid that pitfall he was led into dangers on the opposite flank. Thus, for example, he has been charged with so obliterating the distinction between thought and reality that with it goes the distinction between reality and illusion and hence that between truth and error.[157] Certainly he asserts a distinction between thought and reality, but it cannot be said that he is altogether precise as to the nature of this distinction. Knox quotes him thus:

> Undoubtedly there is something other than thought. Feeling is so; the whole system of nature, on which feeling depends, is so; its otherness from thought makes it what it is, but this is the same as saying that relation to thought makes it what it is, that but for thought it would not be.[158]

To Knox this is an 'empty formula' since if all relation is in and for thought, how is relation to thought possible? It does seem that what Green gives with one hand he takes away with the other. Again, Green, as we have seen, grounds upon a self-distinguishing eternal self-consciousness as the foundation of the system of reality. Can he, asks Calderwood, 'now escape from this self-distinguishing characteristic of "the spiritual principle", so as logically to maintain the unification of existence?'[159] Iverach presses the question further in a theological direction:

> What is the relation of the universal self-consciousness to the self-consciousness of finite beings? Are we to conclude that God is personal only in man, and man immortal only in God? . . . Is God anything in

Himself? Is there a divine centre of thought, activity, blessedness; and is there an existence of God for Himself? Green's way of speaking about the universal self-consciousness seems to imply that it has no reality in itself; the only reality it has consists in the fact that it is the logical subject of all possible experience. The attempt to unify the divine and human subject seems to destroy the reality of both.[160]

As to the human side of the equation, Green contends that 'our consciousness' may mean

> either a function of the animal organism, which is being made, gradually and with interruptions, a vehicle of the eternal consciousness; or that eternal consciousness itself, as making the animal organism its vehicle and subject to certain limitations in so doing, but retaining its essential characteristic as independent of time, as the determinant of becoming, which has not and does not itself become.[161]

Either way, Pringle-Pattison's complaint that this 'is of a piece with the Scholastic Realism which hypostasized *humanitas* or *homo* as a universal substance, of which individual men were, in a manner, the accidents',[162] seems entirely justified. Upton's verdict upon Green was no less stern:

> If the ultimate reality be the indivisible unity of the eternal self-consciousness and the sum-total of ideas which that self-consciousness embraces and knows, it becomes wholly inconceivable that this Eternal Being should originate other self-conscious beings in some way distinct from himself. The activity of thought may give rise to other *thoughts,* but it is ... impossible that it should give rise to other *thinkers.*[163]

When we turn to Caird we find that he faces the same problem as Green: his understanding of an eternal self-consciousness makes it difficult for him to allow, as he wishes to do, for distinct finite self-consciousness. '[T]he infinite itself', he writes,

> must be conceived, not merely as that which the finite is not, but as that which includes and explains it; not merely as an indeterminate background of the finite but as a self-determining principle, which manifests itself in all the determinations of the finite without losing its unity with itself. It *must* be so conceived; otherwise the negative or regressive movement by which we rise to the infinite would itself be impossible.[164]

The scales seem here to be weighted in favour of the infinite, or spiritual, or God – all of which are terms used interchangeably by Caird. How then can there be genuinely finite individuals? Conversely, in passages where Caird emphasizes our existence as subjects for which all objects exist[165] (a not entirely clear notion), how can he speak so eloquently of an underlying unity of subject and object? And what is the nature of this unity? In Iverach's poignant words, 'He calls it God, but the use of that sacred name does not make the meaning more clear.'[166] At least as puzzling is the notion of relative reality, as when Caird declares that

> it is possible to maintain that every intelligible object is a partial form or expression of the same principle which is fully expressed in the intelligence, without denying the relative reality either of the inorganic or the organic world, and without, on the other hand, treating every mind as an absolutely self-determined being.[167]

Although the general tenor of Caird's remarks is in the direction of the diminishing of the individual, it must in fairness be noted that he was more than alive to the dangers of Spinozism. He repudiated Spinoza's way of seeking an all-embracing unity by the path of abstraction, so that, for example, God might have an infinite number of attributes or none at all.[168] Instead, he advocated the ideas of organic unity attained by a process of evolution. The latter concept, he thought, 'enables us to escape from the conception of this unity as a substance, to which all things are *equally* related',[169] and thereby allowed for the less than perfect. Humanity could thus be seen not simply as one object among, and level with, others, but as 'including in himself the life of all the others, and reaching beyond it'.[170] But the nature of the inclusion and the manner of the reaching are left unexplained, and identifiable human individuality seems under threat once more.

In the wake of his teacher, Henry Jones assures us time and again that 'every rational contrast falls within a unity of some kind', and that if we endeavour to give independent existence to contrasting terms we are guilty of irrationality: there is always the whole within which they are elements.[171] Not indeed that he wishes to deny difference:

> [T]he differences *are* real, the activities of each subject *are* its own, and no one thing is another thing, or fulfils *its* function. But I am not

concerned to deny difference; nay, I go all the way with the critics in asserting it. What I *am* concerned with is the assumption implied, that the mere assertion of difference and distinctions is tantamount to the denial of unity, and that we are shut up to the choice between the exclusive alternatives of abstract unity and abstract difference.[172]

Elsewhere he elaborates the point as follows:

[I]f difference and unity imply each other and are not conceivable apart, then reason does not, as is ordinarily thought, aim at *introducing* systematic continuity amongst its objects, in the sense of forming connections where none existed before. Its object must already be a system, for it presents itself as one thing, and also as a thing which has some quality or character of some kind: it is not a mere many, nor is it mere sameness.[173]

On this basis Jones sallied forth against materialists and dualists of all kinds. For example, he teases Huxley for the distinction in the latter's *Evolution and Ethics* between ethical nature and cosmic nature:

It is said of an ancient sage that he went out and looked upon the universe and pronounced that 'All is one.' Professor Huxley went down to Oxford the other day and pronounced that All is two, and that there exists between them a strife which is inextinguishable.[174]

'All our halting dualisms . . . rend asunder the seamless garment of the real', he proclaims.[175]

It cannot be denied that at times Jones's language carries him away. In one place he can say, 'I refuse to regard opposites which are supplementary and positive aspects of the same reality as being contradictory; contradiction, as a last word, is a confession of failure.'[176] Elsewhere, and more cautiously, he remarks that the idealist 'repudiates all distinction between outer and inner, *except that which is relative*'.[177] More boldly, as I pointed out in the previous chapter, he thunders, 'The unity is as real as the differences, and the differences as ideal as the unity.'[178] But if this is so it must apply to all differences – not least those thrown up by the problem of evil; and as we shall see in the next chapter, there is no graver threat to the monistic position than this perennial monstrosity. As to the individual, there is an ambivalence in Jones's thought, both sides of which are in one place expressed within ten lines. In connection with the believer's union with God in Christ he says that 'There is not . . . any limit to the identification of the worshipper and his God in a true religion. From that point of view not a shred or shadow of the old self remains',[179] (though Paul, whom Jones has just quoted, found himself engaged in a constant struggle with his 'old man').[180] Six lines later, and now with reference to morality, we are advised that 'The identification with the ideal must not be by the annihilation of the self.'[181]

It was, however, precisely the fear that individual selves would be annihilated by absolutism which prompted the response of the personal idealists. Clearly, we are here concerned not with the absolute as the one eternal reality of which all other entities are but imperfect aspects or elements, but with the idea that the individuals we encounter in the phenomenal realm have their own reality which may, at times, be over against whatever absolute there may be.[182] Some decades before personal idealism was placed squarely on the philosophical map by Pringle-Pattison and others, Martineau and Campbell Fraser (Pringle-Pattison's teacher) had premonitions of things to come, and accordingly uttered cautionary words.[183] The former observed that

> As the parts of our nature which . . . enter into relation with God are precisely those which make us *Persons* and distinguish us from other 'living things', it is difficult to see why the same term should not be given to the corresponding attributes of rational and moral Will in him . . .[184]

The latter, distressed by what he regarded as creeping idealistic 'gnosticism', warned that 'He who is elaborating a science of *what must be* in thought is in danger of excluding from his regard not a little of *what is* in man.'[185] Consistently with this Pringle-Pattison, who was highly thought of by both Martineau and Fraser,[186] was guided in his religious philosophy by the principle that 'We must interpret the divine on the analogy of what we feel to be profoundest in our own experience.'[187] And for them the profoundest reality was personality morally conceived.

In this they had learned not only from the Britons to whom I have just referred, but also from Lotze and, to some extent, from Ritschl.[188] They applied their lessons as appropriate to Green, Caird, Jones, Bradley and Bosanquet in particular. Webb, though not uncritical of some forms of personal idealism, as we shall see, nevertheless exalted personality in God and man and found Green wanting in that he understood personality to be 'the activity which goes on in all minds that think or reason and which, so far as they reason correctly, must be the same in all', and not as that which distinguishes one person from another.[189] This could only place complications in the way of genuine personal relations between humanity and God – though Webb acknowledges that Green desired to maintain the possibility of such relations to a degree that Bosanquet would have thought impossible, and in a way which Lotze thought essential.[190]

Matters were certainly exacerbated by Bosanquet's blunt description of finite individuality as an 'adjectival mode of being'.[191] In criticism of Green, Upton had earlier driven to the heart of the matter thus:

> [I]t makes a momentous difference . . . whether we regard God's self-revealing presence in the soul, in the form of our higher reason and moral ideals, as the presence of a supreme Personality in a certain sense distinct from our personality, or whether, on the other hand, we conceive of ourselves as, in one aspect, human and finite, but, in another aspect, identical with God, the self-existing, self-evolving thought.[192]

But Pringle-Pattison took Bosanquet directly to task:

> Professor Bosanquet completely fails to realise the elementary conditions of selfhood. In his theory there is no real self at all, either of God or man, but only a logical transparency called the Absolute. In speaking of finite selves he seems never to look at them from the inside . . . but always from the point of view of a spectator momentarily concentrating attention upon them in abstraction from the social whole which is their setting.[193]

His own position is that 'belief in the relative independence of human personalities and belief in the existence of God as a living Being are bound up together.'[194]

Among the motivating concerns of the personalists in general was the conviction that the absolutist position(s), by virtue of their intellectualism, allowed insufficient scope to moral, aesthetic and religious values (though most of the personalists did not have as much to say concerning aesthetics as did Bosanquet).[195] If our philosophy cannot accommodate the highest we know it is an inadequate thing indeed. Illingworth was convinced all human thought must start from the idea of personality, which is the most real thing we know and our canon of reality. We find that we come to know other persons, and by analogy we come to know God as personal also.[196] Of course, we could only do this, thought Illingworth, because the transcendent God was already immanently present to us.[197] The nub of his case is that human personality is a spiritual thing as is 'the highest category under which we can conceive of God'.[198] But under the same moral impetus we also become aware of the imperfect and the morally evil. This causes us to see ourselves as we are in the light of the holy, and opens the door to the response of Christian doctrine. These matters will occupy us in the next two chapters.

A second prominent motive behind religious varieties of personal idealism was the conviction that religious experience was not to be overlooked and that, at least in the Christian religion, it was centrally concerned with personal God–humanity relations, and with disrupted ones at that. No one was stronger on this point than Webb. Fully cognizant of the fate suffered by the traditional arguments for the existence of God at the hands of Hume, Kant and others, he contends that 'neither the existence of the religious experience nor of an appropriate object thereof requires or even admits of a preliminary proof.'[199] Further, whereas William James drew attention more particularly to abnormal and eccentric varieties of Christian experience, Webb maintains that many people in fact have religious experiences but would not immediately label them as such.[200] He is quite clear that 'The Object of Religious Experience is always God revealing himself, since it is inconceivable that God should be known or experienced except through his own act.'[201] His next step is to argue that while we are conscious of the object of our religious experience, the existence of that object does not depend upon our being conscious of it.[202] He then proceeds to characterize the object as one with whom we have personal relations. Indeed, that

> the denial that there is truly Personality in God must in the end lead to the denial that religious experience is an independent and autonomous form of experience at all, I feel for my own part no doubt whatever.[202]

For example, the 'characteristic religious emotion of Reverence' is one which is hard to refer to an impersonal object;[204] and the acknowledgement of personality in God adds to the intelligibility and moral power of such leading religious ideas as sin, forgiveness, justice, sacrifice, union. Thus, for example,

> to regard Sin as an offence against a personal authority, and still more to regard it as an affront to a loving Father, is a more intelligible and a more ethically significant way of thinking about it than it is to conceive it after the analogy of a physical defilement or an automatic mechanism.[205]

Here once again by the pathway of morality we approach the threshold of Christian doctrine; and here, with Webb's starting-point in relgous experience, we are at the furthest remove from all idealism of the abstracter kind.

As might be expected, those who emphasized personality in their writings did not emerge unscathed. Pringle-Pattison, for example, drew fire for his view that different selves are 'absolutely and for ever exclusive', and that 'each Self is a unique existence, which is perfectly *impervious* . . . to other selves – impervious in a fashion of which the impenetrability of matter is a faint analogue.'[206] His substantive point was that 'I have a centre of my own – a will of my own – which no one shares with me or can share – a centre which I maintain even in my dealings with God Himself.'[207] In a letter of December 1887 to W. P. James, he wrote,

> My contention is that our knowledge of a thing, *even if supposed adequate,* is one thing and the existence of the thing itself is another . . . Ordinary Hegelians seem to me to make one centre do duty for all, thus denying the separateness or imperviousness of the different selves. It is here, as I think, that the confusion of an epistemological with a metaphysical result comes in harmfully. At the same time I fully admit that the problem of this relative independence remains as dark as ever, and is not even touched in my book. Theosophy is a dreadful bog to get into. The British public won't stand it. Better write a treatise on golf than a third course on such a subject.[208]

But the word 'impervious' rankled, and in the second edition of *Hegelianism and Personality* we find instead the following words concerning selves:

> Whatever be the mode of their comprehension within the all-

containing bounds of the divine life, it is certain that, as selves, it is of their very essence to be relatively independent and mutually exclusive centres of existence.[209]

In all of this Pringle-Pattison's underlying motivation was supplied by his conviction that the absolutists moved illegitimately from epistemological to metaphysical questions (something which Jones strenuously denied), and hence made one thinking reality assume the rational responsibilities of all.[210] For him, as one of his pupils put it,

> Idealism is . . . the end of the argument and not the beginning, and because it is so it is able to include the truth of realism as a subordinate moment in a more complete and profound philosophy.[211]

D. G. Ritchie was satisfied by Pringle-Pattison's recasting of his words, but Jones persisted in holding 'impervious' against his colleague.[212] Small wonder that in yet a further presentation of his recast views Pringle-Pattison 'many times regretted' his use of the term 'impervious' in view of the way it had been interpreted and the uses to which it had been put.[213] But on the main point he did not yield:

> The reality of both God and man depends on the reality of the difference between them . . . The process of the finite world is not a game of make-believe which the Absolute plays with itself; it means the actual origination of new centres of life and agency, not created by a magical word of evocation, but given the opportunity to make themselves.[214]

Webb levelled charges similar to that brought against Pringle-Pattison's 'impervious' against Rashdall,[215] and he concluded a criticism of Bradley and Bosanquet with these words:

> What seems to be required is a whole-hearted recognition at once of the genuine unity of the *content*, or (as I should prefer to say) of the *object* of Reason – of that which we may call the world of Ideas, in the Platonic sense of that word – and also of the unity of each personal subject as a substantial element in the system of Reality, and not merely an adjective qualifying it.[212]

In his turn Webb was criticized by Bosanquet for his view that at the heart of religious experience is contact with the ultimate reality. 'Surely', retorted Bosanquet, 'personal intercourse must be with what is one among others and ultimate reality must be what is all-inclusive.'[217] In subsequent works Webb granted the 'mystery' in all of this,[218] and still later, perhaps with a certain relish, he declared,

> Philosophy can never without serious risk of impoverishment ignore the testimony of the religious consciousness, whereof alone indeed, according to a remarkable saying of Bernard Bosanquet, 'metaphysic comes to be little more than the theoretical interpretation.'[219]

When we ask, 'What is the nature of the God with whom we may be in relation?' doctrine beckons once again. For the present, and as a harbinger of things to come, we may conclude this chapter with some words of Iverach:

> If we take the religious consciousness as our guide and as our means of interpretation [and this, of course, is to beg a huge question], and take it in its highest reach as given in the New Testament, then we shall no longer speak of God as absolute, and so on, but we shall borrow the grand words, God is spirit, God is life, God is love. In other words we shall think of God as a determinate Being existing in relations, and these relations are abiding distinctions within the circle of the divine life. God is not an abstract unity, nor an absolute and inclusive self-consciousness, God is a living, concrete, complex Being, and in the Godhead there are relations and activities always in relations and always in action. The relations within the Godhead come to our help and rescue us from the paralysis of thought wrought by the abstractions of metaphysics, and we are not compelled to think in terms of an abstract order, nor driven to the necessity of deriving a manifold universe from a simplicity in which there are no relations.[220]

4

Ethics, Society and the Idealists

The words of Iverach quoted at the end of the preceding chapter alert us to the possibility that, as religious believers, our seven idealists may wish to entertain more than their idealism – certainly more than that of the more absolutist of them – would properly permit. We may find that analogous suspicions are engendered as we approach the territory of ethics and society. A quotation from Charles B. Upton will caution us in this matter. Referring to absolute idealism he writes,

> [I]n quiet intellectual moods, we may, perchance, fondly imagine that we and all things are but phases of manifestation in the inevitable evolution of self-existent, eternal thought. But no sooner do we find ourselves living in contact with practical life and its moral problems, than we wake from this 'metaphysic dream' . . . and the conviction forces itself upon us that there exists much, both in our own character and in the character of many around us, which need not have been; and in respect of which we feel that it would have been both better for society and more acceptable to God if it had never been.[1]

The possibility is here raised that ethical reflection introduces concepts – notably that complex of issues which travels under the umbrella title of the problem of evil – which absolutism, at least, cannot adequately accommodate. We shall conclude that this is undeniably the case. It must, however, be noted that of our seven idealists none were more socially concerned, or wrote more on ethics, than Green and Jones; and none had more to say concerning the reality of evil and imperfection than Green and the later Taylor. Thus where Green and Jones are concerned we shall have to be alive to the possibility that their metaphysics are not all of a piece with their ethics. And in the case of the later Taylor we shall have to bear in mind the fact that by now his thought had become more eclectic – which is to say that he was open to insights supplied by Aquinas and Reid – and that he had lived through the horrors of two World Wars.

We must further reckon with the possibility that whereas the theistic idealism of our seven thinkers operated at a remove from their most important ideas of God (though this, as we saw, was less true of Webb and the later Taylor than of Green and Caird), their philosophical ethics seem to be at an even greater distance from Christian ethical thought insofar as the latter concerns ethical behaviour as motivated by a grateful response to God's love, and the question of the source of power to act.

As before, I shall be selective in my approach to a vast literature. In particular, I shall not linger over the ways in which some of my idealists found fault with such alternative ethical approaches as utilitarianism and evolutionary ethics by which they were surrounded;[2] and I shall not describe and assess their social prescriptions which, though relevant when first propounded, are only of historical interest today. My quest is of the relation of the ethical and social stances of the idealists to Christian doctrine. We shall find that their diverse, philosophically prompted attenuations raise specifically doctrinal issues in a clamant way. In view of the general outlines of their thought already provided, I shall offer only brief encapsulations of the socio-ethical approaches of the seven idealists with whom we are concerned, beginning with the less doctrinally orthodox Green, Caird, Jones and Pringle-Pattison, and ending with the more orthodox Illingworth, Webb and (the later) Taylor.

I

T. H. Green's ethics are pervaded by the importance of the moral agent. Indeed, the agent's perceptions of his or her own 'higher self' provide the foundation for a true understanding of both morality and theology (the conjunction is significant for our purposes). He writes,

> There is a conception to which every one who thinks about himself as a moral agent almost instinctively finds himself resorting, the conception variously expressed as that of the 'better', the 'higher', the 'true' self. This conception, I believe, points the way to that true interpretation of our moral nature, which is also the only source of a true theology.[3]

Lest it be suspected that this conviction was Green's only when he was wearing his homiletic hat (for the words come from a fragment of an address on Romans 10: 8 and Deuteronomy 30: 14, 'The Word is nigh thee'), I hasten to cite a consistent and even crisper affirmation from the *Prolegomena*: 'Our ultimate standard of worth is an idea of *personal* worth. All other values are relative to value for, of, or in a person.'[4] We may observe in passing that Green here affords an instance of the truth that where ethics are concerned the British idealists are for the most part (Caird and Jones excepted) closer to Kant than to Hegel. The former's second formulation of the categorical imperative, 'So act as to treat humanity whether in thine own person or in that of any other, in every case as an end withal, never as means only',[5] is much more in accord with their convictions than is Hegel's hierarchy which ascends from the imperfect individual through the more perfect society to the supremely perfect absolute.[6] Indeed, the priority of the person is the sword which Green wields against materialistic, deterministic, naturalistic and evolutionary ethics, none of which, he thinks, can accord due place to personal moral obligation: '[I]t is obvious that to a being who is simply a result of natural forces, an injunction to conform to their laws is unmeaning.'[7] Nothing may threaten self-consciousness, spiritually conceived, still less make it into a naturally produced aspect of humanity.

Moral beings are, for Green, undetermined, free beings. In the line of Aristotle he holds that coerced actions are not moral actions. Whereas Kant postulated freedom as an ethical requirement, Green thinks that the freedom of the will can rationally be demonstrated from his principle of self-consciousness. Accordingly, he repudiates Kant's distinction between phenomena and noumena, maintaining only that between finite minds and the perfect mind.[8] But freedom is more than the absence of restraint. Persons are able to make moral choices which conduce to self-realization, or not. Those choices which advance a person in this respect are those whose objects are good. In this sense freedom is 'a positive power or capacity of doing or enjoying something worth doing or enjoying'.[9] Nor is there anything inherently selfish about this, for such choices, declares Green, have clear social implications. Indeed, they are only possible because of the help and security given by others.[10] The upshot is that

> The spiritual progress of mankind is . . . an unmeaning phrase, unless it means a progress *of* personal character *to* personal character – a progress of which feeling, thinking, and willing subjects are the agents and sustainers, and of which each step is a fuller realisation of the capacities of such subjects.[11]

It cannot be denied that in the position thus described Green offered a number of hostages to fortune. In the first place, some were not slow to suggest that, for all his desire to uphold freedom, Green actually tumbled into a version of determinism, thereby vitiating his ethics. They fastened upon such a claim as that an agent's moral action 'is as necessarily related to the character and circumstances as any event to the sum of its conditions'.[12] For

> A philosophy which accounts for all things by the 'action of a free or self-conditioned and eternal mind', has by its own structure created a difficulty in the way of shaping a theory of personal obligation; for an injunction to conform to law seems as unmeaning in a nature which is the 'reproduction of an eternal consciousness', as in a 'being who is simply a result of natural forces'.

Thus Henry Calderwood's *tu quoque*.[13] Robert Mackintosh went so far as to describe Green's idealism as 'a determinism masked by quibbles',[14] and Taylor spoke of Green's 'at least nominally disguised' determinism.[15] It would follow that when Green complains that 'The burden of moral obligation is got rid of in the philosophy of Hume, but only to be replaced by that of natural necessity',[16] we have a case of the pot calling the kettle black.

Secondly, the use made by Green of the idea of self-realization raised questions in the minds of some. Green followed Aristotle in defining the true good for humanity as 'the full exercise or realisation of the soul's faculties in accordance with its proper excellence, which was an excellence of thought, speculative and practical'.[17] From the standpoint of the religious consciousness, declared W. G. de Burgh, this was to miss the point. For the self requires not realization, but redemption.[18] More particularly, de Burgh subjects the concept of 'self-realization' to close analysis. He argues that it is contradictory to suppose that God, the timelessly real, could realize himself, for realization implies a temporal process. With specific reference to Green he contends that the latter's 'conception of a transcendent God as a timelessly actual self' lacks justification.[19] On the supposition that the moral life consists in our own realization of our timeless self, de Burgh is pungent indeed:

> This doctrine lends itself readily to edification, and has given rise to more nebulous vapourising, in the pulpit and elsewhere, during the last forty years, than any other ethical theory of modern times . . . I confine myself to one of its many ambiguities, viz. the apparent partition of human nature into a timeless or rational and an animal self. If we take this dualism literally, the theory is open to the [following] objection . . . If, as Green doubtless intends, the command is directed to our lower nature, which is to be conformed to the law of the timeless self, why should a self that is timelessly real thus enjoin an otiose reproduction of its reality? It is obvious, and Green sees this as he goes forward, that our natural capacities furnish the materials for the process, that the timeless self is not a given factor in our personality, but an ideal goal, a 'possible self' evoking a response from our animal nature, and that, consequently, the animal nature is no mere animality, but is informed from the outset of the moral life by the guiding principle of reason and conscience.[20]

Again, on Green's view that 'The rational soul, in seeking an ultimate good necessarily seeks it as a state of its own being', de Burgh comments,

> If this means merely that ultimate good must lie within my capacity of attainment, and that in attaining it I find my satisfaction, the statement is true but unilluminating; if it means that the nature of the good that satisfies me consists in my satisfaction, it is palpably false. The seemingly edifying principle proves to be egoism in disguise, and loses all claim to moral authority.[21]

On the other hand, and thirdly, some philosophers have argued that Green's ethic of self-realization can stand without the metaphysical underpinning which he sought to provide: indeed that the latter vitiates the former: 'That Green tried to ground his ethics in his metaphysics is true; that he did not have to do so is also true.'[22] The early Taylor was to the fore in arguing that

Green's metaphysics were ethically redundant. This was the burden of his work *The Problem of Conduct*, in which he sought to shun metaphysics and to provide grounding for ethics in the empirical facts of human life. As he wrote,

[E]thics, unless it is to consist of mere barren tautologies, must be based not on general principles of metaphysics, but upon the study of human nature in its concrete empirical entirety, as it reveals itself to the student of psychology, sociology, and anthropology.[23]

He does not deny that there is a place for a 'Metaphysics of Ethics', but considers that this should come at the end, not at the beginning, of an examination of morals.[24] He roundly declares that

(1) There is no such thing as the Eternal Self in Green's sense of the term; (2) If there were such a thing as the Eternal Self, it would be of no value for the purposes of the student of ethics.[25]

It is only proper to point out that Taylor's reduction of the basis of ethics to matters empirical displeased some, like the theologian James Orr, who were not wedded to Green's philosophy, and who were convinced that Taylor's approach threatened the crucial ethical concept of free will.[26] Others seriously questioned Taylor's critique of Green, one of them going so far as to declare that 'Taylor's argument is radically uncomprehending. The real relation of metaphysics to ethics in Green's philosophy is not remotely what Taylor supposes it to be.'[27] We may certainly say that for Green, as for Caird and Jones, the practical is deemed to be continuous with the theoretical and, from this point of view, however it may be with self-realization ethics in general, we could not have had *their* ethics without their metaphysics.[28] Taylor subsequently abandoned his earlier position and became a convinced ethical theist. This entailed his repudiation of the empiricism which had so troubled Orr, and prompted him utterly to eschew his early view that religion is simply complete devotion to any object, whether good or bad.[29] Suffice it to say that in appreciating the way in which Samuel Alexander exposed the fallacy residing in Green's concept of a transcendental and timeless self, Pringle-Pattison, with reference to Alexander's 'conception of an organism of individual and social conduct demanding at every point a certain line of action for the preservation of its equilibrium', made the point which can equally be levelled against the early Taylor if we substitute his favoured sciences for biology: 'a conception is not less metaphysical because it is borrowed from biological science.'[30]

In the fourth place, and on the other hand, some were little helped by the concept of self-realization – with or without Green's metaphysics. Robert Adamson, for example, while confessing that he had 'a friendly and companionable feeling' towards idealism, nevertheless declared that ' "Self-realisation" has always impressed me as a conundrum rather than as its solution.'[31]

Fifthly, Green is adversely criticized by those who believe that he too readily identifies God with our moral self. Green writes,

> God is identical with the self of every man in the sense of being the realization of its determinate possibilities, the completion of that which, as merely in it, is incomplete and therefore unreal; that in being conscious of himself man is conscious of God, and thus knows that God is, but knows what he is only in so far as he knows what he himself really is.[32]

Clearly, Green here seeks to avoid the pitfall of making God so remote from human beings as to be irrelevant to them, whilst at the same time noting that human imperfection as a matter of fact makes the identity of humanity and God less than complete. In characteristic fashion Green's biographer explains that 'The identity of two things not only admits but implies difference.'[33] While it may be doubted whether this takes the measure of the gulf of alienation between humanity and God which Christians call sin, it does seem disconcertingly in line with Green's own remark that 'Sin is very much an illusion. People are not as bad as they fancy themselves.'[34] This is not unconnected with his view that conscience addresses us without ambiguity, and that it is not in principle unduly difficult to heed its commands.[35] Not surprisingly, some saw here a blurring of the Creator-creature distinction which is nowhere more acutely perceived than in the moral realm on those occasions when we determine to spurn the highest we know. We may also observe that from the point of view of Christian doctrine Green's ethical attenuations are significant; for divine aid to the human will is not a concern *of his ethics*, sin's reputed devastation of our best intentions is scarcely alluded to, and the concepts of love and atonement are absent. Christianity is, no doubt, of general assistance in encouraging the best efforts of human beings; but this again, though among his general convictions, is not a concern of his ethics; and in any case it would be a strangely utilitarian justification of religion for one who in other contexts inveighed so ardently against utilitarianism. The upshot is that while Green's ethics are those of a (less than fully orthodox) Christian, they are not Christian ethics in the sense of theological ethics. To say this is to recognize a fact, not to express a judgement. Neither does Green attempt to construct an ethical theism after the fashion of the later Taylor.

Caird's biographer remarked upon the apparently surprising fact that although he spent a lifetime teaching moral philosophy, Caird published no systematic work on that subject. We are left to read between the lines of his discussions of the theories of others. When we do this we find that, self-consistent as ever, Caird focused upon the ethical implications of the principle of self-consciousness, and thus had 'much to teach but little to say'.[36]

What Caird had to say emerges, interestingly enough, in some critical remarks upon Green's *Prolegomena*. He thinks that Green is inhibited by Kant's distinction between the noumenal and phenomenal realms from specifying more clearly than he does the nature of the self-conscious principle to which he refers all things. In particular, he dissents from Green's view:

> *That* there is such a consciousness is implied in the existence of the world; but *what* it is we only know through its so far acting in us as to enable us, however partially and interruptedly, to have knowledge of a world or an intelligent experience.[37]

To this Caird replies:

> It is true that we cannot explain the spiritual principle, which is implied in all explanation, by reference to anything else than itself, but this does not imply that we only know *that* it is, and not *what* it is. Our knowledge of the self is rather the type to which all other knowledge imperfectly approximates, than an inferior kind of knowledge. And, on the other hand, if it is possible for us to carry back the world of experience to conditions that are spiritual, there seems to be nothing that should absolutely hinder us from regarding the world *positively* as the manifestation of spirit . . .[38]

It may be suggested that Caird distorts Green's meaning here, for the latter does not say that we have no knowledge of the nature of the eternal self-consciousness at all, only that our knowledge of it is partial. But Caird's motive is the elevation of self-knowledge above other kinds of knowledge, and thus the verdict of his pupil J. S. Mackenzie is justified, namely, that while both Green and Caird utilized substantially the same conceptions in adumbrating their thought, the latter 'carried them farther, both on the metaphysical and on the ethical side, and passed over more completely, by means of them, from the point of view of Kant to that of Hegel'.[39]

All of which is consistent with Caird's critique of Kant, which is expressed clearly and concisely with reference to the latter's *Dialectic*:

> The problem with which Kant's *Dialectic* attempts to deal, and which it treats as insoluble, is . . . simply the problem of *raising consciousness to the form of self-consciousness*; in other words, of attaining to a knowledge of the world of experience as not merely a 'synthetic', and therefore imperfect, unity of things external to each other, but as an organic unity of transparent differences, a self-differentiating, self-integrating unity, such as seems to be presented to us in pure self-consciousness. Nor can this problem be regarded as insoluble; for the unity of self-consciousness is identical with the unity of consciousness; it is only that unity become self-conscious. Hence the point of view at which consciousness and self-consciousness seem to be absolutely opposed to each other, – the highest point of view which Kant *distinctly* reaches, – can be regarded only as a stage of transition from the point at which their relative difference and opposition is not yet developed, to the point at which they are seen to be the factors or elements of a still higher unity.[40]

Under the influence of Hegel, Caird sought to make good Kant's deficiency. For him God is 'the spiritual principle of unity which is above the distinction of subject and object, and which is at once the presupposition and the goal . . . of our finite lives'.[41] Proceeding in ignorance of this insight, ordinary consciousness treats the finite as if it were infinite, and ordinary morality wrongly seeks self-realization in finite ends and objects. On the contrary, the first principle of Christian ethics is to condemn the love of the world.[42]

Like that of Green, Caird's ethical thought is pervaded by the notion of self-realization. He sought to explicate the meaning of that elusive term in a variety of ways. In the familiar context of a letter to a friend he said, '[W]e want a Christianity more set upon realising the "life" in "dying to live".'[43] More formally, and now with specific reference to ethics, he wrote,

> [T]he practical impulse, whenever it goes beyond . . . a craving for the satisfaction of immediate wants, implies the presence in our minds of an idea of absolute good, which is at once the realisation of the self and of a divine purpose in the world.[44]

For all his high-flown rhetoric, Caird had his feet firmly on the ground. In his sermons and addresses he advocated social engagement in the interests of the disadvantaged and, as we saw, he was personally active in such work. His great objection to ritualism and sacerdotalism was that they tempted their devotees to think that

> the truly sacred part of life lies in some special acts of religious service or in some form of emotional religious experience, and not in the simple duties of our station . . . But the moment we begin to make these things ends in themselves or to separate them as a higher class of duties from the work of our profession and the ordinary obligations of our domestic, social and political life, we are on the way to desecrate our natural existence by dividing the spiritual from it, to lose the value of that *power of idealising* which is the salt of our life, sanctifying it and devoting it to higher issues than life itself.[45]

No one could accuse Henry Jones of losing any value that was to be had from the power of idealizing. And, undeniably, he was at one with his teacher in socio-political activism. Somewhat surprisingly, however, he finds a chink in his teacher's Hegelian armour, declaring that Caird was not wholly innocent of the dualism he sought to surmount. While ever insisting upon 'the unity behind the difference of subject and object', Caird nevertheless posits a 'certain isolation' of the individual subject from the world around him. Caird 'does not plainly state that man does nothing, attempts nothing, conceives nothing, in which his long antecedents and limitless environment do not participate more or less directly'.[46] In Jones's view, by contrast, the world presents us with no isolated facts, still less with 'that empty phantom, an isolated personality'.[47] It must be admitted that while Jones proceeds to insist upon both 'the unity and continuity of the moral being with the world, *and* his independence and freedom',[48] he provides no clear account of how this may be. Neither does he show that what can be only a relative independence differs from the 'certain isolation' of the individual of which he complains in the writings of his teacher. Instead, he lapses into homily: 'Man is free but not isolated; he loses himself in his God, but only because in that act he has found himself.'[49] However moving this may sound when declaimed with passion, however true to religious experience it may be, it here enables Jones to overlook the crucial point that he was concerned with the isolation of the individual from the *world*. Or are we to understand a pantheistic identification of the phenomenal world with God?

However this may be, it would seem that Jones goes to extraordinary lengths in order to repudiate Kantian dualism of the moral and natural worlds. Kant, he declares, 'lifts man, *as a moral being* clean out of the natural system'.[50] To be consistent, Kant, he avers, ought to have denied the possibility of conflict between the spiritual and the natural, for the existence of such conflict implies that human beings live in both worlds. While Green moderated Kant's vitiating dualism, he gave such precedence to the spiritual over the natural, that he leaves us with 'the natural *plus* the spiritual, *plus* a relation between them'.[51] This relation remains external and contingent, and thus the natural and the spiritual are not seen by Green to be aspects of a single real. In all of this we have a further demonstration of the fact that the closer one draws to the individual idealists the greater appear to be the differences between them.

Positively, it is Jones's belief that if we would grasp the nature of humanity we must understand it as ethical. With Caird he maintains that 'Morality is not the pursuit of an abstract universal good, but of the good as particularized in this or that duty.'[52] And the assumption (his word) on which his entire philosophy rests, and which, on his own admission, he makes no attempt to justify, is that 'the moral life has a value which is final, unlimited and absolute.'[53] Hence, for example, although the approach to the doing of one's duty may be hard, 'There is happiness at the heart and sweetness at the core of right action . . .'[54] It is not that we create the moral world by performing our duty – any more than we create the objective world by our knowing it. In morality, we engage in a process of interpretation, and in morality, as in epistemology, we presume that the ideal is real and the real ideal.

Accordingly, in morality we press on to our goal which is perfection, sustained and motivated by 'the ideal, the divine, the perfect good'.[55]

Like his fellow-idealists, Pringle-Pattison finds fault with Kant, and his complaint was consistent throughout his career. In his early work of 1881 he accuses Kant of conceiving the moral order 'in the spirit of the baldest Individualism, as the final adjustment of happiness and virtue'. What is more, God becomes simply 'a *Deus ex machina* to effect this combination'. He grants that

> The noumenal and self-legislative Self is, indeed, when properly conceived, identical with the will of God, and leaves no room for any extraneous Deity. But the thoroughly mechanical idea of such a Power weighing happiness against virtue cannot be charmed out of the letter of Kant's theory.

Thus the ghost of the older metaphysic of transcendent reality is not laid.[56]

Pringle-Pattison returns to the charge eighteen years later. He welcomes Kant's idea that the moral law be self-imposed – God is no external lawgiver – but he fails fully to see 'that if its imposition is referred only to the self of the isolated individual, we are thrown back into subjectivity . . .' and are quite unable to account for the law as an obligation upon all rational beings.[57] The truth is, according to Pringle-Pattison, that the moral law is not self-imposed in ethics and then ratified in religion by the external lawgiver. Rather, 'God is the source and author of the law, but only in the sense that he is the higher self within the self which inwardly illuminates all our lives.'[58] In his first series of Gifford Lectures, Pringle-Pattison reiterates his charge, adding the thought that

> if, as Kant insists, it is wrong to treat a human being merely as a means, it must be a false way of putting things to present God himself in this merely instrumental light.[59]

At the same time, Pringle-Pattison was quite content that since the time of Kant, and as a result of his contention, the 'conception of intrinsic value as the clue to the ultimate nature of reality' had become 'the fundamental contention of all idealistic philosophy . . .'[60] He finds it morally impossible to conceive of anything devoid of value as ultimately real or self-subsistent, and in this

realization lies 'the driving-power of the idealistic argument'.[61] As
he had much earlier declared,

> Every idealistic theory of the world has for its ultimate premiss a
> logically unsupported judgment of value – a judgment which affirms an
> end of intrinsic worth, and accepts thereby a standard of unconditional
> obligation.[62]

This is why we cannot explain the higher from the lower.
Judgements of value are not detached and mutually independent
as were the intuitions of 'an older philosophy' (presumably the
Scottish common-sense philosophy):

> They represent rather so many parts of one fundamental judgment in
> which the nature of reality, as exhibited in the system, may be said to
> affirm itself. Every particular judgment depends for its ultimate
> sanction on the recognition of its object as a contributory element in
> this inclusive whole.[63]

At this point Pringle-Pattison laid himself open to the quite
understandable twofold charge of W. L. Davidson. First,

> Have we such a full, accurate, and unerring knowledge of the inclusive
> whole, and such a clear and constant vision of it, as to be able to form a
> complete and satisfactory scale of values, and to determine with
> precision and decisively the exact place of each?

To this he returned a negative answer. Secondly, what are we to
make of the discordant estimates of ultimate values which we find
among supporters of the theory under discussion? Davidson cites
Pringle-Pattison as denying that the finite individual can
ultimately be swamped by the absolute, while Bosanquet seems to
hold that within the ultimate reality the preservation of
individuality ceases. 'Surely', he argues,

> a principle of value that fails to decide as to the value of personality
> itself as determinative of a future life for the individual, at the point
> where authoritative decision is most required, leaves something to be
> desired.[64]

Davidson concluded that the test of consequences and the place of
desire may not be left out of account.

In Clement Webb, as in Pringle-Pattison, we find gratitude to
Kant coupled with a sense of Kant's deficiencies. Unlike Caird,

and more forcefully Jones, Webb does not seek to 'Hegelianize' the dualisms with which Kant leaves us by reference to absolute spirit, so much as to contend that Kant has failed to see how his categorical imperative demands, quite specifically, the God of religion.

Ever ready to give praise where it is due, Webb acknowledges Kant's 'immensely important' attack upon the scholastic theistic arguments, and the significance of his assertion that God is postulated by our moral consciousness: 'he thereby established the essential connexion of the idea of God with an experience not merely theoretical.'[65] Again, Kant has taught us once and for all the distinction between a natural history of morals and a moral philosophy; and also that 'we can impute to ourselves, as sin or as righteousness, that – but only that – which genuinely originates in our own [free] will.'[66]

On the other hand, Kant leaves something to be desired in general terms with his loathing of religious fanaticism which blinds him to the importance of the emotions, and his 'markedly *unhistorical* temper' of mind.[67] More particularly, his holding apart of religion and morality – except symbolically – does justice to neither; for 'the sentiment of reverence for the moral law written on our hearts assumes a form intellectually more satisfactory . . . when it becomes a reverence for the God whom that law reveals.'[68] This is not to deny that Kant's reverence for the moral law may be described as religious, or to doubt that he regarded the law as divinely given and is to be honoured as such, but he does make it appear that the two great commandments are telescoped, and that to love our neighbour is coextensive with loving God.[69] This is a consequence of his epistemology, according to which we cannot know God as such. This, thinks Webb, caused him to miss the true outcome of his proper emphasis upon our consciousness of moral obligation, and of his conviction that the natural law is intrinsically authoritative and divine. In this connection Webb quotes James Martineau with approval:

> In the act of Perception, we are immediately introduced to an *other than ourselves that gives us what we feel*; in the act of Conscience, we are immediately introduced to a *Higher than ourselves that gives us what we feel.*[70]

In Webb's own words:

We must acknowledge . . . in obligation not only, as Kant insisted, an aspect of autonomy, of self-imposed law, but also of a *heteronomy*, of a law imposed by another, which turns out on inspection to be really a *theonomy*, a law imposed by God. Such a heteronomy, however, is not a heteronomy in Kant's sense, in which he felt that it was inconsistent with the genuine notion of moral obligation or duty; for a law given by God is not a law given by one who is another, since it is involved in our notion of God that he is immanent in our reason and will, which notwithstanding he transcends.[71]

Unless the autonomy of morals be preserved – and this is what Webb's understanding of heteronomy is intended to ensure – there can be no non-circular ethical theism. It is not without significance that neither Green, Caird nor Jones proposed an ethical-theistic *argument* – they hardly could have done, given their strong immanentism and their equation of the moral with spirit. Of all our idealists, the later Taylor (though now influenced by other streams of philosophy) made the most earnest attempt to construct a viable ethical theism, and to him we now turn.[72]

Like Webb, and unlike Caird and Jones, Taylor cannot make sense of morality on the basis of radical immanentism; the transcendent must be preserved at all costs. He goes so far as to say that 'No philosophy of pure "immanence" can take the moral life seriously.'[73] Not only would such a philosophy repudiate the transcendent, it would not allow for the givenness of phenomenal reality. Such givenness is not to be understood apart from the idea of value, which is equally a given in human experience. Indeed, there are no value-free facts:

What confronts us in actual life is neither facts without value nor values attached to no facts, but fact revealing value, and dependent, for the wealth of its content, on its character as thus revelatory, and values which are realities and not arbitrary fancies, precisely because they are embedded in fact and give it its meaning.[74]

The concept of value is integrally related to that of character. It is a weakness of Kant that he thinks too much in terms of individual acts, rather than of the character which is revealed in such acts. He thus fails to emphasize that the crucial question is not what I ought to do, but what sort of person I ought to be.[75] A further weakness in Kant is that while he is content to think that the moral law is of divine inspiration, and that the good will with its law is to be reverenced, his insistence that the moral law is imposed by one's own will, while it stands as a bulwark against a utilitarianism which would justify actions in terms of end results, may degenerate into self-worship. Taylor thus wishes to agree with Kant that the demands of the moral law are absolutely reasonable, but to add the consideration, as Kant did not, that they are so because of the 'open possibility' that they originate in

> a supreme and absolute reason into likeness with which I have to grow, but which remains always beyond me . . . Only by some such conception do we escape the intolerable dualism of Kant's account of man's nature as compounded of a rationality which is already full-grown and perfect, and an animality which never grows into anything better at all.[76]

Here we have the ground of Taylor's teleology (which becomes an eschatology) and supernaturalism (which, in one form, becomes a pneumatology). While Kant is applauded for maintaining the dualism of humanity as natural phenomenon and as supernatural reality, on the ground that 'To deny the reality of this antithesis is to eviscerate morality',[77] Taylor regretted that this insight did not serve as a corrective to Kant's method. For Kant unwarrantably requires our consciousness of moral obligation to bear the entire weight of the theistic proposal, whereas Taylor regards it as one strand in the argument, to be supplemented by cosmological/teleological and experiential considerations: '[W]e need to integrate Bonaventura and Thomas and Butler with Kant to appreciate the real strength of the believer's position.'[78] Not, indeed, that the cumulative approach will ever yield demonstrative certainty of God's existence: a commitment of faith will ever be required.[79] We may further note that while Kant rightly defended the objectivity of ethics, Taylor takes much more account of the reality of self-surrender and moral struggle, which are the stuff of life as it is lived.[80]

Morality is thus a prominent factor in prompting Taylor's faith (mark the word) that humanity cannot be its own ultimate source (hence his anti-naturalism), and that the good is freely to be sought after (hence his anti-determinism):

> [T]here is much in human life, including all the thoughts which have inspired religion in all its forms, which must be dismissed unexamined

as mere illusion if our interior life is to be made part of the natural order pure and simple. I do most earnestly protest that it is intolerable assumption in a moralist to assume *ab initio* that there are not influences at work in man's soul (the free grace of God, grace given in response to the prayer of faith . . .) of which, from the nature of the case, scientific determinism can take no account.

Such an Indeterminism as I would advocate naturally does not simply *assume* that these influences from beyond 'nature' are real. On that question the last word must remain with those who have received the gifts, and it is, no doubt, a logical *possibility* that the class of 'recipients of grace' is empty. But Indeterminism, unlike Determinism, is not wedded to the view that the natural order is the only order there is.[81]

Thus is underscored Taylor's view that the human being is not his or her own ultimate source: 'Only to a being who has in his structure the adaptation to the eternal can you significantly say "You ought".'[82] We are being transformed into 'the likeness of that which we contemplate',[83] and God, the 'concrete unity of all good',[84] is the one to whom we aspire. If we ask 'What kind of God?' doctrine hovers close.

So it does in Illingworth's account of ethics. Indeed, to him doctrine and ethics are well-nigh inseparable. He does not, in fact, produce a system of ethics; rather, he reflects upon the moral life from a theological standpoint. Furthermore, there is a pastoral-cum-experiential motif running through Illingworth's work which makes him the most alive of all our idealists to the personal tragedy of the rupture of relations with God and the alienation from him in which sinful humanity is involved. To him, therefore, I shall (apart from passing references) return when, at the end of this chapter, I consider the supreme challenge to idealism which is posed by that complex of problems which goes under the name of the problem of evil. For the present we must consider the bridge from the ethical to the social which, to differing degrees, all our idealists were eager to erect.

II

A. E. Taylor's successor at Edinburgh, John Macmurray, stood at a considerable remove from his predecessor, though both were

Christians. Macmurray defines an idealist religion as being concerned with the spiritual life and not with the material, and as holding that 'the life of the spirit can be achieved only at the expense of the material life.'[85] On this ground he faults Plato, and especially neo-Platonism which has had, he feels, a disastrous impact upon Christianity:

> Religion is concerned in its reality with two things – with action and with community. Idealism seeks to escape from action into meditation; and from the tensions of life in common into the solitariness of one's own spirit.[86]

Indeed in the sentence immediately preceding the two just quoted he declares, 'I have grave doubts . . . whether idealism, in any form, is compatible with religion.'[87] I am not here concerned with the justice or otherwise of Macmurray's rebuke of neo-Platonism; but in adding the words 'in any form' he does seem to slight the more activist of those post-Hegelian idealists who are our present concern.

In this respect Caird was typical of them all. While finding that the mystical language of self-renunciation was in order within its own sphere, he regretted that it was not usually 'brought down to the region of the ordinary understanding . . .' Hegel is commended for having brought the two realms together. Accordingly, Jesus' saying concerning 'dying to live' is not to be construed as if the living were reserved for the next life, but with reference to life in the present.[88] In connection with the religion of Jesus he further wrote,

> I hesitate . . . to introduce the names of philosophic schools, for they are apt to bring with them confusing associations: otherwise I should be inclined to say that Jesus was the most consistent of all idealists, – one who worked out his idealism not in abstract theory, but by the unflinching application of a spiritual measure alike to the simplest and to the most mysterious facts of our existence.[89]

Consistently with this, albeit in the more familiar context of a personal letter, Green writes, 'True citizenship "as unto the Lord" (which includes all morality) I reckon higher than "saintliness" in the technical sense.'[90] Webb justly remarks that the post-Hegelian idealists were above all things concerned to find within *this* world, within the life of the family, of the State, of secular civilization, those religious values which had so often been thought of as belonging to another world than this . . .[91]

Caird may here be summoned in evidence:

[T]he Christian must not live mainly for another world, and seek to reach purity by escaping from earthly interests and affections; [for] the way to salvation here and hereafter lies in a deeper understanding of the wonderful world in which we are placed, and a higher conception of all the ties, material and spiritual, that bind us to our fellow men.[92]

Against Macmurray, it is scarcely an exaggeration to say that the more monistic their tendencies, the more eager the idealists were to realize in the world around them the all-embracing harmony they proclaimed.[93] Caird thus testifies:

As it is a condition of our intellectual life that we exist for ourselves only as other things and beings exist for us, so it is a condition of our practical life that we can realise ourselves or live for ourselves only as we live for other ends and beings than ourselves.[94]

My point is not to raise again the problematic nature of the ontological claim here made, or the question of the viability of self-realization as an ethical goal. I simply wish to show that, however inadequate its piers, this was the bridge over which our seven idealists proceeded to their social concerns. The inherent spiritual thrust was their bulwark against naturalism and materialism; their heritage of socially concerned evangelicalism motivated a Green and a Jones, however much their doctrinal reductionism might have distressed a Nicene Anglican or a Westminster Presbyterian. These factors facilitated and motivated their self-sacrificial altruism – something which their idealism, strictly construed, would have denied, its concern being only the enlightened self-interest of the rational individual.

Where Green is concerned, we find that he not only crosses the bridge from the ethical to the social, but that there is within himself, so to speak, a bridge to be crossed. For when we were discussing the main thrust of his ethics we found him in accord with Kant that virtue is the highest good. Where matters social are concerned, however, he is much more the Hegelian in holding that morality is inherently social, and that we cannot seek anything for ourselves without at the same time seeking it for society.[95] As he writes, a person 'cannot contemplate himself as in a better state, or on the way to the best, without contemplating others, not merely as means to that better state, but as sharing it with him'.[96] Since society is 'the condition of all development of our personality',[97] we may say that apart from their social relationships individuals could not be what they are.[98] Society is founded upon the unity of self-consciousness,[99] and of this foundation the eternal spirit is the originator and the guarantor. Moreover,

> There is no clearer ordinance of that supreme reason, often dark to us, which governs the course of man's affairs, than that no body of men should in the long run be able to strengthen itself at the cost of others' weakness.[100]

Here is the check upon self-realization narrowly construed which, as we saw, was the concern of some critics of Green's ethics. Here also, in the reference to the supreme reason, is the beginning of the bridge from socio-ethical to doctrinal considerations.

Among more recent commentators, Vincent has done well to observe that a reading of Green's sermons makes plain the influence of the Pauline 'dying to live' motif upon his ethical thought.[101] (Caird concurs, as we saw.) It is not that Paul sits lightly to the Cross and Resurrection as historical events, but

> his attitude towards them was not that of a man believing certain events to have happened upon evidence. He seemed to himself to die daily and rise again with Christ, and it was this moral and personal experience that gave reality in his eyes to the supposed historical events . . .[102]

Vincent properly remarks that Green's greatest indebtedness to Baur is in this view that 'Christ is the eternal act of God perpetually reenacted in man.'[103] Such a view, as we shall see later, can all too easily tend towards an 'automaticism' which minimizes both the historic Cross and the tragedy of sin.

I earlier cast doubt upon the suggestion that Green's ethics could have survived apart from his metaphysics. It is in my view more certain that his Kantian-cum-Hegelian social theory could have survived without his Pauline 'dying to live' motif. At the very least it must be admitted that the joins in his theory show. It is not made clear how 'dying to live' is integral to the idea of the social good which I have just outlined; and it is quite certain that while 'dying to live' may be a most attractive religious theme to a philosopher not uninfluenced by Hegel's developmental immanentism, a more Johannine approach emphasizing the 'eleventh commandment' – 'Love as I have loved you' – would have focused attention much more directly upon the manner, cost and results of Christ's love: in a word, upon the historically anchored Cross–Resurrection event; and also upon our inability unaided to obey, with all that that entails concerning grace and pneumatology. This is not to deny that the Johannine theme of 'abiding in Christ' could also be put to good Hegelian use; it is simply to suggest that 'By their texts ye shall know them.'

The importance of the social dimension was willingly conceded, at least in general terms, by all of our idealists. We find Illingworth observing that 'a person has two aspects, the one individual and the other social, and his true life involves the development of both.'[104] Against John Stuart Mill's individualism Pringle-Pattison declares that

> the human being nowhere exists . . . he is, indeed, unthinkable – save as a member of some society, whose laws and customs have entered into his very being, making him the manner of man he is.[105]

And Clement Webb, following Plato's *Republic*, averred:

> the structure of the individual soul is repeated in that of society, and . . . the individual soul first learns what its own structure is as writ large in the community.[106]

None was more adamant on the point, however, than Henry Jones. In his early paper on 'The social organism', which he contributed to the memorial volume to Green, *Essays in Philosophical Criticism*,[107] he rejoices that 'English ethical philosophy is no longer purely individualistic . . . Modern speculation . . . endeavours to . . . fit the individual into his surroundings',[108] and insists against Herbert Spencer that the relation of the parts to the whole in a socio-spiritual society such as he envisages exceeds in concreteness that of any allegedly autonomous physical organism. To Jones,

> The real meaning of the doctrine that society is an organism is, that an

individual has no life except that which is social, and that he cannot realise his own purposes except in realising the larger purposes of society . . . The social organism is . . . a concrete, living, self-integrating, self-differentiating whole, apart from which neither the universal – the abstract society, nor the particular – the abstract individual, can be . . . They exist in and through each other, and are constituted by their relation.[109]

A quarter of a century on, Jones underlined his conviction regarding 'the practical validity of [the] conception of the mutual implication of man with mankind';[110] a decade later we find him warning that citizenship is vitiated if we ignore the truth that 'individuality is to be measured by its comprehensiveness.'[111] Indeed, apart from society, he continues, there is no such thing as an individual self, for selves are inherently social.[112]

In an interesting (some might say, an elusive or self-contradictory) way, Jones occasionally goes further than Kant, only to step back towards him once again. Thus, against the sceptic he contends that 'to show that there are no obligations, is to show that there is no human society, which is just a system of obligations.'[113] Hence, '[A]ll moral questions for the individual . . . are social questions. The bad man cannot help being a public calamity, and the good man . . . cannot help being the stay and strength of his people.'[114] At this point Jones's thought is much more socially orientated than is Kant's. However, three pages later he seems to revert to Kant:

> The recognition of mutual obligation is not adequate, and the obligation itself is not completely binding until it is known to be self-imposed; and it is genuinely self-imposed only when the agent recognizes it as *his own good*.[115]

We may ask: (a) Is Jones not in danger of espousing the very individualism which he elsewhere finds deficient ('The simple creed of Individualism . . . will no longer work')[116]? (b) How does a self-imposed obligation square with Jones's notion of the divine being whose nature is love? The latter question is thrown into relief when we are informed that a person's 'obligations to society are as sacred as his obligations to himself'.[117]

Sentiments of the kind expressed in the remark just quoted were seen by some as conducing to the worship of humanity – of human society – as such. Hence Taylor's caution that the virtues which ennoble human life 'are all to be found at their best only where human society is not made the *principal* end and the supreme object of loyalty'.[118] Humanity, he continues, is best served by those whose supreme loyalty is to something more august and worthy than humanity as such. On this point the early and the later Taylor are agreed. In *The Problem of Conduct* he argued (a) that for the ideal of the perfect society to serve as an ultimately consistent moral end, it must be capable of being realized; (b) that if it were realized and all our aspirations were fulfilled, we should no longer be ethical beings; and (c) that since the perfect society is unrealizable, it can be no more than 'a useful but ultimately illusory ideal'.[119] Thirty years on, we find Taylor inveighing against 'vulgar Utopias', and declaring that

> The merely 'natural' man has only the choice, at best, between satiety and disappointment. To achieve felicity, one must first learn to set one's heart on a good which can neither cloy nor be taken from one . . .[120]

A further frequently reiterated charge levelled against the idealists was that however compelling the vision for society as a whole, on the empirical details concerning what was to be done to ameliorate this political state of affairs or to solve that social problem, the idealists were often unhelpfully vague. Thus A. C. Ewing noted that reference to the conception of the organic whole does not by itself assist us to know how the principle is to be applied in practice, and he implies that even advocates of coherence may legitimately be asked 'What, precisely, is to be done?'[121] John Macmurray went so far as to say that 'Idealist religion makes the realization of community impossible by its preoccupation with the idea of a universal community and of its realization.'[122] With special reference to Jones, J. B. Baillie thought that far too much was built upon the spiritual unity of opposites – a unity which was, on Jones's own admission, but a hypothesis.[123]

As with ethics, so with the social thought of the idealists: at certain points doctrine hovers close. It is frequently not clearly articulated, however, and, as with the 'dying to live' motif, the doctrinal references are highly selective. As I have pondered the social thought of my seven idealists, the most surprising omission I have detected is that of the concept of the Kingdom of God. For they were writing in the heyday of the Social Gospel, and at a time when some enthusiastic hymn-writers were exhorting worshippers actually to bring in the Kingdom (the fact notwithstanding that it is God's gift). It is true that in one of his oratorical flourishes Jones testifies that society is 'the kingdom of heaven upon earth where all are kings because all are subjects',[124] but this, quite apart from the fact that it appears to overlook society's less desirable characteristics, seems far removed from a theological affirmation of God's kingly rule. Perhaps this silence lends credence to those critics who complained that the idealists inadequately traced the inferential path from their vision of society as a realized whole to the specific obligations, the meeting of which would lead to that realization. If this is the case, the worthy social endeavours of a Green, a Caird and a Jones, which were undertaken in response to sometimes dire empirical conditions, were no doubt inspired by their vision, but not directed specifically by it. In a word, and to some extent against their theory, they were more in the tradition of nineteenth-century *individualist* philanthropy than of ethical communitarianism. Not insignificantly, we shall later discover that their ecclesiological sense was less than robust. For the present I turn to the bridge from ethico-social matters to doctrinal.

III

The seven idealists with whom we are primarily concerned did not propound a theological ethical-*cum*-social theory as such, but they alluded to, and invoked, theological considerations as appropriate. This, however, raises the question of the nature and soundness of the bridge between ethico-social thought and Christian doctrine. What is the relation between religion and morals? Does and can philosophical idealism accommodate all that it may be necessary to say concerning God's holiness and human sin?

To begin on a unanimous note, the seven idealists are in no doubt that religious faith has moral implications. Webb expressed this as clearly as any and, indeed, his conviction on the matter is emphasized by the fact that in a later work he quotes directly from an earlier thus:

> It is Religion – that is, the experience in which the soul is aware of itself as one or as capable of being one with the heart of Reality – which guarantees what we perceive of Beauty and of Goodness alike as no

merely subjective or superficial appearances, but as intimations of the ultimate nature of that Reality whose essential attributes are manifested therein. Not only does Religion in this way guarantee Art and Morality as laying hold of Reality, but also, by its interpretation of both as witnesses to different attributes of one Reality it secures each against the dangers which threaten it from its complete separation from the other. The selfishness and cruelty which sometimes attend upon one-sided aestheticism lose their inspiration when those elements of value in the world to which the sense of Beauty testifies are held to be secure in God, although certain modes of their expression are found to be incompatible with Duty. And that censoriousness of a one-sided moralism, which is constantly imposing limits upon artistic expression . . . is corrected by the faith which, even in denying the legitimacy of certain modes of artistic expression, affirms that that which they fain would express is, so far as it is beautiful, also divine, and, even though it remain here and thus unexpressed, eternally secure in God.[125]

Again, in more personal terms he writes,

I could not be a Christian if I did not regard Christianity as providing, so to say, a focus from which objects which meet the eye of the explorer of the field of ethics may be seen in their right proportions; yet I neither suppose that all ethical knowledge is historically derived from Christianity, nor yet that historical Christianity has done equal justice to all the ethical principles which it has acknowledged; nor yet that Christianity has nothing to learn in this or other fields from other religions, which have served to convey to the souls which have devoutly practised them a genuine revelation of that divine love and goodness whereof Christ is to me . . . the highest manifestation.[126]

Taylor is equally convinced that to suppose that our moral, aesthetic and religious being throws no light at all upon the nature of reality is to fall prey to an arbitrary assumption,[127] and of all our idealists he had most to say concerning the vision of God, 'from whom what I shall be must come'.[128] So much for the illumination of morality by religion.

Matters are more complicated, however, when we turn to the question of the precise relations between ethics and religion. As we have seen, Kant profoundly influenced the idealists and, as Webb rightly observed, Kant's attitude towards the moral law was deeply religious.[129] But the idealists seem to oscillate between holding that the religious is given in and with the moral and that the two are thus inseparable, and contending that for the good of both a distinction between morality and religion must be maintained. As we might expect, the more influenced by absolutism they are, the less rigorous their assertion of the distinction. Green, for example, declares that

> It is our very familiarity with God's expression of himself in the institutions of society, in the moral law, in the language and inner life of christians, in our own consciences, that helps to blind us to

God's revelation in all of this.[130] In a private letter he is still more direct:

> A morality that reflects on itself must needs refer itself to God, i.e., be religious. If there seems now to be a reflective morality, which yet is not religious, this is not really unreligious, but its religion is for the time dumb . . .[131]

Pringle-Pattison is more cautious in not proceeding so readily from value and teleology to a theistic mode of expression:

> Every idealistic theory of the world has for its ultimate premiss a logically unsupported judgment of value – a judgment which affirms an end of intrinsic worth, and accepts thereby a standard of unconditional obligation.[132]

For his part Jones oscillates rhetorically. In one place he asks a question expecting an affirmative answer:

> Do [religion and morality], at their best, pass into each other; or, as we have hinted, is there a difference between them that, while leaving them both necessary to man, still holds them apart, complementary perhaps in practice but . . . not reducible to sameness . . . ?[133]

Elsewhere he speaks of 'that region where morality and religion merge in one another; and man finds *himself* in God.'[134]

From most of our idealists we are divided by the advent on the ethical scene of a highly articulate secular humanism, and by the positivistic onslaught upon metaphysics which found its ethical form in the emotivism of C. L. Stevenson and others; and those of our seven philosophers (Webb and Taylor) who lived into the period to which I refer did not critically engage the then newer approaches. No matter what our judgement upon secularist and emotivist ethics may be, it cannot be denied that the entire complex of theories which travel under those names has made it much more difficult to sustain Green's confidence that an ethically reflective person will reach religious conclusions as to his moral foundations; and Jones's oscillations are now less intellectually tolerable than once they seemed to some to be. It may well be – and, indeed, this is my own position – that while the Christian Gospel has the most profound ethical implications, we cannot with integrity deny moral insight and worth to the non-religious who yet lead exemplary lives, for this, apart from slighting those concerned, would be to deny the providence of God, the non-ecclesiastically-confined work of the Spirit, and humanity's creation in the image of God; neither can we with integrity muse to ourselves – still less advise them – that they are, if only they knew it, crypto-Christians.[135] In other words, whereas Christian faith is ethically conditioned, morality as such is not religiously conditioned. This is by no means to deny that there is a considerable amount of ethical common ground as between Christians and others, and this must be capitalized upon in manifold practical ways. But where fundamental motivation (in the Christian's case the response of faith and gratitude for God's love in Christ) and power to act (the new life in Christ, the work of the Holy Spirit) are concerned, the Christian *account of* what is occurring in ethical activity, while it will overlap with that of the secular humanist (the desire for the good of others; the concern to do one's duty), will by no means be identical with it.[136]

We are now in a position to ask why it is necessary that the ethics–religion distinction be maintained. As has just been suggested, the religious may not deprive the non-religious of the entire field of ethics! But failure to observe the distinction would not only adversely affect the non-religious; it would vitiate theology and religion alike. In the first place, it has too often been supposed, not least by some Christians, that Christianity is simply a way of life in the sense of a collection of noble, uplifting, challenging ethical teachings. No doubt Christianity is a way; but it is a way into which one is drawn by grace, and which entails discipleship founded upon a new relationship initiated by the Father, effected by the Son and communicated by the Spirit. It is far from being exclusively a matter of code-following. Accordingly, to present it as such is to leave on one side a large slice of Christian experience which has been processed through the centuries in the form of doctrine. For this reason Illingworth opened his book on *Christian Character* with these words:

> The Christian life presupposes the Christian religion. When, therefore, we speak of Christian ethics, we do not mean a series of precepts, or a course of conduct which may be adopted by the adherents of any other creed, but the life which is the practical outcome of belief in the Incarnation, and which it was the object of the Incarnation to introduce into the world.[137]

For all the value of his insight concerning the categorical obligatoriness of the moral law and of the impossibility of pleasing God by ceremonial or emotional means apart from it, Webb was convinced that Kant had seriously erred in not seeing that although the connection between morality and religion is close, 'there is in Religion something besides Morality, which is distinct from Morality and independent of it.'[138] In particular, there is the experience of personal relationship with the One conceived to be the ultimate reality. Kant was barred from giving due weight to this characteristic of religion by his epistemology which confined knowledge to the phenomenal realm. Moreover,

> Any attempt to make Morality depend upon Religion which rests the obligation to do right upon what has often been called a 'religious sanction' – on a command of God, obedience to which is enforced by promises or threats, rewards or punishments – as much violates the essential nature of Morality as the Utilitarian view which rests it upon the tendency of right action to produce pleasure; and indeed comes in the long run to the same thing.[139]

With the reference to rewards and punishments we come to a further discontinuity between morality and Christianity, for whereas in the former we should not be surprised to find a theory according to which rewards and punishments were deemed to follow upon good or bad actions respectively, where Christianity is concerned, any reward is of grace, is un-earnable ('The idea of merit is foreign to the genuinely moral consciousness')[140] and, what is more, it is not necessarily immediate. That is to say, the performance of right actions by religious persons has frequently been followed by pain and rejection, not by happiness and pleasure. To this the Cross bears the supreme witness.

Above all, Christianity is grounded upon an existential fact which bears supreme value. Otherwise the Christian religion, entailing as it does worship and adoration, is vitiated. Taylor insisted upon this point:

> The possibility of genuine worship and religion is absolutely bound up with a final coincidence of existence and value in an object which is at once the most *real* of beings and the good . . .[141]

While both philosophy and religion may offer a view of the world, the central characteristic of religion, Webb agreed, is worship – 'our natural need of which cannot be satisfied by Philosophy apart from Religion'.[142] Before God, however, we are the abased before the holy; a radical re-centring of our personality is required: an ethical religion is a religion for those whom William James called the 'twice born'.[143] Such a religion's God is not creator only, but redeemer and sanctifier.[144]

It is precisely these ideas which are at risk in the writings of some of our idealists. Pringle-Pattison, for example, begins a sentence thus: 'But if it is in the needs of the moral life that we find our deepest principle of explanation . . .',[145] and he believes that it is so. This, however, is to beg a huge question: may not the holy, as Taylor suggests, radically transform our understanding of the moral?

> If we reflect carefully upon what happens in our minds when we are in a specifically *reverent* mood [writes Pringle-Pattison's pupil H. R. Mackintosh], we can make out that reverence is not compounded merely of things like gratitude, trust, love, or confidence; for all these we might feel towards an exceptionally good man. There is something over and above; there is an awareness of the Holy One. To use a natural expression, we are 'solemnized'.[146]

Among the products of this solemnization is the recognition that our status is not so much that of defaulters before the law as sinners before the holy One. We see, in the words of Illingworth, that 'Sin is the disease that is killing us, and it must be removed before we can live.'[147] But when he proceeds to write, 'Hence the primary place which is occupied in Christian ethics by the consideration of sin. It must come first. Everything else must be postponed to it',[148] I can only dissent. The first thing in Christian ethics as in theology is holy love; and it is only when we stand in the presence of holy love that we begin to see what sin is.

It is not without significance that of our idealists it is

Illingworth, the most theological of them, and Webb and Taylor, the least Hegelian and the most intellectually eclectic of them, who see most clearly the tragic nature of the fact of sin and the necessity of atonement. Are others prohibited from this insight by their 'purer' idealisms? If we juxtapose two quotations – the first from Caird, the second from P. T. Forsyth – the question will be thrown into relief:

> If there is no warrant for the Christian faith which finds God in man, and man in God, which makes us regard the Absolute Being as finding his best name and definition in what we most reverence and love; or, what is the same thing from the other side, makes us see in that growing idea of moral perfection, which is the highest result of human development, the interpretation or revelation of the Absolute; then we must give up the hope of a revival of religion . . .[149]

> A God supremely immanent has no . . . freedom, independence, holiness, or absolute initiative. He is acted on by the world. His relation to it is not free, He has no self-revelation. He really has no ethic. And it is easy thus to see how those who are engrossed with the idea of God's immanence should sink in their ethic. They have little use or affinity for the fundamental moral idea of God's holiness. They have no response to its actions as grace, or its conditions of judgment. They not only do not find such a thing as atonement to be a central principle of the moral life, but they must think it quite otiose or even mischievous to their conception of a God who is but immanent love and commingled identity. For want of the dualism that a holy love implies, their moral world flattens, and the moral practice of their successors must succumb.[150]

In a most pointed way these two quotations bring us to the crucial issue in our entire discussion of philosophical idealism *vis-à-vis* Christian belief. We are here in the midst of something which was at the time far more than a local squall. From North America the idealist Josiah Royce announced, '[T]his very presence of ill in the temporal order is the condition of the perfection of the eternal order.'[151] From Scotland came the curt retort of James Orr, Caird's favourite pupil at Glasgow: 'Sin is that which ought not to be *at all*.'[152] H. R. Mackintosh declared that 'the most complete of Absolutism's failures' was 'its sophistical manipulation of moral evil';[153] and James Iverach was no less affronted by idealism's weakness on this matter:

Any philosophy which obliterates moral values, and which apologizes for ugliness, evil and sin, and makes these to be essential to the perfection of the eternal order, is under the necessity of revising its procedure, and of bringing its conclusions into something like harmony with the moral convictions and aspirations of mankind.[154]

The urgency in the remarks of the theologians just quoted arises from their conviction that if sin is not a most serious affront to God's holiness and repudiation of his love, but is, rather, an unfortunate blemish upon humanity's condition which is in process of eradication; if, still worse, evil is somehow required in order that good may come, the heart of the Christian Gospel is removed, and any understanding of the work of Christ is unlikely to rise above the idea of Christ as one who by his suffering sets us an example to follow (if we can); or as one who is the paradigm case of the ultimate triumph of good over evil. But this is to anticipate the next chapter. Let us for the moment take soundings in the writings of our seven idealists on sin and evil. The objective is to indicate their general approach with a view to illustrating the attenuation to which attention has now been drawn.

As we have seen, T. H. Green had a good deal more to say about Paul than about the synoptic gospels; and even the most cursory expositor of Paul cannot avoid the concept of sin. But Green's exposition is, not surprisingly, shaped by his conviction that morality is at the foundation of the historical process, and that the eternal self-consciousness is ever active and advancing towards complete realization in the moral life of the individual. Green does not deny the reality of evil, and in his social philosophy and practice he sought to combat it in a variety of ways. But far from taking a radical view of evil as sin against a holy God requiring a God-initiated atonement, he considers that the relations of good and evil will inevitably be adjusted appropriately in the end. His doctrinal attenuation emerges in his various definitions of 'sin'. Sin 'consists in the individual's making his own self his object';[155] 'the sin of humanity means its incompleteness, and is in perpetual process of disappearing . . .';[156] 'the sense of Sin is very much an illusion. People are not as bad as they fancy themselves.'[157] In mingled puzzlement and dismay Robert Mackintosh lamented that Green refuses to recognise that sin is an abnormal condition requiring exceptional remedies. Indeed, for so good a man, Mr Green has a singularly dull sense of sin. No awakened conscience could tolerate the doctrine that 'forgiveness *is the moral act of putting off the old man*'.[158]

J. S. Mackenzie fully granted that the fact of evil presented idealism with a serious problem – indeed, he thought it was the only serious problem to be met by that philosophical system.[159] In concluding that 'the only possible way of meeting it is by saying that what presents itself to us as evil is somehow a necessary condition of what is, in the ultimate sense, good',[160] Mackenzie showed himself the true disciple of his teacher, Caird. Where Green's philosophical optimism resulted in an attenuated hamartiology, we might almost say that Caird was temperamentally unsuited to any kind of hamartiology. In sketching his life I drew attention to his non-pugilistic nature, and his way of looking for the best in people, ideas and circumstances. As Henry Jones wrote of him, 'If he could not find the germ of good in things evil, he not only turned away from them, but seemed to delete them.'[161] In a private letter Caird himself admitted, 'I sometimes feel as if I was callous, when I can absorb myself so completely in my work, and get too rapidly to the idealistic proof of good in evil.'[162] Two months earlier he had written to the same correspondent that the ideal which underlies our condemnation of evil and misery 'is the witness that evil is not the ultimate fact'.[163] Caird was not blind to the fact that 'there is a real battle between good and evil going on in the world',[164] but he held that

> The prayer, 'Father, forgive them, for they know not what they do', with its reduction of evil to ignorance, is perhaps the most victorious assertion of the relativity of evil that has ever been made.[165]

The development of human personality is under way, and although there is turmoil in the earliest stages of human existence, 'the turbidity of the waters only proves that the angel has come down to trouble them, and the important thing is that when so disturbed they have a healing virtue.'[166] In the mean time, while 'the sense of division of man from God' remains, 'it can no longer overpower the consciousness of oneness',[167] and the path ahead is that of self-sacrifice, 'dying to live'.[168]

All of which, as we may by now suspect, led some to charge

Caird with *religious* unreality. Among them was Pringle-Pattison's brother, James Seth:

> I cannot see how, on the unitary theory, evil is a necessary phase of the process of the good; how, in a universe such as Mr Caird's, the evil which is an indubitable fact of moral experience, should occur; how human sin can be a part or stage of the necessary process of the divine life; how this unreason should affect a universe which is rational through and through. The explanation offered may be satisfactory, as an explanation of how the knowledge of evil is instrumental to the life of goodness; but it is not satisfactory as an explanation of the existence of evil, it does not justify the occurrence of evil as a real fact in the universe.[169]

At the end of his review of Caird's *Essays* E. H. Blakeney utilized exotic and Gothic references to express his concern:

> [T]he Hegelian dialectic seems too easy. How will it explain that hardest of the riddles of the Sphinx – sin? Can it exorcise that grim phantom? Hegel, indeed, clearly recognises sin and its consequences; but his philosophy seems, in some ways, to give an inadequate *rationale* of its presence in a divinely-ordered universe.[170]

A. E. Garvie's rueful epitaph was, '[I]t was the fact of sin and its consequences which made me break away from the attractive Neo-Hegelianism of my loved and honoured teacher Edward Caird.'[171]

It will come as no surprise that the thought of defection never occurred to Henry Jones. If anything, he is more enthusiastic in his acknowledgement of the reality of evil than his teacher:

> Even if evil *is* evanescent, or is overcome, abolished, or turned into its opposite in a way which Good is not, it does not follow that it lacks reality in any sense or degree.[172]

Indeed, evil is positively useful. The possibility of moral evil is a necessary condition of the free moral growth and progress of human beings as they overcome evil and strive for the good. It 'is necessary as a condition of what is best'.[173] According to Jones, 'Where there is no real evil to resist – and not merely its barren possibility – there cannot be good.'[174] A world in which moral growth was not possible would not be a spiritual world at all. But if a spiritual world is the best of all possible worlds, 'then it justifies what is incidental to it.'[175]

For many, then as now, the questions will not so easily be silenced. Even if some moral victories are won through the conquest of evil, would it not have been better had there been no evil in the first place? How can we be sure that good will always – even usually – flow from evil? Is it not the case that while some have undoubtedly been ennobled by the challenge of suffering, many others have been embittered or stunted by it? Caird's fear that he may have been callous in reaching an optimistic view too easily did not, perhaps, haunt his Welsh pupil as much as it might have done.

Undeterred, Jones's optimism was as strong in his earliest papers as in his post-war Gifford Lectures. He was ever to the fore in condemning a shallow optimism. The result of a hedonistically based optimism is disappointment; true optimism grounds upon a supreme criterion of good which is not definable in terms of pleasure. As he viewed civilization on the day of his Glasgow Inaugural Lecture of 1894, he saw 'a larger hope and a surer promise', and was hopeful that 'man, as he grows morally better, may find means to make the world happier . . .'[176] This hopeful faith never left him, and he spoke of the moral life as 'a progressive attaining'.[177] Chastened by the hideousness of the First World War, Taylor's conclusion was quite otherwise:

> Our own experience of the life of Europe since the opening of the present century might, indeed, suggest an uneasy doubt whether the 'advance of civilisation' may not have been progressive only in the sense in which a physician speaks of a patient's progress towards dissolution or a moralist of the 'rake's' progress in debauchery.[178]

Real though evil is said to be, Jones is far from wishing to make God its author. God must not be made to 'participate in the evil doings of men and responsible for the inequalities under which they live and the injustice they suffer'.[179] A number of Jones's critics were rightly perplexed at this point. Given Jones's immanentism, his assertion of the fundamental unity of all things, how could God *not* be involved in evil if evil is, as Jones insists, a reality in the world? Hastings Rashdall, for example, who found more heat than light in Jones's *Idealism as a Practical Creed*, declared that

> The popular religious consciousness has never accepted Professor Jones's notion of a deity who includes in himself good and bad men

alike, to say nothing of devils and animals . . . or his theory that what appears to be evil in the universe is really good.[180]

Many theologians were not unduly keen on the notion either. With reference to the necessary dualism of the profane and the holy, Forsyth expostulated, '[W]e must have a Dualism with a unity of Reconciliation, and not a Monism with a unity of Identity as real in the sin as in the Saviour.'[181] The philosophical concern has more recently been posed by A. C. Ewing: '[I]t is difficult to see how perfection could be ascribed to a mind which really included in itself beings such as Nero or Caesar Borgia or, as far as that goes, myself.'[182] Jones did not demonstrate that what he said was so and, not insignificantly, he disarmingly acknowledged that he was proceeding from a 'fundamental assumption'.[183]

No doubt those who seek to adumbrate a view of the world cannot avoid a fundamental assumpton of some kind. Their critics then have the task of assessing how far the structure erected accords with reason and fact. Campbell Fraser, for example, did not hesitate to designate his starting-point a faith, but his faith prompted a significantly different conclusion from that of Jones and the absolutists. In his account of his teacher's philosophy Pringle-Pattison points out that Fraser reiterates the quotation *Omnia exeunt in mysteria*. Human experience is inherently mysterious and, conditioned by space and time as it is, thought is always left 'under a sense of intellectual incompleteness and dissatisfaction'.[184] Faith is Fraser's answer to this agnosticism and, as Pringle-Pattison says, this makes for a different temper as between his work and that of the absolutists. To Fraser mystery is inexpungible; where the absolutists are concerned 'the acknowledgment of an unexplained remainder of mystery appears to be wrung, as it were, unwillingly, under the pressure of controversy . . .'[185] Thus, while agreeing with Jones that the ideas of moral probation and education are important, and while affirming that moral beings 'must *be able to make themselves bad*',[186] Fraser's optimism makes room for a real difference between right and wrong, and upholds human responsibility to the full. Above all, like Orr, he insists that evil, far from being a stage on the way to good, ought not to exist.[187]

With his teacher's position Pringle-Pattison was in entire accord. Of Hegelian absolutism he wrote, '[T]he difficulties of such a system are always found in accounting for contingency, for imperfection, for suffering and evil.'[188] While not blind to the darker side of human nature, Hegel is the fountain-head of the modern view that evil is a stage on the way to good and this, as we have seen, raises the question of God's implication in it. Pringle-Pattison insists that

> belief in the relative independence of human personalities and belief in the existence of God as a living Being are bound up together. The reality of both God and man depends on the reality of the difference between them.[189]

The absolutists' difficulty is not, he is convinced, to be evaded by the introduction of a finite God, for this would be to fly in the face of our deepest convictions concerning God, who is and must be omnipotent in the sense of an 'all-compelling power of goodness and love to enlighten the grossest darkness and to melt the human heart'.[190] Omnipotent, atoning love is found 'unweariedly creating good out of evil'.[191]

Webb and Taylor were no less opposed to the notion of a finite God. The former concluded that the idea 'relieves God of the responsibility for the evil in the world only at the cost of depriving him of Godhead';[192] to Taylor the finite God was a *tertium quid* – neither God nor ourselves, at whose door the world's evil might be laid.[193]

However much Green, Caird, Jones and Pringle-Pattison may have drawn upon biblical motifs and theological insights – 'dying to live', 'good from evil' – they did not derive their hamartiology and theodicy directly from the holiness of God's love or the victory of the Cross–Resurrection. Webb, for example, regretted that Pringle-Patttison had not reflected more directly upon Christianity's traditional answer to the problem of evil.[194] What was his own position on the matter?

Webb takes the fact of sin with full seriousness. When older theologians spoke of original sin, and when Kant spoke of the radical propensity to evil in the will, they had the same phenomenon in mind. But Webb will not endorse the more recent interpretation of sin as being a defect surviving from a lower order of existence which is on the way to its final developmental purgation:

[I]t is extremely difficult not to regard the consciousness of sin as something very different from the consciousness of lower instincts surviving at a higher stage of development than that at which they were useful; the consciousness of sin is rather the consciousness of the voluntary surrender of oneself to such instincts where a different course of action was open.[195]

But he immediately proceeds to observe that for such voluntary actions 'sin' is not, strictly, the most appropriate word, for 'I do not . . . regard a propensity to evil whose origin is not traceable to my own individual will, as my own sin.'[196] Hence 'In the sense in which sin can only be individual, Original Sin is not sin.'[197] (Illingworth defined original sin as 'the solidarity of human nature viewed in its sinful aspect'.)[198] There is, Webb suggests, an environment of sin which drags us down, and an environment of grace to which religious people attribute their good actions. Citing Article IX of the Church of England, Webb affirms that the 'infection of nature doth remain, yea even in those that are regenerated', and observes, 'Both alike are present because [the religious person] *was* formerly something other than he now *is*. What he now is, he is by the grace of God.'[199]

Underlying Webb's entire philosophy, and not least his views concerning sin and evil, is his doctrine of personality. He does not deny that the concepts of probation, judgement, atonement, repentance, forgiveness may be construed in a non-personal context, but declares that 'they will gain infinitely in significance . . . when they are translated into the language of a personal relation to a Spirit wherein "we live and move and have our being" ',[200] and to whom, although ever distinguished from it, we are related by a voluntary act of self-surrender. Indeed,

the recognition of Personality in God harmonizes better than any other conception of the Supreme Reality with the experience for which the problem of Evil reveals itself in its acutest form, namely with the experience which may be described as that of 'conviction of Sin'.[201]

Again,

[T]o regard Sin as an offence against a personal authority, and still more to regard it as an affront to a loving Father, is a more intelligible and a more ethically significant way of thinking about it than it is to conceive it after the analogy of a physical defilement or an automatic mechanism.[202]

The restoration of broken divine–human relations is by the way of a divinely initiated atonement which is met by the sinner's repentance,[203] and which secures and ensures ultimate victory. Accordingly Webb quotes R. M. Benson with approval:

> God does not merely get out of evil by a wonderful device, leaving the evil as a thing that had better not have been. God comes to triumph over evil and therefore we must regard it not merely as antagonistic to God, but as subservient to him.[204]

The note of victory is present too in the writings of the later Taylor, and it strives to break through into the thought of Illingworth. Of Taylor we may fairly say that nowhere is the change between the earlier and the later seen more dramatically than in connection with the problem of evil. Consider the *volte-face* represented by the two following quotations from 1903 and 1930 respectively:

> [I]t clearly appears that the sense of fruitlessness and futility which is so characteristic of our moral life, is due less to the radical self-contradictoriness of the moral experience than to the want of a thorough-going organisation of the forces of society for moral purposes.[205]

> To be quite plain, in all moral advance the *ultimate* 'efficient cause' must be the real eternal source of both becoming and value. The initiative in the process of 'assimilation to God' must come from the side of the eternal; it must be God who first comes to meet us, and who, all through the moral life itself, 'works in us', in a sense which is more than metaphorical. Our moral endeavours must genuinely be ours, but they must be responses to intimate actual contacts in which a real God moves outward to meet His creatures, and by the contact at once sustains and inspires the appropriate response on the creature's part.[206]

While not doubting that morality can exist without religion, the later Taylor (and it is he with whom I am concerned henceforth in this chapter) finds Kant wanting in not realizing that religion, which entails the transcendence of the distinction between 'ought' and 'is', is the inspiration of what is best in morality. Moreover, that inspiration may enable the conversion of heavy afflictions into means of moral enrichment ('whom the Lord loveth, He chasteneth') – something for which there is no place in Kantian ethics.[207]

Against those who complain that theology has contaminated ethics with the notion of sin, Taylor contends that 'it is morality which has brought the notion into theology.'[208] For this reason he cannot be content with neo-Platonism which, with its doctrine of the inevitable rise of the soul and the obliteration of the distinction between humanity and divinity, leaves no room for a real fall and a real work of redemption.[209] He laments the absence of the sense of human sinfulness from the writings not only of Aristotle, Descartes, Spinoza, Leibniz, Hegel and Hume, but even from such champions of an 'eternal and immutable' morality as Cudworth, Clarke and Price.[210]

Taylor more than makes good the deficiency. In fact he is the most sombre analyst of sin and moral guilt of all of our seven idealists, maintaining that a properly ethical attitude towards sin entails the recognition that our guilt requires punishment; that we are polluted, and that it is really God against whom we have sinned.[211] All of which requires the practical remedy which, Taylor believes, Christianity provides. Christianity does not profess to explain or justify the existence of evil, or to provide a final account of how good may be derived from evil, but it shows us how to triumph over it. 'The "proof" of the love is the victory it inspires; if we reject that proof there is no other to be given.'[212]

To the challenge 'How can a good and loving God create a being who could sin?' Illingworth responds,

> [I]t is not in this abstract form that the Christian can view the problem. For he has his presuppositions – on the one hand all the evidence of beneficent design in creation, including the great argument from the beauty of the world; and on the other hand the Incarnation, with the ability that it has given men practically to overcome sin.[213]

We may nowadays feel less confidence in the teleological argument than did Illingworth, but in the second part of his statement he, albeit cryptically, anticipates Taylor by adverting to the practical and sufficient (if, *pace* Illingworth,[214] not completely speculatively satisfying) solution which Christianity supplies. Elsewhere he remarks that the human capacity willingly to choose moral evil is indicative of the divine self-limitation in creating finite free will.[215]

Of the seven idealists with whom we are concerned, Illingworth devoted the greatest attention to that aspect of the problem of evil which is summed up by the words 'pain' and 'suffering'. In the light of earlier comments upon Jones, we may not, however, find his exposition entirely satisfactory. '[P]ain,' he declares, 'makes men real. It indurates their character. It endows them with spiritual insight.'[216] (Does it always in fact, or necessarily in principle, do this?) He finds so many uses for pain in a sinful world, 'that it cannot be called, in any true sense of the world, evil'.[217] In such a world any inference drawn from the fact of pain is in favour of, rather than against, the love of God. As for animal pain, we are at a loss to understand their destiny and the final cause of their creation, and hence we have to be content in the knowledge that 'Pain, in the only region where we can test it, is not incompatible with love.'[218] I think that many theologians would now wish, in the light of the Cross, to say that while pain may not be incompatible with love, this does not permit the idea of its indefinite continuance on the grounds of its alleged usefulness. Rather, pain is among those phenomena from which redemption is needed, and in principle it has been vanquished once and for all. It would be much harder to justify Illingworth's view that 'So far from being our greatest enemy [pain] is our safest ally in the battle of life'[219] towards the end of the twentieth century than it was a decade from the end of the nineteenth. While, as Illingworth knew full well, we may have to walk the way of the Cross, this does not make pain a good. Nevertheless, he valued pain because

> It unites us to God because it purifies us, because it detaches us from earth, because it quickens our sense of dependence, because it opens our spiritual vision, and above all because He too, as man, has suffered.[220]

His writing at this point has the air of a confession of faith (there is, in any case, no guarantee that the things he specifies as happening will occur in the lives of those who have not first become believers), yet the note of victory is so strangely absent from it that I am reminded of Robert Mackintosh's judgement upon the atonement theory of another High Church Anglican, R. C. Moberly:

One feels as if one were worshipping in some thronged crypt, dark with stained glass, the air heavy with incense, where sacred rites are performed by an emaciated priest, who is bowed with sorrow almost to the ground. The whole scene is exquisitely beautiful, but crushing in its sadness. Then, as we close the High Church volume, and open the New Testament our eyes light upon such words as these: 'I write unto you, My little children, because your sins are forgiven you for His name's sake.' We are in fresh air! We are in the sunshine! We are in the presence of God, of a victorious Saviour! How much better God's sunshine is than the Church's crypt![221]

But I have already strayed into the field of Christian doctrine . . .

5

The Idealists and Christian Doctrine

We have already seen that the more absolutist of our seven idealists left us with both a doctrinal attenuation and a logical howler when they spoke as if 'spirit,' 'the Absolute,' 'God' were terms which, having the same connotation, were mutually interchangeable. We saw, further, that while the idealists asserted the need to maintain both the transcendence and immanence of God, their metaphysical immanentism unduly slanted their endeavours, while their less than full-blooded understanding of sin (partly consequent upon a lack of emphasis upon God's love as holy), coupled with their optimistic view of humanity was not calculated to redress the balance. On the contrary, and notwithstanding their acknowledgement of its importance, the Creator–creature distinction was seen to be at risk in their writings.

From time to time we have found the idealists articulating orthodox-sounding convictions which do not, however, sit comfortably with their underlying metaphysical presuppositions. It is as if, having begun elsewhere, they subsequently wish to import considerations deriving from their religious experience, or to give weight to religious convictions reached by a route which is at most tangential to their metaphysical starting-point; and this would seem to apply regardless of the Kantian–Hegelian proportions of their work.

I have observed that Webb and Taylor are most alive to the perils thus enumerated and, significantly, their philosophical positions are the most eclectic among our seven and, indeed, are the most recent. Not that eclecticism necessarily makes for a secure philosophical resting-place; but it does imply that the facts and/or experiences to be accommodated cannot adequately be marshalled under the rubrics of a narrower idealism, however internally coherent it may have been. This consideration will come to the fore when we seek to take with due seriousness the rootedness of the Christian Gospel in history. Webb and Taylor wished to do this but, as we shall see, despite his theological sensitivity and his suggestion that in the doctrines of the Trinity and the Incarnation we have the key to the harmonization of transcendence and immanence, the natural and the supernatural, Illingworth, no less than Green, Caird and Jones, tends to leave us with an idealized Christianity.

Towards the end of the preceding chapter we noted the less than radical view of sin and evil entertained by some of our idealists, and their optimistic view of humanity. These strands of thought, when coupled with the evolutionary and developmental motifs which were so powerfully present in the air they breathed, and with hostility towards a penal substitutionary theory of the atonement which Caird, for example, came to regard as immoral, influenced them against a radical atonement, and led them towards inadequate Christologies, minimal ecclesiologies, and truncated views of immortality. I shall now attempt to justify these serious charges and then, in a conclusion, I shall summarize my findings and indicate the continuing importance of the methodological question which underlies this entire study.

I

To pose the crucial question bluntly: can philosophical idealism accommodate the notion of a divinely initiated atoning act wrought in the midst of human history by one who is God incarnate?

Consider this view of Green's:

> God is identical with the self of every man in the sense of being the realisation of its determinate possibilities . . . in being conscious of himself man is conscious of God, and thus knows that God is, but knows what he is only so far as he knows what he himself really is.[1]

We may now leave on one side the consideration that this formulation suggests 'pantheizing tendencies'. More important for our present purpose is the underlying idea of progress, and the analysis of the penultimate word, 'really'. Presumably Green intends us to understand that we know ourselves as we really are when we see ourselves in God, and that our progression through life is towards the realization of this knowledge. Such a view would harmonize with the evolutionary intellectual tendencies of Green's day; it might even be said to recapitulate an Irenaean view of humanity, or to be compatible with the idea of deification. But what if we 'really' are not what we ideally may become, but sinners? What if 'The soul needs not a development from within, but a rescue from without . . .'?[2] Less dramatically, though prompted by a similar concern, W. L. Walker commented directly upon Green thus:

> It is true that, as Mr T. H. Green has said, 'It is the God in you which strives for communication with God.' But in us alas! the spirit is 'weak through the flesh' . . . [T]hough 'the spirit may be willing the flesh is weak', yea, sadly weak.[3]

To Henry Jones the invocation of the category of self-consciousness alone permits a satisfactory account of the nature of humanity; certainly, the physical and biological sciences are quite unable to account fully for humanity.[4] Further, he considers that as between the naturalistic or materialistic views of humanity and the spiritual there can be no commerce: a choice has to be made for 'It is gradually realised that both the natural and the spiritual method of explaining man claim him *as a whole*.'[5] If we opt for the spiritual account of humanity, then we will come to see that the human being's

> nature *is* a process. He is . . . moving from promise to fulfilment, in so far as he is true to himself. He is *becoming* free, and *acquiring* reason; and it is only because he can *become* that we can call him either free or rational.[6]

The human being is 'the infinite in process'.[7] But what if, with Forsyth, we believe that

> Any theology that places us in a spiritual *process*, or native movement between the finite and the infinite, depreciates the value of spiritual *act*, and thus makes us independent of the grace of God . . . If it speak of the grace of God it does not take it with moral seriousness.[8]

If we give due place to an atoning act of God (and I readily accept that there is a hornet's nest of linguistic analytical issues within that claim, and that these need to be teased out more thoroughly than has so far been done), we shall not be able to give wholehearted assent to Jones's claim that 'It is possible that religion is not so much an introduction of new facts as a new light upon the familiar facts of the previous secular life.'[9] No doubt those who become Christians frequently do view their previous life and the world around them in a new light; but this is because they are a 'new creation'.[10] The heart of the matter is not a new way of looking at things, but a new life. And even when Jones's teacher Caird posits the notion of 'dying to live' as fundamental to Christianity, and when Green speaks of 'the power of a present and spiritual resurrection', they do not relate it to the once-for-all Cross–Resurrection event in anything like the full-blooded Pauline way.[11] No doubt Christians are becoming what they are in Christ; but this becoming is the becoming of a redeemed humanity, not of an automatically progressive 'natural' humanity.

The reference to Caird returns us directly to his writings. To Mary Sarah Talbot he wrote,

> I have – as you know – the greatest reluctance to say anything that would annoy or perplex the good people, but I feel that the time has come for the old bottles to be broken, and that it is the new wine of Christianity itself that must break them, if Christianity and humanity are ever to be one.[12]

According to J. H. Muirhead, Caird's sermons 'showed how religious subjects could be treated without offending the conscience of any or remotely stirring the dregs of theological controversy'.[13] No doubt doctrine – particularly the doctrines of predestination and election and the penal substitutionary theory of the atonement – had from time to time been propounded in Scotland as elsewhere in ways calculated to offend (and there is a profound difference between the offence of the Cross and the offensiveness of preachers); certainly Scotland had experienced more than its fair share of theological and ecclesiastical controversy, and both the Caird brothers saw themselves as peacemakers.[14] Nevertheless Caird lends himself to characteristic idealist confusion in this remark culled from one of his sermons:

[T]he root of the matter lies in the spirit of Christ, and not in doctrines about Him; in the living realisation of the nearness of our finite life to the infinite, and not in the theological exactness of our creed . . .[15]

It is not necessary to assert the plenary inspiration of creeds and confessions, or to suggest that subscription to them is what saves, in order to observe that Caird's view that Christ imparts his spirit to believers is a doctrine about him as well as a believing testimony, and that Caird begs the question by asserting the spirit of Christ as the root of the matter. Suppose that redemption through atoning, victorious sacrifice is the heart of the matter? The point is underlined when Caird elsewhere writes that 'the essential lesson of the gospel of Jesus' is the 'union between the human and the divine'.[16] That this is a peculiarly Hegelian Jesus should by now be clear.

On this basis Caird announces the moral principle which, following Hegel, he deems to be central to Christianity, namely, the principle of self-realization through self-sacrifice.[17] I use the verb 'announces' advisedly, for Caird does not stay to defend this view (perhaps that might have landed him in controversy?), though it is not difficult to think of a number of alternative candidates for Christianity's central moral principle; and Caird's upbringing was permeated by one of them: 'Man's chief end is to glorify God, and to enjoy Him for ever.'[18] Be that as it may, what is important here is the way in which Caird's commitment to his principle leads him to attenuations of Christian teaching which can only be described as serious. The simplest way to illustrate this contention is to enter into dialogue with Caird, placing my own remarks within square brackets:

It is not, as St Paul represents it, that Christ dies to save us from death, as the penalty for sin: for he does *not* save us [What are the grounds of this observation which seems to run counter to Paul's teaching?]: it is that he makes death itself the greatest means of manifesting and realising the new principle of life [But is not the new life realized by and in the Spirit?], and enables us also to take death in the same way, and so to overcome its power [We overcome by virtue of Christ's victory, and not because we have learned the right way of regarding death] . . . In this way the resurrection of Christ becomes the pledge and proof that all who have his spirit will rise again: and that, not merely as the result of any arbitrary reward attached to their faith [Quite so, it is a natural consequence of it, and the faith itself is a gift, so that none may boast], but because they have the same seed of immortal life in them, and cannot be holden of death any more than he. [But for Paul this is our situation by grace and not by nature, and what Caird omits is any reference to the ground of the new life as being the atoning work of Christ at the Cross – and this in an exposition of Paul's thought. Can it be denied that Paul gloried not, indeed, in crucifixion, but in the Cross?][19]

It is not at all surprising that Caird's pupil, D. W. Forrest, with reference to Caird's extolling of the principle of dying to live and symbolized by Christ, expostulated,

[W]hat Christ reveals to us is not simply that self-sacrifice is the principle of all spiritual life, and therefore common to Him and to us, but that *He* realised it, and that *we* do not . . . As a mere example, He is no encouragement to us, for His moral experience has different conditions from ours.[20]

Clearly, behind Caird's principle of self-realization is his conviction that there is already and eternally continuity as between the human and the divine. What he wrote of his brother John is no less true of himself: '[H]e dwelt less upon doctrines about Christ, and more upon identification with him as a living person; less upon atonement by his death, and more and more upon unity with him.'[21] It would not be just, however, to suggest that Caird had nothing at all to say about the Cross, but in the following typical statement he seems so near and yet so far:

[T]he cross, combining as it did the loftiest and the lowest things of human existence, the deepest outward shame and the manifestation of the highest energy of spiritual life to which the soul of man can rise, was the appropriate, and, we might even say, the *necessary* symbol of a religion which, in breaking down all the walls of division between man and man, class and class, nation and nation, at the same time awoke man, in all the weakness of his finitude, to a consciousness of unity with God.[22]

It seems undeniable that the conclusion to be drawn from this is that humanity's fundamental problem is finitude rather than sin, and hence it is not surprising that there is no suggestion that anything radical had to be *done* at the Cross in respect both of that sin and of God's holiness; rather, the Cross remains a symbol of the eternal truth concerning life through death on the ground of the eternal God–humanity continuity. The moral gulf is not thereby bridged, it is bypassed. The affirmation that '[T]his belief, in the revelation of God in man, in itself constitutes the *articulus stantis vel cadentis ecclesiae*'[23] seems, by its (unacknowledged) quotation of Luther, to be a direct challenge to the heart of Luther's Gospel, namely, that justification is by grace through faith – and this on the ground of Christ's atoning work. And does not Caird offer a hostage to fortune when he writes, '[W]e should not gather from St Paul's Epistles that he knew anything, or cared to know anything, of the life of Christ, except that he suffered and died and rose again'?[24] To the extent that this is true (and Caird admits that it is an exaggeration) why did not Caird ask himself why this might be so? Had he done so, he might have ended with something a little more full-blooded than this:

> The death of Jesus was thus . . . the first clear demonstration that the idea of a Universal God which underlies all religion is not merely the abstract idea of an infinite Being in which everything finite is merged and lost, but that it is a productive principle which can restore out of itself all, and more than all, it seems to take away.[25]

Here immanence wins out over transcendent (albeit immanent) holiness, the divine–human continuity takes precedence over the moral gulf between Creator and creature, and the Cross remains a visual aid rather than the place where love is victorious and holiness vindicated. As Caird's pupil James Denney wrote, 'St Paul felt that the sin of the world made a difference to God; it was a sin against His righteousness, and His righteousness had to be vindicated against it.'[26] On the general tendency of some to identify the human with the divine life, Denney expostulated,

> One can only regret that this short and easy method was not discovered till the close of the nineteenth century; anything less like the terrible problem sin presented to the apostles, and their intense preoccupation with it, it would not be easy to conceive.[27]

On the monists in general Forsyth's sepulchral verdict was, 'For want of the dualism that a holy love implies, their moral world flattens, and the moral practice of their successors must succumb.'[28] On the other hand William James welcomed Caird's philosophy as giving 'a quasi-metaphysical backbone which [liberal] theology has always been in need of'.[29]

Be that as it may, the contrast between Caird and Illingworth, for example, on this matter is considerable. Illingworth writes,

> Christ came . . . essentially in order to work what, in the existing state of human society, would be a transcendent miracle by living and dying in perfectly sinless obedience to the will of God . . . He came to restore human nature to that harmony with the divine law, which had been broken by the unique miracle of sin . . . His purpose was to effect a complete reversal of what had come to be the normal state of things. This was the absolutely central and cardinal object of His advent . . .[30]

Another way of putting the point is to say that Caird leaves us with an exemplary Christ rather than with Christ the mediator. Webb made the point in his review of Caird's *The Evolution of Theology in the Greek Philosophers*:

> [N]either in the present series of Gifford Lectures nor in the earlier series on the *Evolution of Religion* does the Master of Balliol seem to us to have done full justice to the place of the Mediator in Christianity.[31]

Webb clearly expresses his positive view of the matter in one of his later writings:

> It is because man has separated himself from God by sin that he needs to be reconciled to him. It is because, to effect this reconciliation, Christ's body was broken and his blood shed upon the cross that man is spiritually nourished in the Eucharist by the life thus sacrificed. Nevertheless, it is difficult for a Christian to think of the cross of Christ as something the very existence of which is so wholly the consequence of sin that, in condemning the sin which gave occasion to his death thereon, one could say that one wished the Passion had not been . . . Instead of looking upon the cross merely as a remedy for sin, which it would have been better had it not been needed, the devout soul tends to see in the surpassing worth of the remedy the final cause of the permission of the sin, and to cry *O felix culpa, quae talem et tantum meruit habere Redemptorem!* When this stage is reached, the cross itself passes in some sense into the 'supralapsarian' sphere, and we remember that the seer of the Apocalypse speaks of the Lamb as 'slain from the foundation of the world'.[32]

With this testimony we come to the threshold of Christology. For if in Christ God has wrought redemption, who must Christ be? It is certainly the case that logically Christology takes precedence over soteriology: Christ can only do what he does because he is who he is. But in history and in the believer's experience we come to an understanding of who Christ is via what he has done. The apostles preached the Cross, not the two-nature doctrine. 'Atonement itself', wrote Nels Ferré, 'is the starting-point for full Christology.'[33]

II

In the course of a paper on 'Recent philosophy and Christian doctrine' Robert Mackintosh declared,

> Philosophy, however well disposed, and however competent in its own sphere, must not lay down the law to Christian doctrine; which strives to answer the other, the immense question, *What thinkest thou of Christ?*[34]

But none knew better than Mackintosh that in his own time many philosophers were making assertions which could only be described as Christological. Among them were our seven idealists. How far, if at all, did their philosophical presuppositions influence, for good or ill, their references to the person of Christ? I begin my answer to this question by reference to Illingworth, for of the thinkers with whom we are principally concerned none was more doctrinally inclined than he, and no other was, so to speak, professionally required to propagate Christian doctrine. We might therefore expect that he would have the greatest interest in clarity on the Christological issue; what we find is a considerable degree of ambivalence.

On the one hand, as we have seen, Illingworth regards the atoning work of Christ as crucial to Christian ethics and doctrine. He knew that he was thus far standing within a long tradition of Christian witness. Of 'the great thinkers of the early Church' he writes, '[T]he very completeness of their grasp on the Atonement led them to dwell upon the cosmical significance of the Incarnation, its purpose to "gather all things into one".'[35] He can thus aver that 'the Christian conviction that . . . God is love, depends mainly . . . upon belief in the Incarnation in its atoning aspect.'[36] As he elsewhere says, 'the love of the Father for sinners is plainly recognised in the New Testament as the cause of the coming of Christ.'[37]

Thus far orthodox doctrine seems to have the upper hand. On the next page he cautions that we must never consider the Christ's vicarious sacrifice 'in abstraction from the correlative truth of His progressive union with believers . . .'[38] We are still in good doctrinal territory here, and the Johannine notion of abiding in Christ, and Paul's so-called 'Christ mysticism' come to mind. But Illingworth's proper concern that we should not see in the Incarnation only the atonement from sin, still less regard it as 'a Divine afterthought . . . consequent upon human sins',[39] comes to be transformed by a philosophical immanentism which lies at the root of Illingworth's many oscillations. Thus, he can regret that the Incarnation came to be 'regarded as contingent upon or directly due to human sin',[40] and also say that the Incarnation was an atonement.[41] He then welcomes the scholastic line of thought according to which the Incarnation is 'the pre-destined climax of creation, independently of human sin',[42] and as late nineteenth-century man, imbued with evolutionary optimism, he exults, '[S]ecular civilization is . . . nothing less than the providential correlative and counterpart of the Incarnation.'[43] Indeed the Incarnation is the coping-stone of the development of human religious experience from natural religion to spiritual.[44] Alasdair Heron was not without justification when he concluded that in his *Lux Mundi* essay ('by far the outstanding christological contribution to *Lux Mundi*'[45]) 'Illingworth is much less concerned with the Incarnation as such than with the implications of *an incarnational understanding of creation and human life.*'[46] This is all of a piece with Illingworth's desire in one of his sermons to end the isolation of the Incarnation from its context in theology, history and nature,[47] a task he accomplishes without any reference to its connection with the atonement. His claim that 'The Incarnation . . . is no exceptional intervention in human affairs, but the natural continuation of God's original purpose in creating man . . .'[48] hardly squares with his claim elsewhere that

> the Incarnation is emphatically presented to us in the New Testament as an advent; no mere event in the ordinary line of human evolution, but the coming of One from a transcendent sphere,[49]

or with the view, 'Christ and the members of Christ must always differ as the creator and the creature.'[50] It is all very confusing, and I suggest that it is so because Illingworth's religion depends upon insights and convictions which cannot but overflow the mould of his preferred philosophy. Christ's purpose, he declares, was 'to restore human nature to that harmony with the divine law, which had been broken by the unique miracle of sin'.[51] But had he raised more directly than he ever does the question 'What kind of person alone could do this?' he would have been led into a discussion of the nature of the person of Christ, and brought face to face with the tension between his undoubted Chalcedonianism and his idealistic philosophy; and the way in which the incarnation of Christ makes for the proper relations of transcendence and immanence, as he says it does, would have been more plainly evident.

If Illingworth, the most professionally theological of our authors, is thus in difficulties, we cannot expect that others of our subjects will be in less of a predicament – unless, of course, they restrict the doctrinal claims they wish to make – as Green, Caird, Jones and Pringle-Pattison do; or widen their philosophical basis – as Webb and Taylor do.

Of our seven idealists – and this may be as much a function of his temperament as of his philosophy – Pringle-Pattison is the most cautious in ascribing honorific titles to Jesus (Jones uses them, but means something less than fully orthodox by them). In his *Studies in the Philosophy of Religion* (1930) Pringle-Pattison provides his fullest consecutive account of Jesus. Jesus is one who came preaching 'the near approach of the Kingdom of God, and the need of repentance as the condition of admission to that Kingdom . . .'[52] Jesus' gospel was 'independent of any theory as to his own person; and it is difficult to gather with certainty from the gospels what his own beliefs about himself and his mission were.'[53] To Paul he attributes the transformation of the gospel of the Kingdom into the gospel about Jesus.[54] (I shall not stay to demonstrate my own view that Paul was among the first to see the point of the life and ministry of Christ, huge clues to which are scattered throughout the gospels.) He could even make his own the words of his pupil, H. R. Mackintosh (who, as we have seen, had both respect for, and reservations concerning, Pringle-Pattison's position):

[F]aith in Christ is not a disputable belief that He was this or that, but a confident perception of the divinity of His love, of the righteousness of God, which shone forth in His words and deeds.[55]

But, with characteristic reticence, Pringle-Pattison will not press too far. On the one hand he thinks that 'We are far too apt to limit and mechanise the great doctrine of the Incarnation, which forms the centre of the Christian faith.' On the other hand he continues, 'Whatever else it may mean, it means at least this – that in the conditions of the highest human life we have access, as nowhere else, to the inmost nature of the divine.'[56] Pringle-Pattison has more than one way of suggesting the kind of access we have. Thus in one place he argues that '[I]n order to give us authentic tidings of the character of God, Jesus did not require actually to *be* God'[57] – a view which lends itself to the exemplary, first-among-equals Christ, and which begs the question whether the giving of authentic tidings of God's character is all we need.[58] Pringle-Pattison comes closer to the heart of the matter when, elsewhere, he concludes to

> a God who lives in the perpetual giving of himself, who shares the life of his finite creatures, bearing in and with them the whole burden of their finitude, their sinful wanderings and sorrows, and suffering without which they cannot be made perfect.[59]

But there is no discussion of the place of Christ in all of this, or of his nature as competent to reveal such a God – still less to effect a saving act. This is not surprising since there is no strong sense of the holy one whose love sinners spurn. If the doctrine of God is thus emaciated, sin will not appear so sinful, a radical atonement will not appear so necessary and, hence, the nature of the one who saves will not appear to be of such critical importance.

Having placed Illingworth, our most Chalcedonian idealist and Pringle-Pattison, our least Chalcedonian idealist, side by side, we may now turn briefly to the succession of Green, Caird and Jones. It cannot be denied that Green writes movingly on the Pauline view of our dying and rising with Christ:

> God was in [Christ], so that what he did, God did. A death unto life, a life out of death, must, then, be in some way the essence of the divine nature – must be an act which, though exhibited once for all in the crucifixion and resurrection of Christ, was yet eternal – the act of God himself. For that very reason, however, it was one perpetually re-enacted, and to be re-enacted, by all men. If Christ died for all, all died in him: all were buried in his grave to be all made alive in his resurrection.[60]

Again: 'God has died and been buried, and risen again, and realised himself in all the particularities of a moral life.'[61] But in the absence of an analysis of the person of Christ – indeed, in Green's case, in the absence of much reference at all to the life and ministry of Jesus – what we have here is the result of his policy that 'Christian dogma . . . must be retained in its completeness, but it must be transformed into a philosophy.'[62] But in the process no clear answer is given to the question, 'What has been done for human redemption, and who alone could do it?' There is a skirting of the historical here, about which I shall say more in the next section. For the present we may note the justice of D. W. Forrest's observation that even Green's construction of the Pauline message entails our assent to two 'propositions on evidence' – the very things Green wishes to avoid – namely, 'the remarkable purity of Christ's life, and His crucifixion'.[63]

Of Caird it was said that while

> His ethical teaching is impregnated with the spirit of the Gospels . . . it is difficult to escape the conclusion that in his thought he has in the last resort no place for a doctrine of Jesus Christ . . . [He] teaches in the end a doctrine of Incarnation in history, but scarcely a doctrine of a historical Incarnation.[64]

It would be as tedious as it is unnecessary to amass passages from Caird's writings to demonstrate the justice of this verdict. I shall content myself with a random selection. Jesus, Caird writes, may properly be called divine, as being the one who first and fully

> realised in its full meaning the truth which we philosophically express by saying that the consciousness of God is presupposed and implied in the consciousness of the world, and even more directly in the consciousness of self . . .[65]

This would seem to be a Green-like 'translation' of dogma into philosophy with a vengeance, and one which bypasses what traditional Christianity has ever believed was necessary to be done for human redemption. Again,

> By [Jesus] as by no other individual before, the pure idea of a divine humanity was apprehended and made into the great principle of life . . . [S]o long as it was regarded as embodied in him only in the same sense in which it flowed out from him to others, so long the primacy attributed to Christ could not obscure the truth.[66]

The Cross is 'the *necessary* symbol' of a religion which breaks down inter-human, class and national barriers, and awakens our consciousness of union with God.[67] But with a holy God? And if so, at what cost? Who dies and is raised? It all seems so automatic in Caird's writings – as one might expect, given the impact of evolutionary immanentism upon him. Be that as it may, the closest he comes to the two-nature doctrine is to say that

> Christ is divine *just because* he is the most human of men . . . he is the ideal or typical man, the Son of Man who reveals what is in humanity, *just because* he is the purest revelation of God in man.[68]

The upshot is that the advent of Christ was a critical turning-point in human history because

> man rose to an idea of himself and of his world toward which all the movement of the ancient world had been converging, and from which all the modern world has started.[69]

The last clause begs a number of questions in a pluralistic world, but the main difficulty with the assertion as a whole is Caird's characteristically confident positing of the ever-developing consciousness of divine–human unity, God's holiness and human sin notwithstanding. Small wonder that he can write:

> Any necessity for an irruption of the spiritual into the natural world, would seem inconsistent with the idea that the latter is spiritual in its own right – as the common doctrine of the divinity of Christ can only be very artificially reconciled with the idea of the revelation of God in man.[70]

On the contrary: properly regarded, the doctrine of the two natures, yielding as it does both transcendence and immanence, unites the material and the spiritual as nothing else that we have seen does or can do. The question which needs to be pressed on Caird and others of his general stance is this: do you leave us with a real incarnation, or merely with a doctrine of divine immanence which would be complete and sufficient even if Christ had never lived as the exemplar of it?

Henry Jones will give us little consolation at this point, though he is refreshingly cheeky on the matter. His biographer records that having preached an apparently well-received sermon at Llanfair PG, Anglesey, Jones did not receive an expected return invitation. He asked John Morris Jones why this was, and the latter, following consultations with the deacons, replied, ' "They are told . . . that you deny the divinity of Christ." "I!" said Henry, "I deny the divinity of Christ! I do not deny the divinity of any man!" '[71] Jones never modified his view, though he did express it more formally. Thus towards the end of his life he observes, 'God incarnates himself anew in all his children. What is merely human is lost to view.'[72]

Jones's Christological views emerge as concisely as anywhere else in his paper on 'The idealism of Jesus', which he contributed to the provocative (some would say, notorious) Supplement to *The Hibbert Journal* of 1909, *Jesus or Christ?* He here takes issue with his former fellow-student at Glasgow, James Denney. Denney is insistent that Jesus of Nazareth is not a Son of God but the Son of God. This, argues Jones, is to drive an unacceptable wedge between Jesus and everybody else. Against this he asserts the divinity of all, and seeks to show that this assertion does not empty the term 'divine man', when applied to Jesus, of significance, for he is the supreme exemplar of the divine–human unity, who came to show God's love for all. Denney, however, claims that, as compared with ourselves, Jesus is on the side of the divine. If that is so, retorts Jones, the value of Jesus as an example is destroyed, our own divinity is denied, and his victory cannot become ours. The root of the error, he continues, is not the denial of the divinity of Jesus, but the denial of the divinity of humanity.[73] His own view is that '[T]he humanity of God and the divinity of man are two aspects of the same truth.'[74] But, as William Sanday pointed out, 'The distinction between sonship real but not realized and sonship brought into unclouded consciousness is of vital importance for this discussion.'[75] By failing to make this distinction Jones is less than just to Denney. Moreover, as A. E. Garvie observed, 'If the divinity of Christ were an individual monopoly, we should deny man's sonship in affirming Christ's; but the uniqueness of Christ is *mediatorial*.'[76] There is thus exposed, once again, the 'atonement-shaped-blank' in the writings of an idealist; and until that blank is filled the resultant Christology will be less than adequate.

The fact that Webb takes action at this point makes his Christology much more satisfactory. He insists upon the atonement as meaning that 'through the union of God with man the taking away of man's sin is accomplished. What man cannot do without God, God in man can do.'[77] We breathe a different air here and, not surprisingly, Webb is led to a strong assertion of the two-nature doctrine of Christ. To him it is of central importance, together with the doctrine of the Trinity.[78] But there is something else in Webb: the seriousness of his grasp of the importance of history, and his refusal in general to avoid the scandal of particularity which is entailed by the Cross–Resurrection event. I say, 'in general', because there is a certain ambivalence in Webb's writings, as was pointed out by Leonard Hodgson.[79] Thus while asserting that, for all its difficulties, the idea of the Incarnation of the ideal personality in the historical Jesus is to be maintained, he can almost immediately proceed to say of the doctrine of the mediator that it is

> [A] doctrine which may appear, and has appeared, in contexts other than Christian; while it must not be forgotten that Christianity itself, in its identification of the Logos or Mediator with Jesus, sees in his earthly life as a man among men no more than one stage of the manifestation of the Son of God . . .[80]

Here we detect the pull of idealistic metaphysics upon the most empirically-historically conscious of our seven idealists; and it is not without significance that the pull is exerted where the reference is to 'contexts other than Christian'. The more resolutely absolutist idealists needed no such contextual encouragement to minimize the historical particularity of the Christian claim.

III

With his conviction that the object of the Christian faith 'is not past events, but a present reconciled and indwelling God',[81] Green shows himself to be so far a true son of Hegel; while Taylor, in affirming that

> the actual history of Gnosticism is a sufficient warning against repetitions of the attempt to divorce the spiritual life, which we know in fact only as mediated by religions with roots in historical facts and happenings, wholly from its historical attachments,[82]

suggests not only the extent of his assimilation of the epistemologies of Aquinas and Reid, but also his much profounder grasp of the human condition and what needed to be *done* to ameliorate it. At no point in our study are the differences between our seven subjects wider.

As we have seen, it is not that Green, or any other of the thinkers here under review, took over Hegel's theory of history in its entirety – far from it; but faced with naturalistic and materialistic philosophy at home, and with the historically agnostic implications of such German biblical scholarship as that of Baur and Strauss, Green thought that in Hegel was to be found a metaphysic which, however much it might require to be tempered by Kantianism, could be deployed in such a way as to serve the Christian faith. As Arnold Toynbee put it,

> Mr Green sought to establish . . . an intellectual position for the Christian faith which should not be called in question by every advance in historical evidence and in physical science. It is with no eagerness to impair the existing religious creeds that he insists on the incorrectness of the theories on which they are professedly based; other thinkers have assailed the orthodox foundations of religion to overthrow it, Mr Green assailed them to save it.[83]

More positively, Green's quest, like that of Hegel, was of a comprehensive, true (and hence on their terms, not historically conditioned) philosophy. Although Jowett thought that Green had undertaken a difficult task, he conceded that '[S]omething like this is what the better mind of the age is seeking – a religion independent of the accidents of time and place.'[84]

While welcoming the fact that Hegel had given 'a new dignity to historical study' by insisting that 'the true significance of things and of reality as a whole could not be understood apart from the way in which they had come to be',[85] Webb who, we recall, regretted Kant's unhistorical temper of mind,[86] was no less insistent that 'the Christian Church has worshipped as God a real historical person, of whose life and character it has preserved a genuine record . . .'[87] He could even be quite dismissive of others on the point: 'I know . . . that there are those who would deny the historicity of Jesus; but I regard this denial as the mere wantonness of doubt.'[88]

Be that as it may, Green was convinced that great harm had been done to the Christian faith by the externalizing and mystifying of Christ, whereby 'The miraculous overpowered the moral and spiritual . . .'[89] To the extent that this has happened, Green is right to protest. But there is no need to draw the conclusion that what is required in consequence is a withdrawal from the particularities of history. Green grants that Paul believed in the 'objectivity' of Christ's death and resurrection, but maintains that

> his attitude towards [these facts] was not that of a man believing certain events to have happened on evidence. He seemed to himself to die daily and rise again with Christ, and it was this moral and personal experience that gave reality in his eyes to the supposed [mark the word] historical events . . .[90]

In justice to Green it must be observed that he did not minimize the importance of the life of Jesus as having initiated the Christian movement, but he did not believe that our present-day grasp of the faith depended upon access to the historical details of that life.[91] More generally, he declares that

> The more strongly we insist that faith is a personal and conscious relation of the man to God, forming the principle of a new life . . . the more awkward becomes its dependence on events believed to have happened in the past.[92]

In a private letter he is even stronger on the point: he holds

> that the belief in the events was derived from the ideas (of which philosophy is the true intellectual expression), not the ideas from the real happening of the events . . . [He hopes one day to write a book in which he will] exhibit the essential truth of Christian ideas about God, the Spirit, Eternal life, and prayer – but to do that I should have to maintain the '*a priori* impossibility of miracles', for to me the philosophic condition of Theism is that there is nothing real apart from thought, whereas the doctrine of miracles implies that there is something real apart from thought, viz. 'nature', but that thought has once or twice miraculously interfered with it.[93]

The disjunction between ideas and facts upon which Green here rests is too strong, for there seems much to be said for the view that there are no facts without interpretation. Moreover, 'It is a rather desperate expedient to try to prove anything about the course of history without inspection of the historical facts themselves.'[94] More particularly, the Christian ideas of Christ and atonement are yielded by what is taken to be the Cross–Resurrection event; and it is highly significant that Christological and soteriological ideas are conspicuous by their absence from the list of topics to which Green hopes one day to turn. Neither need we endorse the definition of 'miracle' as that which entails an intervention from without. Small wonder that Robert Mackintosh, like other by no means reactionary theologians, warned,

> Our redemption is no mere complex of ideas. It is a fact in history; the central fact of that long story. And we must be on our guard as Christians against the tyranny of several types of idealist philosophy which sterilize such belief at the outset.[95]

It may not be inappropriate to point out that for all Green's obvious sympathy with the evolutionary theme, his philosophy, which seems to explain away the empirical, has little room for a doctrine of creation.[96] *A fortiori*, we should not be surprised to find a lack of attention to re-creation. There is little encouragement in Green's writings to do other than endorse the lament of his contemporary, Iverach: '[F]or Green the historical Christ has vanished, and has been succeeded by the idea.'[97]

From the point of view of orthodox Christian doctrine, Caird's position represents no improvement upon that of Green:

> It is a law of human history that principles and tendencies which are really universal, should at first make their appearance in an individual form, as if bound up with the passing existence of a particular nation or even of a single man. The general idea needs, so to speak, to be embodied or incarnated, to be 'made flesh and to dwell among men' in all the fulness of realisation in a finite individuality, before it can be known and appreciated in its universal meaning. And it is only after such individual presentation had produced its effect that reflexion is able to detach the idea from accidents of time and place and circumstance, and present it as a general principle.[98]

Over and above the difficulties attaching to the analysis of 'a law of human history' – and these are not my present concern – here is clear endorsement of the intellectualist position that the Incarnation is a temporary expedient to engender the universal idea, rather than a decisive divine act with a view to the redemption of the world. The supremely important thing about Jesus is that from him, as from nowhere else, we obtain 'the . . . impression of reconciliation with self and God . . .'[99] Indeed, Christianity's 'first and last word is the unity or reconciliation of the human and the divine'.[100] Accordingly, Christ symbolizes what is humanity's goal. But the nature of the reconciliation, and what had to be done to achieve it, is not spelled out. On the contrary, such ideas are refused admittance by a philosophical idealism which manages without 'any extraneous support from vision or miracle', and in which, Caird declares, 'the principle of Christianity has come to self-consciousness.'[101] But the overpowering principle is that of divine–human continuity. It can be illustrated by historical particularities, but it cannot accommodate an atoning scandal of particularity. As A. M. Fairbairn judged,

> The theory controls the history; the history does not suggest and verify the theory. Thus particular instances which happen to illustrate the philosophical principle are raised to the dignity of universal laws.[102]

The idea of the natural development of religious consciousness replaces that of a supernatural divine intervention;[103] but if 'natural' humanity is powerless to save itself, talk of natural development is reduced to a sad and solemn missing of the point.

In face of Caird's intellectualism, Illingworth's basic Christianity may appear naïve: 'It was of the essence of the Christian life to be founded on fact – the fact of the life and death and resurrection and teaching of Jesus Christ.'[104] But it is refreshing, and I believe it to be true. It was, as Webb clearly saw, the Church's watchword against the Gnostics 'who sought to see in her Gospel only a symbol of something not historical at all';[105] and, like the poor, the Gnostics are ever with us.[106]

Where Green and Caird played down the supernatural – indeed, repudiated it – Taylor cannot do without it: '[T]he moral life of man, rightly studied, bears impressive testimony to three great strictly *supernatural* or *other-world* realities – God, grace, eternal life.'[107] He does not, however, shirk the question of the relation between historical facts and spiritual life, and fully appreciates the distinction between assent to the truth of historical claims and the faith which saves. Nevertheless,

> The whole 'power of the Gospel' to remake human personality is intimately bound up with the conviction that the story of the passion

and exaltation of Christ is neither symbol nor allegory, but a story of what *has been done* for man by a real man, who was also something more than a real man, a story of a real *transaction* at once divine and human.[108]

IV

We may not unreasonably surmise that the different stances adopted by our seven idealists towards history will be reflected in their view of the Church as an institution; and this is exactly what we find. Webb and Taylor have a much more rooted and realistic ecclesiology than any of the others – not excluding Illingworth, the professional parson. There is something odd about this, for while we need not expect philosophers to have a great deal to say upon questions of polity, ministry and sacraments (though on the last Taylor has a good deal to offer), we might have expected that the general idealist contention that persons are not atoms but beings in relation would have fostered a more definite ecclesiology than it seems in some cases to have done: the more so, given the social thrust of Green, Caird and Jones, and the charge of individualism which, with varying degrees of intensity, they were prone to level against eighteenth-century thinkers. Thus, for example, Caird rebukes Stoics and sceptics who strive 'to realise in isolation a life whose essential characteristic is community';[109] Jones denies that the individual's self is private;[110] and Pringle-Pattison, opposing Mill's individualism, welcomes the insight learned from anthropological and historical studies, that

the human being nowhere exists – that he is, indeed, unthinkable – save as a member of some society, whose laws and customs have entered into his very being, making him the manner of man he is.[111]

But neither Caird, Jones nor Pringle-Pattison apply these convictions in any systematic way to ecclesiology. The lacuna is emphasized when the last-named writes on 'The communal or social character of early religion' near the beginning of his second series of Gifford Lectures, but has no corresponding chapter when he reaches the Christian era.[112] The effect of this, when coupled with the already detected tendency to skirt historical particularity, is to lead us in the direction of a new Gnosticism – and this despite Jones's assertion that idealism is a practical creed.

Not surprisingly, some of the idealists' remarks upon the Church are influenced by the times in which they lived. This is especially so in the case of Green. For example, he gave an address on the establishment question in which he argued that the struggle for disestablishment and disendowment would embitter social relations; that it would yield a faction-ridden episcopalian sect; and that it would reduce the future clergyman to the roles of mere priest or preacher, whilst removing from him the social and administrative functions which he currently performs, and which are not undertaken by the state. Green's proposal was 'To congregationalise the church, without disestablishment and disendowment'. But this would entail the restoration of congregational life in the parishes, and he feared it might now be too late for this to be a possiblity.[113] What is noticeable here is Green's characteristically Church of England pragmatism on the matter. He does not attempt to mount a theological justification of church establishments as such in relation to such questions as 'Who are the Church?' 'How is the Lordship of Christ to be honoured in the Church?' 'Does the idea of a national Church run counter to the notion of genuine catholicity?' 'Is the Church the kind of institution which can properly have a monarch as its temporal head and a secular parliament as its legislating body?' or even to counter those Dissenters who were attempting to move the discussion in these directions.[114]

Again, situated at Oxford as he was, Green could not be blind to Anglo-Catholic activity on the traditionalist and dogmatic fronts. He thought it most unfortunate that the Church should be regarded as a 'depositary of a dogma', rather than as 'the slowly articulated expression of the crucified and risen life'.[115] In his sermon on 'The witness of God' he urged his hearers not to follow 'hasty and passionate theologians' in assuming that 'God . . . suddenly set up the christian church as a miraculous institution owing nothing to the other influences of the world, within which all is light, without it all darkness.'[116] Richter suggests that Jowett's verdict upon *Lux Mundi*, which Green did not live to see, would surely have been endorsed by Green:

> I have read a considerable portion of *Lux Mundi*, but am a good deal disappointed in it. It has a more friendly and Christian tone than High Church theology used to have, but it is the same old haze and maze –

no nearer approach of religion either to morality or to historical truth.[117]

But it cannot be said that Green's primary concern was with historical truth. What he was undoubtely distressed by was the High Church emphasis upon churchly authority, this being deemed to afford security in face of the attacks upon Scripture, and his ground of concern was the implicit anti-rationalism of the suspect position.

It is interesting at this point to summon Pringle-Pattison, who distinguishes between scientific and religious authority thus:

> We accept scientific authority simply to save ourselves the trouble of verifying the conclusions for ourselves – or the trouble of educating ourselves till we are able to test it all. This is purely provisional and a matter of personal convenience. Whereas the religious authority is supposed to deal with matters which reason is incompetent to settle, and accordingly puts forward claims to permanent submission. Again, so far as 'revelation' is a revelation of spiritual truth, I do not see that it needs any authority behind it. Its authority lies in its own content. It appeals to the spiritual nature of man, and the response it evokes is its verification. Spiritual truth is judged by the spiritual nature of man just as intellectual truth by his intellectual nature, and neither in the one case nor in the other is there ultimately a place for external revelation or external authority.[118]

We may suppose that Green would have been in agreement with Pringle-Pattison up to the last two sentences quoted here. It was not his way, however, to appeal to intellectual as over against spiritual faculties as if the latter had nothing to do with reason; and it was not characteristic of Pringle-Pattison to do so either.

His concern about anti-rationalism also lay behind Green's warning to Scott Holland against the tendency

> to substitute, for the moral presence of God in the Church, a miraculous and mystical one; in other words, against 'Sacerdotalism and Sacramentalism'. Opinions about evidence don't affect the essence of Christianity; but these demoralise it.[119]

Green does not deny the importance of the sacraments, however. But he cautions,

> We do wrong to ourselves and them, if we allow any intellectual

vexation at the mode in which they may be presented to us to prevent us from their due use. If we are really seeking to live as members one of another in the general assembly of the first-born, why do we not gladly approach the table where in the simplest of all rites that mutual membership is expressed?[120]

The Lord's Supper is but an outward expression of that hidden life of the Church wherein the true Lord's table is spread.[121] Clearly, there is much more that might be said about the Lord's Supper as remembrance, communion, earnest of the 'marriage supper of the Lamb' – and this by those who do not stand for sacerdotalism. It cannot be denied that Green's sacramental theology is minimalist.

Not so that of Illingworth, our contributor to *Lux Mundi*. In one of his sermons he defines the Church as a 'great sacramental system', and declares that 'no one part of a coherent system can be overlooked without loss to the whole.' Why does he speak in this vein?

> I have called the Church a sacramental system, because its function is to embody and communicate, through outward and visible agencies, as in their ways do the special sacraments, the inward, invisible, infinite life of God. And by thinking and speaking of it in this aspect we best remember its connection, not only with the several sacraments and sacramental ordinances which go to make up its sum, but also with the whole created universe outside it, which in its measure is sacramental also – i.e. created to exhibit things eternal through the agencies of time . . . [122]

Here is a thoroughly idealistic way of construing the sacramental but, be it noted, it is not necessarily sacerdotalist in intention.

Before leaving the sacraments we may note that the idealists have very little to say about baptism. Webb does indeed refer to it with reference to baptismal discipline, thus:

> Thoughtful apologists of infant baptism would admit that, apart from a genuine guarantee of Christian upbringing, infant baptism is a mockery, all the more profane the less it is thought of as a mere ceremony and the more there is attributed to it, at least potentially, a supernatural efficacy. The real defence against a superstitious view of sacraments is not a reduction of them to the position of mere outward

ceremonies, having no organic connection . . . with the spiritual experiences which they symbolize, but a grasp of their social character and of sociality as an essential feature of spiritual life.[123]

This is a surprising attenuation of the significance of infant baptism. No doubt church discipline is as important as it is often neglected in this connection; certainly sacraments are neither vehicles of superstition nor mere outward signs. But neither are they simply witnesses to, or agents in fostering, the sociality of spiritual life. Primarily they are witnesses to the grace of God in the Gospel, infant baptism declaring God's prevenient grace which acts before we can respond, and the Lord's Supper dramatizing the redeeming acts which lie at the heart of the Good News.

By writing at length on the Church as an institution, Taylor sailed as close to the wind as any Gifford Lecturer. He reports the suggestion made to him that the topic lay outside the bounds of Lord Gifford's directions. Taylor's reply was characteristically crisp:

I do not see how the instruction that the subject of religion is to be treated 'from the point of view of natural reason' can in any way preclude us from raising the question whether natural reason does, or does not, demand from those who would be loyal to it an attitude of hostility to, or at least detachment from, the organised life of the religious community.[124]

His own conclusion is that natural reason, far from requiring hostility or detachment, requires loyalty to the institutional Church, its imperfections notwithstanding. On the way to this conclusion he argues strongly for the inevitability in religion of the supernatural; he cannot, like Green and others, exclude it. Neither can he dispense with authority in the way that Green does. Philosophy, indeed, is committed to the principle of private judgement, but in any positive religion there is always an authority before which private judgement is properly bidden to submit.[125] Moreover, this authority is not a 'God within', but 'a supra-individual supreme authority', a 'God without'.[126] As we might expect, Taylor, by now a convert from Methodism, does not endorse a 'not-rational' authoritarianism towards which, in their revolt against 'the domination of individual judgment', Methodism,

Evangelicalism and Anglo-Catholicism, in their different ways, tended.[127] But that religion posits an absolute authority which is not of ourselves cannot, he thinks, be denied.

This, however, is 'the *scandalum* offered by all positive and historical religions to the philosophical mind, honestly bent on the understanding of things'.[128] There is ineradicable mystery here, and while the intellect should not be idle, the mystery cannot be removed, and

> *Christianity not Mysterious* is no proper title for a work on the Christian religion by a writer who seriously believes that religion to be something more than an invention of ingenious moralists and statesmen . . . A theology which finds mystery it cannot explain away at the centre of things may not be true, but it is certain that a theology which professes to have cleared away all the mystery out of the world must be false.[129]

It cannot be otherwise, he continues, for whether we immediately apprehend the supernatural or the natural, 'we are dealing with concrete, individual, historical, experiences which resist complete intellectual analysis, at the same time that they demand it.'[130]

It goes without saying that Taylor has no concern to uphold the infallibility of Pope, Councils or Bible; rather, the authority of the universal Church is not dead and canalized, but alive: 'The "catholicity" of the community is precisely that which gives the driving force to the appeal to its authority.'

I must here record my conviction that any idealism which sets out to 'understand all mysteries', or even believes that it is in principle possible to achieve such understanding, needs to heed Taylor's words concerning mystery. Of all our idealists he is the most insistent upon this point. It must also be said, however, that his conclusion to the authority of the living community is lame apart from reference to the authoritative action of God in Christ on the basis of which the community is called into being and to which, elsewhere as we saw, Taylor paid so much attention. Indeed, in the next chapter he bluntly declares of God: 'He can only reach us by an activity striking down into the temporal and historical.'[131] It is surprising that he seems not to follow through to this crucial point when discussing authority.[132]

This is not to deny the importance of Taylor's emphasis upon the communal nature of religion: it is not merely a 'personal and private transaction between [a person] and . . . God'.[133] Religion is more than a moral support; it concerns more than the individual's salvation; with aspects of its corporate expression the individual may on occasion feel ill at ease – hence the necessity of guarding against 'the ever-present danger of the spiritual sin of priggishness'.[134] Even in the early Taylor there is recognition of the importance of the social aspect of religion. He charges McTaggart with overlooking this, and of treating religion 'as simply the convictions of an individual thinker on certain momentous questions', and as 'a form of emotion arising from a conviction of harmony between ourselves and the nature of ultimate reality'.[135] Above all,

> worship, like . . . morality, art, the pursuit of knowledge, and the rest, is a supra-individual activity, needing for its maintenance . . . all the support afforded by organised fellowship, definite institutions, and a great historical tradition.[136]

With all of which Webb is in full accord. While recognizing that, on the one hand, religion is profoundly inward, he insists that, on the other hand, it is characterized by what he calls sociality.[137]

There is much concerning the nature and the 'matter' of the Church which the idealists do not bring within their purview. As to the former, there is no reason why, as philosophers, they should treat of the biblical images of the Church, or of polity. As to the latter, we may not uncharitably suspect that, however much such corporate imagery of the Church as many-limbed body, household of faith and royal priesthood might have undergirded their social teaching, the more monistic of them would have had more than a little difficulty with any notion that, for all the imagery they invoke concerning dying to live, there is a radical distinction of eternal significance between believers and others, between Church and world. This is consonant with their attenuated understanding of God's holiness, human sin and, hence, of grace and redemption; and the root of the difficulty is that 'automaticism' which derives from their optimistic faith in the divine–human continuity and the ongoing progress of the human race. But what of the end?

V

Ever since the days of Lessing and Kant mankind has been travelling away from the narrow infinitude and hard-lined limitedness of the days of Hume. Philosophers and poets alike – almost all of the greatest of them – Fichte and Schelling, Hegel and Goethe, Coleridge and Wordsworth, Shelley, Tennyson, and Browning, have steeped the present life in the life to come . . . The universe is spirit-woven, God is immanent in it, and every meanest object is in its way 'filled full of magical music, as they freight a star with light'.[138]

Of the idealists under consideration in these pages, Jones alone could have written those words. He is here at his most irrepressible and, as some may feel, at his most impossible. Cocooned within a grand rhetorical flourish, questions are begged, and the writers cited are said collectively to have engineered a superhuman feat. More soberly, Jones goes on to show that Tennyson and Browning require the presupposition of immortality to make sense of sin, sorrow and God;[139] and with this Kant-inspired line of thought he himself is in entire sympathy. Not, indeed, that Jones had a great deal to say concerning immortality; neither did his teacher, Caird: 'It must be confessed . . . that Caird had no definite theory as to the nature of . . . personal immortality',[140] wrote another of his pupils. From one point of view this is not surprising, for given the strength of the immanence-continuity focus of their work, they would not need to think of one life in succession to another, or of death as a catastrophic interruption. On the other hand, their conviction that belief in immortality was tenable – even required – if God were to be God and morality justified might have been expected to quicken their interest in the persons who are deemed immortal. But at this point, as in connection with their view of history, the individual is in danger of being lost. In lofty manner Caird rules certain questions out of order:

> We need not ask questions about the future state or trouble ourselves about the answer, but wait in tranquillity, and confidence in the justice of God, who has not made the world for nothing, or lighted the fires of spiritual life in order to produce nothing but ashes. In the meantime there is work to do. I think there is perhaps a kind of Stoical-

Epicurean-Christianity which may serve these latter days better than more apparently aspiring doctrines.[141]

Somewhat more surprisingly, the doctrine of immortality/ eternal life does not play a prominent part in the writings of the clergyman, Illingworth. True, he has a sermon on death, and another on eternity. But the former, though ostensibly an exposition of Revelation 1: 18 ('I am he that liveth, and was dead; and, behold, I am alive for evermore . . .'), becomes in Illingworth's hands a call to the noble path of self-sacrifice in the company of Christ; while the latter, on II Corinthians 4: 18 ('The things which are seen are temporal; but the things which are not seen are eternal'), is an extended affirmation of eternity as 'a fact, a plain, palpable, inevitable fact, as familiar as the experience of our everyday lives', without any reference to union with a victorious Christ.[142]

Webb, more philosophically eclectic and less tied to absolutist dogma than Caird and Jones, might have been expected to accommodate a more distinctly theological treatment of immortality in his works on human and divine personality. But he seems to have had a temperamental uneasiness with the subject. He grants the difficulty of constructing a theodicy which does not 'include at least such a survival of death as shall suffer the individual to "see of the travail of his soul and be satisfied" ';[143] but he doubts if he has ever felt what Tennyson calls 'the sacred passion of the second life'.[144] While he admits to a prejudice in favour of a belief historically associated with religious experience, he has a greater prejudice 'against a belief which jars upon and distresses my imagination, and from the consideration of which my mind has an instinctive tendency to turn'.[145]

Green, as we shall see, has an abiding conviction of eternal life which does not sit easily with his metaphysical position, while Pringle-Pattison, the most reserved of our idealists, and A. E. Taylor, the most vociferous, have the most to say upon immortality. I shall set out from Pringle-Pattison's survey-*cum*-construction, which forms his second series of Gifford Lectures, and then refer to themes which recur in several of our writers.

In the first sentence of *The Idea of Immortality*, and with characteristic caution, Pringle-Pattison declares, 'The universality of a belief is no sufficient guarantee of its truth.'[146] At the same

time, he recognizes that such a long-standing and widespread
belief as that in immortality is not to be treated lightly. He
discusses primitive ideas of the soul and the after-life, and outlines
the development of the doctrines in Hebrew and Greek thought.
Plato's importance is emphasized. With his doctrine of ideas was
introduced for the first time in the history of thought 'the
conception of a mode of being which was eternal, not in the sense
of persisting changelessly through time . . . but in the sense of
absolute timelessness'.[147] For Plato, the soul is related both to the
eternal world of intelligible reality and to the 'quasi-real world of
. . . Becoming, with which we have to do in sense-perception and
in the everyday conduct of our lives'.[148] We need not pursue
Pringle-Pattison through Plato's arguments for immortality. It will
suffice us to note his view that they are 'for the most part,
singularly unconvincing'.[149] The underlying problem is Plato's
dualism of soul and body, and his own preference is for Aristotle's
starting-point, namely, the living organism, with 'conscious
experience as the final form or expression of biological facts'.[150]
Accordingly, he sets his face against soul-substances, whether
Scholastic or Cartesian, as being 'superfluous for the explanation
of our conscious experience during the present life', and hence as
not 'essential for the continuance of that experience after
death'.[151] Locke is quoted as agreeing that 'all the great ends of
morality and religion are well enough secured, without philosophical proofs of the soul's immateriality', but he does not
'definitely abandon the conception whose uselessness he so
triumphantly demonstrates'.[152] Moreover, to adopt the Cartesian
standpoint is to leave the material world in the hands of the
mechanists, so that the human being becomes 'a mechanical union
of a corpse and a ghost'.[153] The moral is that 'If we start with the
living body as the embodied soul, the problem of interaction
ceases to exist and laboured schemes of parallelism become
unnecessary.'[154] While Hume rightly saw that the self was
something other than a simple, atomic unit, and that it was
complex, he was mistaken in concluding that it was not a unity at
all.[155] For Pringle-Pattison the soul is 'the systematic unity of the
conscious experiences of a particular individual centre – the
individual centre being defined or determined at the outset by the
bodily organism'.[156]

We pass over Pringle-Pattison on the intricacies of karma and reincarnation, though we should note that in his chapter on eternal life, he construes this not as a life which is 'end-on' to our present existence, but rather as 'an experience, a state of being, to be enjoyed here and now' as well as hereafter.[157] He sets his face against any limitation of individual life to this world – whether such teaching emanates from Spinoza or Bosanquet – and he welcomes Bradley's later, less negative, view of the matter. It goes without saying that Pringle-Pattison's emphasis upon the individual personality prompts his rejection of alternatives of absorption or annihilation at death, while his understanding of the practical implications of religious truth explains his warning against immersion in eschatological speculations – especially those concerning the eternal destiny of others. But it is possible for the individual to be humbly confident – on which matter Pringle-Pattison quotes Caird: 'Unbelief in death seems to be the necessary characteristic or concomitant of true spiritual life.'[158]

While there is no specific exposition here of eternal life as a gift divinely imparted with reference to Christ's atoning work, Pringle-Pattison's view of the nature of the human person is very often consonant with the biblical understanding of personality, and his realism tempers his idealism to such a degree that his thought may be said to run parallel to important Christian insights. 'Very often', but not always; for Pringle-Pattison can speak both of the individual's absorption in the divine object of contemplation, and of the folly of supposing that this entails the surrender of the individual's personality.[159] It is not clear how these contradictory positions are to be harmonized. At the very least we need an analysis of that ambiguous term 'absorption' which, as Taylor pointed out, can mean either that one's mind is utterly concentrated – in prayer, for example – and this with no violence to the individual personality; or that it has been annihilated.[160] Such an analysis is not forthcoming from Pringle-Pattison; neither does Jones supply the need. 'I am tempted', he confesses, 'to believe that there is a higher for man and a greater for God than absorption.'[161] *I* am tempted to reply, 'Let us hope so!' But Jones's metaphysical presuppositions, strictly construed, do not make it easy to understand why he should be thus tempted.

The views of Green and Caird seem further removed than those of Pringle-Pattison from Christian eschatological teaching. With them, the emphasis upon the divine–human continuity has the effect of bypassing the redemptive act and skirting the scandal of particularity, also, when doused in optimism concerning humanity, make eternal felicity almost a foregone conclusion. Thus Caird in one of his sermons:

> Direct proof of immortality cannot be had, or not in a conclusive form, but if we believe in God, immortality seems to follow as a natural, perhaps we should say as a necessary consequence. For if we think of the world as the manifestation of a rational and moral principle – and that it must be so conceived seems to be a necessary presupposition of all our mental and moral life – we must regard it as existing for the realisation of that which is best and highest; and that best and highest we can hardly conceive as anything but the training and development of immortal spirits. The outcome of a world which is the realisation of the Will of God, must be either immortality for beings who are made in his image, or something better – and what better can there be that does not involve immortal life? . . . [T]he existence of God carries with it the continued existence of those who have lived for His service.[162]

Green is in agreement that

> There must be eternally such a subject which is all that the self-conscious subject, as developed in time, has the possibility of becoming; in which the idea of the human spirit, or all that it has in itself to become, is completely realised.[163]

Again we may ask, What has Christ to do with all of this? In his Ellerton Essay of 1860, Green wrote that 'In Christ [the believer] becomes one with God, he partakes of the divine nature, and even in the flesh lives an eternal life by the faith of the Son of God.'[164] It is not easy to see how this Christological position is to be squared with Green's metaphysics, which proceeds along idealistic lines without it, and which is summarized by Green thus:

> [T]he 'immortality of the soul', as = the eternity of thought = the being of God, is the absolute first and absolute whole. To deny the 'immortality of the soul' in this sense is to maintain the destructibility of thought, and this is a contradiction in terms, for destruction has no meaning except in relation to thought.[165]

These assertions of a 'pious if undogmatic mind'[166] show concisely how Green's epistemology bears upon the question of immortality. Presupposing the divine–human union in self-consciousness, the knowing subject transcends phenomena, and participates in the timeless being of God. Yet Green also advises us that the human soul partakes of eternal self-consciousness in a manner limited by physical constraints. When those constraints are no more, is the individual lost and the soul absorbed? Charles Upton raised the question and, with some justification, concluded that

> [I]t is impossible to harmonize the absolute idealism of Green, first, with the sense of sin and of personal merit and demerit; second, with the spiritual experience of the action of the Spirit of God on the inner life of man; and, lastly, with the rational hope of a continued individual existence after physical death.[167]

From such considerations, thought Taylor, Green shied away, fearing the charge of other-worldliness.[168] For his part, Taylor observes that whereas in earlier days he had been 'carried off my feet' by Bradley, and notwithstanding his puzzlement over Green's conception of 'a world composed of relations between terms of which we could say nothing, except that they were the terms of the relation', he had now come to see that 'the great danger of the whole Hegelian way of regarding things [is] that it dissevers the "eternal verities" from all contact with "historical" actuality.'[169]

If Green seems to make immortality an inevitable consequence of our being at all, Pringle-Pattison denies that the individual is necessarily immortal. He denies that

> we are to think of personal immortality as an inherent possession of every human soul . . . We talk very loosely of 'souls' and 'persons', as if these were static entities . . . But it is manifestly a question of degree: *how much* personality . . . has the experience of life developed within the animal creature?[170]

This is distinctly odd. From the point of view of standard Christian eschatology, it is not easy to determine a preference between Green's quasi-biological, and hence morally neutral, view of immortality, according to which we could not be other than in communion with God eternally, and Pringle-Pattison's quantitative suggestion that we may weigh too little on the heavenly scales to qualify for eternal fellowship of any kind at all. Pringle-Pattison's point is that eternity must be won by way of the development of character; and here, however much he may have been in the wake of muscular Christianity, not to mention Pelagius, he seems a long way from eternity as a gift of grace.[171]

Moreover, how can one who declares that the idea of personal immortality is not 'an absolute necessity, in the sense that without it the world becomes a sheer irrationality',[172] consistently hold to the eternity of value if, as he thinks, personality is at the heart of value?[173]

Quite apart from the life to come, a number of our idealists emphasize their conviction that in the absence of belief in immortality we cannot make sense of the facts of this earthly life. 'Our ultimate reason', wrote Caird,

> for believing anything that goes beyond our immediate sensible experience is that we cannot give a rational account of the facts, cannot conceive them as part of an intelligible order, if it be not true.[174]

He continues (apparently oblivious to the distinction between immortality as implicit in self-consciousness and the possibility of rational reflection, and immortality as implicit in successful moral striving):[175]

> If the world is a rational, and therefore a moral system, it cannot be that . . . a character built up and nurtured in goodness through all the trials of life, should pass away and be lost for ever.[176]

It is difficult to resist the feeling that at this point too firm a conclusion is based upon too shaky a foundation. What we have here is more in the nature of an aspiration (which in itself is understandable enough) than an argument. We shall not be surprised to find that Jones concurs, and that he invokes God by name: 'It is not possible to maintain the limitless love and power of God if the soul be not immortal,' and the strivings of the worthy are not 'to go for nothing when death comes'.[177] Furthermore, immortality 'extends man's spiritual chances' so that somewhere at some time the soul will 'awake and apprehend its true nature and destiny'.[178]

Less inclined to such flights, Taylor is no less convinced that moral considerations are intimately connected with viable views of immortality; but more than that, he requires an adequate doctrine of God as his foundation, especially when, unlike our other authors, he pays considerable attention to the fate of the 'finally impenitent'.[179] On this subject he is properly reticent, concluding that 'there is just one man, of the many whom I have known, about whom I feel it is salutary not to be over-sanguine, myself.'[180]

While at certain points in his argument Taylor makes surprising assertions – such as that the only logical alternative world views are Christianity or pessimistic atheism[181] (a view contradicted by Pringle-Pattison, who instanced Stoicism as a 'standing refutation' of Taylor at this point)[182] – he frequently swashbuckles to good effect, as when he proclaims that it is no argument against the reality of the faith of a person who has sought and found God to say that those who have not searched have not found.[183] In his later writings, and not least in *The Christian Hope of Immortality* (1938), Taylor comes closer than any others under review to a theological exposition of the matter, emphasizing as he does human renewal into the likeness of Christ, with whom to live is life eternal: and this as being all of grace.

One way, additional to those already specified, of indicating a lacuna which I detect in the writings of the idealists on immortality is to say that while many of them have a good deal to say about spirit, they are virtually silent on the Holy Spirit. The implications for the idea of eternal life of a clause in Luther's *Smaller Catechism* do not appear to have struck them forcibly:

> I believe that I cannot by my own reason or power believe in Jesus Christ my Lord or come to him; but the Holy Spirit has called me through the gospel, enlightened me with his gifts, sanctified and preserved me in the true faith.

'We do not', wrote Lovell Cocks,

> become Christs, nor are we absorbed into the divine substance, but we are remade after the pattern of Him who is the image of God. We have fellowship with Him in his death and resurrection . . .[184]

This is the work of the Spirit, and, to reiterate our earlier theme, it is grounded in the Son's finished work. For this reason,

> [W]e still preach Jesus as Lord and Saviour; to the Pragmatist a stumbling block and to the Idealist foolishness; but to them who are called, whether from the one camp or the other, Christ the power and the wisdom of God.[185]

In view of the attenuations now detected, what, finally, will the idealists make of the doctrine of the Trinity – at once the presupposition and the culmination of Christian theology?

VI

The short answer is that some of them do not make very much of the Trinity at all. This is true of Green, Caird and Jones. We have already noticed that our selected idealists do not take over Hegel's doctrine of history in its entirety, and it is not perhaps surprising that those just mentioned do not pursue Hegel's dialectical method of construing the doctrine of the Trinity as a stage on the way to pure philosophical formulation, according to which the Father is God as he eternally is in himself; the Son is God as eternally finite and becoming; the Spirit is God as eternally recovering his otherness. This is all to the good for, as has often been pointed out,[186] Hegel's method denies the independence of the created order and blurs the Creator–creature distinction. Furthermore, it makes God dependent on that which is other than himself. Nevertheless, the tendency towards absolutism is hard to resist, as we shall see.

Illingworth has a good deal to say in his various writings concerning the personality of God as triune. This, he feels is a more conceivable position than the Unitarian, for it accords with human personality which is, he says, triune – albeit only potentially so.[187] Far from being a 'metaphysical invention' like the Platonic ideas or the Aristotelian form, the Trinity is a statement in philosophical language of the fact that there is triune plurality in God. This plurality is elaborated along the lines of the social analogy, with love being the key to the inner-trinitarian relations.[188] The Christian doctrine of the Trinity concerns

> that Divine Society, whose co-equal members are one in infinite eternal love, and who in that love's exuberance come forth, in a sense, from out themselves, to create, to sustain, to redeem, to sanctify, to bless.[189]

(No doubt, were we to ask, 'In what sense?' we should be reminded of the mystery at the heart of things. D. W. Forrest thought that Illingworth 'puts the case very mildly [with respect to the Spirit] when he says that "a personal object is easier to imagine than a personal relation." '[190]). In the doctrine of the Trinity, teaches Illingworth, the necessary aspects of the divine transcendence and the divine immanence are combined.[191] Furthermore, it is the doctrine of the Trinity which enables us to conceive of God as personal 'without at the same time derogating from His absolute character'.[192] By this Illingworth means that a Unitarian God could have relations only with the world of relative and finite beings; such a God would attain self-realization only through them, and hence would not be in himself absolute. We should then be denied the assurance that all things are moving towards their divinely ordained end.[193] Again – and here we have a theme which was later to be resumed by Webb[194] – the doctrine of the Trinity is the necessary condition of the Incarnation which has, in turn, made known to us the mutual relations of Son, Father and Spirit.[195]

Precisely how this is done is none too clear. More than one reviewer felt cheated by Illingworth's *Doctrine of the Trinity*. In a private letter James Denney confessed that he had thought of Illingworth as the ablest of the *Lux Mundi* men, but found this work

> obscurantist and irrelevant to an incredible degree. I have written as polite a notice of it as I could, but it is impossible to praise anything in it which is related to the subject.[196]

The reviewer in *The Expository Times* found the book

> a deep disappointment. It seems as if Dr Illingworth had made up his mind, not to describe the doctrine of God, but to write another book . . . he manoeuvres very prettily all round it . . .[197]

while A. S. Martin, who found Illingworth's result 'meagre', put his finger upon the weakness:

> The immanent rationality of the doctrinal process corresponding to and in concurrence with the living experience of the historic Body – this is what has to be proved. The proof will be found along the lines here, not too strongly, traced.[198]

These judgements may be too sweeping, though it must be said that as with his Christology, so with his trinitarian exposition: Illingworth does not always relate his master themes of transcendence, immanence and development to what he also believes concerning Father, Son, Spirit, history and Christian experience – and this despite his cautionary remark against the substitution of 'an ideal for an eventful religion'.[199] The result is that his writings betray a certain ambivalence, for all that his faith shines through them.[200]

Both Pringle-Pattison and Webb offer comments on Kant's view of the Trinity,[201] but the former has relatively little to say on his own account. What he does say is less than fully orthodox. Thus, he regrets that the spiritual fact for which such expressions as the influence of God and the indwelling of God in the human person stand has been materialized in such a way as 'to suggest the existence of a third personality or agency distinct from both the Father and the Son'.[202] The problem here, however, is that while immanence may be safeguarded along Pringle-Pattison's line, it is doubtful whether transcendence can be; and the result once again is that the line between Creator and creature is blurred, with consequent attenuations of Christian doctrines concerning the human condition and the need of redemption. This is not to minimize the difficulty of distinguishing between the work of Son and Spirit in the cosmological and moral spheres, but it is to sympathize with Forrest's remark, 'It is only when we realise His function in the order of God's redemptive revelation of Himself in history that the personality of the Spirit becomes to us a clear conviction.'[203] Or, as it was put long before, 'The Spirit applieth to us the redemption purchased by Christ, by working faith in us, and thereby uniting us to Christ in our effectual calling.'[204]

Like Illingworth, Webb favours the social analogy of the Trinity over against the monistic view, and this despite the danger of tritheism, and as a safeguard against modalism. However, he places much greater emphasis than Illingworth upon history and religious experience, with the result that his treatment of the doctrine has a decidedly empirical flavour. The doctrine of the Trinity, though developed under the influence of Greek philosophy, was nevertheless 'an outcome of religious experience, the speculative account given by the Church of its own social life as a manifestation of the divine nature'.[205] Taylor underlines the point when he suggests that the reason why the early divines could not rest content with a merely 'economic' Trinity was that such a Trinity did not 'make *giving* as fully and inwardly characteristic of the divine life as it requires to be made'.[206]

As we might expect, Webb has much to say concerning the personality of the God conceived as triune. In particular, he shows that in the development of Christian doctrine, personality as such was not ascribed to God – indeed, anti-trinitarians spoke of the one personality of God; rather, reference was made to 'Personality *in* God',[207] and this with a view to maintaining the idea of persons within the Godhead. Webb does not deny that attributes have been applied to God by many theologians – Christian, Jewish and Muslim – which apply only to persons, but personality as such was not so applied.[208]

Some have wondered whether Webb does not protest too much at this point. Miall Edwards, for example, replied that 'in affirming that the very *ousia* of God is ethical spirithood we are affirming the personality *of* God.'[209] Others, among them H. Wheeler Robinson, repudiated the social Trinity as ineffective in helping us to conceive of the unity of divine personality, and as tending towards pluralism.[210] Hodgson sprang to Webb's defence, and attributed Robinson's conclusion to his idealist, Pringle-Pattisonian predilections, which prompted him to think of 'Spirit' as 'fundamentally the medium through which God realises Himself in the universe'.[211] Webb remained grateful for the fact that the received trinitarian theology

> has not set up for worship a Unity beyond all distinctions, and therefore unknowable, but one to whose inmost nature it belongs to reveal itself in the very processes of knowledge and love by which the worshipper apprehends it.[212]

He is here at his most alert to the dangers of monism.

James Patrick has written that

> The religion to which idealism led most effortlessly . . . remained after a century a religion to which the deep things – grace, glory, sanctity, the virtues, the vision of God, sin, Jesus, his cross, his resurrection and ascension – were strangers.[213]

The operative words here must surely be 'most effortlessly'. For where Christian doctrine is concerned we have seen that Webb (to whom Patrick refers) and Taylor in particular had no intention of forsaking the themes which Patrick enumerates. Their degree of success was directly proportional to their willingness to fertilize their idealism from experiential, historical and realist sources. Where the more thoroughgoing absolutists were concerned, and even where their religious views approached those of traditional Christianity, they had either to remain silent on some of them, or risk doctrinal attenuations. With this we come to the legacy of post-Hegelian philosophical idealism and, in particular, to the methodological crux.

The Legacy of Post-Hegelian Idealism

At the outset I described this inquiry as a meditation upon remarks of Morell and McTaggart to the effect that philosophical idealism is a dangerous ally of Christianity because of its propensity to engulf the genuinely religious. I have not undertaken to discuss criticisms of philosophical idealism which have been levelled from all possible points of view, or to show how, under the impact of realism and empiricism, its armour was dented. Nor have I dwelt upon the considerable service which, to differing degrees and with varying emphases, the post-Hegelian idealists performed in their repudiation of naturalism, materialism and scepticism, and in their determination to tackle substantive issues. In face of more conservative expressions of the Christian faith they set an example of openness towards society; they welcomed light from modern biblical critics, and they realized that some accommodation had to be made towards those who lived by religions and world views other than the Christian. For good measure they sought to 'moralize dogma' – notably in connection with the penal substitutionary theory of the atonement, miracles, and predestinarian 'scholasticism'. On all of this much might be written.

I, however, have concentrated upon the narrower, albeit important, questions: How far were those philosophical idealists who were closest to Christian belief able to express their religious convictions in terms of idealism? Could they consistently do this? Were distinctively Christian beliefs thereby attenuated, or left out of account? Inevitably some of the problems I have diagnosed refer to post-Hegelian idealism of every hue – for example, the tendency towards the loss of the individual, and the difficulty of accommodating the manifest problem of evil; but the impact of idealistic presuppositions and doctrines upon the articulation of Christian convictions by philosophers who were not hostile to the faith has been my particular concern.

My method was first to analyse the soil in which British post-Hegelian idealism took root. The home-grown interests and influences by which they were surrounded – Humean scepticism, Scottish realism, nineteenth-century naturalism, materialism and agnosticism – were shown to have suggested the shapes their idealism took. In particular, they did not imbibe Hegel's under-standing of history in its entirety, and the influence of Kant remained strong upon them. I refer to the 'shapes' their idealism took because it became clear that the closer one's inspection of the idealists, the less monolithic the 'ism' appeared. The idealists were temperamentally diverse – the ebullient Jones, the sometimes acerbic Taylor; and their literary styles varied greatly, as any who place Green's sometimes tortuous language alongside Illing-worth's limpid prose may see at a glance. But the serious point concerns their content. Over and above the major distinction (itself blurred at times in Illingworth, Pringle-Pattison and Webb) between the absolute and the personal idealists, we saw, for example, that whereas Green doubted that a universal philo-sophical synthesis could be made, Caird declared that 'If philosophy is incapable of a universal synthesis, it cannot make any synthesis at all.'[1] Where Green, questioning whether knowledge of God was truly open to us, said, 'To know God we must be God',[2] Caird contended that 'if we cannot . . . know God, we cannot know anything.'[3] Again, if Pringle-Pattison faulted Green for leaving us with a formal ego only,[4] Webb, unlike Pringle-Pattison, did not see how we could 'without self-contradiction, attempt to postpone knowledge to an enquiry into the nature of knowledge'.[5] Taylor thought that Green's deity was 'an only half-baptized Aristotelian God',[6] while Webb wondered how the particularity of phenomena and of persons could be sustained along Green's line.[7] As for Caird's bald and abstract 'principle of unity', Pringle-Pattison found it philosophically inadequate and religiously unsatisfying.[8] For his part Henry Jones charged Green with failing to make it clear that the natural and the spiritual are aspects of a single reality.[9] As we saw in the previous chapter, Illingworth's Christ is much more the incarnate mediator than is Caird's exemplary Jesus; Webb was more theologically disturbed by the tragedy of humanity's sin than were Caird or Jones; Webb and Taylor paid much more heed to historical, redemptive actions than did the absolutists; Taylor sought to reinstate the supernatural over against Green and Caird; and whereas to Green immortality was a characteristic of humanity as such, Pringle-Pattison did not so regard it.

Differences such as these should be borne in mind when phrases such as 'the heyday of idealism' are bandied about, for they call our attention to the fact that the phenomenon alleged to be having its hour of glory was diverse indeed – even internally contradictory at times. The glib phrase is, however, questionable for the further reason that there was a good deal of non- and even anti-idealistic thought current between 1870 and 1930 (tailing off into the 1950s). If it has not been to our purpose to dwell upon realists, pragmatists and empiricists in this study, we have most certainly taken account of those who, like our seven idealists, wished to articulate Christian convictions, but found that philosophical idealism was a less than satisfactory vehicle for this purpose. It has been especially instructive to observe the way in which Caird's pupils divided on this issue, with Jones, Watson, Mackenzie and Muirhead remaining more or less faithful to their master's vision, while James Orr, James Denney, D. W. Forrest, Robert Mackintosh, and A. E. Garvie departed from it. It is not without significance for our study that of Caird's pupils, those who came to distance themselves from him were, for the most part, theologians who felt that the philosophical shoe pinched the theological foot, so to speak. The work of these men, as well as of such hinterland philosophers as C. B. Upton and of theologians like James Iverach, reinforces my conviction that we shall not fully have understood the great names in philosophy or theology until we have observed the nature of the soil in which their ideas took root, and the reception which was accorded to them, positively and negatively, by their lesser-known contemporaries.

Before recapitulating my findings I must enter a caveat. Whereas those who write learned treatises upon, say, Hilary of Poitiers or the Labadists are not necessarily expected to show the relevance of their subjects to twentieth-century theological or philosophical discussion, those who treat of the nearer past are sometimes reproved if they do not show how their studies feed into current debate. I believe that the thought of any period can be studied for its own sake, and that students are under no obligation necessarily to do obeisance to the 'god' Relevance. Moreover, attempts to draw lines too easily between thinkers from the past (even the nearer past) and those of today can falsify matters by overlooking significant differences of both logical and societal kinds. In the former case meanings may be unwarrantably assimilated (Anselm in his ontological argument did not have the modern concept of logical necessity in mind, for example); in the latter, an insufficiently empirical approach can, for example, issue in the perils of restorationism – as when some present-day Christians seek to reproduce 'the' Church polity of the New Testament as if little had changed in society between the first century and the twentieth. This is not to deny that there can be echoes of the past in the present; it is only to absolve authors of the necessity of tracing links in detail if that is not their intention. On the other hand, there is no harm in hearing whatever echoes there may be, provided that one's hearing is tempered by the realization that if a later thinker sounds like a former, he or she is not necessarily indebted to the former thinker either consciously or unconsciously: positions may be reached by independent reflection (as well as, on occasion, by unacknowledged indebtedness). All of which considerations underlie my resolution, when rehearsing the points at which idealism's shoe pinches Christianity's foot, to allude to, though not exhaustively to investigate, some lingering traces of post-Hegelian idealism in the writings of some of our own contemporaries, against which this study may stand as a cautionary word.

Among the issues which were raised by the concept of the absolute were the following: (a) The unsatisfactoriness of the apparent jump from epistemology to ontology which surfaced in the writings of Green in particular. (b) The justifiability of the *decision* by such idealists as Jones that the absolute spirit must have the character of love, which raised the question how far it is legitimate to clothe the absolute with content derived from the Christian revelation – and even to name the absolute 'God'. (c) The failure on the part of the more monistically inclined in particular to take due account of the analogical procedure which is involved when terms are rebaptized from one world view to another, and to suppose that direct translation is possible. (d) The questionable nature of Green's determination to continue to use traditional Christian language, whilst meaning something quite different by it.

Our discussion of the idealists' ethico-social vision revealed still further differences between them, notably again that between the older monists and the later Taylor, who declared, 'No philosophy of pure "immanence" can take the moral life seriously.'[10] Again, we saw that Green did not make it clear how his biblical motif of 'dying to live' was integral to his idea of the social good, or why he opted for that phrase rather than, for example, 'Love as I have loved you.' We observed Jones's oscillations between the view that moral obligations are self-imposed, and the conviction that there is a divine lawgiver whose nature is love. The striking omission from the idealists' social thought of the then widely current notion of the Kingdom of God inclined us to the view that, notwithstanding their all-embracing vision, they were in the line of nineteenth-century philanthropy (estimable though much of that was) rather than of communitarian ethics. Their relative weakness on ecclesiology reinforced this view. On the other hand, such a claim as Jones's that there is 'no such thing as individual self-consciousness'[11] flashes like a warning light, given the idealists' tendency to slide from epistemological insight into ontological assertion, with the resultant loss of the individual. With hindsight it would seem that for all their sometimes high-flown and optimistic language concerning society, the idealists were not strong on the need for detailed empirical investigation of what might be required to set society more firmly on its allegedly upward-tending course.

It was intriguing to observe the way in which the note of divine transcendence could become muffled by a monistic pantheistic immanentism which could become a mirror image of the materialism so resolutely opposed by the idealists. This further accelerated the tendency towards the submergence of the individual human being, and for the blurring of the Creator–creature distinction in such a way as to undermine worship, ethics and doctrine alike. The ideas of sin against a holy God, and of the saving action of such a God on the stage of human history, became difficult to accommodate and were either inconsistently held, or bracketed, with humanity's tragedy sometimes being couched in terms of finitude rather than of sin. Christology could be transmuted into an incarnational principle of a suspiciously immanentist kind, and evil could too easily be accepted as a stage on the way to good. Ironically, despite the concern of the absolutists for truth, the blurring of the Creator–creature distinction made it harder to sustain the conviction that religion 'involves the recognition of an independent Reality about which its doctrinal statements are either true or false'.[12]

As far as the matters raised in the preceding paragraph are concerned, it is impossible not to hear echoes of the older idealism in current thought. Thus, on the one hand we have Moltmann's stipulation that we should think not so much of the God of history as of history in God[13] – a Hegelian-sounding notion indeed, and one which recalls Creed's criticism of Caird to the effect that 'he teaches in the end a doctrine of Incarnation in history, but scarcely a doctrine of a historical Incarnation.'[14] It is not altogether surprising (though admittedly the phrase requires careful qualification) that when Moltmann and Pannenberg were introduced to British readers they were labelled 'the new Hegelians'.[15] In a markedly different key we have the multifaceted New Age phenomenon, concerning which John W. Cooper has said that

> It denies the personal nature of God, erases the Creator–creature distinction, denies a stable creation order, blurs creation and fall, removes the difference between good and evil, lacks an abiding moral order, refuses to admit sin and guilt, relativizes Jesus Christ, believes in self-salvation . . .[16]

Cooper's list, upon which I chanced after having reached my conclusions concerning the earlier idealism, contains a surprising number of identical 'neuralgic' points. However, as with Webb and immortality, I suspect that I am temperamentally disinclined to delve further into New Age thought. Different again, and of more central importance to the theology of the last fifty years, has been Bultmann's claim that truths – for example that concerning the risen Christ – may be grasped existentially notwithstanding the dubiety of the historical event to which 'resurrection' traditionally refers. This is a notoriously complex and subtle matter and, to repeat, I am simply suggesting allusions and hearing echoes of an older idealism: I am not advancing a thoroughly argued case with respect to more recent writers. Nevertheless the comment of a careful student of Bultmann to the effect that for the latter 'The Gospel . . . becomes something that God *says* instead of something that he *did*'[17] lends some support to my here unsubstantiated suspicion that the conclusion *vis-à-vis* God's redemptive act which Bultmann reached along his existentialist pathway is not, as far as its historical rootedness is concerned, markedly dissimilar to that reached by the more monistically inclined idealists.

Further echoes of the older idealism are heard in connection with the pluralistic societies which many of us now inhabit. It was interesting to observe that, for all his emphasis upon the importance of the historical events of Jesus's life, Webb was never nearer to lapsing into immanentism than when he had world faiths other than the Christian in view. Heirs of evolutionary optimism, our seven idealists, to differing degrees, had little difficulty in regarding Christianity as the coping-stone of the world's faiths, the terminus on the way to which all other religious movements were staging-posts.[18] Thus Illingworth avers that '[I]n the light of the Incarnation we see the true drift and meaning of all the other religions of the world . . .';[19] or again, 'The pre-Christian religions were the age-long prayer. The Incarnation was the answer.'[20] R. L. Ottley thought this last phrase 'beautifully said',[21] but, as I pointed out earlier, many in our own time feel distinctly uncomfortable with such language as Illingworth's. It appears to them to be imperialistic, patronizing, and unwilling to take other faiths at their own estimation. At the same time, whilst repudiating the hierarchical model, some of those currently in quest of a theology of religions, and especially those who proclaim an immanent ground of being behind and beyond the phenomenal world and the several religious claims, are nearer to Illingworth and the idealists than may at first sight appear. Some of these advocate a relativism which would have been anathema to Illingworth[22] who, like Webb, wished to maintain the distinctiveness and supremacy of Christianity. But the challenge of the scandal of particularity may be posed to older idealist and modern aspirant after a theology of religions alike.

This is indeed the crucial question – crucial because upon it depends the philosophico-theological method we choose to employ: Can idealism accommodate the scandal of particularity? It would seem from all that we have discovered that it cannot.

With a view to preserving Christianity from the onslaughts of sceptical historians and others, T. H. Green declared that 'Christian dogma . . . must be retained in its completeness, but it must be transformed into a philosophy.'[23] But, as we have seen, the kind of philosophy he had in mind was such as to remove the decisive redemptive act of God from the stage of human history, thereby leaving us with an exemplary Christ only, and it was over this question that Taylor, as we saw, severed relations with absolutism.[24] At point after point we have seen that idealism cannot accommodate the central witness of the Gospel to a once-for-all act of redemption. Its way is too narrowly intellectualist. It relies too heavily upon its understanding of the God–humanity continuity. It cannot fail to leave out much of what Christians wish to assert – concerning God's holy love *vis-à-vis* sin, the nature of the Church, and eternal life, for example; and those who succumb to its charms have been shown either to land in inconsistency if they wish at the same time to entertain Christian teaching in anything like its full scope and traditional sense, or to banish certain important features of Christian doctrine from their philosophy. What Taylor said of Spinoza applies to a number of our idealists: '[H]e clearly had a personal religion which finds no adequate expression in his professed metaphysic.'[25] We saw that Webb and Taylor in particular sought to accord due place to the historicity of Jesus, but the pull of old paths upon both was strong, as when Taylor says, 'It is our unending task to divine the supreme pattern of the real.'[26] And when Green avers that 'philosophy and theology are related simply as the critical and uncritical methods of dealing with one and the same question',[27] it is in the best interests of Christian thinkers to protest vigorously; for this is altogether to overlook the question of diversity of subject matter and of objectives on either side. Moreover, where any given type of philosophy is concerned, if it is (wrongly) assumed that there is a necessary connection between its presuppositions and conclusions and those of the Christian faith, it is salutary to reflect upon the condition of the Christian faith should the philosophy be overturned or simply left on one side.

Let it clearly be understood that in showing the ways in which philosophical idealism fails Christian doctrine I am by no means siding with those who would banish metaphysical considerations from theology altogether. Indeed I suspect that this could be done

only by practitioners of a covert metaphysics; and it is arguable
that some current theological writing is the poorer for its failure to
address metaphysical questions. What more appropriate metaphysic may invite Christian exploration is a large question, but
already some clues to its nature have begun to emerge.

A Christian philosophy, or world-and-life view, cannot, I judge,
bypass the historic act of redemption wrought once for all by
God-in-Christ. Time and again this criterion has emerged as the
rock on which idealism founders. This throws into relief the
question of starting-points, and it seems quite clear by now that
we shall end with distinctly different theoretical accounts of the
nature of existence, of morality, of aesthetics, according as we set
out from the presuppositions of monism, personalism, realism,
existentialism, Christianity. But the intellectual account of faith
and its implications will always be at one remove from faith itself,
and if the account be overturned, the faith need not be. The
account will be as orderly a testimony as possible of what those
making it have seen and heard. As Webb put it,

> [T]houghtful men [and, as I should wish to add, women] who make
> the claim [to divine sonship and daughterhood] will desire to set forth
> to themselves in some coherent form a view of the world which will
> place their experience of reconciliation in an intelligible connexion with
> the other facts of which they are conscious.[28]

With some significant deviations – especially on the part of
Taylor and Webb – the idealists ploughed a relatively straight
philosophical furrow, but (to change the agricultural metaphor)
their swathe was not wide enough to accommodate some of
Christianity's most basic claims. Thus, for all the value of their
repudiation of the constricted view of the materialists and
naturalists of their day, they were in their own way in the same
case as their opponents. What Taylor had to say of physicists and
biologists could be said of some of the idealists themselves:

> If . . . sin and the remission of sins are real facts of life – and the
> physicist or biologist assuredly cannot pretend to settle *that* question by
> his physics or biology – it is idle to dismiss the theologian's doctrines of
> sin and grace on the plea that the biologist, for the purposes of his
> biology, can dispense with the notions.[29]

Of one variety of idealism, Pringle-Pattison's pupil H. R.

Mackintosh expostulated in homely fashion,

> Increasingly one feels that a purely logical construction of things, like that of Absolute Idealism, is quite irrelevant and non-committal in regard to those elements of human life that make it best worth living.[30]

Since the terrain to be traversed by Christian testimony is wide, involving a texture of historical, existential, theological, metaphysical, ethical, aesthetic, liturgical assertions, its method must be correspondingly hospitable. Taylor, for example, thought that 'we need to integrate Bonaventura and Thomas and Butler with Kant to appreciate the real strength of the believer's position.'[31] For all his tendencies to lapse into immanentism, Illingworth fully appreciated the inevitability of a certain eclecticism:

> [T]he same person who . . . finds himself to be rational, and the inhabitant of a material world which is rationally ordered, finds himself also to be a moral and spiritual being; with a conscience, however acquired, that distinguishes right from wrong; and with a desire for spiritual communion with other persons and, in its deepest analysis, with God.[32]

Accordingly, he felt that Christian apologetics comprised an amalgam of philosophical, historical and experiential components.[33] If, in the end, recourse was had to faith, that did not matter, for faith

> is not weak reasoning, it is strong sight. It does not act independently of evidence, but it interprets the evidence in the light of its own inner experience, to which a thousand subtle coincidences, secret influences, special providences, give a cogency far too deep for words.[34]

To put it bluntly: responding and witnessing to the alpha and omega is at once more simple (because a child can do it) and more complicated (because the greatest minds will sooner or later balk at mystery) than proceeding along the idealistic road from A to B. It is also more exciting and worthwhile. 'The human mind will not permanently renounce the attempt to find a theory of the universe which shall include all being, even the highest', declared William Sanday.[35] But if the attempts are to be Christian, let those making them give heed to their starting-point, and have the humility to understand that, given the nature of their God and the limitations of themselves, their efforts can be provisional only, and that neither their salvation nor that of anyone else depends upon assent to their results. As to their manner, they may take a leaf out of Anselm's book, concerning whom Webb writes:

> Two opposite dangers beset [those of a philosophical bent]: the indulgence in contemplation, which weakens the sense of personal sinfulness; and the fear of consequences, which refuses to follow the argument, in Plato's words, whithersoever it leads us. The study of Anselm, a pattern of humble penitence and of indefatigable intellectual curiosity, should discourage both these tendencies, and encourage at once sound thought and genuine devotion.[36]

Thus cautioned, we may proceed, with the following words of hope (which one only of our idealists could have written) ringing in our ears:

> Pressing God's lamp close to our breast, carrying within our inmost selves the sense of His indwelling and presence, though we step into a dark, tremendous cloud, it is but for a time:

> > 'Its splendour soon or late will pierce the gloom.
> > We shall emerge the day.'[37]

Notes

Chapter 1: The Provenance of British Idealism

[1] Henry Jones, 'Modern scientific and philosophical thought regarding human society', in *Christ and Civilization,* ed. J. B. Paton *et al.,* London: National Council of Evangelical Free Churches, 1910, 495–6.

[2] See J. B. Baillie, *Studies in Human Nature,* London: Bell, 1921, and with it compare his earlier work, *An Outline of The Idealistic Construction of Experience,* London: Macmillan, 1906. The American philosopher Ralph Barton Perry was convinced that, on the ground of suspicion of all things German, anti-idealistic philosophy had 'gained great impetus from the war'. See his *The Present Conflict of Ideals: A Study of the Philosophical Background of the World War,* New York: Longmans, 1918, 199.

[3] H. Jones, in *Christ and Civilization,* 496.

[4] J. R. Illingworth, *Divine Transcendence,* London: Macmillan, 1911, 1.

[5] C. C. J. Webb, *Religious Experience,* London: OUP, 1945, 35.

[6] B. Russell, *Our Knowledge of the External World,* Chicago: Open Court, 1914.

[7] R. Metz, *A Hundred Years of British Philosophy,* London: Allen & Unwin, 1938, 258.

[8] For an account of these and other trends, with special reference to the philosophy of religion see Alan P. F. Sell, *The Philosophy of Religion 1875–1980,* London: Croom Helm [now Routledge], 1988. Although idealism never entirely vanished from the British philosophical scene, there is some point in A. M. Quinton's quip concerning the fact that idealists 'continued to be the largest group in the philsophical professoriate until 1945'. He continues,

Nothing shows the intellectually anachronistic character of this state of affairs more poignantly than the very high level of technological unemployment of idealists within the philosophical profession. A remarkable number of them nimbly overcame this misfortune by becoming vice-chancellors. The Hegelian mode of thought, with its combination of practical realism and theoretical nebulosity, is a remarkably serviceable instrument for the holders of high administrative positions.

See his 'Absolute idealism', *Proceedings of the British Academy,* LVII, 1971, 304–5. In R. G. Collingwood's opinion 'the philosophy of Green's school had never been predominant among teachers' at Oxford. See his *An Autobiography,* London: OUP, 1939, 17.

9   J. D. Morell, *An Historical and Critical View of the Speculative Philosophy of Europe in the Nineteenth Century,* London: William Pickering, 1846, II, 159.

10   J. M. E. McTaggart, *Studies in Hegelian Cosmology,* Cambridge: CUP, 1901, 250.

11   A. E. Taylor in *The Philosophical Review,* XV, 1906, 414.

12   C. C. J. Webb, *Divine Personality and Human Life,* London: Allen & Unwin 1920, 252. But see a letter of Bradley to A. S. Pringle-Pattison in which he says that now 'I certainly would *not* say that "a future life must be taken as decidedly improbable."' See G. F. Barbour's Memoir of Pringle-Pattison prefixed to the latter's *The Balfour Lectures on Realism,* Edinburgh: Blackwood, 1933, 145.

13   J. H. Muirhead, *The Platonic Tradition in Anglo-Saxon Philosophy,* London: Allen & Unwin, 1931, 197.

14   For a succinct account of this see Alan P. F. Sell, *The Philosophy of Religion 1875–1980,* 39–61.

15   For an account of Edward Caird's older brother John, see Alan P. F. Sell, *Defending and Declaring the Faith: Some Scottish Examples 1860–1920,* Exeter: The Paternoster Press, and Colorado Springs: Helmers & Howard, 1987, ch.4. In the present work 'Caird' will always refer to Edward Caird; John will be so designated. For Rashdall see Margaret Marsh, *Hastings Rashdall: Bibliography of the Published Writings,* Leysters, Herefordshire: Modern Churchpeople's Union, 1993. It may be asked why I exclude R. G. Collingwood from the discussion of substantive issues. Rightly or wrongly, I prefer to see him as an inspirer of subsequent hermeneutical enquiry, rather than as a representative of idealism in (at least temporary) decline. But to have passed through the door of hermeneutics would have taken me well beyond my chosen period and into an area of continuing, prolific activity. I offer brief remarks on Collingwood, Rashdall and Ward in *The Philosophy of Religion 1875–1980.*

16 C. C. J. Webb, *A Study of Religious Thought in England from 1850,* Oxford: Clarendon Press, 1933, 28–9.

17 B. Spinoza, *Ethics,* [1677], I.15.

18 See the appendix to Book I of Spinoza's *Ethics,* and *The Correspondence of Spinoza,* trans. and ed. A. Wolf, London: Allen & Unwin, 1928, letters XXXI, XXXII. Cf. A. Seth Pringle-Pattison, *The Idea of God in the Light of Recent Philosophy,* 2nd rev. edn, New York: OUP, 1920, 221–2. This author, who, as we shall see in the next chapter, added Pringle-Pattison to his name in order to meet legal inheritance requirements, will be known as Pringle-Pattison in our text, and by the chronologically correct name in bibliographical references.

19 See R. Descartes, *A Discourse on Method,* 1637, pt.IV.

20 Andrew Seth, *Scottish Philosophy,* Edinburgh: Blackwood, 2nd edn, 1890, 11.

21 C. C. J. Webb, *Studies in the History of Natural Theology,* [1915], Oxford: The Clarendon Press, 1970, 148; cf. 55.

22 Henry Jones, *The Working Faith of the Social Reformer and Other Essays,* London: Macmillan, 1910, 44.

23 I. Kant, *Critique of Pure Reason,* [1781], trans. J. M. D. Meiklejohn, London: Dent, 1964, 12. For summary comments on Kant, Schleiermacher, Hegel and others in relation to immanentism see Alan P. F. Sell, *Theology in Turmoil: The Roots, Course and Significance of the Conservative–Liberal Debate in Modern Theology,* Grand Rapids: Baker Book House, 1986, ch.I.

24 H. Jones, 'Mr. Balfour as Sophist', *Hibbert Journal,* III, 1904–5, 458.

25 H. Jones, *A Critical Account of the Philosophy of Lotze,* Glasgow: Maclehose, 1895, 371–2.

26 T. H. Green, *Works,* ed. R. L. Nettleship, London: Longmans, Green, 1891, III, 127. This is a review of Caird's *The Philosophy of Kant.*

27 Ibid., 135.

28 As Donald Mackinnon has remarked, 'Caird for all his scholarship saw Kant as the morning star (faintly glimmering) of the Hegelian dawn.' See his *Themes in Theology: The Three-fold Cord,* Edinburgh: T. & T. Clark, 1987, 66n.

29 E. Caird, *The Evolution of Theology in the Greek Philosophers,* Glasgow: Maclehose, 1904, I, 362, 365.

30 Ibid., 370.

31 Idem, *Hegel,* Edinburgh: Blackwood, 1891, 131.

32 R. Mackintosh, 'Theism', in *Encyclopaedia Britannica,* 11th edn. For this sadly neglected theologian see Alan P. F. Sell, *Robert Mackintosh: Theologian of Integrity,* Berne: Peter Lang, 1977.

33 A. Seth, *Scottish Philosophy,* 130.

34 T. H. Green, *Works,* ed. R. L. Nettleship, London: Longmans, Green, 1891, III, 228.

[35] A. Seth, *Hegelianism and Personality,* Edinburgh: Blackwood, 1887, 11, 12.

[36] A. S. Pringle-Pattison, *The Idea of God,* 38.

[37] Henry Jones and John Henry Muirhead, *The Life and Philosophy of Edward Caird,* Glasgow: Maclehose, Jackson, 1921, 282.

[38] H. Jones, *The Immanence of God and the Individuality of Man,* Manchester, 1912, 14.

[39] See C. C. J. Webb, *Kant's Philosophy of Religion,* Oxford: Clarendon Press, 1926, 17, 21, 45.

[40] F. D. E. Schleiermacher, *On Religion: Speeches to its Cultured Despisers,* New York: Harper Torchbooks, 1958, 15.

[41] Ibid., 16.

[42] Ibid., 18.

[43] Ibid., 31.

[44] Ibid., 40.

[45] W. B. Selbie, *Schleiermacher: A Critical and Historical Study,* London: Chapman and Hall, 1913, 241.

[46] Schleiermacher, *On Religion,* 101.

[47] A. Seth, *Hegelianism and Personality,* 57. The entire chapter constitutes an illuminating exposition of Fichte.

[48] Ibid., 58; cf. 39.

[49] Ibid., 72, 73.

[50] E. Caird, *Essays on Literature and Philosophy,* Glasgow: Maclehose, 1892, II, 435.

[51] E. Caird, *Hegel,* 127–8.

[52] See A. Seth, *Two Lectures on Theism,* Edinburgh: Blackwood, 1897, 16.

[53] Quoted ibid., 20.

[54] H. Jones, 'Idealism and epistemology', *Mind,* NS II, 1893, 304.

[55] E. Caird, *Hegel,* 184.

[56] Ibid., 138.

[57] Ibid., 163.

[58] Ibid., 174.

[59] See idem, *Essays on Literature and Philosophy,* II, 518.

[60] Idem, *Hegel,* 31.

[61] Ibid., 21.

[62] *Hegel: The Letters,* trans. Clark Butler and Christiane Seiler, Bloomington: Indiana University Press, 1984, 114; letter of 13 October 1806 to F. I. Niethammer.

[63] John Edward Toews, *Hegelianism. The Path Toward Dialectical Humanism, 1805–1841,* Cambridge: CUP, 1980, 38. In the chapter from which I quote, Toews provides a lucid account of the broader socio-political context to which I but briefly allude.

[64] A. S. Pringle-Pattison, *The Philosophical Radicals and Other Essays: With Chapters Reprinted on the Philosophy of Religion in Kant and Hegel,* Edinburgh: Blackwood, 1907, 288.

65 F. D. E. Schleiermacher, *On Religion,* 55.

66 E. Caird, *Essays on Literature and Philosophy,* II, 436. Cf. idem, *Hegel,* 55; C. C. J. Webb, *A History of Philosophy,* London: Williams and Norgate, 1915, 218.

67 A. Seth, *Hegelianism and Personality,* 83.

68 Idem, *Scottish Philosophy,* 198.

69 O. Pfleiderer, *The Development of Theology in Germany since Kant, and its Progress in Great Britain since 1825,* London: Swan Sonnenschein, 1890, 343.

70 See, for example, R. F. A. Hoernlé, *Idealism as a Philosophical Doctrine,* London: Hodder & Stoughton, [1924], ch.III.

71 [B. Whichcote], *Moral and Religious Aphorisms,* Norwich, 1703, no. 916 (though misprinted 216 ad loc.), 129; cf. *Proverbs* 20: 27. In the remainder of this paragraph I draw on my 'Platonists (ancient and modern) and the Gospel', *The Irish Theological Quarterly,* XLIV no. 3, 1977, sect. III, 161–4.

72 H. More, *An Explanation of the Grand Mystery of Godliness,* 1660, 408.

73 See P. Lamprecht, 'The role of Descartes in seventeenth-century England', *Studies in the History of Ideas,* III, 1935, 181–240; J. Passmore, *Ralph Cudworth,* Cambridge: CUP, 1951; C. Webster, 'Henry More and Descartes: some new sources', *British Journal for the History of Science,* IV, 1969, 359–77.

74 See e.g. H. More, *Divine Dialogues,* Series I.

75 R. Cudworth, *The True Intellectual System of the Universe,* 1820, III, 397.

76 See J. Passmore, *Ralph Cudworth,* 9–11.

77 See his 'Editor's Introduction' to Locke's *An Essay Concerning Human Understanding* (abridged), Oxford: Clarendon Press, 1924, xii–xiv.

78 J. Locke, *Essay,* IV.xxi.4.

79 A. S. Pringle-Pattison, 'Editor's Introduction', xxxix.

80 Thus Pringle-Pattison's exposition in *The Idea of God,* 116–17, 160–1. On p.161 he adverts to Berkeley's 'delicate irony' at the beginning of the *Three Dialogues between Hylas and Philonous,* that philosophers are 'ignorant of what everybody else knows perfectly well'. He continues, 'Yet what Berkeley put forward in irony was propounded at a later date in sober earnest by Sir William Hamilton' – and he cites the latter's *Discussions,* London, 1852; 2nd enlarged edn, 1853, 36. It is interesting to note that Pringle-Pattison's teacher, A. Campbell Fraser, maintained that Hume was the true heir to Locke, and that far from Berkeley's being a sceptic who mistrusted sensation, he was a spiritual realist. See Alan P. F. Sell, 'In the wake of the Enlightenment: the adjustments of James Martineau and Alexander Campbell Fraser', *Enlightenment and Dissent,* IX, 1990, 75; reprinted in idem, *Commemorations: Studies in Christian Thought and History,* Calgary: University of Calgary Press and Cardiff: University of Wales Press, 1993, ch.X.

[81] G. Berkeley, *A Treatise Concerning the Principles of Human Knowledge*, in Berkeley's *Works*, ed. A. Campbell Fraser, Oxford: Clarendon Press, 1871, I, 200.

[82] J. S. Mackenzie, 'Edward Caird as a philosophical teacher', *Mind*, NS XVIII, 1909, 519. Incidentally, this 'false idealism' was G. E. Moore's principal target in his celebrated article 'The refutation of idealism', *Mind*, NS XII, 1903, 433–53, rather than the post-Hegelian or neo-Kantian idealisms which were current at the time. On comparing Moore's paper with Berkeley's text Collingwood concluded that 'the position actually criticized in that article is not Berkeley's position; indeed, in certain important respects it is the exact position which Berkeley was controverting.' See R. G. Collingwood, *An Autobiography*, 22.

[83] D. Hume, *A Treatise on Human Nature*, in Hume's *Works*, ed. T. H. Green and T. H. Grose, London, 1874, I, 327.

[84] A. S. Pringle-Pattison, *The Balfour Lectures on Realism*, Edinburgh: Blackwood, 1933, 202.

[85] Ibid., 206.

[86] Percival Chubb, 'The significance of Thomas Hill Green's philosophical and religious teaching', *The Journal of Speculative Philosophy*, XXII nos. 1 and 2, January, April 1888, 8.

[87] A. S. Pringle-Pattison, 'Philosophy as criticism of categories', reprinted in *The Philosophical Radicals*, 332.

[88] J. S. Mackenzie, 'Edward Caird as a philosophical teacher', 520.

[89] Cf. A. S. Pringle-Pattison, 'Editor's Introduction' to Locke's *Essay*, xlvii.

[90] J. H. Muirhead, *Reflections by a Journeyman in Philosophy*, London: Allen & Unwin, 1942, 29. Cf. A. Seth, *Scottish Philosophy*, 96–7. For this reason, Muirhead continues (with a reference to James Seth's *English Philosophers and Schools of Philosophy*, London: Dent, 1912, 236), the Scottish philosophy made its way in France, where it was widely taught between 1816 and 1870, and in America, where its supreme representative was James McCosh, for whom now see J. David Hoeveler, Jr, *James McCosh and the Scottish Intellectual Tradition*, Princeton: Princeton University Press, 1981.

[91] T. Reid, *Works*, ed. W. Hamilton, Edinburgh: Maclachlan and Stewart, 6th edn, 1863, I, 283.

[92] A. Seth, *Scottish Philosophy*, 76–7.

[93] Ibid., 214.

[94] Idem, *The Balfour Lectures on Realism*, 198–9.

[95] William Hazlitt, *Lectures on English Poets and The Spirit of the Age*, London: Dent, 1910, 198–200.

[96] Thomas Love Peacock, *Nightmare Abbey*, London: OUP, 1929, 140n.

[97] Ibid., 141–2.

[98] Ibid., 174. There is probably a double irony here for, as Hazlitt reminds us,

> Mr Coleridge named his eldest son . . . after Hartley, and the second after Berkeley. The third was called Derwent, after the river of that name. Nothing can be more characteristic of his mind than this circumstance. All his ideas indeed are like a river, flowing on for ever . . . (op. cit., 198n.)

Well, almost: at one point, in the midst of a transcendentalist flight, 'Mr Flosky suddenly stopped; he found himself unintentionally trespassing within the limits of common sense' (*Nightmare Abbey*, 189).

[99] For the marginalia see Coleridge's copy of Hegel's *Wissenschaft der Logik*, held at the British Library, and printed in Alice D. Snyder, *Coleridge on Logic and Learning*, New Haven: Yale University Press, 1929, 162–5; cf. ibid., 68–71. See also *The Philosophical Lectures of Samuel Taylor Coleridge, hitherto unpublished*, ed. Kathleen Coburn, London: Pilot Press, 1949.

[100] Neither of whom, incidentally, is mentioned in Hazlitt's lengthy catalogue of Coleridge's intellectual forebears.

[101] A. Seth, *Two Lectures on Theism*, 15.

[102] J. S. Mill, *Dissertations and Discussions*, London: J. W. Parker, 1859, I, 331.

[103] F. D. Maurice, *Moral and Metaphysical Philosophy*, London: Macmillan, 1882, II, 620.

[104] So A. Seth, *Hegelianism and Personality*, 33; and see the note, in which the author refers to Kant's *Werke*, ed. Gustav Hartenstein, Leipzig, 1838, VIII, 719.

[105] Ibid., 35. This judgement is more charitable and more accurate than that of the idealist John Watson, a pupil of Caird:

> Hume had in the eighteenth century aroused Kant from his dogmatic slumbers, but he had been less successful in his native land, where the so-called 'common sense' philosophy of Reid and Dugald Stuart [*sic*] allowed men to jog along contentedly, with no very strong faith and no very disquieting disbelief.

See his 'The idealism of Edward Caird', *The Philosophical Review*, XVIII, 1909, 150.

[106] See C. Villers, *Philosophie de Kant*, Paris, 1801. For a full account of Kant's reception in England see René Wellek, *Immanuel Kant in England 1793–1838*, Princeton: Princeton University Press, 1931.

[107] The chapter appears in Stewart's *Dissertation Exhibiting the Progress of Metaphysical, Ethical and Political Philosophy*, in Stewart's *Works*, ed. W. Hamilton, 1854, I. It was a supplement to the 4th and 5th editions of the *Encyclopaedia Britannica*, V, 1824.

[108] D. Stewart, *Works,* I, 389n.

[109] C. C. J. Webb, *A Study of Religious Thought in England from 1850,* 90.

[110] See J. S. Mill's *An Examination of Sir William Hamilton's Philosophy,* London: Longman, 1865; 3rd edn, 1867.

[111] David Masson, *Recent British Philosophy,* [1865], 3rd edn, London, 1877, 196.

[112] See F. D. Maurice, *What is Revelation?,* Cambridge, 1859, and *Sequel to the Inquiry, What is Revelation?,* London, 1860.

[113] C. C. J. Webb, *Religious Thought in England from 1850,* 92. This is a characteristic example of Webb's Latinate style.

[114] A. Seth, *Scottish Philosophy,* 183, quoting Reid's *Works,* 636. In fact Reid's first words here are 'Other good men, by a like zeal . . .' In the preceding sentence he refers to 'Some good men' who 'have been led, by zeal for religion, to deprive us of all active power'.

[115] P. Chubb, 'The significance of Thomas Hill Green's philosphical and religious teaching', 5–6.

[116] J. H. Muirhead, *The Platonic Tradition,* 148. Muirhead's informative chapter is entitled, 'How Hegel came to England'. His line of intepretation has been questioned by James Bradley, 'Hegel in Britain: a brief history of British commentary and attitudes', *The Heythrop Journal,* XX, 1979, 1–24, 163–82. See also Peter Robbins, *The British Hegelians 1875–1925,* New York: Garland Publishing, 1982, ch.II.

[117] J. H. Muirhead, *The Platonic Tradition,* 159–60.

[118] A. M. Quinton, 'Absolute Idealism', 318ff.; J. Bradley, 'Hegel in Britain', 2. It is true, and not jingoistic, gently to observe that parochialism is not always one-way. Thus, for example, the distinguished theologian Wolfhart Pannenberg, in a work entitled *Metaphysics and the Idea of God,* Edinburgh: T. & T. Clark, 1990, 113, recounts that he discovered the process philosophy of Whitehead (d. 1947) in 1963. And communications then were vastly improved upon those of 1831.

[119] J. S. Mackenzie, 'The idealism of Edward Caird', 151, 152.

[120] Not that Jones was uncritical of Browning – especially of his later distrust of reason. See H. Jones, *Browning as a Philosophical and Religious Teacher,* Glasgow: Maclehose, 1901. Jones's biographer remarks that Jones knew Wordsworth and Browning 'almost as well as he knew his Bible', and that 'to them – in his last book as in his first – he turned for the imaginative expression of the hypothesis which his philosophical masters had sought to sustain by the more laborious methods of reasoning.' H. J. W. Hetherington, *The Life and Letters of Sir Henry Jones,* London: Hodder & Stoughton, 1924, 44.

[121] Stirling's story is recounted by G. E. Davie, *The Democratic Intellect: Scotland and the Universities in the Nineteenth Century,* Edinburgh: Edinburgh University Press, 1961, 335.

[122] H. D. Lewis, 'The British idealists', in *Nineteenth-Century Religious*

Thought in the West, ed. Ninian Smart *et al.,* Cambridge: CUP, 1985, 275.

123 E. Caird, *Hegel,* vi.

124 Quoted by J. H. Muirhead, *The Platonic Tradition,* 171.

125 J. H. Stirling, *The Secret of Hegel,* Edinburgh: Oliver & Boyd, new edn, 1898, xxii. For the view that 'in terms of a deeper and more imaginative understanding of Hegelianism, of scholarly criticism and new departures in philosophy', Stirling's contribution was 'negligible', see P. Robbins, *The British Hegelians,* 40.

126 Wallace prefaced his translation with *Prolegomena to the Study of Hegel's Philosophy.*

127 See E. Caird, art. 'Benjamin Jowett', in *The Dictionary of National Biography;* P. Robbins, *The British Hegelians,* 29–32 and ch.5.

128 A. M. Quinton, 'Absolute idealism', 320.

129 F. H. Bradley, *The Principles of Logic,* [1883], London: OUP, 2nd edn, corrected, 1928, I, x.

130 T. H. Green, *Works,* III, 145, 146.

131 H. Jones, 'Idealism and epistemology', 304.

132 T. H. Green, *Works,* III, 125.

133 H. Jones, *Idealism as a Practical Creed,* Glasgow: Maclehose, 1909, 241.

134 R. Mackintosh, *Essays Towards a New Theology,* Glasgow: Maclehose, 1889, 367.

135 H. Scott Holland, in a letter to Mrs T. H. Green, quoted in *Henry Scott Holland, Memoirs and Letters,* ed. Stephen Paget, London: John Murray, 1921, 113.

136 A. S. Pringle-Pattison, *The Idea of God,* 166.

137 E. Caird, *Essays on Literature and Philosophy,* I, 193.

138 Idem, *The Social Philosophy and Religion of Comte,* Glasgow: Maclehose, 1893, xvii.

139 Idem, *The Problem of Philosophy at the Present Time,* Glasgow: Maclehose, 1881, 19.

140 C. C. J. Webb, *Studies in the History of Natural Theology,* 358.

141 J. O. Johnston, *Life and Letters of Henry Parry Liddon,* London: Longmans, 1904, 113, in a letter to Lord Beauchamp of 22 June 1868.

142 So C. C. J. Webb, *Religious Thought in England from 1850,* 132.

143 J. R. Illingworth, *Personality Human and Divine,* London: Macmillan, 1904, 48.

144 H. Jones, 'Mr Balfour as Sophist', *Hibbert Journal,* III, 1904–5, 474.

145 Henry Calderwood, 'Another view of Green's last work', *Mind,* X, 1885, 74.

146 A. S. Pringle-Pattison, *The Idea of God,* 82.

147 See Alan P. F. Sell, *Theology in Turmoil,* ch.III.

[148] See C. C. J. Webb, *Religious Thought in the Oxford Movement,* London: SPCK, 1928, 18.

[149] J. R. Illingworth in *Lux Mundi: A Series of Studies in the Religion of the Incarnation,* ed. Charles Gore, London: John Murray, 15th edn, 1904, 132.

[150] See further, Alan P. F. Sell, *Theology in Turmoil,* ch.II on 'The rise and reception of modern biblical criticism'. F. H. Bradley's *The Presuppositions of Critical History,* Oxford: J. Parker, 1874, reveals a certain debt to Baur. Melvin Richter, in the course of commenting upon the crisis for evangelical faith posed by the new science and scholarship, says that he uses the term 'evangelicalism' to cover 'that revival of fundamentalist and ascetic Protestantism begun by the Wesleys'. Now (a) this is an anachronistic use of 'fundamentalist' which, as the word indicates, refers to that series of apologetic booklets, *The Fundamentals,* 1911–15 (see my *Theology in Turmoil,* 101); (b) to confine the attention to the stream of evangelicalism 'begun' by the Wesleys is to overlook the Calvinist (and earlier) wing of the English Revival, some of whose heirs were as disturbed by the new scholarship as their Arminian counterparts; and (c) it is better not to describe Methodism as a 'dissenting denomination' as Richter proceeds to do. Nonconformists they became (reluctantly in the case of many Wesleyans); but 'dissent' is best reserved to the older orthodox and heterodox dissenters, whose *raison d'être* was ecclesiological rather than evangelistic and religious. See Melvin Richter, *The Politics of Conscience: T. H. Green and his Age,* London: Weidenfeld and Nicolson, 1964, 15.

[151] William Sanday, *Christologies Ancient and Modern,* Oxford: Clarendon Press, 1910, 61.

[152] A. S. Pringle-Pattison, *The Idea of God,* 42.

[153] C. C. J. Webb, *Religious Experience,* Oxford: OUP, 1945, 26–7.

[154] For Fairbairn see *The Dictionary of National Biography*; R. S. Franks, 'The theology of Andrew Martin Fairbairn', *Congregational Historical Society Transactions,* XIII, 1937–9, 140–50; W. B. Selbie, *The Life of Andrew Martin Fairbairn,* London: Hodder & Stoughton, 1914; Alan P. F. Sell, *Dissenting Thought and the Life of the Churches: Studies in an English Tradition,* Lewiston, NY: Mellen Research University Press, 1990, ch.XIX.

[155] A. M. Fairbairn, 'Experience in theology: a chapter of autobiography', *The Contemporary Review,* XCI, January–June 1907, 557–8.

[156] Ibid., 567–9. Not indeed that Fairbairn was an uncritical Hegelian. His younger colleague at Mansfield College, T. M. Watt, wrote that Fairbairn

was never wholly mastered by the Hegelian system . . . He broke away from it in his treatment of history; and his Theology would never completely submit itself to the cast-iron mould of the Hegelian categories. Hegelian thought was useful as an ally, but dangerous as a master. On the other hand, he saw that Christian Theology, in alliance with speculative idealism, would be brought into line with the great constructive periods of Christian thought, when philosophy and theology were in harmony with each other. (Quoted by W. B. Selbie, *The Life of Andrew Martin Fairbairn*, 239–40)

In a collection of essays presented to Fairbairn on his seventieth birthday (4 November 1908) a pupil, A. E. Garvie, by now Principal of New College, London, writes, 'Probably Hegelianism is the boldest attempt yet made completely to catch the universe in a network of logical categories; but to-day we marvel more at its audacity than we recognise its adequacy.' See *Mansfield College Essays*, London: Hodder & Stoughton, 1909, 165.

[157] For Denney see *The Dictionary of National Biography;* Alan P. F. Sell, *Defending and Declaring the Faith: Some Scottish Examples 1860–1929*, Exeter: Paternoster Press and Colorado Springs: Helmers & Howard, 1987, ch.IX.

[158] James Denney, *Letters of Principal James Denney to his Family and Friends,* ed. James Moffatt, London: Hodder & Stoughton, [1922], 49; letter dated 15 February 1893. Nearly twenty years on, in a characteristic outburst to his friend William Robertson Nicoll, Denney declared, 'Philosophers used to be our botheration, now it is economists, but they all have souls above parsing.' See *Letters of Principal James Denney to W. Robertson Nicoll 1893–1917*, London: Hodder & Stoughton, 1920, 167–8; letter dated 14 December 1910.

[159] J. Denney, *The Atonement and the Modern Mind,* London: Hodder & Stoughton, 1903, 27, 28.

[160] Quoted in *Letters of Principal James Denney to W. Robertson Nicoll*, xxxv.

[161] A. Campbell Fraser, *Biographia Philosophica: A Retrospect*, Edinburgh: Blackwood, 1904, 184, 186. Cf. idem, *Berkeley,* Edinburgh: Blackwood, 1881, 232–4, and *Thomas Reid,* Edinburgh: Oliphant, 1898, 155.

Chapter 2: Seven British Idealists

[1] While I think it helpful to sketch the lives of the seven idealists, my interests are not primarily biographical. Accordingly, I confine myself to the consideration of published works and letters. Had the seven constituted a closely knit, regularly corresponding school,

unpublished papers would have assumed greater importance. As it is, the most important letters of those who did correspond with one another have been published in whole or in part, and to these I shall refer as appropriate.

2   T. H. Green, *Works,*ed. R. L. Nettleship, London: Longmans, 3rd edn, 1891, III, 250. For Green see *The Dictionary of National Biography*; Nettleship's 'Memoir' in Green's *Works*; Melvin Richter, *The Politics of Conscience: T. H. Green and His Age,* London: Weidenfeld and Nicolson, 1964; Geoffrey Thomas, *The Moral Philosophy of T. H. Green,* Oxford: The Clarendon Press, 1987.

3   William Sanday, *Christologies Ancient and Modern,* Oxford: The Clarendon Press, 1910, 66. Against which sentence the first owner of my copy of Sanday writes, 'Good combination!'

4   Quoted (unattributed) by J. H. Muirhead, *Reflections by a Journeyman in Philosophy,* London: Allen & Unwin, 1942, 41.

5   Quoted by R. L. Nettleship, 'Memoir' in Green's *Works,* III, xiv.

6   T. H. Green, *Works,* III, 118.

7   See Henry Jones and J. H. Muirhead, *The Life and Philosophy of Edward Caird,* Glasgow: Maclehose, 1921, 30–1.

8   See M. Richter, *The Politics of Conscience,* 88–9.

9   From R. L. Nettleship's 'Notes for T. H. Green's Memoir', Bibliography II, T. H. Green Papers, Balliol College, Oxford; quoted by Geoffrey Thomas, *The Moral Philosophy of T. H. Green,* 10.

10   Quoted by R. L. Nettleship, 'Memoir', xxxv.

11   See Green's letter to James Bryce, quoted by M. Richter, *The Politics of Conscience,* 93.

12   Quoted by M. Richter, *The Politics of Conscience,* 153.

13   See R. L. Nettleship, 'Memoir', xli. For cautionary tales concerning the influence of ecclesiastical parties upon Scottish academic appointments see G. E. Davie, *The Democratic Intellect: Scotland and her Universities in the Nineteenth Century,* Edinburgh: Edinburgh University Press, 1961.

14   Quoted by Mrs Oliphant in *A Memoir of the Life of John Tulloch, D.D., LL.D.,* Edinburgh: Blackwood, 3rd edn, 1889, 198–9.

15   From the *Instructions to Assistant Commissioners,* quoted by R. L. Nettleship, 'Memoir', xlv.

16   R. L. Nettleship, ibid., lvi.

17   Quoted by A. W. W. Dale, *The Life of R. W. Dale of Birmingham,* London: Hodder & Stoughton, 1898, 496, and by W. B. Selbie, *The Life of Andrew Martin Fairbairn,* London: Hodder & Stoughton, 1914, 163. Cf. *Mansfield College, Its Origin and Opening,* London: James Clarke, 1890, 32. Are we to infer from Green's very 'Oxford' first sentence that London was either not national, or not a university, or neither? Selbie remarks that the advent of Nonconformist students at

Cambridge 'created no difficulty', for there 'Nonconformity was already strong, and . . . there were churches able and willing to meet the needs of Free Church members of the university. But at Oxford the circumstances were very different' (op. cit., 163).

18 R. L. Nettleship, 'Memoir', lxi.

19 T. H. Green, *Liberal Legislation and Freedom of Contract*, 1881, 22. Reprinted in his *Works*, III, 386.

20 Robert Mackintosh, *Hegel and Hegelianism*, Edinburgh: T. & T. Clark, 1903, 99.

21 R. G. Collingwood, *An Autobiography*, London: OUP, 1939, 17.

22 See M. Richter, *The Politics of Conscience*, 118–19; Klaus Dockhorn, *Die Staatsphilosophie des englischen Idealismus: ihre Lehre und Wirkung*, Bochum, 1937.

23 Quoted by R. L. Nettleship, 'Memoir', cxxvi.

24 Geoffrey Thomas supplies the medical details in *The Moral Philosophy of T. H. Green*, 56, n.76.

25 Quoted by R. L. Nettleship, 'Memoir', clx.

26 Geoffrey Thomas, *The Moral Philosophy of T. H. Green*, 40, citing W. H. Walsh, *Hegelian Ethics*, London: Macmillan, 1969, 4, and H. Sturt, *Idola Theatri: A Criticism of Oxford Thought and Thinkers from the Standpoint of Personal Idealism*, London: Macmillan, 1906, 221. Sturt declares that Green 'arms himself with German principles when he attacks the traditional English philosophy and the modifications of it brought into vogue by John Mill, Herbert Spencer, and the Comtists'. The relevant pages in Edgeworth's work are 83, 85.

27 Henry Calderwood, 'Another view of Green's last work', *Mind*, X, 1885, 73–84.

28 A. M. Quinton, 'Absolute idealism', *Proceedings of the British Academy*, LVII, 1971, 318.

29 Robert Mackintosh, *Hegel and Hegelianism*, 87, 284.

30 Geoffrey Thomas, *The Moral Philosophy of T. H. Green*, 40–1, citing H. Sturt, *Idola Theatri*, 221, and H. Sidgwick, *Lectures on the Ethics of T. H. Green, Mr Herbert Spencer, and J. Martineau*, London: Macmillan, 1902, 3.

31 R.G. Collingwood, *An Autobiography*, 15.

32 A. Seth, *Scottish Philosophy*, Edinburgh: Blackwood, 1890, 125.

33 This point is not made by Geoffrey Thomas when accounting for the difficulty of labelling Green as anything other than an 'idealist' in the sense of one who holds that ultimate reality is constituted by mind. See his *The Moral Philosophy of T. H. Green*, 41.

34 T. H. Green, *Works*, III, 141–2, 143, 144, 146. For Edward Caird's reservations concerning his brother's Hegelianism see his 'Memoir' of John, prefixed to the latter's *The Fundamental Ideas of Christianity*, Glasgow: Maclehose, 1899, lxvii, lxxvi.

[35] Edward Caird in *Essays in Philosophical Criticism,* ed. A. Seth and R. B. Haldane, London: Longmans, 1883, 5.

[36] T. H. Green, *Works,* I, 5.

[37] I thus indicate a certain sympathy with H. V. Knox: 'Locke, the sworn foe of meaningless phrases and unreasoned assumptions, never appears in Green's pages at all . . .' See his 'Has Green answered Locke?', *Mind,* NS XXIII, 1914, 336. Knox refers to A. Campbell Fraser, *Locke,* Edinburgh: Blackwood, 1891, and it is difficult after careful examination not to agree that as compared with Green's, Fraser's exposition (see especially Part II, chs.III and IV) is more accurate and less tendentious.

[38] Idem, *Prolegomena to Ethics,* Oxford: The Clarendon Press, 4th edn, 1899, 11.

[39] Idem,, *Works,* II, 15.

[40] Idem, *Prolegomena to Ethics,* 53.

[41] Idem, *Works,* II, 74.

[42] Percival Chubb, 'The significance of Thomas Hill Green's philosophical and religious teaching', *The Journal of Speculative Philosophy,* XXII nos. 1 and 2, January, April, 1888, 12.

[43] Quoted by R. R. Marett, *A Jerseyman at Oxford,* London: OUP, 1941, 110–11. Marett says that Bywater had Hegel, or possibly Green, in mind.

[44] As recalled by Donald Mackinnon in *Themes in Theology: The Three-fold Chord,* Edinburgh: T. & T. Clark, 1987, 52.

[45] T. H. Green in a letter to Henry Scott Holland of 29 December 1868; see Stephen Paget, *Henry Scott Holland: Memoir and Letters,* London: John Murray, 1921, 29–30.

[46] R. L. Nettleship, 'Memoir', c.

[47] H. D. Lewis, 'The British Idealists', in *Nineteenth Century Religious Thought in the West,* ed. Ninian Smart *et al.,* Cambridge: CUP, 1985, 302.

[48] T. H. Green, *Works,* III, 260.

[49] Ibid., 236.

[50] Ibid., 182.

[51] Letter of Green to H. Scott Holland, quoted by Stephen Paget, *Henry Scott Holland: Memoir and Letters,* 66. Cf. Green's 'Essay on Christian dogma', *Works,* III.

[52] T. H. Green, *Works,* III, 274.

[53] See Albert Peel and J. A. R. Marriott, *Robert Forman Horton,* London: Allen & Unwin, 1937, 75, 109.

[54] T. H. Green, *Prolegomena to Ethics,* 222–3.

[55] Robert Mackintosh, *Christianity and Sin,* London: Duckworth, 1913, 122.

[56] T. H. Green, *Works,* III, 239.

57 Ibid., 276.

58 James Iverach, 'Professor Thomas Hill Green. II', *The Expository Times*, IV, 1892–3, 164.

59 Henry Jones, 'Modern scientific and philosophical thought regarding human society', in *Christ and Civilization*, eds. J. B. Paton *et al.*, London: National Council of Evangelical Free Churches, 1910, 501.

60 T. H. Green, *Works*, III, 273.

61 Ibid., 237.

62 Ibid., 183.

63 James Iverach, 'Professor Thomas Hill Green. II', 168.

64 James Martineau, in a letter of 24 April 1889 to Professor William Knight. See James Drummond and C. B. Upton, *The Life and Letters of James Martineau*, London: Nisbet, 1902, II, 226.

65 John Herman Randall, Jr, *Philosophy After Darwin: Chapters for the Career of Philosophy*, New York: Columbia University Press, 1977, III, 65.

66 C. D. Broad, *Five Types of Ethical Theory*, London: Routledge & Kegan Paul, 1930, 144.

67 J. H. Randall, Jr, *Philosophy After Darwin*, 67.

68 Roger B. C. Johnson, *The Metaphysics of Knowledge: Being an Examination of Some Phases of T. H. Green's Theory of Reality*, Princeton: Princeton University Press, 1900, 48.

69 See M. Richter, *The Politics of Conscience*, 14; H. Scott Holland, *A Bundle of Memories*, London: Wells Gardner, [1915], 145. Scott Holland's remark occurs in his chapter on Hugh Price Hughes.

70 [Dorothea Price Hughes], *The Life of Hugh Price Hughes*, London: Hodder & Stoughton, 1905, 134. Green called on Hughes shortly after the latter's arrival in the Oxford circuit. The minister managed to persuade himself that in Green's view that the ego might be perfected by the union of altruism with enlightened egoism 'you have the philosophical expression of the good old Methodist doctrine of entire sanctification' (ibid.).

71 J. B. Lancelot, *Francis James Chavasse, Bishop of Liverpool*, Oxford: Basil Blackwell, 1929, 26.

72 Henry Jones, *A Faith that Enquires*, London: Macmillan, 1922, 141.

73 For Edward Caird see *The Dictionary of National Biography* (which records his birth date as 22 March); Henry Jones and J. H. Muirhead, *The Life and Philosophy of Edward Caird*. For John Caird see *The Dictionary of National Biography*; Alan P. F. Sell, *Defending and Declaring the Faith: Some Scottish Examples 1860–1920*, Exeter: Paternoster Press and Colorado Springs: Helmers & Howard, 1987, ch.IV.

74 For David Duff see Robert Small, *History of the Congregations of the United Presbyterian Church from 1733 to 1900*, Edinburgh: David M. Small, 1900, I, 237.

75   H. Jones and J. H. Muirhead, *The Life and Philosophy of Edward Caird,*15.

76   Ibid., 19.

77   Ibid., 23.

78   Edward Caird, *Essays on Literature and Philosophy,* Glasgow: Maclehose, 1892, I, 231, 232, 234.

79   H. Jones and J. H. Muirhead, *The Life and Philosophy of Edward Caird,* 370–1.

80   John Watson, 'The Idealism of Edward Caird, I', *The Philosophical Review,* XVIII, 1909, 147.

81   R. M. Wenley, 'An unborn idealism', in *Contemporary American Philosophy,* ed. George P. Adams and Wm. Pepperell Montague, London: Allen & Unwin, 1930, II, 389, n.4.

82   Letter of 18 August 1893 to Henry Jones, in H. Jones and J. H. Muirhead, *The Life and Philosophy of Edward Caird,* 191. In the same year Jones averred that 'truth is essentially combative in nature.' See his 'The nature and aims of philosophy', *Mind,* NS II, 1893, 160.

83   Letter of 14 January 1906 to Miss Mary Sarah Talbot, in H. Jones and J. H. Muirhead, *The Life and Philosophy of Edward Caird,* 241. For 'The faith of Job' see E. Caird, *Lay Sermons and Addresses Delivered in the Hall of Balliol College, Oxford,* Glasgow: Maclehose, 1907, 283–312.

84   J. S. Mackenzie, 'Edward Caird as a philosophical teacher', *Mind,* NS XVIII, 1909, 510.

85   H. Jones and J. H. Muirhead, *The Life and Philosophy of Edward Caird,* 67. Although Caird's intention was the positive one of undertaking the 'difficult task' of separating 'what is permanent from what is transitory in the traditions of the past' (see his *The Evolution of Religion,* Glasgow: Maclehose, 1894, I, viii), it is difficult entirely to quell the feeling that the neglect of a prominent tradition of thought by a philosophical teacher whose method is historical verges upon censorship and vitiates the objectives of a liberal education.

86   In his inaugural lecture on assuming Glasgow's Chair of Moral Philosophy, Caird did, however, acknowledge his distinguished predecessors, Hutcheson, Adam Smith and Reid, who had made the Chair 'in their day and generation a source of light to their country and to the world'. Quoted by J. H. Muirhead, *Reflections by a Journeyman in Philosophy,* 31.

87   E. Caird, *The Evolution of Religion,* I, 45.

88   H. Jones and J. H. Muirhead, *The Life and Philosophy of Edward Caird,* 36.

89   J. H. Muirhead, *Reflections by a Journeyman in Philosophy,* 35.

90   H. Jones and J. H. Muirhead, *The Life and Philosophy of Edward Caird,* 33.

91   W. B. Selbie (ed.), *The Life of Charles Silvester Horne, M.A., M.P.,*

London: Hodder & Stoughton, [1920], 23; letter from Glasgow of 21 February 1886.

92 Ibid., 28; letter of 5 April 1886.

93 H. Jones and J. H. Muirhead, *The Life and Philosophy of Edward Caird,*125.

94 Letter of 29 December 1892 to Mary Sarah Talbot, ibid., 183.

95 Letters to Mary Sarah Talbot of 4 August 1898 and 28 August 1894, ibid., 224, 202; and ibid., 54.

96 Ibid., 349.

97 Quoted by William Temple, *Nature, Man and God,* London: Macmillan, 1934, 70. Temple, yet another of Caird's distinguished pupils, dedicated these Gifford Lectures to his teacher's memory. Cf. the remark of J. S. Mackenzie, 'The real enemy of idealism, as Caird always recognised, is not materialism, but dualism.' See his 'Edward Caird as a philosophical teacher', 515.

98 E. Caird, *Hegel,* Edinburgh: Blackwood, 1891, 114.

99 T. H. Green, *Works,* III, 145.

100 E. Caird, *Essays on Literature and Philosophy,* I, 205–6.

101 Idem, *The Evolution of Theology in the Greek Philosophers,* Glasgow: Maclehose, 1904, I, 193. Caird here refers to Plato's *Republic,* 477A.

102 Idem, 'Idealism and the theory of knowledge', *Proceedings of the British Academy,*1903–4, 108.

103 So J. S. Mackenzie, 'Edward Caird as a philosophical teacher', 517. Caird concludes his *Hegel* with these words:

> The only important question now is, not whether we are disciples of Hegel, – the days of discipleship are past, – but whether we recognise the existence of a living development of philosophy, and especially of that spiritual or idealistic view of things in which philosophy culminates – a development which begins in the earliest dawn of speculation, and in which Kant and Hegel are, not indeed the last names, but the last names in the highest order of speculative genius, *i Maestri di color che sanno.* (op. cit., 224)

104 E. Caird, *Essays on Literature and Philosophy,* I, 256–7.

105 Idem, *The Evolution of Religion,* I, 4.

106 Ibid., I, ix, x.

107 Idem, *Lay Sermons and Addresses,* 162.

108 Idem, *The Evolution of Religion,* I, 51. This view is echoed by many, notably by John Hick in a number of his works, at the time of writing.

109 Ibid., I, 88.

110 Ibid., II, 321.

111 [Leslie Stephen] in *The Dictionary of National Biography,* s.v. 'Caird, Edward.'

112 W. Temple, *Nature, Man and God,* 58.

[113] H. Jones and J. H. Muirhead, *The Life and Philosophy of Edward Caird*, 79.

[114] J. S. Mackenzie, 'Edward Caird as a philosophical teacher', 512–13.

[115] Cf. P. Carnegie Simpson, *The Life of Principal Rainy*, London: Hodder & Stoughton, popular edn, n.d., I, 407: Caird 'taught men to think, though indeed he took many inquiring minds out into new and deep seas – not, in all cases, piloting them to port'.

[116] A. E. Garvie, *Memories and Meanings of My Life*, London: Allen & Unwin, 1938, 77, 78.

[117] Robert Mackintosh, *Hegel and Hegelianism*, 96.

[118] Ibid., 98.

[119] Ibid., 98–9.

[120] C. C. J. Webb, *Natural and Revealed Religion*, Oxford: The Clarendon Press, 1912, 29.

[121] J. R. Illingworth, *University and Cathedral Sermons*, London: Macmillan, 1893, 140–1.

[122] [Agnes Louisa Illingworth], *The Life and Work of John Richardson Illingworth, M.A., D.D.*, London: John Murray, 1917, 24; in a letter to the Revd Charles Seaman.

[123] Ibid., 316–17.

[124] Ibid., 30.

[125] Ibid., 241.

[126] Ibid., 61.

[127] Ibid., 78. (Quite right too!)

[128] So H. Scott Holland, ibid., 319.

[129] Ibid., 239, 242.

[130] Ibid., 238.

[131] J. R. Illingworth, *The Gospel Miracles*, London: Macmillan, 1915, v–vi.

[132] Ibid., 185.

[133] See further Alan P. F. Sell, *Theology in Turmoil: The Roots, Course and Significance of the Conservative–Liberal Debate in Modern Theology*, Grand Rapids: Baker Book House, 1986, 35–6, 154.

[134] J. R. Illingworth, *Divine Transcendence and its Reflection in Religious Authority*, London: Macmillan, 1911, 12, 13.

[135] See *The Life and Work of John Richardson Illingworth*, 174–5.

[136] Ibid., 173.

[137] Ibid., v, xi.

[138] Ibid., 177.

[139] Ibid., 25.

[140] Ibid., 90; letter of 14 December 1888.

[141] Ibid., 46; letter of 26 September 1878 to the Revd H. E. Trimmer.

[142] C. Gore, preface to *Lux Mundi*, [1889], 15th edn, 1904, vii.

[143] J. R. Illingworth, *The Church and Human Thought in the Present Day* (Pan Anglican Papers no. 2), London: SPCK, 1907, 3 (my pagination).

[144] Idem, 'The Incarnation and development', in *Lux Mundi,* 137. Cf. idem, *Sermons Preached in a College Chapel,* London: Macmillan, 1882, 67.

[145] Idem, *Sermons Preached in a College Chapel,* 41–2.

[146] See letters to the Revd Wilfrid Richmond of 19 March 1875 and 1889, in *The Life and Work of John Richardson Illingworth,* 36, 160.

[147] Idem, *Reason and Revelation,* London: Macmillan, 1902, 103. I am, of course, well aware of many subsequent philosophers who would hotly contest this definition of the philosopher's task – in the interests, for example of the 'humbler' (yet sometimes so arrogantly prosecuted!) role of linguistic analysis. In recent years there has been sometimes cordial, sometimes grudging recognition that some of the meta-physicians of the past were no mean analysts of discourse, albeit they had construction and not simply the therapeutic dissolution of problems in mind.

[148] J. R. Illingworth, *Divine Immanence: An Essay on the Spiritual Signi-ficance of Matter,* London: Macmillan, [1898], 2nd edn, reprinted 1903, 2.

[149] Ibid., 69.

[150] Idem, *Reason and Revelation,* 116.

[151] Idem, *Personality Human and Divine,* London: Macmillan, 1904, 167. These words have a hierarchical flavour which many would today find offensive; and it is not a foregone conclusion that all those of faiths other than the Christian would welcome the conviction that the world's religion is too much of a piece to be torn asunder. It goes without saying that Illingworth's form of words is infinitely to be preferred to that of some in his time who announced with varying degrees of lurid detail that followers of other faiths than the Christian were *ipso facto* hell-bound. For some further reflections on this matter see Alan P. F. Sell, *Aspects of Christian Integrity,* Calgary: University of Calgary Press, 1990, and Louisville: Westminster/John Knox Press, 1991, ch.V.

[152] Idem, *The Doctrine of the Trinity Apologetically Considered,* London: Macmillan, 1907, 18.

[153] Idem, *Personality Human and Divine,* 4.

[154] Idem, *University and Cathedral Sermons,* London: Macmillan, 1893, ch.I.

[155] Idem, in *Lux Mundi,* 133.

[156] Idem, *Christian Character,* London: Macmillan, 1914, 17.

[157] [A. L. Illingworth], *The Life and Work of John Richardson Illingworth,* vi.

[158] Samuel M. Crothers in *The International Journal of Ethics,* VI, 1896, 265f.

[159] H. Scott Holland in *The Life and Work of John Richardson Illingworth,* 321, 322.

[160] Ibid., 336.

[161] James Iverach in *The Critical Review of Theological and Philosophical Literature*, XIII, 1903, 31.

[162] Quoted in *The Life and Work of John Richardson Illingworth*, 308; from a sermon preached on 22 August 1915.

[163] For Jones see *The Dictionary of National Biography*; *The Dictionary of Welsh Biography down to 1940*, London: The Honourable Society of Cymmrodorion, 1959; H. Jones, *Old Memories*, London: Hodder & Stoughton [1923]; J. H. Muirhead, 'Sir Henry Jones, 1852–1922': *Proceedings of the British Academy*, X, 1921–3; H. J. W. Hetherington, *The Life and Letters of Sir Henry Jones*, London: Hodder & Stoughton, 1924; [Huw Morris-Jones], 'The life and philosophy of Sir Henry Jones', in *Henry Jones, 1852–1922. Centenary Addresses delivered at the University College of North Wales on the first day of December, 1952*, Cardiff: University of Wales Press, 1953; David Boucher and Andrew Vincent, *A Radical Hegelian: The Political and Social Philosophy of Henry Jones*, Cardiff: University of Wales Press, 1993. See my review of this book in the *British Journal for the History of Philosophy*, III no.1, 1995, 201–4.

[164] H. Jones, *Old Memories*, 38.

[165] Quoted by H. J. W. Hetheringon, *The Life and Letters of Sir Henry Jones*, 20n.

[166] H. Jones, 'Modern scientific and philosophical thought regarding human society', in *Christ and Civilization*, ed. J. B. Paton *et al.*, London: National Council of Evangelical Free Churches, 1910, 500.

[167] H. Jones, *Idealism as a Practical Creed*, Glasgow: Maclehose, 1909, 162, 101.

[168] H. Jones and J. H. Muirhead, *The Life and Philosophy of Edward Caird*, 168, 212; letters to Mary Sarah Talbot of 3 June 1891 and 18 January 1896.

[169] H. J. W. Hetherington, *The Life and Letters of Sir Henry Jones*, 71.

[170] H. Jones and J. H. Muirhead, *The Life and Philosophy of Edward Caird*, 228; letter of 17 January 1899 to Mary Sarah Talbot.

[171] *Letters of Principal James Denney to W. Robertson Nicoll 1893–1917*, London: Hodder & Stoughton, [1920], 78, 82; letters of 19 and 29 January 1907.

[172] Quoted by H. J. W. Hetherington, *The Life and Letters of Sir Henry Jones*, 148.

[173] Ibid.

[174] H. Jones, *Christ and Civilization*, 513.

[175] Idem, 'The nature and aims of philosophy', *Mind*, NS II, 1893, 160.

[176] Ibid., 162.

[177] Ibid., 163.

[178] Idem, *Is the Order of Nature Opposed to the Moral Life?* (Inaugural Lecture at Glasgow University), Glasgow: Maclehose, 1894, 28.

[179] Idem, 'The nature and aims of philosophy', 170.

[180] Idem, *Idealism as a Practical Creed*, 7.

[181] A. S. Pringle-Pattison, *The Philosophical Radicals*, Edinburgh: Blackwood, 1907, 148. The context is the author's review of Jones's *A Critical Account of the Philosophy of Lotze*.

[182] Robert Mackintosh, *Hegel and Hegelianism*, 124.

[183] A. S. Pringle-Pattison, *The Balfour Lectures on Realism*, Edinburgh: Blackwood, 1933, 194. These lectures were originally delivered in 1891, and published in *The Philosophical Review*.

[184] H. Jones, 'Idealism and epistemology', *Mind*, NS II no. 7, July 1893, 291.

[185] A. Seth, 'Hegelianism and its critics', *Mind*, NS III no. 9, January 1894, 1.

[186] Ibid., 5.

[187] See Pringle-Pattison's further critique reprinted in *The Philosophical Radicals*.

[188] H. Jones, *A Faith that Enquires*, 161.

[189] A. Seth, 'Hegelianism and its critics', 19.

[190] Idem, *The Balfour Lectures on Realism*, 173.

[191] In which connection Illingworth's remark on coming to breakfast one morning may be noted: 'How are we to have any speculative peace as long as cats kill mice?' [A. L. Illingworth], *The Life and Work of John Richardson Illingworth*, 336.

[192] H. J. W. Hetherington, *The Life and Letters of Sir Henry Jones*, 216–17; letter of 22 May 1909.

[193] H. Jones, *Is the Order of Nature Opposed to the Moral Life?*, 5–6.

[194] H. Jones, *The Immortality of the Soul in Tennyson and Browning*, (the Essex Hall Lecture for 1905), London: Green, 1905, 33.

[195] Idem, *The Philosophy of Martineau in Relation to the Idealism of the Present Day: Being an Address delivered in Manchester College, Oxford, at the celebration of the Centenary of Dr Martineau*, London: Macmillan, 1905, 37.

[196] Idem, *Idealism as a Practical Creed*, 127.

[197] Idem, *Social Powers: Three Popular Lectures on the Environment, the Press and the Pulpit*, Glasgow: Maclehose, 1913, 90–1, 114. Cf. idem, 'The present attitude of reflective thought towards religion', *Hibbert Journal*, I, 1902–3, 252.

[198] Idem, 'Modern scientific and philosophical thought regarding human society', in *Christ and Civilization*, 498.

[199] Ibid., 502. Cf. *Idealism as a Practical Creed*, 224–5; *A Faith that Enquires*, vii, 15.

[200] Idem, *A Faith that Enquires*, 51.

[201] J. Denney, *Letters of Principal James Denney to W. Robertson Nicoll 1893–1917*, 149.

[202] H. J. W. Hetherington, *The Life and Letters of Sir Henry Jones,* 82.

[203] H. Jones, *Old Memories,* 128. This is the kind of charge which, as we have seen, Denney turned against philosophers.

[204] Idem, 'Tennyson', *Hibbert Journal,* VIII, 1909–10, 277.

[205] Huw Morris-Jones, *Henry Jones 1852–1922,* 5.

[206] See H. J. W. Hetherington, *The Life and Letters of Sir Henry Jones,* 81, 111, 153.

[207] C. A. Campbell, quoted by Huw Morris-Jones, *Henry Jones 1852–1922,* 8.

[208] H. Rashdall, *International Journal of Ethics,* XXI no. 1, October 1910, 110.

[209] H. J. W. Hetherington, *The Life and Letters of Sir Henry Jones,* 154.

[210] See Alan P. F. Sell, 'In the wake of the Enlightenment: the adjustments of James Martineau and Alexander Campbell Fraser', *Enlightenment and Dissent,* IX, 1990, 63–92; reprinted in idem, *Commemorations: Studies in Christian Thought and History,* Calgary: University of Calgary Press, and Cardiff: University of Wales Press, 1993, ch.X.

[211] For Pringle-Pattison see *The Dictionary of National Biography;* J. B. Capper and J. B. Baillie, 'Andrew Seth Pringle-Pattison,1856–1931', *Proceedings of the British Academy,* XVII, 1931; E. N. Merrington, 'A Scottish thinker: Andrew Seth Pringle-Pattison', *Australian Journal of Psychology and Philosophy,* IX no. 4, December 1931, 241–5; G. F. Barbour, 'Memoir of Andrew Seth Pringle-Pattison', prefixed to *The Balfour Lectures on Realism;* H. F. Hallett, 'Andrew Seth Pringle-Pattison 1856–1931', *Mind,* NS XLII, 1933, 137–49.

[212] A. Seth, *On the Present Position of the Philosophical Sciences,* Edinburgh: Blackwood, 1891, 2; reprinted in *Man's Place in the Cosmos,* Edinburgh: Blackwood, 2nd edn, revised and enlarged, 1902.

[213] A. S. Pringle-Pattison, 'Memoir of James Seth' prefixed to the latter's *Essays on Ethics and Religion,* Edinburgh: Blackwood, 1926, xv. James Seth dedicated his *English Philosophers and Schools of Philosophy,* London: Dent, 1912, to the memory of Campbell Fraser.

[214] Quoted by G. F. Barbour, 29, and J. B. Capper, 9, in their 'Memoirs'.

[215] Reprinted in part in A. S. Pringle-Pattison, *The Philosophical Radicals.*

[216] For Begg and his *milieu* see Alan P. F. Sell, *Defending and Declaring the Faith: Some Scottish Examples 1860–1920,* ch.II.

[217] His letter of application for the Principalship is extant, as are testimonials from Sir Alexander Grant, A. Campbell Fraser, Henry Calderwood, A. J. Balfour, James Hutchinson Stirling, Edward Caird, Henry Sidgwick, G. Croom Robertson, Robert Adamson, Shadworth H. Hodgson, A. M. Fairbairn, Robert Flint, W. Y. Sellar, David Masson, Simon S. Laurie, James Donaldson, R. B. Haldane and twenty members of the Select Advanced Class at Edinburgh.

Supplementary testimonials were submitted by Edward Zeller, William Wallace, William Peterson and J. W. Mackail. Clearly this was no 'party' list: Fraser would never have eulogized Hegel as Stirling did; both Calderwood and Sidgwick criticized Caird from their respective vantage points; and Robert Flint was his own man. In addition we note the names of Fairbairn the theologian and Masson the Professor of English. These materials may be consulted at the Bodleian Library, Oxford.

218 Green, we recall, had been a candidate for the Chair when Baynes was appointed.

219 So William Menzies, quoted by G. F. Barbour, 'Memoir', 61, 66.

220 J. Laird in *The Dictionary of National Biography*, s.v. 'Pattison, Andrew Seth Pringle-'. His brother James had more rapport with the students in class; he discouraged, and eventually forbade, the interruption of note-taking, and was more adept at initiating beginners into philosophy. So G. F. Barbour, 'Memoir', 95–6; A. S. Pringle-Pattison's 'Memoir of James Seth', vii.

221 H. F. Hallett, 'Andrew Seth Pringle-Pattison', 148.

222 A. Campbell Fraser, *Biographia Philosophica: A Retrospect*, Edinburgh: Blackwood, 1904, 279. Pringle-Pattison's application contained thirty-four testimonials from individuals, others from St Andrews students, a list of his publications, extracts from press notes; it ran to seventy pages in all, and may be consulted at the Bodleian Library, Oxford.

223 A. S. Pringle-Pattison, *The Philosophical Radicals*, 336.

224 Ibid., x.

225 Ibid., 336. Cf. *The Idea of God*, 67.

226 Idem, *The Idea of God*, 108–9.

227 Ibid., 129.

228 Idem, *Scottish Philosophy*, 219.

229 Idem, *Man's Place in the Cosmos*, 61-2.

230 Idem, *Two Lectures on Theism*, 62.

231 Idem, *Man's Place in the Cosmos*, vi. Cf. ibid., vii; *The Idea of God*, 200, 236.

232 Idem, *The Idea of God*, vi–vii.

233 A. Seth, 'Three years under the new ordinances: a graduation address', *The Scottish Review*, XXVI, 1895, 174.

234 Idem, *The Idea of God*, 127.

235 Ibid., 42.

236 J. B. Baillie, 'Andrew Seth Pringle-Pattison', 19, 45.

237 A. Seth, *Scottish Philosophy*, 200–1.

238 Ibid., 187.

239 Idem, *Hegelianism and Personality*, 215.

240 Ibid., 218.

[241] Idem, *Two Lectures on Theism,* 19.

[242] Idem, *The Idea of God,* 57.

[243] H. F. Hallett, 'Andrew Seth Pringle-Pattison', 144.

[244] A. S. Pringle-Pattison in a letter of 28 November 1915 to Lord Balfour; quoted by G. F. Barbour, 'Memoir', 118. On the other hand he greatly valued Green's teaching concerning the eternal Self which creates 'manifold individual selves', and he recalled 'the thrill with which the meaning of the new principle first flashed upon him, and the light which it seemed to throw upon old difficulties'. See his *Hegelianism and Personality,* 59. Concerning this book Caird wrote to Mary Sarah Talbot on 2 June 1893:

> Seth's book is a reaction from Idealism upon common sense. He says that he combines Idealistic Ontology and Realistic Epistemology – which really seems to mean a dualism of knowledge with a faith that somehow the dualism is not absolute tho' for us in thinking it is so. He represents and tried to make rational a very common state of mind, and so finds a good deal of acceptance.

See H. Jones and J. H. Muirhead, *The Life and Philosophy of Edward Caird,* 188.

[245] A. Seth, *Scottish Philosophy,* 219.

[246] J. B. Capper and J. B. Baillie, 'Andrew Seth Pringle-Pattison', 45. It is difficult to suppress the conviction that Baillie's must be among the most jaundiced of 'appreciations' ever published under the auspices of the British Academy. As with bad (in the sense of tendentious, ill-tempered and unjust – not unfavourable) reviews, to respond to his comments would be to take them too seriously. At least he did not patronize with sentimental eulogy!

[247] Quoted by J. B. Capper, 'Andrew Seth Pringle-Pattison', 17. See also H. R. Mackintosh, 'A philosopher's theology', in his *Some Aspects of Christian Belief,* London: Hodder & Stoughton, [1923], ch.XIII.

[248] W. R. Inge, *God and the Astronomers,* London: Longmans, 1933, 9; *Mysticism and Religion,* London: Rider, [1947] 1969, 203.

[249] Denis M. Gallagher, *Pringle-Pattison's Idea of God,* Washington: Catholic University of America, 1933, 138.

[250] It is interesting (I do not say significant or ominous) that the entry on Webb in *The Dictionary of National Biography* is not by a philosopher, but by the distinguished medieval historian, F. M. Powicke.

[251] For Webb see his 'Biographical' at n.252 below; *The Dictionary of National Biography;* W. D. Ross, 'Clement Charles Julian Webb', *Proceedings of the British Academy,* XLI, 1955; James Patrick, *Idealism and Orthodoxy at Oxford,1901–1945,* Macon, GA: Mercer University Press, 1985; L. W. Grensted (Webb's successor in the Nolloth Chair), 'Foreword' to C. C. J. Webb, *Religious Experience,* Oxford: OUP, 1945;

and numerous autobiographical references scattered through Webb's works.

252 C. C. J. Webb, 'Biographical', prefixed to his 'Outline of a philosophy of religion', in *Contemporary British Philosophy*, ed. J. H. Muirhead, London: Allen & Unwin, Second Series, 1925, 336.

253 Idem, *Religious Thought in the Oxford Movement*, London: SPCK, 1928, 82.

254 Idem, *A Century of Anglican Theology*, Oxford: Blackwell, 1923, 31.

255 Idem, 'Biographical', 336.

256 Ibid.

257 Ibid., 336–7.

258 Ibid., 338.

259 Ibid., 339.

260 Idem, *Religious Experience*, 35.

261 Idem, 'Biographical', 340. See further John D. Root, 'The correspondence of Friedrich von Hügel and Clement C. J. Webb', *The Downside Review*, XCIX no. 337, October 1981, 288–98.

262 In *The Oxford Magazine*, 12 February 1890, suppl. 3–4.

263 L. W. Grensted, 'Foreword' to C. C. J. Webb, *Religious Experience*, 21.

264 C. C. J. Webb, 'Outline of a philosophy of religion', 342.

265 Idem, *Divine Personality and Human Life*, London: Allen & Unwin, 1920, 22. This volume was dedicated to Charles John Shebbear 'in the fortieth year of our friendship'. On the following page he writes, 'I have never made any attempts to engage for myself in investigations of the kind carried on by the Society of Psychical Research.'

266 See idem, *Religious Experience*, 43–5.

267 Idem, *A Century of Anglican Theology*, 4.

268 Idem, *A Study of Religious Thought in England from 1850*, Oxford: The Clarendon Press, 188; cf. 179–80.

269 Idem, *A Century of Anglican Theology*, 7–11.

270 Idem, *God and Personality*, London: Allen & Unwin, 1918, 21.

271 See idem, *A Century of Anglican Theology*, 22–6, 33.

272 Idem, *God and Personality*, 82.

273 Idem, 'Outline of a philosophy of religion', 341–2.

274 Ibid., 342–3.

275 Ibid., 359.

276 Ibid., 345.

277 Ibid., 348.

278 Ibid., 349.

279 Idem, *Religious Experience*, 41.

280 Idem, *Problems in the Relations of God and Man*, London: Nisbet, 1911, 58. Cf. ibid., 17 and ch.II. This book is dedicated to his wife. Cf. idem, *Religious Experience*, 42.

281   Idem, *Religious Experience*, 43–5.

282   Idem, *Studies in the History of Natural Theology*, 50.

283   E.g. idem, 'Outline of a philosophy of religion', 358.

284   L. W. Grensted, 'Foreword' to C. C. J. Webb, *Religious Experience*, 16.

285   For Taylor see *The Dictionary of National Biography*; W. D. Ross, 'Alfred Edward Taylor 1869–1945', reprinted from *Proceedings of the British Academy*, XXXI, 1945.

286   W. D. Ross, 'Alfred Edward Taylor', 3.

287   See W. F. Lofthouse, 'Alfred Edward Taylor', *The London Quarterly and Holborn Review*, 6th series, XV, 1946, 97–107. There is some difference of opinion as to how High Church an Anglican Taylor became. Lofthouse (105) denies that he was an Anglo-Catholic, points out that he wrote as a defender of the faith against unbelief and never as one recalling others to 'the' Church, and notes that in his Gifford Lectures Taylor, while upholding the sacraments, does not pronounce upon the threefold ministry or upon the 'validity' of sacraments administered outside such a ministerial tradition. On the other hand Donald Mackinnon, in his article on Taylor in *The Dictionary of National Biography*, declared that 'Taylor was a strong Anglo-Catholic'; and W. L. Knox and Alec R. Vidler described Taylor's Gifford Lectures as 'The most important achievement of Anglo-Catholic theology since the War in this field . . .' See *The Development of Modern Catholicism*, London: Philip Allan, 1933, 287. Certainly in one of his articles Taylor made it clear that he was not for traditionalism for its own sake. As another name for indolence, traditionalism, he thought, was the enemy of philosophy. See his 'Philosophy', in *Recent Developments in European Thought*, ed. F. S. Marvin, London: OUP, III, 1920, 49. Taylor retained to the end objections to catholicism of the Roman variety: 'I cannot find the abode of the supreme truth in a society which has not renounced the right of persecution.' See his 'Why I am not a Roman Catholic' in *Why I am, and Why I am not a Roman Catholic*, ed. Alban Goodier, London: Cassell, 1931, 180.

288   R. G. Collingwood, *An Autobiography*, 16.

289   C. C. J. Webb, *Religious Experience*, 34–5.

290   W. D. Ross, 'Alfred Edward Taylor', 3.

291   A. E. Taylor, 'Biographical' preface to 'The freedom of man', in *Contemporary British Philosophy*, ed. J. H. Muirhead, First Series, 1924, 271.

292   Quoted by W. D. Ross, ibid., 4.

293   Quoted ibid., 5–6.

294   Unless otherwise stated quotations are from A. E. Taylor, 'Biographical' preface to his 'The freedom of man', in *Contemporary British Philosophy*, First Series, 270–2.

295   A. E. Taylor, 'The metaphysical problem, with special reference to its

bearing upon ethics', *International Journal of Ethics*, X, 1899–1900, 356.

296 Idem, 'Mind and nature', *International Journal of Ethics*, XIII, 1902–3, 59.

297 G. E. Moore, 'The refutation of Idealism', [1903], reprinted in his *Philosophical Studies*, London: Routledge & Kegan Paul, [1922], 1965, 8.

298 A. E. Taylor, *The Problem of Conduct*, London: Macmillan, 1901, 169. I have been guided in my choice of quotations for this paragraph by the illuminating article of Charles F. Sawhill Virtue, 'The axiological theism of A. E. Taylor', *Philosophy*, XXVII, 1952, 110–24. For a theologian's critique of Taylor's early ethical views see James Orr, *Sin as a Problem of Today*, London: Hodder & Stoughton, 1910, 49–52.

299 Ibid., 277. Cf. F. H. Bradley, *Ethical Studies*, London: OUP, 2nd edn, 1927, 201.

300 Idem, *The Faith of a Moralist*, London: Macmillan, 1930, I, 223–4.

301 Ibid., II, 1931, 195.

302 J. E. Creighton, review of A. E. Taylor, *The Elements of Metaphysics*, in *The Philosophical Review*, XIV, 1905, 60.

303 Robert Mackintosh, 'Recent philosophy and Christian doctrine', *Proceedings of the Third International Congregational Council*, ed. John Brown, London: Congregational Union of England and Wales, 1908, 83. Cf. A. E. Taylor, *The Elements of Metaphysics*, London: Methuen, 1903, 343–7, 354–8.

304 A. E. Taylor, 'The vindication of religion', in *Essays Catholic and Critical*, ed. E. G. Selwyn, London: SPCK, 1926, 79.

305 W. F. Lofthouse, 'Alfred Edward Taylor', 103.

306 A. E. Taylor, 'Religion and present-day thought', in *The Recall to Religion*, London: Eyre & Spottiswoode, 1937, 245.

307 Idem, *Does God Exist?*, [1945], London: Collins Fontana, 1961, 25, 41.

308 Ibid., 101ff, 111, 141, 157–8.

309 Idem, *The Faith of a Moralist*, II, 377. Cf. his 'Ancient and modern philosophy', in *European Civilization: Its Origin and Development*, ed. Edward Dyre, London: OUP, 1935, 739.

310 Idem, 'Theism', in *The Encyclopaedia of Religion and Ethics*, ed. James Hastings, Edinburgh: T. & T. Clark, 1921, XII, 286(b).

311 A. E. Taylor, *The Christian Hope of Immortality*, London: The Unicorn Press, 1938, 71.

Chapter 3: *God, the Absolute and the Idealists*

1 E. H. Blakeney, review of E. Caird, *Essays on Literature and Philosophy*, in *The Churchman*, VII, August 1893, 591, and ibid., VIII, October 1893, 15.

2   Robert Mackintosh, *Hegel and Hegelianism,* Edinburgh: T. & T. Clark, 1903, 195, 192.

3   Although many idealists – Caird, Illingworth, Webb and Taylor among them – devoted considerable attention to the several arguments for the existence of God, I bypass these theistic efforts in this book in order to concentrate upon the relations between post-Hegelian idealism and specifically Christian doctrinal affirmations. Illingworth's view of the theistic arguments is broadly representative of that of all of our seven idealists:

> [W]hen we come to consider the various evidences, arguments, proofs by which this belief [i.e. belief in a personal God] is commonly supported, we must remember that these are all attempts to account for, and explain, and justify something which already exists; to decompose a highly complex, though immediate, judgement into its constituent elements, none of which when isolated can have the completeness or the cogency of the original conviction taken as a whole.

See his *Personality Human and Divine,* London: Macmillan, 1904, 81.

4   T. H. Green, *Works,* London: Longmans, 1893, II, 80.

5   Ibid., 179.

6   Ibid., I, 91.

7   Ibid., III, 143, 144. Cf. 146.

8   Ibid., 145.

9   Ibid.

10 T. H. Green, *Prolegomena to Ethics,* Oxford: The Clarendon Press, 4th edn, 1899, para. 69.

11 Ibid., para. 52. Sidgwick quotes these words among others in his 'The philosophy of T. H. Green', *Mind,* NS X, 1901, 22.

12 T. H. Green, *Prolegomena to Ethics,* para. 187.

13 Ibid., para. 182.

14 Melvin Richter, *The Politics of Conscience: T. H. Green and His Age,* London: Weidenfeld and Nicolson, 1964, 185.

15 James Orr, *Sin as a Problem of To-day,* London: Hodder & Stoughton, 1910, 81–2.

16 Charles B. Upton, 'Theological aspects of the philosophy of T. H. Green', *New World* (Chicago), I, 1892, 142. Upton quotes the unnamed student of Balliol. Cf. Taylor's quip: 'The Hegelians, to be sure, made merry of the Unknowable of Mr Spencer, but their own Absolute is really just the Unknowable in its "Sunday best".' See his 'Philosophy', in *Recent Developments in European Thought,* ed. F. S. Marvin (The Unity Series, III), London: OUP, 1920, 53. Illingworth said of the absolute, construed in the sense of 'unrelated to anything outside itself' and as applicable only to 'the totality of all existence',

that it thereby 'becomes a practically meaningless thing'. See his *Divine Transcendence*, London: Macmillan, 1914, 14.

[17] A. E. Taylor, *William George de Burgh, 1866–1943*, reprinted from the *Proceedings of the British Academy*, XXIX, 1943, 22. Taylor compares de Burgh favourably with Green in this respect.

[18] T. H. Green, *Works*, III, 239–40. Andrew Vincent and Raymond Plant write that Green is here commenting upon Baur's progressive view of the Christian revelation adumbrated in *Geschichte der Christlichen Kirche*. See their *Philosophy, Politics and Citizenship*, Oxford: Blackwell, 1984, 12. But in the text of the sermon, 'The witness of God', from which Green's words are taken, there is no explicit reference to Baur. This is not to deny the latter's influence upon Green. The more general influence of evolutionary thought should not go unnoticed either. See further, Alan P. F. Sell, *Theology in Turmoil: The Roots, Course and Significance of the Conservative–Liberal Debate in Modern Theology*, Grand Rapids: Baker Book House, 1986, ch.III.

[19] C. C. J. Webb, *A Century of Anglican Theology*, Oxford: Blackwell, 1923, 52–3.

[20] H. Jones, *A Faith that Enquires*, London: Macmillan, 1922, 132.

[21] Ibid., 273.

[22] H. Jones and J. H. Muirhead, *The Life and Philosophy of Edward Caird*, Glasgow: Maclehose, Jackson, 1921, 185; letter of 25 February 1893.

[23] H. Jones, *A Faith that Enquires*, 299.

[24] A. S. Pringle-Pattison, *The Idea of God in the Light of Recent Philosophy*, New York: Oxford University Press, 2nd rev. edn, 1920, 383.

[25] For a fuller exposition of these points see J. S. Mackenzie, 'Edward Caird as a philosophical teacher', *Mind*, NS XVII, 1909, 521–6.

[26] E. Caird, *Hegel*, Edinburgh: Blackwood, 1891, 176.

[27] Idem, *The Evolution of Religion*, Glasgow: Maclehose, 2nd edn, 1894, I, 68. In a footnote Caird admits the abstract nature of this summary statement, which he subsequently elaborates.

[28] Ibid., 163.

[29] Idem, *Hegel*, 149.

[30] See, for example, R. Adamson's review of *The Evolution of Religion*, in *International Journal of Ethics*, IV, 1893–4, 101–11.

[31] A. E. Garvie, *A Handbook of Christian Apologetics*, London: Duckworth, 1913, 18–19.

[32] E. Caird, *The Evolution of Philosophy in the Greek Philosophers*, Glasgow: Maclehose, 1904, I, 33.

[33] A. S. Pringle-Pattison, *The Idea of God*, 334.

[34] A. E. Garvie, *Apologetics*, 18.

[35] E. Caird, *The Evolution of Religion*, II, 84.

[36] Ibid., I, 138.

[37] H. Jones, *A Faith that Enquires*, 5.

[38] Ibid., 33. His criticisms of Lotze rest upon this principle to a considerable extent.

[39] Idem, *The Philosophy of Martineau in Relation to the Idealism of the Present Day,* London: Macmillan, 1905, 33.

[40] Idem, *Idealism as a Practical Creed,* Glasgow: Maclehose, 1909, 205.

[41] Ibid. The reference to Luke 15 could hardly be clearer.

[42] Ibid., 106–7.

[43] Idem, *A Faith that Enquires,* 323.

[44] Ibid., 358, 360.

[45] H. J. W. Hetherington, *The Life and Letters of Sir Henry Jones,* London: Hodder & Stoughton, 1924, 265; letter dated 7 May 1920.

[46] J. A. Smith, review of H. Jones, *A Faith that Enquires,* in *Hibbert Journal,* XXI, 1922–3, 395.

[47] H. Jones, *A Faith that Enquires,* 244.

[48] Ibid., 271.

[49] Ibid., 332.

[50] Ibid., 36.

[51] Idem, *The Working Faith of the Social Reformer,* London: Macmillan, 1910, 70.

[52] Idem, *A Faith that Enquires,* 56.

[53] Idem, *The Working Faith of the Social Reformer,* 78.

[54] Idem, *The Philosophy of Martineau,* 31.

[55] See idem, *A Critical Account of the Philosophy of Lotze,* Glasgow: Maclehose, 1895, 105.

[56] Idem, *The Immortality of the Soul in Tennyson and Browning,* London: Green, 1905, 20, 24.

[57] D. Mackenzie, 'Transcendentalism', in *Encyclopaedia of Religion and Ethics,* Edinburgh: T. & T. Clark, 1921, XII, 424(a). William James's *mot* comes to mind: 'I somehow feel as if all prigs ought to end, if developed, by becoming Hegelians . . .' ('Absolutism and empiricism', *Mind,* IX, 1884, 285).

[58] E. Caird in *Queen's Quarterly,* XII; quoted by John Watson, 'The idealism of Edward Caird', *The Philosophical Review,* XVIII no. 3, May 1909, 275.

[59] C. C. J. Webb, *God and Personality,* London: Allen & Unwin, 1918, 137–8, 153.

[60] See F. H. Bradley, *Appearance and Reality,* London: Swan Sonnenschein, 1893, 533.

[61] J. H. Muirhead, *Bernard Bosanquet and His Friends,* London: Allen & Unwin, 1935, 239; letter dated 14 November 1922.

[62] H. Jones, review of B. Bosanquet, *The Value and Destiny of the Individual,* in *Hibbert Journal,* XI, 1912–13, 909. Jones quotes Bosanquet, 255.

[63] A. S. Pringle-Pattison, 'The mode of being of finite individuals',

Proceedings of the Aristotelian Society, NS XVIII, 1917–18, 517.

[64] Ibid., 519.

[65] C. C. J. Webb, *God and Personality,* 129.

[66] See F. H. Bradley, *Appearance and Reality,* Oxford: The Clarendon Press [1893], 9th impression (corrected), 1930, 140–2.

[67] A. S. Pringle-Pattison, *Man's Place in the Cosmos,* Edinburgh: Blackwood, 1902, 98–103, 111, 119, 140–1.

[68] Idem, *Two Lectures on Theism,* Edinburgh: Blackwood, 1897, 53.

[69] F. H. Bradley, *Essays on Truth and Reality,* Oxford: The Clarendon Press, 1914, 428.

[70] Ibid., 436.

[71] H. Jones, *A Faith that Enquires,* 315.

[72] Idem, *The Working Faith of the Social Reformer,* 74.

[73] C. C. J. Webb, *A History of Philosophy,* London: Williams and Norgate, 1915, 213.

[74] Idem, *Problems in the Relations of God and Man,* London: Nisbet, 1911, 188.

[75] A. E. Taylor, *The Problem of Conduct,* London: Macmillan, 1901, 442.

[76] C .C. J. Webb, *God and Personality,* 154–5. Cf. W. R. Sorley's review of Webb's book in *Hibbert Journal,* XVII, 1918–19, 756.

[77] A. Seth, *Hegelianism and Personality,* 185; cf. ibid., 205–7.

[78] Ibid., 100.

[79] For example, in *The Idea of God,* 156.

[80] Ibid., 431.

[81] Ibid., 435.

[82] Defined by Gilbert Ryle as 'the presentation of facts belonging to one category in the idioms appropriate to another'. See his *The Concept of Mind,* London: Hutchinson's University Library, 1949, 8.

[83] A. B. Bruce, *The Humiliation of Christ,* Edinburgh: T. & T. Clark, 2nd revised and enlarged edn, 1881, 12.

[84] H. R. Mackintosh, *Some Aspects of Christian Belief,* London: Hodder & Stoughton, [1923], 296. For the way in which the philosopher A. C. Ewing differentiates between the absolute of philosophical idealism and the 'God of most theology', see his careful work, *Idealism: A Critical Survey,* London: Methuen, [1934], 3rd edn, 1961, 403–4.

[85] A. E. Taylor, *The Faith of a Moralist,* London: Macmillan, 1931, II, 71.

[86] See S. L. Stebbing, *A Modern Introduction to Logic,* London: Methuen, 1930, 250.

[87] I here allude to my article, 'The peril of reductionism in recent thought', *Scottish Journal of Theology,* XXVII, 1974, 48–64, with the general line of which I still agree; and to my book, *The Philosophy of Religion 1875–1980,* London: Croom Helm, 1988, 28–31.

[88] A. Moore, 'The Christian doctrine of God', in *Lux Mundi,* London: John Murray, 15th edn, 1904, 47.

89 Ibid.
90 J. Iverach, *Theism in the Light of Present Science and Philosophy,* London: Hodder & Stoughton, 1900, 307. For this interesting but neglected thinker see Alan P. F. Sell, *Defending and Declaring the Faith: Some Scottish Examples 1860–1920,* Exeter: Paternoster Press and Colorado Springs: Helmers & Howard, 1987, ch.VI.
91 See further, Alan P. F. Sell, *Theology in Turmoil,* ch.I.
92 E. Caird, *The Evolution of Religion,* I, 148. Cf. idem, *The Evolution of Theology in the Greek Philosophers,* II, 215:

> [T]he mystic who finds everything in God seems to speak the same language as the Agnostic who finds nothing in him, or who finds in him only the negation of all that we can perceive or know or think.

Illingworth's critique of mysticism turned on the latter's alleged obliteration of human personality. See his *Christian Character,* London: Macmillan, 1914, 177, 181.
93 A. Seth, *Two Lectures on Theism,* 34.
94 A. C. McGiffert, 'Immanence', in *Encyclopaedia of Religion and Ethics,* VII, 171(a), 172(a).
95 C. C. J. Webb, 'Baron Friedrich von Hügel and his contribution to religious philosophy', *The Harvard Theological Review,* XLII, 1949, 5–6.
96 A. E. Taylor, 'Theism', in *Encyclopaedia of Religion and Ethics,* XII, 262(a).
97 P. T. Forsyth, *Faith, Freedom and the Future,* [1912], London: Independent Press, 1952, 342.
98 So James Patrick, *The Magdalen Metaphysicals: Idealism and Orthodoxy at Oxford, 1901–1945,* Macon, GA: Mercer University Press, 1985, 21.
99 J. R. Illingworth, in *Lux Mundi,* 140.
100 For a discussion of this point in relation to more recent theologians see Alan P. F. Sell, 'Transcendence, immanence and the supernatural', *Journal of Theology for Southern Africa,* no. 29, March 1979, 56–66.
101 John Heywood Thomas, 'Kierkegaard's alternative metaphysical theology', *History of European Ideas,* XII no. 1, 1990, 57.
102 See Alan P. F. Sell, *Defending and Declaring the Faith,* ch.III.
103 Quoted by A. C. Bradley in his 'Biographical sketch' prefixed to *Philosophical Remains of Richard Lewis Nettleship,* London: Macmillan, 2nd edn, 1901, xlix.
104 T. H. Green, *Works,* III, 225. Cf. ibid., xciv.
105 M. Richter, *The Politics of Conscience,* 102.
106 Ibid., 183, quoting W. D. Lamont, *Introduction to Green's Moral Philosophy,* London: Allen & Unwin, 1934, 190; cf. Richter, op. cit., 186. In fact Richter slightly misquotes Lamont, to whose original text I here return.

[107] See, for example, E. Caird, *A Critical Account of the Philosophy of Kant,* Glasgow: Maclehose, 1877, 648.

[108] Idem, *The Evolution of Theology in the Greek Philosophers,* II, 362.

[109] S. S. Laurie, 'The metaphysics of T. H. Green', *The Philosophical Review,* VI no. 2, March 1897, 125. Cf. A. S. Pringle-Pattison, *The Idea of God,* 253.

[110] A. Seth, *Hegelianism and Personality,* 193.

[111] J. R. Illingworth, *Divine Immanence,* London: Macmillan, 1903, 69.

[112] Idem, in *Lux Mundi,* 136.

[113] A. S. Pringle-Pattison, *Two Lectures on Theism,* 47.

[114] C. C. J. Webb, *God and Personality,* 73, 75.

[115] F. von Hügel, *The Reality of God,* London: J. M. Dent, 1931, 66.

[116] A. E. Garvie, 'The limits of doctrinal restatement', *Proceedings of the Third International Congregational Council,* London: Congregational Union of England and Wales, 1908, 96. Cf. idem, *The Christian Certainty amid the Modern Perplexity,* London: Hodder & Stoughton, 1910, ch.IX.

[117] A. C. McGiffert, 'Immanence', in *Encyclopaedia of Religion and Ethics,* VII, 171(b).

[118] A. S. Pringle-Pattison, 'Immanence and transcendence', in *The Spirit,* ed. B. H. Streeter, London: Macmillan, 1928, 21. W. L. Davidson regrets Pringle-Pattison's deficiency at this point. See his *Recent Theistic Discussion,* Edinburgh: T. & T. Clark, 1921, 131.

[119] A. S. Pringle-Pattison, *The Idea of God,* 255.

[120] See Charles Gore, *The Reconstruction of Belief,* London: John Murray, 1926, 71.

[121] N. F. S. Ferré, *The Christian Understanding of God,* London: SCM Press, 1951, 61.

[122] J. R. Illingworth, *Divine Transcendence,* London: Macmillan, 1911, 18.

[123] See Isaiah 6.

[124] E. Caird, *The Evolution of Theology,* I, 257.

[125] See, for example, E. Caird, *The Evolution of Religion,* II, 117.

[126] So J. R. Illingworth, *Divine Transcendence,* 72.

[127] Idem, *Divine Immanence,* ch.III. Cf. idem, *The Doctrine of the Trinity,* London: Macmillan, 1909, 195–6.

[128] See C. C. J. Webb, *Religion and Theism,* London: Allen & Unwin, 1934, 136; cf. idem, *God and Personality,* 248; and for the implications for worship, idem, *Divine Personality and Human Life,* 105–6.

[129] H. Jones, 'Divine immanence', *Hibbert Journal,* V no. 4, July 1907, 751. Cf. idem, *Divine Transcendence,* 18.

[130] See e.g. J. R. Illingworth, *The Doctrine of the Trinity,* 207; *The Church and Human Thought* (Pan Anglican Papers, no. 2), London: SPCK, 1907; *Divine Immanence,* 35; *Sermons Preached in a College Chapel,* London: Macmillan, 1882, 172.

[131]   David Jenkins, *The Glory of Man*, London: SCM Press, 1967, 104; cf. 53.

[132]   C. C. J. Webb, *Religion and Theism*, 137.

[133]   N. F. S. Ferré, *The Christian Understanding of God*, 62.

[134]   J. R. Illingworth, *Personality Human and Divine*, 17.

[135]   A. D. Lindsay, 'The idealism of Caird and Jones', *Journal of Philosophical Studies*, I, 1926, 174.

[136]   T. H. Green, *Works*, III, 227.

[137]   Cf. the criticisms of James Iverach, 'Professor Thomas Hill Green', *The Expository Times*, IV, 1892–3, 166.

[138]   R. Mackintosh, *Hegel and Hegelianism*, 285.

[139]   See, for example, E. Caird, *The Evolution of Religion*, II, 23–4.

[140]   H. Jones and J. H. Muirhead (eds.), *The Life and Philosophy of Edward Caird*, 169; letter of 3 June 1891 to Mary Sarah Talbot.

[141]   A. D. Lindsay, 'The idealism of Caird and Jones', 175.

[142]   E. Caird, 'Idealism and the theory of Knowledge', *Proceedings of the British Academy*, 1903–4, 101.

[143]   Though it is special pleading to say, as Caird does, that that author was a monist in the same sense as was Hegel. See E. Jones and J. H. Muirhead, *The Life and Philosophy of Edward Caird*, 168. For one thing, the ancient writer quoted by Paul in Acts 17: 28 was untroubled by Hegel's doctrine of history. For a further blatant example of special pleading see E. Caird, 'St Paul and the idea of evoluton', *Hibbert Journal*, II no. 1, October 1903, 5, where he accuses Paul of changing the Gospel of a realized reconciliation to one which teaches that the kingdom of God has been in Christ and will be at the second coming, but is not now. In view of Paul's well-known 'Christ-mysticism' (II Corinthians 5: 17) this is a travesty of Paul's teaching.

[144]   P. T. Forsyth, 'Monism', a paper read before the London Society for the Study of Religion on Tuesday, 2 February 1909; privately printed, 8.

[145]   J. R. Illingworth, *The Doctrine of the Trinity*, 199–200.

[146]   H. Jones, *The Philosophy of Martineau*, 13.

[147]   J. R. Illingworth, *Divine Transcendence*, 17. Cf. idem, *The Doctrine of the Trinity*, 206; *Christian Character*, 180.

[148]   A. S. Pringle-Pattison, *The Philosophical Radicals*, 168, where he refers to H. Jones, *A Critical Account of the Philosophy of Lotze*, 330.

[149]   H. Jones, *A Faith that Enquires*, 317.

[150]   J. R. Illingworth, *The Doctrine of the Trinity*, 188. Cf. idem, *Divine Transcendence*, 15.

[151]   This point is strongly asserted by Pringle-Pattison in answer to the charge of ambiguity levelled against him by his pupil, the theologian H. R. Mackintosh. The latter had suggested that his teacher may, mistakenly, have meant to suggest that the God-humanity reciprocity

means that God needs us as much as we need him, or (correctly) to say that God's love is such that it cannot but reveal itself to human beings. Pringle-Pattison decisively opted for the latter. The sequence of works is: A. S. Pringle-Pattison, *The Idea of God,* 254; H. R. Mackintosh, *Some Aspects of Christian Belief,* 266; A. S. Pringle-Pattison, 'Immanence and transcendence', in *The Spirit,* 13, 15. See also, F. von Hügel, *Essays and Addresses on the Philosophy of Religion,* London: Dent, 1926, II, 143–51.

[152] A. S. Pringle-Pattison, *Two Lectures on Theism,* 44.

[153] See further, Diogenes Allen, *The Path of Perfect Love,* Cambridge, MA: Cowley Publications, 1992, 43. Cf. J. R. Illingworth, *The Gospel Miracles,* 161–2.

[154] J. R. Illingworth, *Divine Transcendence,* 16.

[155] A. S. Pringle-Pattison, *The Idea of God,* 289.

[156] John Oman, *The Natural and the Supernatural,* Cambridge: CUP, 1931, 475.

[157] See Howard V. Knox, 'Green's refutation of empiricism', *Mind,* NS IX, 1900, 67. Cf. A. S. Pringle-Pattison, *The Philosophical Radicals,* 165.

[158] Ibid., 62, quoting T. H. Green, *Works,* II, 181.

[159] Henry Calderwood, 'Another view of Green's last work', *Mind,* X, 1885, 77.

[160] J. Iverach, 'Professor Thomas Hill Green', *The Expository Times,* IV, 1892–3, 166. Cf. A. Seth, *Hegelianism and Personality,* 222; idem, *Scottish Philosophy,* 220–1.

[161] T. H. Green, *Prolegomena to Ethics,* para. 67.

[162] A. Seth, *Hegelianism and Personality,* 30.

[163] C. B. Upton, 'Theological aspects of the philosophy of Thomas Hill Green', 150.

[164] E. Caird, *The Evolution of Religion,* I, 108.

[165] Ibid., 189.

[166] J. Iverach, 'Edward Caird', *The Expository Times,* V, 1893–4, 206.

[167] E. Caird, *The Evolution of Theology in the Greek Philosophers,* I, 195.

[168] Idem, *The Evolution of Religion,* II, 70–1.

[169] Ibid., 76.

[170] Ibid., 77.

[171] H. Jones, *A Faith that Enquires,* 60; cf. ibid., 69, etc.

[172] Idem, 'Divine immanence', 763.

[173] Idem, 'The present attitudes of reflective thought towards religion', *Hibbert Journal,* II no. 1, October 1903, 26–7.

[174] Idem, *Is the Order of Nature Opposed to the Moral Life?,* Glasgow: Maclehose, 1894, 7. This is Jones's Inaugural Lecture at Glasgow University.

[175] Idem, *A Faith that Enquires,* 131.

[176] Ibid., 178.

[177] Idem, *The Philosophy of Martineau*, 19. My italics.

[178] Ibid., 27.

[179] Idem, *A Faith that Enquires*, 156.

[180] In Philippians 3: 12, one of three Pauline letters quoted by Jones, Paul says that he has not yet attained perfection.

[181] H. Jones, *A Faith that Enquires*, 156.

[182] For the ambiguity of 'individual' in Hegelian thought see Andrew Vincent, 'The individual in Hegelian thought', *Idealistic Studies*, XII, 1982, 156–68.

[183] See further, Alan P. F. Sell, *Commemorations: Studies in Christian Thought and History*, Calgary: University of Calgary Press, and Cardiff: University of Wales Press, 1993, ch.X.

[184] James Martineau, *A Study of Religion*, Oxford: The Clarendon Press, 2nd rev. edn, 1900, II, 183. It should be remembered that Martineau reached his major positions between forty and fifty years prior to the publication of most of his works.

[185] In a paper of 1852 quoted by A. S. Pringle-Pattison, *Man's Place in the Cosmos*, Edinburgh: Blackwood, 1902, 248.

[186] See C. B. Upton, *Dr Martineau's Philosophy: A Survey*, London: Nisbet, 1905, 155, 156 (though in Martineau's letter quoted on p.155 Andrew is incorrectly described as the younger brother of James Seth); A. Campbell Fraser, *Biographia Philosophica: A Retrospect*, Edinburgh: Blackwood, 1904, 279.

[187] A. S. Pringle-Pattison, *The Idea of God*, 411.

[188] For Ritschl see Alan P. F. Sell, *Theology in Turmoil*, ch.IV.

[189] C. C. J. Webb, *God and Personality*, 113.

[190] Idem, *Divine Personality and Human Life*, 247; *God and Personality*, 106–7. For a comparison of Illingworth's apologetic method with that of Lotze see John Edward Cantelon, 'John Richardson Illingworth: Philosophical Theologian', D.Phil. dissertation, University of Oxford, 1951, especially chs.III, IV.

[191] Bernard Bosanquet in the symposium, 'Do finite individuals possess a substantive or an adjectival mode of being?', *Proceedings of the Aristotelian Society*, NS XVIII, 1917–18. The other contributors to the symposium were Pringle-Pattison, G. F. Stout and R. B. Haldane. With reference to the personal idealist Hastings Rashdall, Webb writes that Bosanquet here 'expresses a theory which is the extreme antithesis of that which Rashdall consistently held, and which was the point on which all his speculation turned'. See 'Rashdall as philosopher and theologian', in P. E. Matheson, *The Life of Hastings Rashdall, D.D.*, London: OUP, 1918, 240.

[192] C. B. Upton, 'The philosophy of Thomas Hill Green', 151.

[193] A. S. Pringle-Pattison, 'The mode of being of finite individuals', 517.

[194] Ibid., 523.

[195] See e.g. A. S. Pringle-Pattison, *Man's Place in the Cosmos*, 158.

[196] J. R. Illingworth, *Personality Human and Divine*, 41, 43, 125. Cf. *Reason and Revelation*, 72. At this point Jones's quip comes to mind:

> The theory that induction proceeds from particulars to universals reminds me of the railway that we used to call the Manchester to Milford Haven Railway. It didn't start from Manchester, and never got to Milford Haven.

See H. J. W. Hetherington, *The Life and Letters of Sir Henry Jones*, 78 n.2. But note the next sentence in the text.

[197] See e.g. J. R. Illingworth, *Divine Immanence*, 71–2.

[198] Idem, *Personality Human and Divine*, vii–viii. It has more than once been noted that for all their talk of personality, Illingworth and others took no advantage of the newer psychology of their day. See e.g. Thomas A. Langford, *In Search of Foundations: English Theology 1900– 1920*, Nashville: Abingdon, 1969, 74. In 'Christology for today', in *Soundings*, ed. A. R. Vidler, Cambridge: CUP, 1962, 155n., H. W. Montefiore, noting that more recent researches of psychologists have revealed the importance of the unconscious, surmised that 'Until the human sciences can give a clearer conception of personality, it is unlikely that any Christological theory that is based on the nature of personality will prove satisfactory.'

[199] C. C. J. Webb, *Studies in the History of Natural Theology*, Oxford: The Clarendon Press, 1915, 68–9; cf. idem, *Problems in the Relations of God and Man*, 3.

[200] Idem, *Religious Experience*, 37–8.

[201] Ibid., 39.

[202] Idem, *Problems in the Relation of God and Man*, 140–1 and n.

[203] Idem, *God and Personality*, 266.

[204] Ibid., 267.

[205] Ibid., 250.

[206] A. S. Pringle-Pattison, *Hegelianism and Personality*, 64, 216.

[207] Ibid., 217. Illingworth held monism to be built on the sceptical foundation that we cannot but distrust what we think we know in ourselves. See his *Divine Immanence*, 71.

[208] Quoted by G. F. Barbour in his 'Memoir' of Pringle-Pattison prefixed to *The Balfour Lectures on Realism*, 53–4. The reference to the 'third course' is to the lectures on realism which had not then been written, the first two courses being *Scottish Philosophy* and *Hegelianism and Personality*.

[209] Ibid., 2nd edn, 69.

[210] See H. Jones, 'Idealism and epistemology', *Mind*, NS II no. 7, July 1893, 289–306 and 457–72. For Seth's reply see his 'Hegelianism and its critics', ibid., NS III no. 9, January 1894, 1–25.

211 H. F. Hallett, 'Andrew Seth Pringle-Pattison 1856–1931', *Mind*, XLII no. 166, April 1933, 144.

212 See D. G. Ritchie, *Darwin and Hegel*, London: Swan Sonnenschein, 1893, 100n.; H. Jones, review of B. Bosanquet, *Individuality and Value*, in *Hibbert Journal*, X, 1911–12, 952.

213 A. S. Pringle-Pattison, *The Idea of God*, 389–90n.

214 Idem, 'The mode of being of finite individuals', 523. Cf. J. R. Illingworth, *Divine Immanence*, 68. Pringle-Pattison was also charged with oscillating between dualism and monism. See H. Rashdall, 'The religious philosophy of Professor Pringle-Pattison', *Mind*, NS XXVII, July 1918, 273; W. Preston Warren, *Pantheism in Neo-Hegelian Thought*, Scottdale, PA: Mennonite Press, 1933, 18–19. See further, J. B. Baillie, *Andrew Seth Pringle-Pattison 1856–1931*, reprinted from *The Proceedings of the British Academy*, XVII, 1931, 28–30.

215 C. C. J. Webb, *Divine Personality and Human Life*, 212–13.

216 Ibid., 237.

217 B. Bosanquet in a letter to Webb of 20 April 1919, referring to Webb's *God and Personality*, 239.

218 C. C. J. Webb, 'God and the world', *Journal of Philosophical Studies*, II, 1927, 297.

219 Idem, 'Religion, philosophy, and history', in *Philosophy and History: Essays Presented to Ernst Cassirer*, eds. R. Klibansky and H. J. Paton, Oxford: The Clarendon Press, 1936, 60.

220 J. Iverach, *Theism in the Light of Present Science and Philosophy*, 307.

Chapter 4: Ethics, Society and the Idealists

1 Charles B. Upton, 'Theological aspects of the philosophy of Thomas Hill Green', *New World* (Chicago), I, 1892, 157.

2 Though I cannot resist quoting Taylor's characteristically trenchant dismissal of evolutionary ethics: 'There is, in fact, no ground for believing that 'evolution' need be the same thing as progress, and this is enough to knock the bottom out of "evolutionary ethics".' See his 'Philosophy', in *Recent Developments in European Thought*, ed. F. S. Marvin, London: OUP, 1920, 38.

3 T. H. Green, *Works*, London: Longmans, 1893, III, 223.

4 Idem, *Prolegomena to Ethics*, Oxford: The Clarendon Press, 4th edn, 1899, para. 184.

5 I. Kant, *Fundamental Principles of the Metaphysics of Ethics*, trans. T. K. Abbott, London: Longmans (1873), 10th edn, 1925, 56.

6 Though James Martineau, commenting upon Green's words, 'It is the very essence of moral duty to be imposed by a man on himself' (*Prolegomena*, para. 324), expressed relief that what he himself had

declared to be impossible was not really entertained by Green, whose 'Hegelian aptitude . . . for unifying contradictions is not easily baffled'. For by 'self' here Green means not a detached finite individual, but a self which owes its being to the communication to humanity of the absolute self. A person is thus not a 'law unto himself' by reason of individual autonomy, but because of the 'self-communication of the infinite Spirit to the soul' (*Prolegomena*, para. 319). See James Martineau, *Types of Ethical Theory*, Oxford: The Clarendon Press, 3rd edn revised, 1891, II, 105–6.

7   T. H. Green, *Prolegomena*, para. 7.

8   See further, Geoffrey Thomas, *The Moral Philosophy of T. H. Green*, Oxford: The Clarendon Press, 1982, 41–5.

9   T. H. Green, *Works*, III, 371.

10 Ibid.

11 Idem, *Prolegomena*, para. 185.

12 Ibid., para. 109.

13 H. Calderwood, 'Another view of Green's last work', *Mind*, X, 1885, 81.

14 R. Mackintosh, *Essays towards a New Theology*, Glasgow: Maclehose, 1889, 126.

15 A. E. Taylor, 'The freedom of man', in *Contemporary British Philosophy*, ed. J. H. Muirhead, London: Allen & Unwin, Second Series, 1925, 275.

16 T. H. Green, *Works*, III, 111.

17 Idem, *Prolegomena*, para. 254.

18 W. G. de Burgh, *Towards a Religious Philosophy*, London: Macdonald & Evans, 1937, 179.

19 Ibid., 181.

20 Ibid., 183.

21 Ibid., 184. Though for some mitigation of this point see below for Green's social construal of self-realization.

22 Ann R. Cacoullos, *Thomas Hill Green, Philosopher of Rights*, New York: Twayne Publishers Inc., 1974, 34.

23 A. E. Taylor, *The Problem of Conduct*, London: Macmillan, 1901, 42.

24 Ibid., 49. Cf. idem, 'The metaphysical problem with special reference to its bearing upon ethics', *International Journal of Ethics*, X, 1899–1900, 370.

25 Ibid., 65.

26 James Orr, *Sin as a Problem of Today*, London: Hodder & Stoughton, 1910, 56–7.

27 Geoffrey Thomas, *The Moral Philosophy of T. H. Green*, 67. See also the perceptive review of Taylor's book by Albert Lefevre in *The Philosophical Review*, XI, 1902, 56–69.

28 Cf. e.g. E. Caird, *The Evolution of Theology in the Greek Philosophers*, Glasgow: Maclehose, 1904, I, 368–9.

29 See A. E. Taylor, *The Problem of Conduct*, 484.

[30] A. Seth, critical notice of S. Alexander, *Moral Order and Progress*, London: Trübner, 1889, in *Mind*, XIV, 1889, 557.

[31] Robert Adamson, *The Development of Modern Philosophy with Other Lectures and Essays*, ed. W. R. Sorley, Edinburgh: Blackwood, 1903, II, 109.

[32] T. H. Green, *Works*, III, 227.

[33] R. L. Nettleship in ibid., xciv.

[34] MS letter, R. L. Nettleship to J. A. Symonds, in Balliol College Library, Oxford.

[35] See e.g. T. H. Green, *Prolegomena*, para. 321.

[36] H. Jones and J. H. Muirhead, *The Life and Philosophy of Edward Caird*, Glasgow: Maclehose, Jackson, 1921, 305.

[37] See E. Caird, 'Professor Green's last work', *Mind*, VIII, 1883, 560. Caird here quotes Green's *Prolegomena*, para. 51.

[38] E. Caird, ibid., 560–1.

[39] J. S. Mackenzie, 'Edward Caird as a philosophical teacher', *Mind*, NS XVIII, 1909, 517.

[40] E. Caird, *Essays on Literature and Philosophy*, Glasgow: Maclehose, 1892, II, 429–30. Cf. e.g. idem, *The Critical Philosophy of Immanuel Kant*, Glasgow: Maclehose, 1889, II, 556.

[41] Idem, *The Evolution of Religion*, Glasgow: Maclehose, 2nd edn, 1894, II, 160–1.

[42] Ibid., 161. An interesting study could be made of what principles have been deemed, by various writers, to be the first principle of Christian ethics. Caird's 'first principle' seems negative and idiosyncratic. Many have thought that 'Love God/love neighbour' are the twin 'first principles' of Christian ethics. But T.W. Manson pointed out that these were advanced by Jesus and received by the scribe 'as the quintessence, not of Christian ethics, but of the Jewish Law'. He therefore followed F. W. Robertson in finding the differentia of Christian ethics in Jesus' new commandment: 'As I have loved you, you are to love one another' (John 13: 34). See T. W. Manson, *Ethics and the Gospel*, London: SCM Press, 1960, 61–2.

[43] E. Caird, letter of 27 August 1897 to Mary Sarah Talbot, in H. Jones and J. H. Muirhead, *The Life and Philosophy of Edward Caird*, 221.

[44] Idem, *Essays on Literature and Philosophy*, I, 223.

[45] Idem, *Lay Sermons and Addresses*, Glasgow: Maclehose, 1907, 111–12.

[46] H. Jones, *A Faith that Enquires*, London: Macmillan, 1922, 141–2.

[47] Ibid., 142.

[48] Ibid., 145.

[49] Ibid., 146.

[50] Ibid., 138. Jones had made this point forty-four years earlier in his *Morality as Freedom: A Lecture given at the Ethical Society*, London: 1888, 4.

51 Ibid., 141.
52 Ibid., 164.
53 Ibid., 350.
54 Idem, *The Principles of Citizenship*, London: Macmillan, 1919, 48.
55 Idem, *Idealism as a Practical Creed*, Glasgow: Maclehose, 1909, 271–2, 281.
56 A. S. Pringle-Pattison, *The Philosophical Radicals*, Edinburgh: Blackwood, 1907, 267.
57 Idem (as A. Seth), *Two Lectures on Theism*, Edinburgh: Blackwood, 1897, 27.
58 Ibid., 28.
59 Idem, *The Idea of God in the Light of Recent Philosophy*, Oxford: The Clarendon Press, 1917, 34.
60 Ibid., 38.
61 Ibid., 200.
62 Idem, *Man's Place in the Cosmos*, Edinburgh: Blackwood, 2nd edn, 1902, vii.
63 Idem, *The Idea of God*, 223.
64 W. L. Davidson, *Recent Theistic Discussion*, Edinburgh: T. & T. Clark, 1921, 126–7, 128.
65 C. C. J. Webb, *Religion and Theism*, London: Allen & Unwin, 1934, 17.
66 Idem, *Studies in the History of Natural Theology*, Oxford: The Clarendon Press, 1915, 127, 128.
67 Idem, *Kant's Philosophy of Religion*, Oxford: The Clarendon Press, 1926, 21.
68 Idem, 'Outline of a Philosophy of Religion', in *Contemporary British Philosophy*, ed. J. H. Muirhead, London: Allen & Unwin, Second Series, 1925, 359.
69 See idem, *The Contribution of Christianity to Ethics*, Calcutta: University of Calcutta Press, 1932, 67.
70 Idem, *Divine Personality and Human Life*, London: Allen & Unwin, 1920, 123. Webb quotes James Martineau, *A Study of Religion*, Oxford: The Clarendon Press, 2nd edn, 1900, II, 27.
71 Idem, *A Century of Anglican Theology and Other Lectures*, Oxford: Blackwell, 1923, 101.
72 All that needs to be said concerning the early Taylor has been said above in connection with Green's ethics.
73 A. E. Taylor, *The Faith of a Moralist*, London: Macmillan, 1930, I, 228.
74 Ibid., 61–2.
75 Ibid., 67–8.
76 Ibid., 152, 153.
77 Idem, 'The vindication of religion', in *Essays Catholic and Critical*, ed. E. G. Selwyn, London: SPCK, 3rd edn, 1929, 63.
78 Ibid. Cf. idem, *The Faith of a Moralist*, II, ch.IX.

79	See further idem, 'Theism', in *Encyclopaedia of Religion and Ethics;* and *Does God Exist?*, London: Collins Fontana, [1945], 1961.

80	See e.g. idem, *The Faith of a Moralist*, I, 223–4.

81	Idem, 'The freedom of man', 303–4. For an example of the early Taylor *contra* determinism see his review of J. M. E. McTaggart's *Some Dogmas of Religion*, in *The Philosophical Review*, XV, 1906, 420–1.

82	Idem, 'The vindication of religion', 63.

83	Idem, *The Faith of a Moralist*, I, 239.

84	Ibid., 101.

85	John Macmurray, *Search for Reality in Religion*, London: Friends Home Service Committee, [1965], 1969, 58. Cf. his boldly entitled *Idealism Against Religion*, London: The Lindsey Press, [1944].

86	Ibid., 59.

87	Ibid.

88	See E. Caird, *Hegel*, Edinburgh: Blackwood, 1891, 211–13. He refers to Mark 8: 35.

89	Idem, *The Evolution of Religion*, II, 151. Once again the context of the remark is the notion of dying to live (John 12: 24).

90	Letter of 29 December 1868 from T. H. Green to Henry Scott Holland. In *Henry Scott Holland, Memoir and Letters*, ed. Stephen Paget, London: John Murray, 1921, 29.

91	C. C. J. Webb, *A Study of Religious Thought in England from 1850*, Oxford: The Clarendon Press, 1933, 107–8.

92	E. Caird, *Lay Sermons and Addresses*, 67–8.

93	Cf. Donald M. Mackinnon, *Themes in Theology: The Three-fold Cord*, Edinburgh: T. & T. Clark, 1987, 59.

94	E. Caird, *Hegel*, 213–14.

95	Cf. W. D. Hudson's exposition of Green in *A Century of Moral Philosophy*, Guildford: Longmans, 1980, 53.

96	T. H. Green, *Prolegomena*, para. 199.

97	Ibid., para. 183.

98	Ibid., para. 184.

99	Ibid., para. 202.

100	Idem, *Works*, III, 372.

101	Andrew Vincent (ed.), *The Philosophy of T. H. Green*, Aldershot: Gower, 1986, 54.

102	T. H. Green, *Works*, III, 258.

103	A. Vincent, *The Philosophy of T. H. Green*, 54.

104	J. R. Illingworth, *Christian Character*, London: Macmillan, 1914, 7.

105	A. S. Pringle-Pattison, Introduction to J. S. Mill, *On Liberty*, London: Routledge, 1910, xxii.

106	C. C. J. Webb, *Divine Personality and Human Life*, London: Allen & Unwin, 1920, 155.

107	R. B. Haldane and A. Seth (eds.), *Essays in Philosophical Criticism*, London: Longmans, 1883.

[108] Ibid., 187.

[109] Ibid., 193, 209. Along this line it is difficult to envisage or accommodate conflicts of real interests, yet such there surely are.

[110] H. Jones, 'Modern scientific and philosophical thought regarding human society', in *Christ and Civilization*, ed. J. B. Paton *et al.*, London: National Council of Evangelical Free Churches, 1910, 514.

[111] H. Jones, *The Principles of Citizenship*, London: Macmillan, 1919, 71.

[112] Ibid., 147; cf. idem, *Idealism as a Practical Creed*, Glasgow: Maclehose, 1909, 35.

[113] Idem, *The Working Faith of the Social Reformer*, London: Macmillan, 1910, 14; cf. 273.

[114] Idem, *Idealism as a Practical Creed*, 113.

[115] Ibid., 116.

[116] Idem, *The Working Faith of the Social Reformer*, ix.

[117] Ibid., 273.

[118] A. E. Taylor, *The Faith of a Moralist*, I, 349.

[119] Idem, *The Problem of Conduct*, 419–21.

[120] Idem, *The Faith of a Moralist*, I, 147.

[121] A. C. Ewing, *Idealism: A Critical Survey*, London: Methuen (1934), 3rd edn, 1961, 430, 432. Cf. H. D. Lewis and D. M. Mackinnon *contra* Green in *Nineteenth-Century Religious Thought in the West*, ed. N. Smart *et al.*, Cambridge: CUP, 1985, II, 289, and *Themes in Theology*, 53, respectively.

[122] J. Macmurray, *Idealism against Religion*, 22.

[123] J. B. Baillie, review of H. Jones, *The Working Faith of the Social Reformer*, in *Hibbert Journal*, X, 1911–12, 501.

[124] H. Jones, 'The social organism', 213.

[125] C. C. J. Webb, *Divine Personality and Human Life*, 111–12. Webb quotes from his *Group Theories of Religion and the Individual*, London: Allen & Unwin, 1916, 187, 188.

[126] Idem, *The Contribution of Christianity to Ethics*, Calcutta: University of Calcutta Press, 1932, 4.

[127] A. E. Taylor, *The Faith of a Moralist*, I, 65.

[128] Ibid., 162.

[129] See C. C. J. Webb, *Kant's Philosophy of Religion*, 62.

[130] T. H. Green, *Works*, III, 270.

[131] T. H. Green quoted in Stephen Paget (ed.), *Henry Scott Holland: Memoir and Letters*, London: John Murray, 1921, 30–1; a letter to Scott Holland of 9 January 1869.

[132] A. S. Pringle-Pattison, *Man's Place in the Cosmos*, vii.

[133] H. Jones, *A Faith that Enquires*, 127.

[134] Idem, *The Philosophy of James Martineau in Relation to the Idealism of the Present Day*, London: Macmillan, 1905, 35.

[135] See further, Alan P. F. Sell, *Aspects of Christian Integrity*, Calgary: The

University of Calgary Press, 1990, and Louisville, KY: Westminster/ John Knox Press, 1991, 119–20.

[136] See further ibid., 72–5.

[137] J. R. Illingworth, *Christian Character,* London: Macmillan, 1914, 1.

[138] C. C. J. Webb, *A Century of Anglican Theology,* 61.

[139] Ibid., 64–5.

[140] A. S. Pringle-Pattison, *The Idea of Immortality,* Oxford: The Clarendon Press, 1922, 179.

[141] A. E. Taylor, *The Faith of a Moralist,* I, 31–2.

[142] C. C. J. Webb, *Philosophy and the Christian Religion,* Oxford: The Clarendon Press, 1920, 15.

[143] A. E. Taylor, *The Faith of a Moralist,* I, 230, 233.

[144] Ibid., 234. Cf. W. G. de Burgh, *Towards a Religious Philosophy,* 179.

[145] A. S. Pringle-Pattison, *Man's Place in the Cosmos,* 23.

[146] H. R. Mackintosh, *The Christian Apprehension of God,* London: SCM Press, 1929, 150.

[147] J. R. Illingworth, *Christian Character,* 9.

[148] Ibid.

[149] E. Caird, *The Social Philosophy and Religion of Comte,* Glasgow: Maclehose, 1893, 139.

[150] P. T. Forsyth, 'Monism', a paper read before the London Society for the Study of Religion, Tuesday 2 February 1909, privately printed for the use of members, 9–10. A copy is in The Congregational Library at Dr Williams's Library, London.

[151] Josiah Royce, *The World and the Individual,* New York: Macmillan, 1901, II, 385.

[152] James Orr, *Sidelights on Christian Doctrine,* London: Marshall, 1909, 94; cf. idem, *The Christian View of God and the World,* Edinburgh: Elliot, 4th edn, 1897, 171. For Orr see Alan P. F. Sell, *Defending and Declaring the Faith: Some Scottish Examples 1860–1920,* Exeter: Paternoster Press, and Colorado Springs: Helmers & Howard, 1987, ch.7; G. G. Scorgie, *A Call for Continuity: The Theological Contribution of James Orr,* Macon, GA: Mercer University Press, 1988.

[153] H. R. Mackintosh, *Some Aspects of Christian Belief,* London: Hodder & Stoughton, [1923], 300.

[154] James Iverach, *The Expositor,* 7th series, IV, 1907, 165.

[155] T. H. Green, *Works,* III, 73.

[156] Ibid., 197.

[157] Letter of J. A. Symonds to R. L. Nettleship in Balliol College Library; quoted by Melvin Richter, *The Politics of Conscience: T. H. Green and His Age,* London: Weidenfeld and Nicolson, 1964, 109.

[158] Robert Mackintosh, *Essays Towards a New Theology,* Glasgow: Maclehose, 1889, 125.

[159] Not indeed that the problem of evil is a challenge only to idealists. It

confronts all who wish to hold that God is both omnipotent and benevolent.

[160] J. S. Mackenzie, 'Edward Caird as a philosophical teacher', *Mind,* NS XVIII, 1909, 530.

[161] H. Jones and J. H. Muirhead, *The Life and Philosophy of Edward Caird,* 36. With reference to Caird's *The Evolution of Religion,* James Orr observes, 'It is instructive to note that the words "Sin" and "Evil" do not occur in Dr Caird's Index.' See his *Sin as a Problem of To-day,* 83 n.2.

[162] Jones and Muirhead, *The Life and Philosophy of Edward Caird,* 177; letter of 30 December 1891 to Mary Sarah Talbot.

[163] Ibid., 173; letter of 28 October 1891.

[164] E. Caird, *Lay Sermons,* 186.

[165] Idem, *The Evolution of Theology in the Greek Philosophers,* II, 365.

[166] Idem, *The Evolution of Religion,* I, 231.

[167] Ibid., II, 147.

[168] Idem, *Hegel,* 217–18.

[169] James Seth, *A Study of Ethical Principles,* Edinburgh: Blackwood, 1899, 441–2.

[170] E. H. Blakeney, *Caird's Essays: A Critical Review,* reprinted from *The Churchman,* August and October 1893, 13.

[171] A. E. Garvie, *Revelation through History and Experience,* London: Ivor Nicholson and Watson, 1934, 139.

[172] H. Jones, *A Faith that Enquires,* 58.

[173] Ibid., 246.

[174] Idem, *The Principles of Citizenship,* 45.

[175] Idem, *A Faith that Enquires,* 245.

[176] Idem, *Is the Order of Nature Opposed to the Moral Life?,* Glasgow: Maclehose, 1894, 19.

[177] Idem, 'The present attitude of reflective thought towards religion', *Hibbert Journal,* II no. 1, October 1903, 25.

[178] A. E. Taylor, *The Faith of a Moralist,* I, 35.

[179] H. Jones, *A Faith that Enquires,* 202.

[180] Hastings Rashdall, review of H. Jones, *Idealism as a Practical Creed,* in *International Journal of Ethics,* XXI no. 1, October 1910, 110.

[181] P. T. Forsyth, 'Monism', 12.

[182] A. C. Ewing, *Idealism: A Critical Survey,* 409.

[183] H. Jones, *A Faith that Enquires,* 360. Cf. J. B. Baillie's acerbic remarks concerning Jones's 'hypothesis' in his review of *The Working Faith of the Social Reformer,* in *Hibbert Journal,* X, 1911–12, 501.

[184] A. Campbell Fraser, *Philosophy of Theism,* Edinburgh: Blackwood, 2nd edn, 1899, 97. See further Alan P. F. Sell, *Commemorations: Studies in Christian Thought and History,* Calgary: The University of Calgary Press, and Cardiff: University of Wales Press, 1993, ch.X, especially sect. IV.

[185] A. S. Pringle-Pattison, 'Alexander Campbell Fraser, 1819–1914', *Mind*, NS XXIV, July 1915, 325.

[186] A. Campbell Fraser, *Philosophy of Theism*, 266.

[187] Ibid., 253.

[188] A. S. Pringle-Pattison, *The Philosophical Radicals*, 289.

[189] Idem, 'The mode of being of finite individuals', *Proceedings of the Aristotelian Society*, NS XVIII, 1917–18, 523.

[190] Idem, *The Idea of God*, 411.

[191] Ibid., 417.

[192] C. C. J. Webb, *God and Personality*, 192; cf. idem, *A Century of Anglican Theology*, 94.

[193] A. E. Taylor, *The Problem of Evil*, London: Benn, 1929, 16–17.

[194] C. C. J. Webb, review of A. S. Pringle-Pattison, *The Idea of God*, in *The Oxford Magazine*, 26 October 1917, 29.

[195] Idem, *Problems in the Relations of God and Man*, London: Nisbet, 1911, 118.

[196] Ibid.

[197] Ibid., 119.

[198] J. R. Illingworth, *Christian Character*, 13; cf. idem, *The Gospel Miracles*, London: Macmillan, 1915, 203.

[199] C. C. J. Webb, *Problems in the Relations of God and Man*, 129.

[200] Idem, *God and Personality*, 190.

[201] Ibid., 191.

[202] Ibid., 250.

[203] Ibid., 195.

[204] Idem, *A Century of Anglican Theology*, 95; cf. idem, *God and Personality*, 195–6. Webb quotes from Richard Meux Benson, *Spiritual Readings for Every Day*, London: J. T. Hayes, 3 vols., 1879–82; the section for Advent, 195–6.

[205] A. E. Taylor, *The Problem of Conduct*, 409.

[206] Idem, *The Faith of a Moralist*, I, 223.

[207] Ibid., 155.

[208] Ibid., 169.

[209] Ibid., 122 and n.

[210] Ibid., 164. It is, however, a lapse on Taylor's part to define the three last-named as 'divines of a Church which teaches a dogma of "Original sin" . . .', since there are two churchly traditions – Anglicanism and Dissent – represented here, the latter by Price.

[211] Ibid., 182, 192, 377. Concerning pollution, H. J. Paton thought we must 'ask ourselves whether such feelings are a mark of spiritual profundity or a symptom of mental disease'. See his *The Modern Predicament*, London: Allen & Unwin, 1955, 134. Given the context of Taylor's remarks this is a shallow response of a peculiarly 'Oxford' kind, for which another Oxford man may atone: H. P. Owen calls attention to

Taylor's 'unusually profound analysis of moral guilt' in his *The Moral Argument for Christian Theism*, London: Allen & Unwin, 1965, 58n.

212 Idem, *The Problem of Evil*, 31.

213 J. R. Illingworth, *Reason and Revelation*, London: Macmillan, 1902, 222; cf. idem, *University and Cathedral Sermons*, London: Macmillan, 1893, 96.

214 Idem, *The Gospel Miracles*, 20, where Illingworth claims that the incarnation and the atonement supply both a practical and a speculative solution to the problem of abused free will.

215 Idem, *Divine Transcendence*, London: Macmillan, 1911, 225.

216 Idem, *Sermons Preached in a College Chapel*, London: Macmillan, 1882, 21.

217 Idem, *Christian Character*, 90.

218 Ibid., 91.

219 Idem, 'The problem of pain', in *Lux Mundi*, London: John Murray, 15th edn, 1904, 90.

220 Ibid., 92.

221 Robert Mackintosh, *Historic Theories of Atonement*, London: Hodder & Stoughton, 1920, 228–9.

Chapter 5: The Idealists and Christian Doctrine

1 T. H. Green, *Works*, ed. R. L. Nettleship, London: Longmans, Green, 1888, III, 227.

2 P. T. Forsyth, *Missions in State and Church*, London: Hodder & Stoughton, 1908, 83.

3 W. L. Walker, *The Spirit and the Incarnation*, Edinburgh: T. & T. Clark, 1899, 167.

4 See H. Jones, *The Working Faith of the Social Reformer*, London: Macmillan, 1910, 41.

5 Idem, 'The child and heredity', in *The Child and Religion*, ed. Thomas Stephens, London: Williams & Norgate, 1905, 44.

6 Idem, *Idealism as a Practical Creed*, Glasgow: Maclehose, 1909, 38–9.

7 Idem, *A Faith that Enquires*, London: Macmillan, 1922, 190.

8 P. T. Forsyth, *Positive Preaching and the Modern Mind*, (1907), London: Independent Press, 1964, 146.

9 H. Jones, *A Faith that Enquires*, 44.

10 Galatians 5: 16.

11 See, for example, E. Caird, *Hegel*, Edinburgh: Blackwood, 1891, 218; T. H. Green, *Works*, III, 238.

12 Quoted in H. Jones and J. H. Muirhead (eds.), *The Life and Philosophy of Edward Caird*, Glasgow: Maclehose, 1921, 175; letter dated 17 November 1891.

[13] Ibid., 146.

[14] For the Scottish theological-ecclesiastical context in general and John Caird in particular see Alan P. F. Sell, *Defending and Declaring the Faith: Some Scottish Examples 1860–1920*, Exeter: Paternoster Press and Colorado Springs: Helmers & Howard, 1987. Cf. Muirhead's remarks upon W. T. Harris, leader of the St Louis Hegelians:

> It was because Harris and his companions thought they saw in the Hegelian philosophy a sword wherewith to smite the three-headed monster of anarchy in politics, traditionalism in religion, and naturalism in science, that they found the courage to undertake and the perseverance to carry through the task of naturalizing it in America.

See his *The Platonic Tradition in Anglo-Saxon Philosophy*, London: Allen & Unwin, 1931, 321–2.

[15] E. Caird, *Lay Sermons and Addresses*, Glasgow: Maclehose, 1907, 194.

[16] Idem, *The Evolution of Religion*, Glasgow: Maclehose, 2nd edn, 1894, II, 214.

[17] Idem, *Hegel*, 43.

[18] *Westminster Shorter Catechism*, A. 1.

[19] E. Caird, 'St Paul and evolution', *Hibbert Journal*, II no. 1, October 1903, 13.

[20] D. W. Forrest, *The Christ of History and of Experience*, [1897], Edinburgh: T. & T. Clark, 7th edn, 1914, 307–8. For Forrest see Alan P. F. Sell, *Defending and Declaring the Faith: Some Scottish Examples 1860–1920*, ch.8.

[21] E. Caird, 'Memoir of Principal Caird', prefixed to J. Caird, *The Fundamental Ideas of Christianity*, Glasgow: Maclehose, 1900, I, xvii.

[22] Idem, *The Evolution of Religion*, II, 232. Cf. idem, *Essays on Literature and Philosophy*, Glasgow: Maclehose, 1892, I, 225.

[23] Idem, *The Evolution of Religion*, II, 320.

[24] Idem, 'St Paul and evolution', 8.

[25] Idem, *The Evolution of Religion*, II, 193.

[26] James Denney, *The Death of Christ*, London: Hodder & Stoughton, 2nd edn, 1902, 168.

[27] Ibid., 324.

[28] P. T. Forsyth, 'Monism', a paper printed for the members of the London Society for the Study of Religion, 1909, 10.

[29] Henry James (ed.), *The Letters of William James*, Boston: The Atlantic Monthly Press, I, 1920, 208.

[30] J. R. Illingworth, *The Gospel Miracles*, London: Macmillan, 1915, 50–1. 'The unique miracle of sin' is an expression which Illingworth would have done well to have elucidated.

[31] C. C. J. Webb in *The Oxford Magazine*, 18 May 1904, 356.

32 Idem, 'Nature and grace', *Journal of Theological Studies*, XXXVII, 1936, 125–6. For a consideration by Webb of the history of the doctrine of the atonement see his *The Devotions of Saint Anselm*, London: Methuen, 1903.

33 Nels F. S. Ferré, *The Atonement and Mission*, London: London Missionary Society, 1960, 19. This is an echo of Denney: '[T]he rationale of the incarnation is in the atonement.' See his *The Christian Doctrine of Reconciliation*, London: Hodder & Stoughton, 1919, 65. For a fuller discussion of this point see Alan P. F. Sell, *Aspects of Christian Integrity*, Calgary: The University of Calgary Press, 1990, and Louisville, KY: Westminster/John Knox Press, 1991, ch.2.

34 Robert Mackintosh, 'Recent philosophy and Christian doctrine', *Proceedings of the Third International Congregational Council*, London: Congregational Union of England and Wales, 1908, 84.

35 J. R. Illingworth, in *Lux Mundi*, London: John Murray, 15th edn, 1904, 134.

36 Idem, *Reason and Revelation*, London: Macmillan, 1902, 227–8.

37 Idem, *The Doctrine of the Trinity*, London: Macmillan, 1909, 156.

38 Ibid., 157–8.

39 Idem, *University and Cathedral Sermons*, London: Macmillan, 1893, 182; cf. idem, *The Doctrine of the Trinity*, 202–3.

40 Idem, *The Doctrine of the Trinity*, 204; cf. *Lux Mundi*, 154–5.

41 Idem, *Divine Immanence*, London: Macmillan, 1903, 92.

42 Idem, *Lux Mundi*, 136.

43 Ibid., 155. A view which A. M. Ramsay dubbed 'naïve optimism'. See his *From Gore to Temple*, London: Longmans, 1960, 4.

44 See J. R. Illingworth, *Divine Immanence*, vi, vii, 77, 132, etc.

45 Alasdair Heron, 'The person of Christ', in Geoffrey Wainwright (ed.), *Keeping the Faith: Essays to Mark the Centenary of Lux Mundi*, Philadelphia: Fortress Press and Allison Park, PA: Pickwick Publications, 1988, 108.

46 Ibid., 117. Though it is only proper to note Illingworth's title, and to remember that a further *Lux Mundi* paper, on 'The Incarnation as the basis of dogma', was allocated to R. C. Moberly.

47 J. R. Illingworth in E. S. Talbot (ed.), *Sermons Preached in the Temporary Chapel of Keble College, Oxford, 1870–1876*, London: Rivingtons, 1877, 319.

48 Idem, *The Doctrine of the Trinity*, 203.

49 Idem, *Divine Transcendence*, 8.

50 Idem, *The Gospel Miracles,*199.

51 Ibid., 50.

52 A. S. Pringle-Pattison, *Studies in the Philosophy of Religion*, Oxford: The Clarendon Press, 1930, 160. When this book was published it was already becoming unusual for material of this kind to be included

in a treatise on the philosophy of religion. For the development of that discipline see Alan P. F. Sell, *The Philosophy of Religion 1875–1980*, London: Croom Helm, 1988.

[53] Ibid., 163.

[54] Ibid., 189.

[55] Idem, *The Duty of Candour in Religious Teaching* (Presidential Address to the Theological Society, New College, Edinburgh), London: Hodder & Stoughton, [1920], 47; quoting a review by H. R. Mackintosh in *Hibbert Journal,* October 1919.

[56] Idem, *The Idea of God in the Light of Recent Philosophy*, New York: Macmillan, 2nd edn, 1920, 157.

[57] Idem, *Studies in the Philosophy of Religion*, 252.

[58] William Temple thought that the intellectualism here displayed constituted the weakness of Pringle-Pattison's position. See his *Nature, Man and God,* London: Macmillan, 1934, 320. This volume was, we recall, dedicated to the memory of Edward Caird.

[59] A. S. Pringle-Pattison, *The Idea of God,* 411.

[60] T. H. Green, *Works*, III, 233.

[61] Ibid., 184. But beware: the Godhead does not die.

[62] Ibid., 182.

[63] D. W. Forrest, *The Christ of History and of Experience,* 304.

[64] J. M. Creed, *The Divinity of Jesus Christ,* [1938], London: Collins Fontana, 1964, 62, 63.

[65] E. Caird, *The Evolution of Religion,* II, 230.

[66] Ibid., II, 230–1.

[67] Ibid., 232.

[68] Ibid., 233.

[69] Ibid., 266–7.

[70] Idem, *The Life and Philosophy of Edward Caird,* 181; letter of 3 June 1892 to Mary Sarah Talbot.

[71] H. J. W. Hetherington, *The Life and Letters of Sir Henry Jones,* London: Hodder & Stoughton, 1924, 43.

[72] H. Jones, *A Faith that Enquires,* 77.

[73] In his critique Jones refers to James Denney, *Jesus and the Gospel,* London: Hodder & Stoughton, 2nd edn, 1909, 264, 373–403.

[74] H. Jones, *The Philosophy of Martineau in Relation to the Idealism of the Present Day,* London: Macmillan, 1905, 15n.

[75] William Sanday, *Christologies Ancient and Modern,* Oxford: The Clarendon Press, 1910, 208n.

[76] Alfred E. Garvie, *The Christian Certainty amid the Modern Perplexity,* London: Hodder & Stoughton, 1910, 432.

[77] C. C. J. Webb, *Problems in the Relations of God and Man,* London: Nisbet, 1911, 276.

[78] Idem, *God and Personality,* London: Allen & Unwin, 1918, 31.

79 See Leonard Hodgson, *The Doctrine of the Trinity,* Welwyn, Herts.: Nisbet, 1943, 225–6.
80 C. C. J. Webb, *God and Personality,* 183.
81 T. H. Green, *Works,* III, 263.
82 A. E. Taylor, *The Faith of a Moralist,* II, 136.
83 Arnold Toynbee, Preface to T. H. Green, *The Witness of God and Faith: Two Lay Sermons,* London: 1883, vi.
84 Evelyn Abbott and Lewis Campbell, *The Life and Letters of Benjamin Jowett, M.A.,* London: John Murray, 1897, II, 77. Cf. R. L. Nettleship, 'Memoir' of Green in the latter's *Works,* III, xcvii.
85 C. C. J. Webb, *A Century of Anglican Theology,* Oxford: Blackwell, 1923, 29. Cf. idem, *Religious Experience,* Oxford: OUP, [1945], 30–1.
86 Ibid., 22; cf. his *Kant's Philosophy of Religion,* Oxford: The Clarendon Press, 1926, 21; *Problems in the Relations of God and Man,* 101–2; *Religious Thought in the Oxford Movement,* London: SPCK, 1928, 49.
87 Idem, *God and Personality,* 81.
88 Idem, 'Christianity as the climax of religious development', *Constructive Quarterly,* VI, 1918, 447.
89 T. H. Green, *Works,* III, 242.
90 Ibid., 258.
91 Ibid., 241 ff.
92 Ibid., 260.
93 Idem, letter to Henry Scott Holland, in Stephen Paget (ed.), *Henry Scott Holland: Memoir and Letters,* London: John Murray, 1921, 66, 67. Cf. idem, *Works* III, 266:

> It is by no means . . . a piece of mere intellectual wantonness to disturb the faithful in that theory of their faith which they have come to think inseparable from faith itself; to inquire whether faith, as a spiritual state, is necessarily dependent on assent to those propositions concerning ostensible matters of fact, which form the basis of theological dogma.

94 H. D. Lewis, *Philosophy of Religion,* London: The English Universities Press, 1965, 190. Cf. idem, 'The British idealists', in Ninian Smart *et al.* (eds.), *Nineteenth-Century Religious Thought in the West,* Cambridge: CUP, 1985, II, 303.
95 Robert Mackintosh, *Historic Theories of Atonement,* London: Hodder & Stoughton, 1920, 2.
96 Henry Jones can declare that

> The spirit of Christianity at its highest is inconsistent with the view that the victory of spirit is to be partial, and that 'Nature' can remain an exception to the benevolent purposes of a benevolent will which can neither fail nor falter.

See his 'Modern scientific and philosophical thought regarding human society', in J. B. Paton *et al.* (eds.), *Christ and Civilization*, London: National Council of Evangelical Free Churches, 1910, 508. As so often, Jones's heart is in the right place, but he does not relate the notion of re-creation to the saving event.

[97] James Iverach, 'Professor Thomas Hill Green', *The Expository Times*, IV, 1892–3, 167. In view of Green's allowing some importance to the fact that Jesus lived, as I have just indicated, the operative word here is 'succeeded'.

[98] E. Caird, *The Evolution of Religion*, II, 220–1.

[99] Ibid., 140.

[100] Ibid., 291.

[101] Ibid., 317, 316.

[102] A. M. Fairbairn in *Critical Review of Theological and Philosophical Literature*, IV, 1893–4, 256. Cf. J. K. Mozley, *Some Tendencies in British Theology*, London: SPCK, 1951, 123.

[103] See e.g. H. Jones and J. H. Muirhead, *The Life and Philosophy of Edward Caird*, 167; letter of 7 May 1890 from Caird to Mary Sarah Talbot.

[104] J. R. Illingworth, *The Doctrine of the Trinity,*70.

[105] C. C. J. Webb, 'Religion and philosophy', in C. F. Nolloth (ed.), *The Christian Faith*, London: John Murray, 1922, 13.

[106] Hegel and Kant remind R. S. Franks of the Gnostics. See his *A History of the Doctrine of the Work of Christ*, London: Hodder & Stoughton, [1918], II, 224.

[107] A. E. Taylor, *The Faith of a Moralist*, II, 2.

[108] Ibid., 117.

[109] E. Caird, *Essays on Literature and Philosophy*, I, 202.

[110] H. Jones, *A Faith that Enquires*, 197.

[111] A. S. Pringle-Pattison, Introduction to J. S. Mill, *On Liberty*, London: Routledge, 1910, xxii.

[112] See idem, *Studies in the Philosophy of Religion*.

[113] T. H. Green, *Works*, III, cxxiii, where Green's biographer refers to the notes of a speech delivered by Green at Merton College, Oxford, in December 1881.

[114] For the witness of historic Dissent on the matter see Alan P. F. Sell, *Dissenting Thought and the Life of the Churches: Studies in an English Tradition*, Lewiston, NY: Edwin Mellen Press, 1990.

[115] T. H. Green, *Works*, III, 237.

[116] Ibid., 239.

[117] Melvin Richter, *The Politics of Conscience: T. H. Green and His Age*, London: Weidenfeld and Nicolson, 1964, 124. Richter quotes E. Abbott and L. Campbell, *The Life and Letters of Benjamin Jowett, M.A.*, 377; letter of 4 May 1890, to the Revd John La Touche.

[118] G. F. Barbour, 'Memoir' of Pringle-Pattison prefixed to the latter's *The Balfour Lectures on Realism,* Edinburgh: Blackwood, 1933, 109–10. Barbour quotes a letter of Pringle-Pattison to A. J. Balfour of January 1899.

[119] Quoted by Stephen Paget (ed.), *Henry Scott Holland,* 68.

[120] T. H. Green, *Works,* III, 251.

[121] Ibid.

[122] J. R. Illingworth, in E. S. Talbot *et al., Sermons Preached in the Temporary Chapel of Keble College, Oxford, 1870–1876,* London: Rivingtons, 1877, 295–6.

[123] C. C. J. Webb, *Religious Thought in the Oxford Movement,* 99.

[124] A. E. Taylor, *The Faith of a Moralist,* II, 12.

[125] Ibid., 197.

[126] Ibid., 203.

[127] Ibid., 206.

[128] Ibid., 208.

[129] Ibid., 211, 212.

[130] Ibid., 223–4.

[131] Ibid., 311.

[132] For some further reflections on this matter see Alan P. F. Sell, *Commemorations: Studies in Christian Thought and History,* Calgary: The University of Calgary Press, and Cardiff: University of Wales Press, 1993, ch.I.

[133] A. E. Taylor, *The Faith of a Moralist,* II, 271.

[134] Ibid., 275.

[135] A. E. Taylor, review of J. M. E. McTaggart, *Some Dogmas of Religion,* in *The Philosophical Review,* XV, 1906, 415, 416.

[136] Idem, *The Faith of a Moralist,* I, 21. The point is reiterated, ibid., II, 19.

[137] C. C. J. Webb, *A Century of Anglican Theology,* 112. Cf. idem, *Problems in the Relations of God and Man,* 245.

[138] Henry Jones, *The Immortality of the Soul in Tennyson and Browning,* London: Green, 1905, 20.

[139] Ibid., 30.

[140] J. S. Mackenzie, 'Edward Caird as a philosophical teacher', *Mind,* NS XVIII, 1909, 525 and n.

[141] H. Jones and J. H. Muirhead, *The Life and Philosophy of Edward Caird,* 184; from a letter of Caird to Mary Sarah Talbot of 29 December 1892.

[142] See J. R. Illingworth, *Sermons Preached in a College Chapel,* London: Macmillan, 1882. I quote from p.45.

[143] C. C. J. Webb, *Divine Personality and Human Life,* 255.

[144] Ibid. This is, I think, the more striking in one who has such a strong sense of the historical continuity of the faith through the ages. There

is nothing of Richard Baxter about Webb at this point:

> As for my friends, they are not lost;
> The several vessels of Thy fleet,
> Though parted now by tempests tost,
> Shall safely in the haven meet.

[145] Ibid., 256. Cf. idem, 'Outline of a philosophy of religion', in *Contemporary British Philosophy*, ed. J. H. Muirhead, London: Allen & Unwin, Second Series, 1925, 357.

[146] A. S. Pringle-Pattison, *The Idea of Immortality*, Oxford: The Clarendon Press, 1922, 1.

[147] Ibid., 38.

[148] Ibid., 39.

[149] Ibid., 44. We may note that W. R. Inge disagreed with Pringle-Pattison's view (ibid., 56) that the ideas of God and immortality were not treated by Plato as 'part of a scientific theory of the unseen world, but primarily as "regulative ideas" for the direction of our life here and now'. See his *God and the Astronomers*, London: Longmans, 1933, 287n.

[150] Ibid., 63.

[151] Ibid., 74.

[152] Ibid., 76. Pringle-Pattison quotes Locke's *Essay*, IV.iii. 6.

[153] Ibid., 91.

[154] Ibid., 92. 'This view', wrote H. Wheeler Robinson, 'has an interesting kinship with Hebrew ideas of psychology, according to which human personality consists of an animated body, and not, as in the Platonic conception, an incarnate soul.' See his *The Christian Experience of the Holy Spirit*, [1928], London: Collins Fontana, 1962, 74–5.

[155] Ibid., 99.

[156] Ibid., 100.

[157] Ibid., 135.

[158] Ibid., 208, quoting E. Caird, *The Evolution of Religion*, 3rd edn, II, 242.

[159] Ibid., 160, 163. Cf. the criticism of J. B. Baillie, *A. S. Pringle-Pattison 1856–1931*, reprinted from *Proceedings of the British Academy*, XVII, 1931, 42.

[160] A. E. Taylor, 'The belief in immortality', in *The Faith and the War*, ed. F. J. Foakes-Jackson, London: Macmillan, 1915, 157n.

[161] H. Jones, 'Divine immanence', *Hibbert Journal*, V no. 4, July 1907, 766.

[162] E. Caird, *Lay Sermons*, 281, 282.

[163] T. H. Green, *Prolegomena to Ethics*, Oxford: The Clarendon Press, 4th edn, 1899, para. 187.

[164] Quoted by R. L. Nettleship in his 'Memoir', Green's *Works*, III, xxvii.

165 T. H. Green, *Works*, III,159.

166 So Robert Mackintosh, *Hegel and Hegelianism*, Edinburgh: T. & T. Clark, 1903, 260.

167 Charles B. Upton, 'Theological aspects of the philosophy of Thomas Hill Green', *New World* (Chicago), I, 1892, 156.

168 A. E. Taylor, 'The vindication of religion', in *Essays Catholic and Critical*, ed. E. G. Selwyn, London: SPCK, 3rd edn, reprinted 1931, 65. Cf. idem, *The Faith of a Moralist*, I, 71.

169 Idem, 'The freedom of man', in *Contemporary British Philosophy*, ed. J. H. Muirhead, Second Series, 1925, 270–1. For the same reason the Christian understanding of creation, and of the Creator–creature distinction is undercut, as we saw in ch.3 above.

170 A. S. Pringle-Pattison, *The Idea of Immortality*, 195–6; cf. his *The Balfour Lectures on Realism*, 141–2.

171 The defence by his pupil, H. F. Hallett, does not convince. See 'Andrew Seth Pringle-Pattison 1856–1931', *Mind*, XLII, April 1933, 146.

172 A. S. Pringle-Pattison, *The Idea of God*, 45.

173 Cf. W. L. Davidson, *Recent Theistic Discussion*, Edinburgh: T. & T. Clark, 1921, 131–2. Cf. A. E. Taylor's review of Pringle-Pattison's *The Idea of Immortality*, in *Hibbert Journal*, XX 1923–4, 598–603.

174 E. Caird, *Lay Sermons*, 275.

175 I am indebted to D. O. Thomas for this remark, which I endorse.

176 Ibid., 276–7.

177 H. Jones, *A Faith that Enquires*, 347.

178 Ibid., 344.

179 A. E. Taylor, *The Faith of a Moralist*, I, 324ff.

180 Ibid., 331.

181 Idem, 'The belief in immortality', 149.

182 A. S. Pringle-Pattison, *The Idea of Immortality*, 183–5.

183 A. E. Taylor, *Human Mind and Will*, The Congress Books no. 22, London: The Society of SS Peter and Paul, [1923], 29.

184 H. F. Lovell Cocks, *By Faith Alone*, London: James Clarke, 1943, 155. For an account of this unfairly neglected theologian see Alan P. F. Sell, *Commemorations: Studies in Christian Thought and History*, ch.13.

185 Robert Mackintosh, 'Recent philosophy and Christian doctrine', 84.

186 See, for example, Patrick Masterson, 'Hegel's philosophy of God', *Philosophical Studies*, XIX, 1970, 146; Leonard Hodgson, *Towards a Christian Philosophy*, London: Nisbet, 1943, 157–60, where Hodgson adversely criticizes William Temple for lingering idealism.

187 See, for example, J. R. Illingworth, *Personality Human and Divine*, London: Macmillan, 1904, 74.

188 Idem, *Divine Immanence*, 154, 155. Cf. idem, *The Doctrine of the Trinity*, 143–4; idem, *Divine Transcendence*, 49–50.

[189] Ibid., 157.

[190] D. W. Forrest, *The Christ of History and of Experience*, 210; Forrest quotes J. R. Illingworth, *Personality Human and Divine*, 73.

[191] J. R. Illingworth, *The Doctrine of the Trinity*, 207.

[192] Idem, *Christian Character*, 179.

[193] See idem, *Sermons Preached in a College Chapel*, 172.

[194] C. C. J. Webb, *God and Personality*, 82–3.

[195] J. R. Illingworth, *The Doctrine of the Trinity*, 147–9.

[196] *Letters of Principal James Denney to W. Robertson Nicoll*, London: Hodder & Stoughton, [1920], 101; letter of 29 November 1907.

[197] *The Expository Times*, XIX, 1907–8, 233.

[198] A. S. Martin, review of J. R. Illingworth, *The Doctrine of the Trinity*, in *Review of Theology and Philosophy*, III, 1908, 735.

[199] J. R. Illingworth, *The Gospel Miracles*, 185.

[200] For this reason it is very easy to misconstrue Illingworth's thought by presenting but one side of it. I am inclined to think that this has happened in *Persons, Divine and Human* (ed. Christoph Schwöbel and Colin E. Gunton, Edinburgh: T. & T. Clark, 1991), which came into my hands after I had completed the text of this chapter. In the Introduction, Dr Schwöbel sets out from Illingworth (whose initials he consistently reverses). Both he and Dr Brian Horne (who has his subject's initials in the correct order) focus exclusively upon *Personality Human and Divine*; and both regret the absence of the influence of the Cappadocian Fathers upon Illingworth. Dr Horne declares that Illingworth was 'too firmly rooted in the thought of Augustine for that' (67). It must be granted that *some* of Illingworth's statements lend credence to this view. But he says other things too – sufficient to place question marks against Dr Horne's allegation that Illingworth was so Augustinian that he could not accommodate the Cappadocians in his thought; and against Dr Schwöbel's statement of what Dr Horne 'notes in passing', namely,

> that for Illingworth the self-reflective structure of human consciousness determines the approach to divine personality by means of analogy, rather than the tri-personal being of God which becomes accessible to us through God's self-communication in the divine economy (19).

It is not difficult to find in Illingworth assertions which reveal his grasp of the priority of revelation and his indebtedness to the Cappadocians. Thus, in the work cited (*Personality Human and Divine*, 212), he displays no discomfort with the fact that the Trinity

> was regarded as a revelation by the men who shaped its intellectual expression; and it was only in . . . the very gradual process of that

expression, that its congruity with human psychology came out; that psychology in fact being distinctly developed in the effort to give it utterance.

He immediately proceeds to cite Augustine, Origen, Athanasius, Hilary, Basil and the Gregories as among those who understood this very well. The point is underscored in *The Doctrine of the Trinity* (264), by means of a lengthy quotation from none other than Gregory of Nyssa. Yet again: 'though at first sight [the Trinity] might seem a mystery too transcendental to be worth revelation, its revelation was in fact a thing of the profoundest practical import' (*Divine Immanence*, 154). It would therefore seem that Illingworth's trinitarian position is more complex, and less one-sidedly Western, than Drs Schwöbel and Horne suggest.

201 See, for example, A. S. Pringle-Pattison, *The Philosophical Radicals*, Edinburgh: Blackwood, 1907, 246; C. C. J. Webb, *Kant's Philosophy of Religion*, Oxford: The Clarendon Press, 1926, 146.

202 A. S. Pringle-Pattison, 'Immanence and Transcendence', in B. H. Streeter (ed.), *The Spirit*, London: Macmillan, 1928, 11. Cf. idem, *The Idea of God*, 409–10.

203 D. W. Forrest, *The Christ of History and of Experience*, 211.

204 *Westminster Shorter Catechism*, A. 30.

205 C.C.J. Webb, *Problems in the Relations of God and Man*, 249.

206 A.E. Taylor, *The Faith of a Moralist*, I, 248.

207 C. C. J. Webb, *God and Personality*, 65; cf. ibid., 102. Leonard Hodgson concurs. See his *Towards a Christian Philosophy*, 150n.

208 C. C. J. Webb, *God and Personality*, 65; idem, *Problems in the Relations of God and Man*, 281.

209 D. Miall Edwards, *Christianity and Philosophy*, Edinburgh: T. & T. Clark, 1932, 351.

210 H. Wheeler Robinson, *The Christian Experience of the Holy Spirit*, 230–1.

211 L. Hodgson, *The Doctrine of the Trinity*, 227. See further D. M. Baillie's discussion of Webb and others on this matter in his *God Was in Christ*, London: Faber & Faber, 1961, ch.VI.

212 C. C. J. Webb, *A History of Philosophy*, London: Williams and Norgate, 1915, 108.

213 James Patrick, *The Magdalen Metaphysicals: Idealism and Orthodoxy at Oxford, 1901–1945*, Macon, GA: Mercer Univesity Press, 1985, 168. Although Webb is the only one of our seven idealists among the Magdalen metaphysicals, and recognizing that Patrick's purpose is not the detailed analysis of philosophical texts, this is nevertheless a most illuminating and evocative account of a group whose other members were J. A. Smith, R. G. Collingwood and C. S. Lewis. For my review

of this book see *Philosophical Studies* (Dublin), XXXII, 1988–90, 350–2.

Chapter 6: The Legacy of Post-Hegelian Idealism

[1] E. Caird, *Essays on Literature and Philosophy,* Glasgow: Maclehose, 1892, I, 205.

[2] T. H. Green, *Works,* ed. R. L. Nettleship, London: Longmans, 3rd edn, 1891, III, 145.

[3] E. Caird, *Essays on Literature and Philosophy,* I, 206.

[4] A. S. Pringle-Pattison in a letter of 28 November 1915 to Lord Balfour, quoted by G. F. Barbour in his 'Memoir' of Pringle-Pattison prefixed to the latter's *The Balfour Lectures on Realism,* Edinburgh: Blackwood, 1933, 118.

[5] C. C. J. Webb, 'Outline of a philosophy of religion', in *Contemporary British Philosophy,* ed. J. H. Muirhead, London: Allen & Unwin, Second Series, 1925, 342.

[6] A. E. Taylor, *William George de Burgh, 1866–1943,* reprinted from the *Proceedings of the British Academy,* XXIX, 1943, 22.

[7] C. C. J. Webb, *A Century of Anglican Theology,* Oxford: Blackwell, 1923, 52–3.

[8] A. S. Pringle-Pattison, *The Idea of God in the Light of Recent Philosophy,* New York: Oxford University Press, 2nd edn revised, 1920, 334.

[9] H. Jones, *A Faith that Enquires,* London: Macmillan, 1922, 141.

[10] A. E. Taylor, *The Faith of a Moralist,* London: Macmillan, 1931, 228.

[11] H. Jones, 'The social organism', in R. B. Haldane and A. Seth (eds.), *Essays in Philosophical Criticism,* London: Longmans, 1883, 211.

[12] C. C. J. Webb, *Problems in the Relations of God and Man,* London: Nisbet, 1911, 67.

[13] See J. Moltmann, *The Crucified God,* New York: Harper & Row, 1974, 246–7.

[14] J. M. Creed, *The Divinity of Jesus Christ,* [1938], London: Collins Fontana, 1964, 63.

[15] By Allan D. Galloway, *Religious Studies,* VIII, 1972, 367.

[16] John W. Cooper, 'Testing the spirit of the Age of Aquarius: the New Age Movement', *Calvin Theological Journal,* XXII no. 2, November 1987, 302.

[17] H. P. Owen, *Revelation and Existence: A Study in the Theology of Rudolf Bultmann,* Cardiff: University of Wales Press, 1957, 36.

[18] See e.g. E. Caird, *The Evolution of Religion,* Glasgow: Maclehose, 1894, I, ix, x; A. S. Pringle-Pattison, *Studies in the Philosophy of Religion,* Oxford: Clarendon Press, 1930, 3; C. C. J. Webb, 'Christianity as the climax of religious development', *Constructive Quarterly,* VI, 1918, 442.

19 J. R. Illingworth, *Christian Character*, London: Macmillan, 1914, 143.

20 Idem, in *Lux Mundi*, ed. Charles Gore, 15th edn, 1904, 150. Cf. idem, 'The "mystical" and "sacramental" temperaments', *The Expositor*, 5th series, X, 1899, 83.

21 R. L. Ottley, *The Doctrine of the Incarnation*, 6th edn, London: Methuen, 1919, 10.

22 See J. R. Illingworth, *Sermons Preached in a College Chapel*, London: Macmillan, 1882, 161–3, where he denies that the comparative method and the evolutionary principle necessarily entail relativism. He does not, however, hesitate elsewhere to say that

> all others are relative religions, and as such cannot claim to have their truth involved in the rationality of the world, while the claim of Christianity is to be the absolute religion which alone can finally satisfy the reason.

See his *The Doctrine of the Trinity*, 187.

23 T. H. Green, *Works*, III, 182.

24 The remark of F. C. Burkitt, who thought that in his Christology Sanday gave insufficient weight to the atonement, comes to mind at this point. In a letter to Sanday of 2 May 1910 Burkitt wrote,

> Don't think me frivolous if I remind you of the aesthete in *Punch* who said to the mother of a handsome youth: '*Do*, my dear madam? But why should he *do* anything? Is it not sufficient that he should exist beautifully?

See Bodleian Library MS Eng.misc. d. 122 (i).

25 A. E. Taylor, *The Faith of a Moralist*, I, 221.

26 Ibid., II, 377. Though twelve pages later he recognizes that for this we should need the intelligence not of the metaphysician, but of God.

27 T. H. Green, *Works*, III, 133.

28 C. C. J. Webb, 'The permanent meaning of propitiation', *Constructive Quarterly*, V, 1917, 140.

29 A. E. Taylor, *The Faith of a Moralist*, II, 396. Cf. idem, in *Essays Catholic and Critical*, ed. E. G. Selwyn, London: SPCK, 3rd edn, 1921, 44.

30 H. R. Mackintosh, *Some Aspects of Christian Belief*, London: Hodder & Stoughton, [1923], 290.

31 A. E. Taylor, in *Essays Catholic and Critical*, 63.

32 J. R. Illingworth, *The Doctrine of the Trinity*, 174.

33 Idem, *Reason and Revelation*, London: Macmillan, 1902, 242–3. James Iverach, not one predisposed to unadulterated idealism as we have seen, nevertheless thought that Illingworth had, with this book, produced 'one of the ablest treatises on apologetics which we have had the good fortune to read'. See his review in *The Critical Review of*

Theological and Philosophical Literature, XIII, 1903, 31.

[34] J. R. Illingworth, *University and Cathedral Sermons,* London: Macmillan, 1893, 78. Cf. idem, *Sermons Preached in a College Chapel,* London: Macmillan, 1882, 118.

[35] William Sanday, *Christologies Ancient and Modern,* Oxford: Clarendon Press, 1910, 96.

[36] C. C. J. Webb, *The Devotions of Saint Anselm,* London: Methuen, 1903, xxxii–xxxiii.

[37] H. Jones, *The Immanence of God and the Individuality of Man,* Manchester: H. Rawson, 1912, 42.

Bibliography

In Part I are listed the principal *relevant* published works of the seven idealists discussed in this book. Thus, for example, Henry Jones's tracts on Welsh affairs, and A. E. Taylor's editions of classical philosophical texts are not included here. In Part II a selection of works consulted is presented. In both parts, works are listed in chronological order under each author's name, and those marked with an asterisk include a bibliography of the author or person concerned. As a general rule the dates of first editions only are given, and works reprinted in composite volumes are not normally listed separately.

Part I: The Principal Published Works of the Seven Idealists

Edward Caird

Ethical Philosophy: An Introductory Lecture, Glasgow: Maclehose, 1866.
'Mr Balfour on transcendentalism', *Mind,* IV, 1879, 111–14.
'The so-called idealism of Kant', ibid., 557–61.
Review of Robert Adamson, *On the Philosophy of Kant,* in ibid., V, 1880, 124–30.
A Critical Account of the Philosophy of Kant, with an Historical Introduction, Glasgow: Maclehose, 1877.

'Professor Green's last work', *Mind*, VIII, 1883, 544–61.

The Social Philosophy and Religion of Comte, Glasgow: Maclehose, 1885.

The Critical Philosophy of Immanuel Kant, Glasgow: Maclehose, 2 vols. 1889.

Hegel, Edinburgh: Blackwood, 1883.

'The modern conception of the science of religion', *International Journal of Ethics*, I, 1890–1, 389–403.

Essays on Literature and Philosophy, Glasgow: Maclehose, 2 vols. 1892. This work contains papers on Dante; Goethe; Rousseau; Wordsworth; The problem of philosophy at the present time; Carlyle; Cartesianism; Metaphysic, which are not separately noted here.

The Evolution of Religion (Gifford Lectures), Glasgow: Maclehose, 2 vols. 1893.

'Professor Jowett', *International Journal of Ethics*, VIII, 1897–8, 40–7.

Biographical introduction to William Wallace, *Lectures and Essays on Natural Theology and Ethics*, Oxford: Clarendon Press, 2 vols., 1898.

'Memoir of Principal Caird', in John Caird, *The Fundamental Ideas of Christianity*, Glasgow: Maclehose, 1899.

'Idealism and the theory of knowledge', *Proceedings of the British Academy*, I, 1903–4, 95–108.

'St Paul and the idea of evolution', *Hibbert Journal*, II no. 1, October 1903, 1–19.

The Evolution of Theology in the Greek Philosophers (Gifford Lectures), Glasgow: Maclehose, 2 vols. 1904.

Lay Sermons and Addresses Delivered in the Hall of Balliol College, Oxford, Glasgow: Maclehose, 1907.

T. H. Green

'Can there be a natural science of man?', *Mind*, VII, 1882, 1–29, 161–85, 321–48.

Prolegomena to Ethics, ed. A. C. Bradley, Oxford: Clarendon Press, 1883.

Works of Thomas Hill Green, ed. R. L. Nettleship, London: Longmans, Green, 3 vols., 1885–8.

J. R. Illingworth

Sermons 22–4 in E. S. Talbot (ed.), *Sermons Preached in the Temporary Chapel of Keble College, Oxford, 1870–1876*, London: Rivington, 1877.

Sermons Preached in a College Chapel. With an Appendix, London: Macmillan, 1882.

'The Incarnation of the eternal Word', *The Expositor*, 3rd series, III, 1886, 161–75.

'The problem of pain: its bearing on faith in God', and 'The Incarnation in relation to development', in Charles Gore (ed.), *Lux Mundi*, London: John Murray, 1889.

University and Cathedral Sermons, London: Macmillan, 1893.

Personality Human and Divine (Bampton Lectures), London: Macmillan, 1894.

Divine Immanence: An Essay on the Spiritual Significance of Matter, London: Macmillan, 1898.

'The "mystical" and "sacramental" temperaments', *The Expositor*, 5th series, X, 1899, 81–91.

Reason and Revelation: An Essay in Christian Apology, London: Macmillan, 1901.

Christian Character: Being some Lectures on the Elements of Christian Ethics, London: Macmillan, 1904.

The Doctrine of the Trinity Apologetically Considered, London: Macmillan, 1907.

The Church and Human Thought in the Present Day (Pan Anglican Papers no. 2), London: SPCK, 1907.

Divine Transcendence and its Reflection in Religious Authority, London: Macmillan, 1911.

Preface to E. F. H. Frere, *Positive Christianity*, Oxford: Mowbrays, 1913.

The Gospel Miracles: An Essay with Two Appendices, London: Macmillan, 1915.

Henry Jones

'The social organism', in A. Seth and R. B. Haldane (eds.), *Essays in Philosophical Criticism*, London: Longmans, 1881.

Morality as Freedom: A Lecture given at the Ethical Society, London: Swan Sonnenschein, 1888.

Browning as a Philosophical and Religious Teacher, London: Nelson, [1891].

Review of J. H. Muirhead, *Elements of Ethics,* in *International Journal of Ethics,* III, 1892–3, 113–15.

'The nature and aims of philosophy' (Inaugural Lecture, St Andrews), *Mind,* NS II, 1893, 160–73.

'Idealism and epistemology', ibid., 289–306; 457–72.

Browning as a Dramatic Poet, Boston: Poet-Lore, 1894.

Is the Order of Nature Opposed to the Moral Life? (Inaugural Lecture, Glasgow), Glasgow: Maclehose, 1894.

A Critical Account of the Philosophy of Lotze: The Doctrine of Thought, Glasgow: Maclehose, 1895.

Principal Caird, Glasgow: Maclehose, 1898.

'The late Professor Adamson', *Mind,* NS XI, 1902, 431–5.

Review of Josiah Royce, *The World and the Individual,* in *Hibbert Journal,* I, 1902–3, 132–44.

'The present attitude of reflective thought towards religion', *Hibbert Journal,* I, 1902–3, 228–52, and II, 1903–4, 20–43.

'Mr Balfour as Sophist', *Hibbert Journal,* III, 1904–5, 452–77.

'The child and heredity', in *The Child and Religion,* ed. Thomas Stephens, London: Williams & Norgate, 1905.

The Philosophy of Martineau in Relation to the Idealism of the Present Day, London: Macmillan, 1905.

The Immortality of the Soul in the Poems of Tennyson and Browning, London: Philip Green, 1905.

Social Responsibilities: Lectures to Business Men, Glasgow: Maclehose, 1905.

Francis Hutcheson, Glasgow: Maclehose, 1906.

'Divine immanence', *Hibbert Journal,* V, 1906–7, 745–67.

Divine Transcendence, Oxford: Manchester College, 1907.

Review of John Watson, *The Philosophical Basis of Religion,* in *Hibbert Journal,* VI, 1907–8, 676–82.

Idealism as a Practical Creed, Glasgow: Maclehose, 1909.

'The idealism of Jesus', *Hibbert Journal,* Supplement entitled, *Jesus or Christ?,* 1909, 81–106.

'Tennyson', *Hibbert Journal,* VIII, 1909–10, 264–82.

'The ethical demand of the present political situation', *Hibbert Journal,* VIII, 1909–10, 523–42.

'Ethics and politics', *Friends' Quarterly Examiner,* XLIV, 1910, 394–412.

The Working Faith of the Social Reformer and Other Essays, London: Macmillan, 1910.

'Modern science and philosophical thought regarding human society', in J. B. Paton *et al.* (eds.), *Christ and Civilization,* London: National Council of Evangelical Free Churches, 1910.

'The corruption of the citizenship of the working man', *Hibbert Journal,* X, 1911–12, 155–78.

Review of B. Bosanquet, *The Principle of Individuality and Value,* in *Hibbert Journal,* X, 1911–12, 949–54.

Review of B. Bosanquet, *The Value and Destiny of the Individual,* in *Hibbert Journal,* XI, 1912–13, 902–9.

The Immanence of God and the Individuality of Man, Manchester: Rawson, 1912.

Social Powers. Three Popular Lectures on the Environment, the Press and the Pulpit, Glasgow: Maclehose, 1913.

'Why we are fighting', *Hibbert Journal,* XIII, 1914–15, 50–67.

Philosophical Landmarks: Being a Survey of the Recent Gains and the Present Problems of Reflective Thought, Houston: Rice Institute Studies, I, 1915.

'Morality and its relation to the War', in J. E. Carpenter (ed.), *Ethical and Religious Problems of the War,* London: Lindsey Press, 1916.

The Obligations and Privileges of Citizenship – A Plea for the Study of Social Science, Houston: Rice Institute Studies, VI, 1919.

The Principles of Citizenship, London: Macmillan, 1919.

The Life and Philosophy of Edward Caird, with J. H. Muirhead, 1919, see Part II under Jones and Muirhead.

A Faith that Enquires (Gifford Lectures), London: Macmillan, 1922.

Old Memories: Autobiography of Sir Henry Jones, C.H., Late Professor of Moral Philosophy in the University of Glasgow, ed. Thomas Jones, London: Hodder and Stoughton, [1922].

Essays on Literature and Education, ed. H. J. W. Hetherington, London: Hodder and Stoughton, 1924.

A. S. Pringle-Pattison

Note: Up to and including *Two Lectures on Theism,* his works appeared under the name of Andrew Seth.

'Hegel : An exposition and criticism', *Mind,* VI, 1881, 513–30.

Review of Robert Adamson, *Fichte,* in ibid., 583–7.

The Development from Kant to Hegel, with Chapters on the Philosophy of Religion, London: Williams and Norgate, 1882; Part II of this work is reprinted in *The Philosophical Radicals,* q.v.

Essays in Philosophical Criticism, ed. with R. B. Haldane, London: Longmans, 1883.

Scottish Philosophy (Balfour Lectures), Edinburgh: Blackwood, 1885, 1889.

Hegelianism and Personality (Balfour Lectures), Edinburgh: Blackwood, 1887.

'Hegel and his recent critics', *Mind,* XIV, 1889, 116–19.

Review of S. Alexander, *Moral Order and Progress: An Analysis of Ethical Conceptions,* in *Mind,* XIV, 1889, 554–64.

Review of E. Caird, *The Critical Philosophy of Immanuel Kant,* in *Mind,* NS XV, 1890, 266–79.

'Hegelianism and its critics', *Mind,* NS III, 1894, 1–25.

Man's Place in the Cosmos and Other Essays, Edinburgh: Blackwood, 1897; 2nd revised and enlarged edn., 1902. This work contains papers on 'Man's place in the cosmos'; 'The present position of the philosophical sciences'; 'The "new" psychology and automatism'; 'A new theory of the absolute'; 'Mr Balfour and his critics'; 'The venture of theism'; and 'The life and opinions of Friedrich Neitzschte'.

Two Lectures on Theism, Edinburgh: Blackwood, 1897.

Chapter on the philosophical works of Calderwood in W. L. Calderwood, and D. Woodside, *The Life of Henry Calderwood, LL.D., F.R.S.E.,* London: Hodder & Stoughton, 1900.

The Philosophical Radicals and Other Essays with chapters reprinted on the Philosophy of Religion in Kant and Hegel, Edinburgh: Blackwood, 1907. This work contains papers on the philosophical radicals; B. Kidd; J. Martineau; H. Spencer; H. Jones; J. Dewey; J. M. E. McTaggart; and 'Philosophy as criticism of categories'; which are not separately noted here.

Review of A. S. and E. M. S[idgwick], *Henry Sidgwick: A Memoir,* and R. L. Nettleship, *Memoir of Thomas Hill Green,* in *Mind,* NS XVII, 1908, 88–97.

Introduction to J. S. Mill, *On Liberty,* London: Routledge, 1910.

'Alexander Campbell Fraser 1819–1914', *Mind,* NS XXIV, 1915, 289–325.

'Mr Balfour's *Theism and Humanism*', *Hibbert Journal*, XIV, 1916, 268–85.

'Do finite individuals possess a substantive or an adjectival mode of being?', *Proceedings of the Aristotelian Society*, NS XVIII, 1917–18, 507–30.

'Immanence and transcendence', in B. H. Streeter (ed.), *The Spirit*, London: Macmillan, 1919.

The Idea of God in the Light of Recent Philosophy (Gifford Lectures), Oxford: The Clarendon Press, 1917; 2nd revised edn, New York: OUP, 1920.

The Duty of Candour in Religious Teaching, London: Hodder & Stoughton, [1921].

The Idea of Immortality (Gifford Lectures), Oxford: The Clarendon Press, 1922.

An Essay Concerning Human Understanding by John Locke, abridged and ed. A. S. Pringle-Pattison, Oxford: The Clarendon Press, 1924.

'The Philosophy of History' (Annual Philosophical Lecture, Henriette Hertz Trust), *Proceedings of the British Academy*, X, 1924, 513–29.

Memoir of James Seth in the latter's *Essays in Ethics and Religion*, ed. A. S. Pringle-Pattison, Edinburgh: Blackwood, 1926.

'Is a philosophy of history possible?', *The Modern Churchman*, XVIII, 1928, 319–34.

'Richard Burdon Haldane, 1856–1928', *Proceedings of the British Academy*, XIV, 1928, 405–44.

Studies in the Philosophy of Religion (partly based on the Gifford Lectures), Oxford: The Clarendon Press, 1930.

The Balfour Lectures on Realism, ed., with a Memoir of the author by G. F. Barbour, Edinburgh: Blackwood, 1933. These lectures were originally delivered in 1891 and published in *The Philosophical Review*.

A. E. Taylor

'Self-realization – a criticism', *International Journal of Ethics*, VI, 1895–6, 356–71.

'The conception of immortality in Spinoza's Ethics', *Mind*, NS V, 1896, 145–66.

'The metaphysical problem, with special reference to its bearing upon ethics', *International Journal of Ethics,* X, 1899–1900, 352–80.

The Problem of Conduct: A Study in the Phenomenology of Ethics, London: Macmillan, 1901

'Recent criticism of Green's ethics', *Proceedings of the Aristotelian Society,* NS II, 1901–2, 62–6.

'Mind and nature', *International Journal of Ethics,* XIII, 1902–3, 55–86.

Elements of Metaphysics, London: Methuen, 1903.

'Mind and body in recent psychology', *Mind,* NS XIII, 1904, 476–508.

'Truth and practice', *The Philosophical Review,* XIV, 1905, 265–89.

'Truth and consequences', *Mind,* NS XV, 1906, 81–93.

'The place of psychology in the classification of the sciences', *The Philosophical Review,* XV, 1906, 380–6.

Review of J. M. E. McTaggart, *Some Dogmas of Religion,* in ibid., 414–24.

Thomas Hobbes, London: Constable, 1908.

'Why pluralism?', *Proceedings of the Aristotelian Society,* NS IX, 1908–9, 201–16.

'Continuity', in James Hastings (ed.), *Encyclopaedia of Religion and Ethics,* Edinburgh: T. & T. Clark, IV, 1911, 89–98.

'Identity', in ibid., VII, 1914, 95–9.

'The belief in immortality', in F. J. Foakes-Jackson (ed.), *The Faith and the War,* London: Macmillan, 1915.

'Philosophy' in F. S. Marvin (ed.), *Recent Developments in European Thought,* London: OUP, 1920.

'Theism', in *Encyclopaedia of Religion and Ethics,* XII, 1921, 261–87.

Human Mind and Will, London: The Society of SS Peter and Paul, [1923].

Review of A. S. Pringle-Pattison, *The Idea of Immortality,* James Y. Simpson, *Man and the Attainment of Immortality,* and L. P. Jacks, *The Living Universe,* in *Hibbert Journal,* XX, 1923–4, 598–603.

'Francis Herbert Bradley 1846–1924', *Proceedings of the British Academy,* XI, 1924–5, 458–68.

'F. H. Bradley', *Mind,* NS XXXIV, 1925, 1–12.

'Philosophy', in *Evolution in the Light of Modern Knowledge,* London: Blackie, 1925.

Platonism and its Influence, London: G. Harrap, 1925.

'The freedom of man', in J. H. Muirhead (ed.), *Contemporary British Philosophy*, 2nd ser., London: Allen and Unwin, 1925.

'The vindication of religion', in E. G. Selwyn (ed.), *Essays Catholic and Critical*, London: SPCK, 1926.

'Some features of Butler's ethics', *Mind*, NS XXXV, 1926, 273–300.

'Francis Bacon', *Proceedings of the British Academy*, XII, 1926, 273–94.

'The scholastic movement', in A. S. Peake and R. G. Parsons (eds.), *An Outline of Christianity*, London: Waverley, 5 vols., 1926, 1927.

Review of John Laird, *A Study in Moral Theory*, in *Mind*, NS XXXV, 1926, 480–9.

David Hume and the Miraculous, Cambridge: CUP, 1927.

'Knowing and believing', *Proceedings of the Aristotelian Society*, NS XXIX, 1928–9, 1–30.

The Problem of Evil, London: Ernest Benn, 1929.

The Faith of a Moralist (Gifford Lectures), 2 vols., London: Macmillan, 1930.

'Why I am not a Roman Catholic', in Alban Goodier (ed.), *Why I am, and Why I am not a Roman Catholic*, London: Cassell, 1931.

'Is goodness a quality?', *Proceedings of the Aristotelian Society*, Supplementary Volume XI, 1932, 146–68.

Philosophical Studies, London: Macmillan, 1934.

'Ancient and medieval philosophy', in Edward Eyre (ed.) *European Civilization*, III, , London: OUP, 1935, 735–845.

'Modern philosophy', in ibid., VII, 1937, 1179–1268.

'Some incoherencies in Spinozism', *Mind*, NS XLVI, 1937, 137–58; 281–301.

'Religion and present-day thought', in W. Temple (ed.), *The Recall to Religion*, London: Eyre & Spottiswoode, 1937.

The Christian Hope of Immortality, London: John Heritage, 1938.

'The ethical doctrine of Hobbes', *Philosophy*, XIII, 1938, 406–24.

'Science and morality', ibid., XIV, 1939, 24–45.

'Freedom and personality', ibid., 259–80.

'The present-day relevance of Hume's *Dialogues concerning Natural Religion*', *Proceedings of the Aristotelian Society*, Supplementary Volume XVIII, 1939, 179–205.

'Back to Descartes', *Philosophy*, XVI, 1941, 126–37.

'Freedom and personality again', ibid., XVII, 1942, 26–37.

'William George de Burgh 1866–1943', *Proceedings of the British Academy*, XXIX, 1943, 371–91.
Does God Exist?, London: Macmillan, 1945.
'St John of the Cross and John Wesley', *Journal of Theological Studies*, XLVI, 1945, 30–8.
'A further word on Spinoza', *Mind*, NS LV, 1946, 97–112.

C. C. J. Webb

Review of *Lux Mundi*, in *The Oxford Magazine*, 12 February 1890, Supplement, 3–4.
'Is religion presupposed by morality or morality by religion?', *Proceedings of the Aristotelian Society*, II no. 3, part i, 1894, 50–4.
'Anselm's ontological argument for the existence of God', ibid., III no. 2, 1896, 25–43.
Review of A. Seth, *Man's Place in the Cosmos, and Other Essays*, in *The Oxford Magazine*, 26 January 1898, 166.
Review of J. S. Mackenzie, *A Manual of Ethics* (3rd edn), in ibid., 11 May 1898, 346–7.
Review of William Wallace, *Lectures and Essays on Natural Theology and Ethics*, in ibid., 31 May 1899, 388.
'The idea of personality as applied to God', *Journal of Theological Studies*, II, 1901, 49–65.
'Two books on mysticism', (i.e. W. R. Inge, *Christian Mysticism*, and Charles Bigg, *Unity in Diversity*), in ibid., 461–9.
Review of Alfred Caldecott, *The Philosophy of Religion in England and America*, in *Oxford Magazine*, 24 April 1901, 296–7.
Review of J. B. Baillie, *The Origin and Significance of Hegel's Logic*, in *Oxford Magazine*, 30 April 1902, 304.
Review of Josiah Royce, *The World and the Individual*, Second Series, in ibid., 21 May 1902, 360–1.
The Devotions of Saint Anselm, London: Methuen, 1903.
'Psychology and religion', *Journal of Theological Studies*, IV, 1903, 46–68.
Review of A. M. Fairbairn, *The Philosophy of the Christian Religion*, in ibid., 291–300.
Review of E. Caird, *The Evolution of Theology in the Greek Philosophers*, in *The Oxford Magazine*, 18 May 1904, 355–6.
'The personal element in philosophy', *Proceedings of the Aristotelian Society*, NS V, 1904–5, 106–16.
Review of A. Caldecott and H. R. Mackintosh, *Selections from the*

Literature of Theism, in *Journal of Theological Studies,* VI, 1905, 128–9.

Review of James Orr, *God's Image in Man and Its Defacement,* in *Journal of Theological Studies,* VII, 1906, 471–5.

The Notion of Revelation (Pan Anglican Papers), London: SPCK, 1908.

Review of H. M. Gwatkin, *The Knowledge of God and its Historical Development,* in ibid., IX, 1908, 28–9.

Review of F. von Hügel, *The Mystical Element in Religion as studied in Saint Catherine of Genoa and her Friends,* in ibid., X, 1909, 84–94.

Review of H. Rashdall, *Philosophy of Religion,* in *The Oxford Magazine,* 3 February 1910, 179–80.

Review of George Galloway, *The Principles of Religious Development,* in ibid., 10 March 1910, 266.

Review of William Sanday, *Christologies Ancient and Modern,* in ibid., 24 November 1910, 103–5.

Problems in the Relations of God and Man, London: Nisbet, 1911.

Natural and Revealed Religion, Oxford: Clarendon Press, 1912.

Review of R. Eucken, *The Truth of Religion, Journal of Theological Studies,* XIV, 1912, 117–22.

Studies in the History of Natural Theology, Oxford: Clarendon Press, 1914.

'Idea', in James Hastings (ed.), *Encyclopaedia of Religion and Ethics,* VII, Edinburgh: T. & T. Clark, 1914, 81–6.

A History of Philosophy, London: OUP, 1915.

Group Theories of Religion and the Individual, London: Allen & Unwin, 1916.

'The conscience', *Journal of the Transactions of the Victoria Institute,* XLIX, [1917], 141–64.

Review of R. G. Collingwood, *Religion and Philosophy,* in *The Oxford Magazine,* 1 June 1917, 281–2.

Review of A. S. Pringle-Pattison, *The Idea of God in the Light of Recent Philosophy,* in ibid., 26 October 1917, 29-30.

God and Personality (Gifford Lectures), London: Allen & Unwin, 1918.

In Time of War: Addresses upon Several Occasions, Oxford: Blackwell, 1918.

'Christianity as the climax of religious development', *Constructive Quarterly,* VI, 1918, 432–55.

Review of B. Bosanquet, *Social and International Ideals,* in *Mind,* NS XXVII, 1918, 375–7.

Review of Henry Jones, *The Principles of Citizenship,* in ibid., 1919, 486–7.

Divine Personality and Human Life (Gifford Lectures), London: Allen & Unwin, 1920.

Philosophy and the Christian Religion, Oxford: Clarendon Press, 1920.

'Obligation, autonomy, and the common good', *Proceedings of the Aristotelian Society,* NS XX, 1920, 113–24.

Review of Hastings Rashdall, *The Idea of Atonement in Christian Theology,* in *The Oxford Magazine,* 27 February 1920, 251.

Review of Josiah Royce, *Lectures on Modern Idealism,* in *Mind,* NS XXX, 1921, 227–8.

'Religion and philosophy', in C. F. Nolloth (ed.), *The Christian Faith,* London: John Murray, 1922.

'Mr Bosanquet on contemporary philosophy' (a review of B. Bosanquet, *The Meeting of Extremes in Contemporary Philosophy*), *Church Quarterly Review,* XCV, 1922–3, 160–5.

Review of S. Alexander, *Space, Time and Deity,* in ibid., 342–56.

A Century of Anglican Theology and Other Essays, Oxford: Blackwell, 1923.

'The religious consciousness in the light of the history of religion', *The Modern Churchman,* XIV, 1924, 322–32.

Review of E. Troeltsch, *Christian Thought: Its History and Application,* in *Hibbert Journal,* XX, 1923–4, 603–8.

'Science, Christianity, and modern civilization', in Joseph Needham (ed.), *Science, Religion, and Reality,* London: Sheldon Press, 1925.

'An outline of a philosophy of religion', in J. H. Muirhead (ed.), *Contemporary British Philosophy,* Second Series, London: Allen & Unwin, 1925.

'The dramatic element in worship', *The Modern Churchman,* XV, 1925, 478–90.

Kant's Philosophy of Religion, Oxford: Clarendon Press, 1926.

'Peace in the will of God', in A. D. Lindsay (ed.), *Christianity and the Present Moral Unrest,* London: Allen & Unwin, 1926.

'Miracles and sacraments', *Theology,* XII, 1926, 258–66.

'Recent thought on the doctrine of God', *The Expository Times,* XXXVII, 1925–6, 359–66.

'God and the world', *Journal of Philosophical Studies,* II, 1927, 291–300.

Review of B. H. Streeter, *Reality,* in *Journal of Theological Studies,* XXVIII, 1927, 217–22.

Religious Thought in the Oxford Movement, London: SPCK, 1928.

'Rashdall as philosopher and theologian', in P. E. Matheson, *Life of Hastings Rashdall,* London: OUP, 1928.

'The significance of the historical element for religion', *The Modern Churchman,* XVIII, 1928, 335–44.

Pascal's Philosophy of Religon, Oxford: Clarendon Press, 1929.

Religion and the Thought of Today (Riddell Memorial Lectures), London: OUP, 1929.

'Christianity in the nineteenth century', in *The History of Christianity in the Light of Modern Knowledge,* London: Blackie, 1929.

'Our knowledge of one another', *Proceedings of the British Academy,* XVI, 1930, 282–96.

'God and man', *Journal of Philosophical Studies,* V, 1930, 559–67.

'Arthur James Balfour', *Proceedings of the British Academy,* XVI, 1930, 5–11.

John of Salisbury, London: Methuen, 1932.

The Contribution of Christianity to Ethics, Calcutta: University of Calcutta, 1932.

'Charles Gore', *The Oxford Magazine,* 18 February 1932, 458–62.

'The Reformation and the Oxford Movement', *The Modern Churchman,* XXII, 1932–3, 389–404.

A Study of Religious Thought in England from 1850 (Olaus Petri Lectures), Oxford: Clarendon Press, 1933.

'The significance of the Oxford Movement in the history of Anglicanism', *Theology,* XXVI, 1933, 25–36.

'Two philosophers of the Oxford Movement', *Philosophy,* VIII, 1933, 273–84.

'The nature of religious experience', *Hibbert Journal,* XXXII, 1933–4, 17–30.

'Man and morality', in Leonard Hodgson (ed.), *God and the World Through Christian Eyes,* London: SCM Press, 1934.

Religion and Theism (Forwood Lectures), London: Allen & Unwin, 1934.

'Personality in God', *The Modern Churchman,* XXIV, 1934, 11–22.

The Historical Element in Religion (Lewis Fry Lectures), London: Allen & Unwin, 1935.

Review of John Baillie, *And the Life Everlasting,* in *Philosophy,* X, 1935, 94–6.

Review of William Temple, *Nature, Man, and God,* in ibid., 225–8.

Review of A. H. Dakin, *Von Hügel and the Supernatural,* in *The Oriel Record,* June 1935, 36–8.

'Religion, philosophy, and history', in R. Klibansky and H. J. Paton (eds.), *Philosophy and History. Essays presented to E. Cassirer,* Oxford: Clarendon Press, 1936.

'Nature and grace', *Journal of Theological Studies,* XXXVII, 1936, 113–31.

'How is it possible for us to be like our Lord Jesus Christ?', in Ronald Selby Wright (ed.), *Asking Them Questions,* London: OUP, 1936.

Review of W. G. de Burgh, *The Relations of Morality to Religion,* in *Philosophy,* XI, 1936, 225–6.

Review of C. E. Raven, *Evolution and the Christian Conception of God,* in ibid., 360–2.

Review of L. A. Reid, *Creative Morality,* in *Journal of Theological Studies,* XXXVIII, 1937, 317–18.

Review of N. Berdyaev, *The Destiny of Man,* in *Philosophy,* XII, 1937, 472–8.

Review of D. S. Cairns, *The Riddle of the World,* in *Journal of Theological Studies,* XXXVIII, 1937, 440–1.

Review of W. G. de Burgh, *Towards a Religious Philosophy,* in *Mind,* NS XLVII, 1938, 98–101.

Review of M. D. Petre, *Von Hügel and Tyrrell,* in *Journal of Theological Studies,* XXXIX, 1938, 214–17.

Review of W. G. de Burgh, *Knowledge of the Individual,* in *Philosophy,* XIV, 1939, 490–1.

Review of A. A. Bowman, *Studies in the Philosophy of Religion,* in *Journal of Theological Studies,* XL, 1939, 305–8.

Review of W. David Ross, *The Foundations of Ethics,* in *Oriel Record,* 1940, 76–81.

Review of John Baillie, *Our Knowledge of God,* in *Philosophy,* XV, 1940, 91–3.

Review of John Laird, *Theism and Cosmology,* in ibid., 429–35.

Review of S. Alexander, *Philosophical and Literary Pieces,* in *Journal of Theological Studies,* XLI, 1940, 345–9.

'Apropos de Kierkegaard', *Philosophy,* XVIII, April 1943, 68–74.

Review of C. E. M. Joad, *God and Evil,* in *Journal of Theological Studies,* XLIV, 1943, 244–51.

Review of Leonard Hodgson, *Towards a Christian Philosophy*, in *The Oxford Magazine*, 21 October 1943, 27–9.

Review of E. L. Mascall, *He Who Is*, in *Journal of Theological Studies*, XLV, 1944, 110–15.

Review of R. Kroner, *The Primacy of Faith*, in ibid., 247–53.

*Religious Experience, London: OUP, [1945].

Review of W. R. Matthews (ed.), *The Christian Faith: Essays in Explanation and Defence*, in *Journal of Theological Studies*, XLVI, 1946, 114–18.

'The revolt against liberalism in theology: A study, in this respect, of E. L. Mascall's *Christ, the Christian and the Church*', in ibid., XLVIII, 1947, 49–56.

'Baron Friedrich von Hügel and his contribution to religious philosophy', *Harvard Theological Review*, XLII, 1949, 1–18.

Part II   Select Bibliography

Abbott, Evelyn, and Campbell, Lewis, *The Life and Letters of Benjamin Jowett, M.A.*, London: John Murray, 1897.

Adamson, Robert, *The Development of Modern Philosophy with Other Lectures and Essays*, ed. W. R. Sorley, Edinburgh: Blackwood, 2 vols., 1903.

Adamson, Robert, review of E. Caird, *The Evolution of Religion*, in *International Journal of Ethics*, IV, 1893–4, 101–11.

Albee, Ernest, review of A. S. Pringle-Pattison, *The Idea of God in the Light of Recent Philosophy*, in *The Philosophical Review*, XXVI, 1917, 649–59.

Allen, Diogenes, *The Path of Perfect Love*, Cambridge, MA: Cowley Publications, 1992.

Ballie, D. M., *God Was in Christ*, London: Faber & Faber, 1961.

Baillie, J. B., review of E. Caird, *The Evolution of Theology in the Greek Philosophers*, in *International Journal of Ethics*, XV no. 1, October 1904, 117–21.

Baillie, J. B., *An Outline of the Idealistic Construction of Experience*, London: Macmillan, 1906.

Baillie, J. B., review of H. Jones, *The Working Faith of the Social Reformer*, in *Hibbert Journal*, X, October 1911–July 1912, 495–501.

Baillie, J. B., *Studies in Human Nature*, London: Bell, 1921.

Barbour, G. F., *Memoir of Andrew Seth Pringle-Pattison*, prefixed to the latter's *The Balfour Lectures on Realism.*

Berkeley, G., *Works*, ed. A. Campbell Fraser, Oxford: Clarendon Press, 1871.

Blakeney, E. H., review of E. Caird, *Essays on Literature and Philosophy*, in *The Churchman*, VII, August and October 1893.

Bosanquet, Bernard, 'Edward Caird, 1835–1908', *Proceedings of the British Academy*, III, 1907–8, 95–108.

Bosanquet, Bernard, 'Do finite individuals possess a substantive or an adjectival mode of being?', *Proceedings of the Aristotelian Society*, NS XVIII, 1917–18, 479–506.

*Boucher, David, and Vincent, Andrew, *A Radical Hegelian: The Political and Social Philosophy of Henry Jones*, Cardiff: University of Wales Press, 1993.

Bradley, A. C. (ed.), *Philosophical Remains of Richard Lewis Nettleship*, London: Macmillan, 2nd edn, 1901.

Bradley, F. H., *The Presuppositions of Critical History*, Oxford: J. Parker, 1874.

Bradley, F. H., *Appearance and Reality*, London: Swan Sonnenschein, 1893.

Bradley, F. H., *Ethical Studies*, London: OUP, 2nd edn, 1927.

Bradley, F. H., *The Principles of Logic*, [1883], London: OUP, 2nd edn corrected, 1928.

Bradley, James, 'Hegel in Britain: a brief history of British commentary and attitudes', *Heythrop Journal*, XX, 1979, 1–24, 163–82.

Broad, C. D., *Five Types of Ethical Theory*, London: Routledge & Kegan Paul, 1930.

Broad, C. D., review of A. E. Taylor, *The Faith of a Moralist*, in *Mind*, NS XL, 1931, 364–75.

Bruce, A. B., *The Humiliation of Christ*, Edinburgh: T. & T. Clark, 2nd revised and enlarged edn, 1881.

Burgh, W. G. de, *Towards a Religious Philosophy*, London: Macdonald & Evans, 1937.

Burkill, T. A., 'Theism and absolutism', *Philosophy*, XIX, 1944, 117–29.

Cacoullos, Ann R., *Thomas Hill Green, Philosopher of Rights*, New York: Twayne Publishers, 1974.

Caird, John, *The Fundamental Ideas of Christianity*, Glasgow: Maclehose, 1899.

Calderwood, Henry, 'Another view of Green's last work', *Mind*, X, 1885, 73–84.

Cantelon, John Edward, 'John Richardson Illingworth: Philosophical Theologian', unpublished D.Phil. dissertation, University of Oxford, 1951.

Capper, J. B., and Baillie, J. B., 'Andrew Seth Pringle-Pattison, 1856–1931', *Proceedings of the British Academy*, XVII, 1931, 447–89.

Chubb, Percival, 'The significance of Thomas Hill Green's philosophical and religious teaching', *Journal of Speculative Philosophy*, XXII nos. 1 and 2, January, April 1888, 1–21.

Coburn, Kathleen (ed.), *The Philosophical Lectures of Samuel Taylor Coleridge, hitherto Unpublished*, London: Pilot Press, 1949.

Cocks, H. F. Lovell, *By Faith Alone*, London: James Clarke, 1943.

Collingwood, R. G., *An Autobiography*, London: OUP, 1939.

Cooper, John W., 'Testing the spirit of the Age of Aquarius: the New Age Movement', *Calvin Theological Journal*, XXII no. 2, November 1987, 295–305.

Coutain, Édouard, 'L'attitude religieuse de T. H. Green', *Annales de Philosophie Chrétienne*, Paris, 1912, 561–86.

Creed, J. M., *The Divinity of Jesus Christ*, [1938], London: Collins Fontana, 1964.

Creighton, J. E., review of A. E. Taylor, *The Elements of Metaphysics*, in *The Philosophical Review*, XIV, 1905, 57–64.

Crothers, Samuel M., review of J. R. Illingworth, *Personality Human and Divine*, in *International Journal of Ethics*, VI, January 1896, 265.

Cudworth, R., *The True Intellectual System of the Universe*, 1820.

Davidson, W. L., *Recent Theistic Discussion*, Edinburgh: T. & T. Clark, 1921.

Davie, G. E., *The Democratic Intellect: Scotland and her Universities in the Nineteenth Century*, Edinburgh: Edinburgh University Press, 1961.

Denney, James, 'Ritschl in English', *Expository Times*, XII, 1900–1, 135–9.

Denney, James, *The Death of Christ*, London: Hodder & Stoughton, 2nd edn, 1902.

Denney, James, *The Atonement and the Modern Mind*, London: Hodder & Stoughton, 1903.

Denney, James, *Jesus and the Gospel*, London: Hodder & Stoughton, 2nd edn, 1909.

Denney, James, *The Christian Doctrine of Reconciliation*, London: Hodder & Stoughton, 1919.

Denney, James, *Letters of Principal James Denney to W. Robertson Nicoll 1893–1917*, London: Hodder & Stoughton, 1920.

Denney, James, *Letters of Principal James Denney to his Family and Friends*, ed. James Moffatt, London: Hodder & Stoughton, [1922].

Descartes, R., *A Discourse on Method*, 1637, etc.

Dewey, John, 'Green's theory of moral motive', *The Philosophical Review*, I, 1892, 593–612.

Dockhorn, Klaus, *Die Staatsphilosophie des englischen Idealismus: ihre Lehre und Wirkung*, Bochum, 1937.

Drummond, James, and Upton, C. B., *The Life and Letters of James Martineau*, London: Nisbet, 1902.

Edgworth, F. Y., *New and Old Methods in Ethics*, 1877.

Edwards, D. Miall, *Christianity and Philosophy*, Edinburgh: T. & T. Clark, 1932.

Elliott-Binns, *The Development of English Theology in the Later Nineteenth Century*, London: Longmans, 1952.

Evans, V. B., review of A. E. Taylor, *The Faith of a Moralist, Series I*, in *International Journal of Ethics*, XLI, 1930–1, 351–3.

Ewing, A. C., *Idealism. A Critical Survey*, London: Methuen, [1934], 3rd edn., 1961.

Fairbairn, A. M., review of E. Caird, *The Evolution of Religion*, in *Critical Review of Theological and Philosophical Literature*, III no. 2, 1893, 198–206.

Fairbairn, A. M., 'Experience in theology: a chapter of autobiography', *Contemporary Review*, XCI, January–June 1907, 554–73.

Fairbrother, William H., *The Philosophy of T. H. Green*, [1896], London: Methuen, 2nd edn, 1900.

Ferré, Nels F. S., *The Christian Understanding of God*, London: SCM Press, 1951.

Ferré, Nels F. S., *The Atonement and Mission*, London: London Missionary Society, 1960.

Forrest, D. W., *The Christ of History and of Experience*, [1897], Edinburgh: T. & T. Clark, 7th edn, 1914.

Forsyth, P. T., *Positive Preaching and the Modern Mind*, [1907], London: Independent Press, 1964.

Forsyth, P. T., *Missions in State and Church*, London: Hodder & Stoughton, 1908.

Forsyth, P. T., 'Monism', a paper read before the London Society for the Study of Religion, 1909, privately printed.

Forsyth, P. T., *Faith, Freedom and the Future*, [1912], London: Independent Press, 1952.

Franks, R. S., *A History of the Doctrine of the Work of Christ*, London: Hodder & Stoughton, 2 vols., 1918.

Franks, R. S., 'The theology of Andrew Martin Fairbairn', *Congregational Historical Society Transactions*, XIII, 1937–9, 140–50.

Fraser, A. Campbell, *Berkeley*, Edinburgh: Blackwood, 1881.

Fraser, A. Campbell, *Locke*, Edinburgh: Blackwood, 1891.

Fraser, A. Campbell, *Thomas Reid*, Edinburgh: Oliphant, 1898.

Fraser, A. Campbell, *Philosophy of Theism*, Edinburgh: Blackwood, 2nd edn, 1899.

Fraser, A. Campbell, *Biographia Philosophica: A Retrospect*, Edinburgh: Blackwood, 1904.

Gallagher, Denis M., *Pringle-Pattison's Idea of God*, Washington: Catholic University of America, 1933.

Galloway, Allan D., 'The new Hegelians', *Religious Studies*, VIII, 1972.

Gardiner, H. N., review of E. Caird, *The Evolution of Theology in the Greek Philosophers*, in *The Philosophical Review*, XIV, 1905, 204–12.

Garvie, A. E., 'The limits of doctrinal restatement', *Proceedings of the Third International Congregational Council*, ed. John Brown, London: Congregational Union of England and Wales, 1908, 90–8.

Garvie, A. E., *The Christian Certainty amid the Modern Perplexity*, London: Hodder & Stoughton, 1910.

Garvie, A. E., *A Handbook of Christian Apologetics*, London: Duckworth, 1913.

Garvie, A. E., *Revelation through History and Experience*, London: Ivor Nicholson & Watson, 1934.

Garvie, A. E., *Memories and Meanings of My Life*, London: Allen & Unwin, 1938.

Gore, Charles, *The Reconstruction of Belief*, London: John Murray, 1926.

Gore, Charles (ed.), *Lux Mundi: A Series of Studies in the Religion of the Incarnation*, London: John Murray, 15th edn, 1904.

Granger, Frank, review of J. R. Illingworth, *Reason and Revelation*, in *International Journal of Ethics*, XIII, 1903, 508–11.

Grensted, L. W., 'Foreword' to C. C. J. Webb, *Religious Experience*.

Haldane, R. B., 'Hegel and his recent critics', *Mind*, XIII, 1888, 585–9.

Haldane, R. B., and Seth, A. (eds.), *Essays in Philosophical Criticism*, London: Longmans, 1883.

Haldar, Hiralel, 'Green and his critics', *The Philosophical Review*, III, 1894, 168–75.

Hallett, H. F., 'Andrew Seth Pringle-Pattison 1856–1931', *Mind*, NS XLII, April 1933, 137–49.

Hegel, G. W. F., *Hegel: The Letters*, trans. Clark Butler and Christine Seiler, Bloomington: Indiana University Press, 1984.

Heron, Alasdair I. C., 'The person of Christ', in Geoffrey Wainwright (ed.), *Keeping the Faith: Essays to Mark the Centenary of Lux Mundi*, Philadelphia: Fortress Press and Allison Park, PA: Pickwick Publications, 1988, 99–123.

*Hetherington, H. J. W., *The Life and Letters of Sir Henry Jones*, London: Hodder & Stoughton, 1924.

Hodgson, Leonard, *The Doctrine of the Trinity*, Welwyn, Herts.: Nisbet, 1943.

Hodgson, Leonard, *Towards a Christian Philosophy*, London: Nisbet, 1943.

Hoernlé, R. F. A., *Idealism as a Philosophical Doctrine*, London: Hodder & Stoughton, [1924].

Hoeveler, J. David, Jr, *James McCosh and the Scottish Intellectual Tradition*, Princeton: Princeton University Press, 1981.

Holland, Henry Scott, *A Bundle of Memories*, London: Wells Gardner, [1915].

Holland, Henry Scott, *John Richardson Illingworth, Rector of Longworth, Honorary Canon of Christ Church, Oxford*, London: Wells Gardner, Darton, [1916].

Hudson, W. D., *A Century of Moral Philosophy*, Guildford: Longmans, 1980.

Hügel, F. von, *Essays and Addresses on the Philosophy of Religion*, 2 vols., London: Dent, 1926.

Hügel, F. von, *The Reality of God*, London: J. M. Dent, 1931.

[Hughes, Dorothea Price], *The Life of Hugh Price Hughes*, London: Hodder & Stoughton, 1905.

Hume, D., *The Philosophical Works*, eds. T. H. Green and T. H. Grose, London, 4 vols., 1878.

*[Illingworth, Agnes Louisa], *The Life and Work of John Richardson Illingworth, M.A., D.D.*, London: John Murray, 1917.

Inge, W. R., *God and the Astronomers*, London: Longmans, 1923.

Inge, W. R., *Mysticism and Religion*, London: Rider, [1947] 1969.

Iverach, James, 'Professor Thomas Hill Green', *The Expository Times*, IV, 1892–3, 102–4 and 164–8.

Iverach, James, 'Edward Caird', *The Expository Times*, V, 1893–4, 205–9.

Iverach, James, *Theism in the Light of Present Science and Philosophy*, London: Hodder & Stoughton, 1900.

Iverach, James, review of J. R. Illingworth, *Reason and Revelation*, in *The Critical Review of Theological and Philosophical Literature*, XIII, 1903, 26–31.

Iverach, James, 'Pantheism', *The Expositor*, 7th ser., III, 1907, 493–507; IV, 1907, 20–35, 152–68.

James, Henry (ed.), *The Letters of William James*, Boston: The Atlantic Monthly Press, 1920.

James, William, 'Absolutism and empiricism', *Mind*, IX, 1884, 281–6.

Jenkins, David, *The Glory of Man*, London: SCM Press, 1967.

Johnson, Roger B. C., *The Metaphysics of Knowledge: Being an Examination of Some Phases of T. H. Green's Theory of Reality*, Princeton: Princeton University Press, 1900.

Johnston, J. O., *Life and Letters of Henry Parry Liddon*, London: Longmans, 1904.

Jones, Alfred H., 'Professor Pringle-Pattison's epistemological realism', *The Philosophical Review*, XX, 1911, 405–21.

Jones, Henry, and Muirhead, J. H., *The Life and Philosophy of Edward Caird*, Glasgow: Maclehose, Jackson, 1921.

Kant, I., *Critique of Pure Reason*, [1781], trans. J. M. D. Meiklejohn, London: Dent, 1964.

Kant, I., *Fundamental Principles of the Metaphysics of Ethics*, [1785], trans. T. K. Abbott, London: Longman [1873], 10th edn, 1925.

Knox, Howard V., 'Green's refutation of empiricism', *Mind*, NS IX, 1900, 62–74.

Knox, T. V., 'Has Green answered Locke?', *Mind*, NS XXIII, 1914, 335–48.

Knox, Wilfred L., and Vidler, Alec R., *The Development of Modern Catholicism*, London: Philip Allan, 1933.

E.H.L., 'A memory of Longworth and the Rector', *The Treasury*, April 1916, 5–11.

Ladd, George Trumbull, review of A. Seth, *Man's Place in the Cosmos,* in *The Philosophical Review,* VI, 1897, 529–32.

Ladd, George Trumbull, 'A defence of idealism', *Mind,* NS XXIII, October 1914, 473–88.

Lamont, W. D., *Introduction to Green's Moral Philosophy,* London: Allen & Unwin, 1934.

Lamprecht, P., 'The role of Descartes in seventeenth-century England', *Studies in the History of Ideas,* III, 1935, 181–240.

Lancelot, J. B., *Francis James Chavasse, Bishop of Liverpool,* Oxford: Basil Blackwell, 1929.

Langford, Thomas A., *In Search of Foundations: English Theology 1900–1920,* Nashville: Abingdon, 1969.

Laurie, S. S., 'The metaphysics of T. H. Green', *The Philosophical Review,* VI no. 2, March 1897, 113–31.

Lefevre, Albert, review of A. E. Taylor, *The Problem of Conduct,* in *The Philosophical Review,* XI, 1902, 56–69.

Lewis, H. D., *Philosophy of Religion,* London: The English Universities Press, 1965.

Lewis, H. D., 'The British idealists', in *Nineteenth-Century Religious Thought in the West,* ed. Ninian Smart *et al.,* Cambridge: CUP, 1985.

Lindsay, A. D., 'The idealism of Caird and Jones', *Journal of Philosophical Studies,* I, 1926,171–82.

Lindsay, A. D., 'T. H. Green and the idealists', in F. J. C. Hearnshaw (ed.), *The Social and Political Ideas of Some Representative Thinkers of the Victorian Age,* New York: Barnes and Noble, 1930, 150–64.

Lofthouse, W. F., 'Alfred Edward Taylor', *London Quarterly and Holborn Review,* 6th ser., XV, 1946, 97–107.

Long, Eugene T., 'The Gifford Lectures and the Glasgow Hegelians', *Review of Metaphysics,* XLIII no. 2, December 1989, 357–84.

MacCunn, John, *Six Radical Thinkers,* London: Edward Arnold, 1907.

McGiffert, A. C., 'Immanence', in *Encyclopaedia of Religion and Ethics,* Edinburgh: T. & T. Clark, 1921, VII.

Mackenzie, D., 'Transcendentalism', in *Encyclopaedia of Religion and Ethics,* Edinburgh: T. & T. Clark, 1921, XII.

Mackenzie, J. S., 'The new realism and the old idealism', *Mind,* NS XV, 1906, 309–28.

Mackenzie, J. S., 'Edward Caird as a philosophical teacher', *Mind*, NS XVIII, 1909, 509–37.

Mackinnon, Donald M., 'Some aspects of the treatment of Christianity by the British idealists', *Religious Studies*, XX, March 1984, 133–44.

MacKinnon, Donald M., *Themes in Theology: The Three-fold Cord*, Edinburgh: T. & T. Clark, 1987.

Mackintosh, H. R., 'A philosopher's theology', in his *Some Aspects of Christian Belief*, London: Hodder & Stoughton, [1923].

Mackintosh, H. R., *The Christian Apprehension of God*, London: SCM Press, 1929.

Mackintosh, Robert, *Essays towards a New Theology*, Glasgow: Maclehose, 1889.

Mackintosh, Robert, *Hegel and Hegelianism*, Edinburgh: T. & T. Clark, 1903.

Mackintosh, Robert, 'Recent philosophy and Christian doctrine', *Proceedings of the Third International Congregational Council*, ed. John Brown, London: Congregational Union of England and Wales, 1908, 76–84.

Mackintosh, Robert, 'Theism', *Encyclopaedia Britannica*, 11th edn, 1910–11.

Mackintosh, Robert, *Christianity and Sin*, London: Duckworth, 1913.

Mackintosh, Robert, *Historic Theories of Atonement*, London: Hodder & Stoughton, 1920.

Macmurray, John, *Idealism against Religion*, London: The Lindsey Press, [1944].

Macmurray, John, *Search for Reality in Religion*, London: Friends Home Service Committee, [1965], 1969.

Macquarrie, John, *Twentieth-Century Religious Thought: The Frontiers of Philosophy and Theology, 1900–1960*, London: SCM Press, 1963.

McTaggart, J. M. E., *Studies in Hegelian Cosmology*, Cambridge: CUP, 1901.

Mansfield College Essays, London: Hodder & Stoughton, 1909.

Mansfield College, Its Origin and Opening, London: James Clarke, 1890.

Manson, T. W., *Ethics and the Gospel*, London: SCM Press, 1960.

Marett, R. R., *A Jerseyman at Oxford*, London: OUP, 1941.

Marsh, Margaret, *Hastings Rashdall: Bibliography of the Published*

Writings, Leysters, Herefordshire: Modern Churchpeople's Union, 1993.

Martin, A. S., review of J. R. Illingworth, *The Doctrine of the Trinity*, in *Review of Theology and Philosophy*, III, 1908, 731–5.

Martineau, James, *Types of Ethical Theory*, Oxford: Clarendon Press, 2 vols., 3rd edn revised, 1891.

Martineau, James, *A Study of Religion*, Oxford: Clarendon Press, 2 vols., 2nd revised edn, 1900.

Marvin, F. S. (ed.), *Recent Developments in European Thought* (The Unity Series, III), London: OUP, 1920.

*Mason, Charles W., *The Value-Philosophy of Alfred Edward Taylor: A Study in Theistic Implication*, Washington: University Press of America, 1979.

Masson, David, *Recent British Philosophy*, [1865], 3rd edn, London, 1877.

Masterson, Patrick, 'Hegel's philosophy of God', *Philosophical Studies*, XIX, 1970, 126–47.

Matheson, P. E., *The Life of Hastings Rashdall, D.D.*, London: OUP, 1918.

Maurice, F. D., *What is Revelation?*, Cambridge, 1859.

Maurice, F. D., *Sequel to the Inquiry, What is Revelation?*, London, 1860.

Maurice, F. D., *Moral and Metaphysical Philosophy*, London: Macmillan, 2 vols., 1882.

Mellone, S. H., review of A. S. Pringle-Pattison, *The Philosophical Radicals*, in *Mind*, NS XVII, 1908, 97–104.

Merrington, E. N., 'A Scottish thinker: Andrew Seth Pringle-Pattison', *Australian Journal of Psychology and Philosophy*, IX no. 4, December 1931, 241–5.

Metz, Rudolf, *A Hundred Years of British Philosophy*, London: Allen & Unwin, 1938.

Mill, J. S., *Dissertations and Discussions*, London: J. W. Parker, 1859.

Mill, J. S., *An Examination of Sir William Hamilton's Philosophy*, London: Longman, 1865.

Milne, A. J. M., *The Social Philosophy of English Idealism*, London: Allen & Unwin, 1962.

Moltmann, J., *The Crucified God*, New York: Harper & Row, 1974.

Montefiore, H. W., 'Towards a christology for today', in *Soundings*, ed. A. R. Vidler, Cambridge: CUP, 1962, 149–72.

Moore, G. E., 'The refutation of idealism', *Mind*, NS XII, 1903,

433–53; reprinted in idem, *Philosophical Studies*, [1922], London: Routledge & Kegan Paul, 1965.

More, Henry, *An Explanation of the Grand Mystery of Godliness*, 1660.

More, Henry, *Divine Dialogues*, 1668.

Morell, J. D., *An Historical and Critical View of the Speculative Philosophy of Europe in the Nineteenth Century*, London: William Pickering, 2 vols., 1846.

[Morris-Jones, Huw], 'The life and philosophy of Sir Henry Jones', in *Henry Jones, 1852–1922. Centenary Addresses delivered at the University College of North Wales on the first day of December, 1952*, Cardiff: University of Wales Press, 1953.

Mozley, J. K., *Some Tendencies in British Theology*, London: SPCK, 1951.

Muirhead, J. H., review of A. Seth, *Man's Place in the Cosmos*, in *International Journal of Ethics*, VII no. 1, October 1897, 102–6.

Muirhead, J. H., 'Sir Henry Jones, 1852–1922', *Proceedings of the British Academy*, X, 1921–3, 552–62.

Muirhead, J. H., review of A. E. Taylor, *The Faith of a Moralist*, in *Hibbert Journal*, XXIX, October 1930–July 1931, 553–9.

Muirhead, J. H., *The Platonic Tradition in Anglo-Saxon Philosophy*, London: Allen & Unwin, 1931.

Muirhead, J. H., *Bernard Bosanquet and his Friends*, London: Allen & Unwin, 1935.

Muirhead, J. H., *Reflections by a Journeyman in Philosophy*, London: Allen & Unwin, 1942.

Muirhead, J. H. (ed.), *Contemporary British Philosophy*, 2nd ser., London: Allen & Unwin, 1925.

Nettleship, R. L., Memoir of T. H. Green prefixed to the latter's *Works*, III.

Oliphant, Mrs, *A Memoir of the Life of John Tulloch, D.D., LL.D.*, Edinburgh: Blackwood, 3rd edn, 1889.

Oman, John, *The Natural and the Supernatural*, Cambridge: CUP, 1931.

Orr, James, *The Christian View of God and the World*, Edinburgh: Elliot, 4th edn, 1897.

Orr, James, *Sidelights on Christian Doctrine*, London: Marshall, 1909.

Orr, James, *Sin as a Problem of Today*, London: Hodder & Stoughton, 1910.

Osmaston, F. P. B., *The Religious Teaching of Thomas Hill Green,* privately printed, 1889.

Ottley, R. L., *The Doctrine of the Incarnation,* [1896], London: Methuen, 6th edn, 1919.

Owen, H. P., *Revelation and Existence: A Study in the Theology of Rudolf Bultmann,* Cardiff: University of Wales Press, 1957.

Owen, H. P., *The Moral Argument for Christian Theism,* London: Allen & Unwin, 1965.

Paget, Stephen, *Henry Scott Holland: Memoirs and Letters,* London: John Murray, 1921.

Pannenberg, Wolfhart, *Metaphysics and the Idea of God,* Edinburgh: T. & T. Clark, 1990.

Passmore, John, *Ralph Cudworth,* Cambridge: CUP, 1951.

Passmore, John, *A Hundred Years of Philosophy,* London: Duckworth, 1957.

Paton, H. J., *The Modern Predicament,* London: Allen & Unwin, 1955.

Paton, J. B. *et al.* (eds.), *Christ and Civilization,* London: National Council of Evangelical Free Churches, 1910.

Patrick, James, *Idealism and Orthodoxy at Oxford, 1901–1945,* Macon, GA: Mercer University Press, 1985.

Peel, Albert, and Marriott, J. A. R., *Robert Forman Horton,* London: Allen & Unwin, 1937.

Perry, Ralph Barton, *The Present Conflict of Ideals: A Study of the Philosophical Background of the World War,* New York: Longmans, 1918.

Peterson, J. B., review of A. Seth, *Two Lectures on Theism,* in *The Philosophical Review,* VII, 1898, 434–6.

Pfleiderer, *The Development of Theology in Germany since Kant, and its Progress in Great Britain since 1825,* London: Swan Sonnenschein, 1890.

Porteous, A. J. D., 'A. E. Taylor (1869–1945)', *Mind,* NS LV, April 1946, 186–91.

Quinton, A. M., 'Absolute idealism', *Proceedings of the British Academy,* LVII, 1971, 303–29.

Ramsay, A. M., *From Gore to Temple,* London: Longmans, 1960.

Randall, John Herman, Jr, *Philosophy After Darwin: Chapters for the Career of Philosophy,* New York: Columbia University Press, 1977.

Rashdall, Hastings, review of H. Jones, *Idealism as a Practical*

Creed, in *International Journal of Ethics,* XXI, no. 1, October 1910, 107–10.

Rashdall, Hastings, 'The religious philosophy of Professor Pringle-Pattison', *Mind,* NS XXVII, 1918, 261–83.

Reardon, B. M. G., 'Hegel today', *Theology,* LXX, 1967, 350–6.

Reardon, B. M. G., *Religious Thought in the Victorian Age: A Survey from Coleridge to Gore,* [1971], London: Longmans, 1980.

Reardon, B. M. G., *Hegel's Philosophy of Religion,* London: Macmillan, 1977.

Reid, Thomas, *Works,* ed. W. Hamilton, Edinburgh: Maclachlan and Stewart, 6th edn, 1863.

Richter, Melvin, *The Politics of Conscience: T. H. Green and his Age,* London: Weidenfeld and Nicolson, 1964.

Ritchie, D. G., *Darwin and Hegel,* London: Swan Sonnenschein, 1893.

Robbins, Peter, *The British Hegelians 1875–1925,* New York: Garland Publishing, 1982.

Robinson, H. Wheeler, *The Christian Experience of the Holy Spirit,* [1928], London: Collins Fontana, 1962.

Root, John D., 'The correspondence of Friedrich von Hügel and Clement C. J. Webb', *The Downside Review,* XCIX, no. 337, October 1981, 288–98.

*Ross, W. D., 'Alfred Edward Taylor', *Proceedings of the British Academy,* XXXI, 1945, 407–24.

Ross, W. D., 'Clement Charles Julian Webb', *Proceedings of the British Academy,* XLI, 1955, 339–47.

Royce, Josiah, *The World and the Individual,* New York: Macmillan, 1901.

Russell, Bertrand, *Our Knowledge of the External World,* Chicago: Open Court, 1914.

Ryle, Gilbert, *The Concept of Mind,* London: Hutchinson's University Library, 1949.

Sanday, William, *Christologies Ancient and Modern,* Oxford: Clarendon Press, 1910.

Schleiermacher, F. D. E., *On Religion, Speeches to its Cultured Despisers,* New York: Harper Torchbooks, 1958.

Schwöbel, Christoph and Gunton, Colin E. (eds.), *Persons, Divine and Human,* Edinburgh: T. & T. Clark, 1991.

Scorgie, G. G., *A Call for Continuity: The Theological Contribution of James Orr,* Macon, GA: Mercer University Press, 1988.

Selbie, W. B., *Schleiermacher: A Critical and Historical Study*, London: Chapman & Hall, 1913.

Selbie, W. B., *The Life of Andrew Martin Fairbairn*, London: Hodder & Stoughton, 1914.

Selbie, W. B. (ed.), *The Life of Charles Silvester Horne, M.A., J.P.*, London: Hodder & Stoughton, [1920].

Sell, Alan P. F., 'The peril of reductionism in Christian thought', *Scottish Journal of Theology*, XXVII, 1974, 48–64.

Sell, Alan P. F., 'Platonists (ancient and modern) and the Gospel', *Irish Theological Quarterly*, XLIV no. 3, 1977, 153–74.

Sell, Alan P. F., *Robert Mackintosh: Theologian of Integrity*, Bern: Peter Lang, 1977.

Sell, Alan P. F., 'Transcendence, immanence and the supernatural', *Journal of Theology for Southern Africa*, no. 29, March 1979, 56–66.

Sell, Alan P. F., *Theology in Turmoil: The Roots, Course and Significance of the Conservative–Liberal Debate in Modern Theology*, Grand Rapids: Baker Book House, 1986.

Sell, Alan P. F., *Defending and Declaring the Faith: Some Scottish Examples 1860–1920*, Exeter: The Paternoster Press, and Colorado Springs: Helmers & Howard, 1987.

Sell, Alan P. F., *The Philosophy of Religion 1875–1980*, London: Croom Helm [now Routledge], 1988.

Sell, Alan P. F., review of James Patrick, *The Magdalen Metaphysicals*, in *Philosophical Studies* (Dublin), XXXII, 1988–90, 350–2.

Sell, Alan P. F., *Aspects of Christian Integrity*, Calgary: University of Calgary Press, 1990, and Louisville: Westminster/John Knox Press, 1991.

Sell, Alan P. F., *Dissenting Thought and the Life of the Churches: Studies in an English Tradition*, Lewiston, NY: Edwin Mellen Press, 1990.

Sell, Alan P. F., 'In the wake of the Enlightenment: the adjustments of James Martineau and A. Campbell Fraser', *Enlightenment and Dissent*, IX, 1990, 63–92, reprinted in idem, *Commemorations: Studies in Christian Thought and History*, Calgary: University of Calgary Press, and Cardiff: University of Wales Press, 1993, ch. X.

Sell, Alan P. F., review of David Boucher and Andrew Vincent, *A Radical Hegelian: The Political and Social Philosophy of Henry Jones*, in *British Journal for the History of Philosophy*, III, 1995, 201–4.

Selsham, H., *T. H. Green: Critic of Empiricism,* New York, 1930.

Selwyn, E. G. (ed.), *Essays Catholic and Critical,* London: SPCK, 1926.

Seth, James, *English Philosophers and Schools of Philosophy,* London: Dent, 1912.

Seth, James, *Essays on Ethics and Religion,* Edinburgh: Blackwood, 1926.

Sidgwick, H., 'The philosophy of T. H. Green', *Mind,* NS X, 1901, 18–29.

Sidgwick, H., *Lectures on the Ethics of T. H. Green, Mr. Herbert Spencer, and J. Martineau,* London: Macmillan, 1902.

Simpson, P. Carnegie, *The Life of Principal Rainy,* London: Hodder & Stoughton, popular edn, n.d.

Small, Robert, *History of the Congregations of the United Presbyterian Church from 1733 to 1900,* Edinburgh: David M. Small, 1900.

Smith, J. A., review of H. Jones, *A Faith that Enquires,* in *Hibbert Journal,* XXI, October 1922–July 1923, 387–95.

Smith, J. S. Boys, review of A. E. Taylor, *The Faith of a Moralist,* in *Journal of Theological Studies,* XXXII, 1930–1, 435–9.

Smith, J. S. Boys, 'The interpretation of Christianity in idealistic philosophy in Great Britain in the nineteenth century', *The Modern Churchman,* XXI, 1941, 251–73.

Sorley, W. R., review of C. C. J. Webb, *God and Personality,* in *Hibbert Journal,* XVII, October 1918–July 1919, 753–6.

Sorley, W. R., review of C. C. J. Webb, *Divine Personality and Human Life,* in *Hibbert Journal,* XVIII, October 1919-July 1920, 814–17.

Snyder, Alice D., *Coleridge on Logic and Learning,* New Haven: Yale University Press, 1929.

Spinoza, B., *Ethics,* 1677 etc.

Stebbing, Susan L., *A Modern Introduction to Logic,* London: Methuen, 1930.

Stewart, D., *The Collected Works,* ed. W. Hamilton, Edinburgh: Thomas Constable, 1854.

Stirling, J. H., *The Secret of Hegel,* Edinburgh: Oliver & Boyd, new edn, 1898.

Storr, Vernon F., *The Development of English Theology in the Nineteenth Century,* London: Longmans, 1913.

Streeter, B. H. (ed.), *The Spirit,* London: Macmillan, 1928.

Sturt, H., *Idola Theatri: A Criticism of Oxford Thought and Thinkers from the Standpoint of Personal Idealism,* London: Macmillan, 1906.

Temple, William, *Nature, Man and God,* London: Macmillan, 1934.

*Thomas, Geoffrey, *The Moral Philosophy of T. H. Green,* Oxford: Clarendon Press, 1987.

Thomas, John Heywood, 'Kierkegaard's alternative metaphysical theology', *History of European Ideas,* XII no. 1, 1990, 53–63.

Toews, John Edward, *Hegelianism: The Path Toward Dialectical Humanism 1805–1841,* Cambridge: CUP, 1980.

Townsend, Henry Gates, *The Principle of Individuality in the Philosophy of Thomas Hill Green,* New York: Longmans, 1914.

Toynbee, Arnold, Preface to T. H. Green, *The Witness of God and Faith: Two Lay Sermons,* London, 1883.

Tsanoff, Radoslav A., review of A. S. Pringle-Pattison, *The Idea of Immortality,* in *The Philosophical Review,* XXXIII, 1924, 316–18.

Upton, Charles B., 'Theological aspects of the philosophy of T. H. Green', *New World* (Chicago), I, 1892, 139–57.

Upton, Charles B., *Dr. Martineau's Philosophy. A Survey,* London: Nisbet, 1905.

Varley, R. S., review of H. Jones, *The Working Faith of the Social Reformer,* in *International Journal of Ethics,* XXI no. 1, October 1910, 114–16.

Vidler, A. R. (ed.), *Soundings,* Cambridge: CUP, 1962.

Villers, C., *Philosophie de Kant,* Paris, 1801.

Vincent, Andrew, 'The individual in Hegelian thought', *Idealistic Studies,* XII, 1982, 156–68.

Vincent, Andrew and Plant, Raymond, *Philosophy, Politics and Citizenship,* Oxford: Blackwell, 1984.

Vincent, Andrew, *The Philosophy of T. H. Green,* Aldershot: Gower, 1986.

Virtue, Charles F. Sawhill, 'The axiological theism of A. E. Taylor', *Philosophy,* XXVII, 1952, 110–24.

Walker, W. L., *The Spirit and the Incarnation,* Edinburgh: T. & T. Clark, 1899.

Wallace, William, *The Logic of Hegel,* Oxford, 1874.

Walsh, W. H., *Hegelian Ethics,* London: Macmillan, 1969.

Warren, W. Preston, *Pantheism in Neo-Hegelian Thought,* Scottdale, PA: Mennonite Press, 1933.

Watson, John, 'Metaphysic and psychology', *The Philosophical Review,* II no. 5, September 1893, 513–28.

Watson, John, 'The idealism of Edward Caird', *The Philosophical Review,* XVIII nos. 2 and 3, 1909, 147–63, 259–80.

Webster, C., 'Henry More and Descartes: some new sources', *British Journal for the History of Science,* IV, 1969, 359–77.

Wellek, René, *Immanuel Kant in England 1793–1838,* Princeton: Princeton University Press, 1931.

Wenley, R. M., *Contemporary Theology and Theism,* Edinburgh: T. & T. Clark, 1897.

Wenley, R. M., 'An unborn idealism', in *Contemporary American Philosophy,* ed. George P. Adams and Wm. Pepperell Montague, London: Allen & Unwin, II, 1930.

[Whichcote, Benjamin], *Moral and Religious Aphorisms,* Norwich, 1703.

Wolf, A. (ed.), *The Correspondence of Spinoza,* London: Allen & Unwin, 1928.

Index of Persons

Biblical and fictional names are not included

Select Index of Subjects

absolute, the, 8, 15, 33, 98, 105, ch. III, 187, 229, 233, 264–5, 267
agnosticism, 11, 33, 39, 62, 84, 89, 111, 125, 227, 268
Alexandrian theology, 36, 52, 70, 292–3
asceticism, 66–7
association of ideas, 22
Atonement, 38, 72, 176, 188–96, 198, 201, 205, 217, 283, 285
authority, 72, 82, 209, 211–12

beauty, 69, 89, 98, 169
Bible, 36, 42

Cambridge Platonists, 19–20, 25
Cappadocian fathers, 292–3
Christology, 54, 188, 195–202, 231, 273
Church, 72, 96, 207–213, 233, 262
common sense 9, 23, 25, 32, 35, 58, 83, 90–1, 96, 158, 227, 242–3
Creator–creature distinction, 17, 109, 124, 128, 131–5, 152, 187, 193, 222, 224, 230–1, 291

deism, 8, 14, 33, 71, 123–5
doctrine, ch. V
doubt, 81

education, 44, 59
empiricism, 25, 34, 47, 49, 58, 66, 71, 104–5, 226
Enlightenment, 39
epistemology, 9–13, 18, 20–3, 32, 78–9, 89–91, 94, 97–8, 133, 144, 159, 229–30, 260
ethics, 11, 53, 72, 104, 106–7, 112, 131, 143, ch. IV, 195, 230
evil, 53, 109, 124, 146, 176–86, 227, 231, 280–1
evolutionary thought, 7, 20, 28, 35–6,

70, 88, 125, 147–8, 189, 205, 232, 265, 274
existentialism, 231–2, 234
experience, 94, 96, 105, 121, 140, 142–3, 172, 204, 223

faith, 30–1, 51, 53, 63, 81, 84, 90, 104, 117–18, 161–2, 172, 180, 197, 204, 234, 287

God, 5, 11–12, 14, 32, 50, 52, 61, 63, 68–9, 71, 106, ch. III, 150, 152, 154, 161, 174–5, 179, 181–2, 189, 198, 222–5, 227, 264
grace, see holy love

history, 103, 165–6, 188, 202–6, 209, 212, 219, 230–4
holy love, 135, 142, 169, 174–6, 189, 198, 200, 213, 230, 233
Holy Spirit, 172, 191, 221

immanence/immanentism, 14, 50, 52, 54, 68–9, 72, 106, 109, 117, 124–31, 133–4, 160, 175, 187, 193, 196, 214, 222–4, 230–2, 235
immortality, 5, 99, 188, 214–21, 233, 238, 290
Incarnation, 36, 69, 72, 97, 130, 173, 188, 194–202, 223, 231, 283, 285
individual, loss of, 109, 124, 135–45

liberty, 128
Lux Mundi, 36, 67, 70, 94, 124, 196, 208, 210, 223

materialism, 10, 13, 19, 22, 33–5, 43, 47, 89, 127, 148, 189, 226–7, 234
methodology, 5–6, 8, 18, 72–3, 88–9, 123–4, 232–6